UNDERSTANDING MUHAMMAD AND MUSLIMS

Ali Sina

Publisher: Felibri.com
felibri@gmail.com
Publication date: November 2014
Distributed by Ingram Book Group

Library and Archives Canada Cataloguing in Publication
Sina, Ali
Understanding Muhammad and muslims / by Ali Sina.
Includes index.
ISBN 978-1-926800-05-9
1. Muhammad, Prophet, d. 632--Psychology. 2. Islam--
Controversial literature. I. Title.
BP169.S55 2011 297.6'3 C2011-904701-2

Picture on the cover: Muhammad on Mount Hira, by Nicholas Roerich 1932,
Courtesy of Roerich Museum, roerich.org

Blurbs

A blisteringly honest, thoroughly documented, and piercingly insightful investigation of the root causes within Islam of the fanaticism and violence that today threatens the entire world. Should be required reading at the State Department and the White House. -- ***Robert Spencer****, director of Jihad Watch and author of The Politically Incorrect Guide to Islam and the Crusades (Regnery)*

With great courage, perspicacity, and trenchant wit, Ali Sina demolishes a host of politically correct myths about Islam, and its founder. One wishes policymaking elites would avail themselves of his insights which shatter the dangerous delusions of their own invented Islam. ***Andrew G. Bostom****, MD, author of "The Legacy of Jihad"*

To understand Muhammad and the malignant "religion" he created, I would recommend that you read Ali Sina's **Understanding Muhammad and Muslims**. It is a masterful, scholarly work that examines the life of Muhammad and reveals him in ways that demonstrate how he created a cult around himself. It was an ugly, violent, narcissistic life and one that now holds more than a billion people around the world in its grasp. -- *Bookviews by* ***Alan Caruba,*** *a charter member of the National Book Critics.*

The war against jihad can and must be won, in spite of the Western elite class that is instinctively prone to appeasement and betrayal. The first task is to analyze frankly the identity and character of the enemy and the nature of the threat. It is essential to discard the taboos and to discuss Islam without fear or guilt, or the shackles of mandated thinking. Ali Sina's new book makes an important contribution to that objective. ***Dr. S. Trifkovic****, Foreign Affairs Editor CHRONICLES*

A powerful, no holds barred look at an ideology of hate and what must be done to eradicate it. This book pulls no punches. A must read for anyone seeking to understand Islamist terrorism"*Professor* ***Kim Ezra Shienbaum,*** *Ph.D Dept. of Political Science, Rutgers University Camden, NJ. Chief Editor of Beyond Jihad.*

Half a century ago Whittaker Chambers in his book "Witness", warned us about the deadly danger of Communism. Now Ali Sina issues this clarion call regarding the threat of Islam. "Witness" could only have been written by one who knew Communism from within; the same can be said of ***The Islam Threat*** that is written from a perspective of one who knew Islam intimately from within. Islam is more dangerous than communism because it is camouflaged as "religion". ***Jacob Thomas,*** *Consultant on Middle Eastern affairs / Columnist*

Foreword

By Ibn Warraq

Ali Sina was born in Iran. Like most educated Iranians he believed that Islam was a humanistic religion that respected human rights. But Mr. Sina was also blessed with an enquiring mind, a rationalistic spirit that questioned, probed, and looked at the evidence unflinchingly. What he slowly discovered about the real Islam shook him morally and intellectually, and what is more, made him realize, long before September 11, 2001, that unless someone spoke the truth about the faith he was born into, the world would be faced with a system of thought and belief that would destroy not just the West, but civilization as a whole. Since his epiphanous moment when he discovered the inhuman nature of this religion, Mr. Sina has dedicated his life to discussing, criticizing, exposing the unacceptable aspects of Islam on his widely quoted website Faith Freedom International.

The West can make use of defectors, like Mr. Sina, from Islam (apostates) in the way the West used defectors from communism.

As I wrote in *Leaving Islam,*[1] there are very useful analogies to be drawn between Communism and Islam, such as the ones Maxime Rodinson[2] and Bertrand Russell have pointed out between the mindset of the communists of the 1930s and the Islamists of the 1990s and 21st century. As Russell said, "Among religions, Bolshevism [Communism] is to be reckoned with Mohammedanism rather than with Christianity and Buddhism. Christianity and Buddhism are primarily personal religions, with mystical doctrines and a love of contemplation.

Mohammedanism and Bolshevism are practical, social, unspiritual, concerned to win the empire of this world."[3] Hence the interest in the present situation and its haunting parallels with the communism of the Western intellectuals in the 1930s. As Koestler said, "You hate our Cassandra cries and resent us as allies, but when all is said, we ex-Communists are the only people on your side who know what it's all

---

[1] Ibn Warraq. *Leaving Islam. Apostates Speak Out*. Amherst: Prometheus Books. p.136

[2] Maxime Rodinson: *Islam et communisme, une ressemblance frappante*, in Le Figaro [Paris, daily newspaper], 28 Sep. 2001

[3] B.Russell, *Theory and Practice of Bolshevism*, London, 1921 pp .5, 29, 114

about."[4] As Crossman wrote in his introduction, "Silone [an ex-Communist] was joking when he said to Togliatti that the final battle would be between the Communists and ex-Communists. But no one who has not wrestled with Communism as a philosophy and Communists as political opponents can really understand the values of Western Democracy. The Devil once lived in Heaven, and those who have not met him are unlikely to recognize an angel when they see one."[5]

Communism has been defeated, at least for the moment, Islamism has not, and perhaps the final battle will be between Islam and Western Democracy. And these ex-Muslims, to echo Koestler's words, on the side of Western Democracy, are the only ones who know what it's all about, and we would do well to listen to their Cassandra cries.

We who live in the free West and enjoy freedom of expression and scientific inquiry should encourage a rational look at Islam, should encourage Quranic criticism. Only Quranic criticism can help Muslims to look at their Holy Scripture in a more rational and objective way, and prevent young Muslims from being fanaticized by the Quran's less tolerant verses. It is the civic duty of all individuals living in the West to inform themselves about Islam. But if they would only consult the works available in the megastores, they will find apologists of Islam. It is only by going through the meticulously documented and impeccably argued website of Mr. Sina and his team of writers that we would be able to obtain a more just appraisal of Islam. Now, of course, we have Ali Sina's book which I urge all responsible citizens whose critical faculties have not been lulled into confusion and befuddlement by oft-repeated slogans about Islam being a religion of peace to read carefully. Thanks to the courageous efforts of independent scholars like Ali Sina, there can no longer be any excuse for remaining ignorant about a religion that may annihilate all that you cherish and hold worth defending.

Ibn Warraq is the author of ***Leaving Islam, What the Koran Really Says, The Quest for the Historical Muhammad, The Origins of the Koran*** *and* ***Why I Am Not a Muslim****, the book that inspired many Muslims to awake and question their cherished faith.*

---

[4] A.Koestler, et al, *The God That Failed*, Hamish Hamilton, London, 1950, p.7
[5] Ibid. p16

Synopsis

Peace cannot be attained as long as there are ideologies that promote hate. People don't naturally do evil. They do evil when indoctrinated. Good people do evil things when they perceive injustice. Often their perception is imaginary. Masses of people can be manipulated to believe that they are victimized. They then become filled with hate, seek revenge and commit atrocities while considering them-selves righteous and justifying every cruelty. Islam is one such a doctrine.

In the 13 years since September 11, 2001, there have been over 24300 terrorst attacks, resulting in the death and injury of hundreds of thousands of civilians throughout the world. This is on average 5 terrorist attacks per day. The perpetrators of these attacks were not monsters; they were Muslims. They believed and acted in accordance with their faith. There are millions more who think like them and are ready to do the same.

If you think Islamic terrorism is a new phenomenon, think again. Islam owes its success to terrorism. Since the day Muhammad set foot in Medina, he started his campaign of terror. His followers have been doing the same ever since.

Muslims are intolerant, supremacist, bullying and violent. They are volatile and can explode if contradicted. At the same time, they abuse and violate the rights of people of other faiths. To understand them, one must understand their prophet. Muslims worship and emulate Muhammad. Islam is Muhammadism. Only by understanding him can one understand them. *Understanding Muhammad* is a psychobiography. It goes beyond the stories. It seeks to unveil the mystery of the man worshipped by 1.5 billion people.

Historians tell us Muhammad used to withdraw to a cave, spending days wrapped in his thoughts. He heard bells ringing and had ghostly visions. He thought he was demon possessed, until his wife reassured him he had become a prophet. Convinced of his prophetic status, he was intolerant of those who rejected him, assassinated those who criticized him, raided, looted, and massacred entire populations. He reduced thousands to slavery, and allowed his men to rape their female captives. All of this, he did with a clear conscience and a sense of entitlement.

He was magnanimous toward those who admired him, but vengeful toward those who did not. He believed he was the most perfect human creation and the universe's raison d'être. Muhammad was no ordinary man. He was a narcissist. Focusing on the "why" rather than the "what," this book unravels the mystique of one of the most enigmatic men in history.

Understanding Muhammad

Muhammad believed in his own cause. He was so certain of the reality of his hallucinations that he expected everyone to believe them too. In his book, he makes Allah, who was none but his own alter ego, indignantly asks "*What! Do you then dispute with him [Muhammad] as to what he saw?*"(Q.53:12) This is psychopathology. Why should others believe in what he saw? Wasn't it up to him to prove what he saw was real? Only a narcissist expects others to believe in his claims without asking for evidence.

Muhammad was an orphan. Spurned by his mother in his infancy and left in the care of a Bedouin couple, he had a loveless childhood. He then passed on to the care of his grandfather and uncle who took pity on him and spoiled him. Not receiving love at a time he needed unconditional love, and not receiving discipline when he needed to learn about boundaries, he developed a narcissistic personality disorder, which is a trait that made him a megalomaniac and bereft of conscience.

Muhammad fantasized about unlimited power, expected praise and admiration, believed he was special, and expected others to believe him and go along with his ideas and plans. He took advantage of others, was jealous, yet believed others were jealous of him, and was extremely hurt when rejected, to the point of killing those who deserted him. He lied and deceived, feeling entitled and justified in doing so. All of these emotional dysfunctions are traits of Narcissistic Personality Disorder.

Thanks to another mental illness, Temporal Lobe Epilepsy, the prophet of Islam had vivid hallucinations, which he interpreted as mystical and divine intimations. When he claimed he heard voices, saw angels and other ghostly entities, he was not lying. He could not distinguish reality from fantasy.

Muhammad also suffered from obsessive compulsive disorder, causing his fixations on numbers, rituals and stringent rules. This explains why he lived an austere life and why his religion is filled with absurd rules and rituals.

In the later years of his life Muhammad was affected by Acromegaly, a degenerative disease caused by excessive production of a growth hormone, resulting in large bones, cold and fleshy hands and feet and coarse facial features such as enlarged lips, nose and tongue. Acromegaly occurs after the age of 40 and usually kills the patient in his early 60s. It causes erectile dysfunction (impotence). On the other hand temporal lobe hyper activism increases libido. This explains Muhammad's sexual vagaries in his old age and why in the later years of his life he had such an insatiable craving for sex, but no children. He would visit all his 9 wives in one night to touch and fondle them without having intercourse. Impotence explains Muhammad's insecurity, paranoia, and intense jealousy in regards to his young wives. He ordered them to cover themselves, lest younger men would cast a lusting eye on them. Today, Muslim women veil themselves, because Muhammad was impotent. Muhammad's illnesses explain many mysteries of Islam.

The combination of all these psychological disorders and his unusual physiognomy made Muhammad a phenomenon that set him apart from ordinary

Synopsis

people. His uneducated followers interpreted those differences as signs of his prophethood. He even convinced them that a large mole on his back was the sign of his prophethood.

Like devotees of all cults, his followers rose to champion his cause with dedication. By defying death and butchering others, they made Islam the world's second largest religion, and now the biggest threat to human civilization.

Why is it important to know Muhammad? It's because over a billion people strive to emulate him. Consequently, his psychological traits are bequeathed to his followers. If he was insane, we cannot expect sanity from those who try to be like him. It is by understanding Muhammad that we can understand Muslims, and predict these unpredictable people.

We live in a dangerous time. When a fifth of humanity worships a psychopath, eulogizes suicide bombing, and thinks killing and martyrdom are ultimate acts of piety, the world becomes a dangerous place. When these people acquire the atomic bomb, the earth becomes a powder keg. Islam is a cult. As long as Muslims believe in Muhammad, they are a threat to others and to themselves.

What is the solution? Muslims must leave Islam. They must discard their culture of hate and join the rest of mankind as fellow humans. Alternatively, non-Muslims must separate themselves from them, ban Islam, end their immigration and send home those who refuse to integrate and plot against democracy.

Islam is incompatible with democracy. It is a warring creed. Muslims take advantage of democracy to promote their cult in order to destroy it. They want to establish a worldwide dictatorship.

Islam is barbarity. *Islamic culture* and *Islamic civilization* are oxymoron. On the other hand, *Islamic terrorism* is redundancy. The only way to avert the clash between this barbarity and civilization is to expose the fallacy of Islam and demystify it. Muslims must be weaned from this cult, for humanity to live in peace.

Understanding Muhammad is imperative for both Muslims and non-Muslims. This book makes that task easy.

Thousands of Muslims have left Islam after reading this book. The evidence presented is overwhelming and the conclusion is inescapable. Understanding Muhammad will put an end to Islam. Before dismissing this claim as hyperbole, read the book and you too will come to the same conclusion. The challenge is to convince Muslims to read it. A great majority of Muslims will not read books that are critical of their religion. The greatest gift one person can give to another is the gift of doubt. Unfortunately that is what Muslims dread most.

Contents

Content

Prologue

After the 9/11 attack on America, a distraught American mother told me that her son, aged 23, had converted to Islam at 14. He had married a Muslim woman whom he had never seen before in an arranged marriage by his imam (Islamic cleric), and now, with a baby, he wanted to go to Afghanistan to fight for the Taliban, killing American soldiers and become a "martyr." She also said that a few years earlier he told her that once Islam takes over America, he will not hesitate to behead her, when the order comes to slay the unbelievers.

****

Samaira Nazir, a bright and well educated 25-year-old British national of Pakistani descent was stabbed to death. Her throat was slashed by her thirty–year-old brother and her seventeen-year-old cousin at her parents' home. Samaira had dishonored her family by falling in love with an Afghan man they thought was of lower caste and had rejected suitors lined up to meet her in Pakistan. In April 2005 she was summoned to the family home and ambushed by everyone. A neighbor witnessed seeing her trying to escape while her father grabbed her by the hair, pulled her back into the house and slammed the door. She was heard screaming, "You are not my mother anymore!" which indicates that her mother was also involved in her cold-blooded murder. Her nieces, aged two and four were made to watch the whole proceeding as the neighbors heard them screaming. The amount of blood on the children suggested that they were only feet from the attack. The family was educated and well to do.

****

Muhammad Ali al-Ayed, a 23-year-old Saudi millionaire's son living in America, one August evening, in 2003, he called Sellouk, his old Jewish Moroccan friend and suggested they get together. The two had drinks at a bar before going to Al-Ayed's apartment about midnight where he took a knife, stabbed, and nearly decapitated his friend. Al-Ayed's roommate told police the two were not arguing before Al-Ayed killed Sellouk. The reason for this cold-blooded murder was "religious differences," said Ayed's attorney.

****

Mohammad Taheri-azar was a 25-year-old Iranian graduate from the University of North Carolina. One day in March 2006, he rented a SUV and drove it slowly onto the campus. Then he suddenly accelerated into the college crowd with the intent to kill as many people as he could. He hit nine people and injured six of them.

He explained the reason of his attack in a letter that he left in his apartment. He wrote, "I live with the holy Koran as my constitution for right and wrong and definition of injustice… Allah in the Koran gives permission for those who follow Allah to attack those who have waged war against them, with the expectation of eternal paradise in case of martyrdom

****

Sanao Menghwar and his wife, a Hindu couple residing in Karachi, Pakistan, were traumatized one November evening in 2005, when upon returning from work they discovered that all their three daughters were missing. After two days of futile searching, they found out that their daughters had been kidnapped and forced to convert to Islam. The police arrested three Muslim youths in connection with the crime, who were later granted bail by a court because they were minors. The girls remain missing.

"Kidnapping Hindu girls like this has become a normal practice. The girls are then forced to sign stamped papers stating that they've become Muslims," says Laljee, a Hindu resident of Karachi. "Hindus here are too frightened to vent their anger — they fear victimization," he added.

Many Hindu girls meet similar fates in Pakistan. They are abducted, forced to convert to Islam, and forced to marry a Muslim man while their parents are denied the right to see or talk to them. "How can a Muslim girl live and maintain contact with kafirs?" remarked Maulvi Aziz, the cleric representing a Muslim kidnapper in another case that was taken to the court.

When a Hindu girl is converted to Islam, hundreds of Muslims take to the streets and chant religious slogans. The cries of the parents fall on the deaf ears of authorities. The unfortunate girls are then threatened that they will be executed as apostates if they recant Islam. Often lawyers avoid taking up these cases, fearing a backlash from the extremists.

****

In October 2005, three girls were walking through a Cocoa plantation near the city of Poso in Indonesia. The girls attended a private Christian school. They were attacked and beheaded by a group of Muslims. Police said the heads were found some distance from the bodies and one of the heads was left outside a church. Muslim militants have targeted central Sulawesi Province and believe that it could be turned into the foundation stone of an Islamic state. In 2001 and 2002, Muslims began attacking the Christians in that province. The fighting drew Islamic militants from all over Indonesia and resulted in the death of more than 1,000 Christians.

****

Preface

On June 18, 2010, Pravda reported the slaughter of a 5-year-old Ukrainian boy in the town of Dneprovka, in the Crimea region. As little Viktor Shemyakin played in a sandpit with his friends, a stranger strolled up to him. He pointing to a tree and said: “Look, there is a bird up there.” When the youngster glanced upwards, the maniac plunged a knife into his throat.

The victim’s three-year-old sister and her five-year-old friend were among a group of young children who witnessed the horrifying attack. Viktor’s mother heard their screams and ran out of the house to find her child lying in a pool of blood.

The 27-year-old knifeman Server Ibragimov, was apprehended three hours later at his parents' house, where he was hiding in the loft. He confessed to the crime, telling police that he was ordered to kill the boy by God. “The man screamed Allahu Akbar when killing the boy, "said a shocked local. “The kid was slaughtered like a goat."

****

Sahnoun DaifAllah, a 42 year old chemist from Gloucester, UK, caused £700,000 damage when in May 2008 he went on spraying a mixture of his urine and feces on foods in two supermarkets, on children books in a bookshop, and in a pub, as his personal campaign of jihad. When caught by the Police, he did not resist, instead he said, you are doing your work and I am doing my work.

****

In the February of the same year two Muslim shop-owners, Saeed Hasmi, 25, and Jan Yadgari, 23, were fined £1,500 for selling chocolate cake - which had been sprinkled with human feces. A horrified customer ate the foul-smelling gateaux but noticed that it didn't taste or smell "quite right" and handed the cake to public health scientists. The analysts soon established that the sweet treat was covered in feces. The pair admitted the charge.

****

Muriel Degauque a 38-year-old Belgian woman who, according to a neighbor who knew her since childhood, was an “absolutely normal” little girl, who liked to go for sled rides when it snowed, married a Muslim man and converted to Islam. On November 9, 2005, she traveled with her husband through Syria to Iraq, where she blew herself up in an attack on an Iraqi police patrol. Five policemen were killed outright and a sixth officer and four civilians were seriously injured.

****

These acts are insane, yet their perpetrators were “absolutely normal” people. What motivated them to commit these crimes? The only answer is Islam. Everywhere Muslims are busy killing people for what they believe.

Why? What makes sane people commit insane things? Why are Muslims, as a lot, so angry with others, so at war with the world and so quick to resort to violence? Millions of Muslims riot and kill completely innocent people anywhere, when someone says something about Muhammad in another part of the world. This is insane. Yet the perpetrators are completely sane. How can we explain this paradox? Taheri-azar later declared: “I live with the holy Koran as my constitution for right and wrong and definition of justice....Allah gives permission in the Koran for the followers of Allah to attack those who have raged [sic] war against them…” Later he sent a detailed exposition of the Koran’s teachings on warfare to the Carolina campus newspaper.[6]

Has Islam been misunderstood by its practitioners? This is the question I am going to answer in this book.

To understand the violence in Islam, we must understand that Muslims want to be, think and act like their prophet. As such, their attitude, thoughts, and actions come to reflect those of his. Since in the eyes of his followers, Muhammad is the model for all that is righteous, they emulate him in every way. As the result, they come to inhabit in his bubble universe, and to the extent that they follow his examples, they become like him and extensions of him. They share his character, his attitude, and his mindset. To them, he is the best of creation, the most perfect human and the perfect model to follow. They believe that if he did something, no matter how egregious, it was the right thing. No question is asked and no judgment is allowed.

As a subject, Muhammad is one very few have engaged. Muslims get offended if one slights their prophet. Any comment, no matter how innocuous, can elicit opprobrium. Though they may allow you to criticize his followers, they do not tolerate any criticism of the prophet himself. You can criticize Allah and get away with it, but you can’t criticize Muhammad.

It is not possible to make a thorough evaluation of the psychological profile of someone centuries after his death. However, our goal is not to prescribe medication, but to get a better insight into the mind of a man who is followed by a fifth of humanity. There is a wealth of information about the life of Muhammad that is recorded meticulously. Many of these accounts are embellished with exaggeration and hyperbole. It is expected of believers to elevate the status of their prophet and attribute miracles to him. In the biography of Muhammad, however, we find thousands of accounts that don’t portray him as a holy man. He is often depicted as a vile, ruthless, cunning, and a pervert. There is no reason to believe these stories are false. It is not characteristic of believers to portray their prophet as a villain. So if such stories exist, narrated by his close companions and votaries, those who believed in him and loved him, in such a large numbers, it is likely that they are true.

Traditions that are diffusely recurrent are called *mutawattir*. These traditions have come down to later generations through chains of narrations, involving diverse transmitters. It is virtually impossible that all of them, who often lived in different localities and espoused (at times radically) different views, would come together, to fabricate the exact same damning lie and attribute it to their beloved prophet.

Availing ourselves of these stories, called hadith, and the Quran, a book believed by every Muslim to be the verbatim word of God, we will peer into Muhammad's mind, as we try to understand him and to figure out why he did what he did. And we will examine him with our understanding of psychology to assess his sanity.

This book does not intend to psychoanalyze a man who lived 1400 years ago, but to unravel his mystique. Muhammad is an enigma to many and particularly to his followers who have accepted his myth, and have embraced his image. His conduct was ungodly, yet he gave all indications that he believed in his cause. How could a man, so vengeful, so ruthless, and so depraved, have so much charisma and leave spellbound, his companions and billions of people for so many centuries?

Michael Hart, in his book, *The 100: A Ranking of the Most Influential Persons in History*, places Muhammad at the very top of his list. How could an illiterate man, become the most influential person in history? As this book will show, the answer to this question has more to do with human psyche than it does with Muhammad.

There is no other cause for which more blood has been shed than Islam. According to some historians, more than 80 million people were massacred by the sword of Islam in India alone. Millions were killed in Persia, Egypt, and in all other countries that were attacked by Muslims, both during their conquests and in the centuries that followed. These bloodsheds continue to this day.

Some estimates put the number of people massacred by Islamic mujahedeen throughout these fourteen centuries at 280 million. If we add the number of Muslims butchered by other Muslims the total becomes staggering.

In an intensive research on the cause and effect of communal riots since 18th century (the topic of her Ph.D. thesis) Zenab Banu of Gujarat has analyzed and documented major Hindu-Muslim riots spread over 250 years and concluded that over 95% of them, which often led to bloodshed, were initiated by Muslims. Her thesis has been published in a book titled 'Politics of Communalism' (1978). The Gujarati Muslims are 9% of the total population of the state. This means that Muslims, as a group, are a whopping 192 times more prone to resort to violence than others. Why?

This book presents two theses. The first is that Muhammad suffered from narcissistic personality disorder. The second is that he was affected by temporal lobe epilepsy. He had other mental disorders as well, but these two morbidities explain the phenomenon of Islam. Muhammad believed in his cause and was sincere in his claim. It's because he could not differentiate the imaginary from the real. Those who knew him best, called him *majnoon* (lunatic, crazy, possessed by jinn). Their voices of sanity were silenced when they succumbed to his brute force. However, modern discoveries in psychology have finally vindicated them.

Understanding Muhammad

Numerous books about Muhammad give full account of his violence. The best are those written by his early disciples. *Understanding Muhammad*, attempts to explain what motivated him.

Enough has been said about Muhammad being a mass murderer, a marauding gangster, a pedophile, an assassin, and a lustful womanizer. Muslims hear all that and continue believing in him without blinking. They have accepted him as a "perfect human" (*al ensan-e kamel*) and the "Mercy of God among in the worlds" (*rahmatan lil alamin*). They don't judge him by the standards of human morality. On the contrary, they believe morality should rest by his standards. For them, right-wrong and good-evil, are not determined by the Golden Rule, a concept that is alien to the Muslim psyche, but by *halal* (permitted) and *haram* (forbidden) – wanton religious values that have no basis in logic, ethics, or morality.

Muslims are genuinely incapable of questioning Islam. They dismiss every doubt and consider things that are incomprehensible as "test." To pass this test and to prove their faith, they must surrender their intelligence and believe in every absurdity. The highway to paradise, for Muslims, is through blind faith. While thinking and doubting are regarded as roads to hell.

The arguments presented in this book are not based on the authority of my background or credentials. They are backed by evidence that I present in every page. Those who read this book can no longer believe in Islam. The insight contained herein will end your faith this religion. This may sound presumptuous, but don't judge me until you read the book. The challenge is to make Muslims read it. They often give up reading when they see their faith threatened.

Chapter One

Who Was Muhammad?

Your Lord has not forsaken you, nor does He hate you. The future will be better for you than the past. And soon your Lord will give you so that you will be content. Did He not find you an orphan and give you shelter? Did He not find you wandering and guide you? Did He not find you in need and enrich you? (Q. 93:3-8)[7]

Let us begin with Muhammad's story. Who was he and what were the circumstances that influenced his thinking? In this chapter we will briefly go through the salient points of the life of a man, whom over a billion people, literally worship. Muslims claim that they worship no one but Allah. Since Allah was Muhammad's alter ego, in practice, it's him whom they worship. Islam is the personality cult of one man. We will read his words as they were dictated in the Quran, claimed by him to be the words of God, and see him through the eyes of his companions and wives. We will take a look at how he rose from a derelict preacher to become a de facto ruler of Arabia in just a decade. We will focus on how he divided people in order to control them, how he instilled sedition and hate, and roused some to wage war against others. And, how he used raids, rape, torture, and assassinations to cast terror in the hearts of his victims and subdue them. We will learn about his genocides and his penchant for

---

[7] Quran Sura 93: Verses 3-8 (Translations of the Quran in this book are either by Yusuf Ali or by Shakir.) My work is not about the sacred scriptures of Islam, but it is based directly on them. The passages I cite are taken from the Quran and the Hadith. The Quran purports to be not the work of any human, but the very words of Allâh himself, from beginning to end. The Ahadith (plural for Hadith) are short, collected anecdotes and sayings about Muhammad regarded by Muslims as essential to the understanding and practice of their religion. It is not necessary for me, in this book, to discuss the innumerable questions raised by the Quran and the Hadith, their translation into other languages, or the disputes over subtle nuances in those texts. For purposes of this book, the passages I cite will mostly speak for themselves. I have taken them from widely accepted sources.

deception as a strategy, the very strategy used by Muslims today to take over the world. By the time you finish reading this chapter, you will come to see that Muslim terrorists are doing exactly what their prophet did. They are the real Muslims, not those who claim to me moderate.

The Birth and Childhood of Muhammad

In the year 570 A.D., in Mecca, Arabia, a widowed young woman (in her teens) named Amina, gave birth to a boy whom she called Muhammad.[8] Though this was her only child, Amina gave him to a Bedouin woman to be raised in the desert when he was only six months old.

Some wealthy Arab women hired wet nurses for their infants. This allowed them to have another child right away. More children meant higher status. However, Amina was not wealthy. She was a widow with only one child to care for. Abdullah, Muhammad's father, had died six months before his birth. Also, this practice was not that common. Khadijah, the first wife of Muhammad who was one of the wealthiest women of Mecca, had three children from her previous two marriages and bore six to Muhammad. She raised them all on her own.[9]

Why would Amina foster her only child? She also did not breastfeed her infant. She gave him to Thueiba, a maid of his uncle Abu Lahab (the same uncle whom Muhammad cursed in Sura 111), to be nursed. Why Amina did not nurse or raise her child is not mentioned. All we can do is to speculate. Was she depressed? Did she think that the child was an impediment to the possibility of a remarriage?

A death in the family can lead to depression. Other factors that may increase a woman's chances of depression are: living alone, anxiety about the fetus, marital or financial problems, and the young age of the mother. Amina had just lost her husband, she was alone, poor, and young. Based on what we know about her, she was a good candidate for depression. Depression may interfere with the mother's ability to bond with her growing baby. Also, during pregnancy, it can place the

---

[8] Nur al-Din al-Halabi (d. 1634), the author of the book Insan al-`uyun fi sirat al-Amin wa-l-Ma'mun, popularly known as al-Sira al-Halabiyya, V.1 page 128, says Muhammad's birth name was Qathem قثم (not to be confused with Qasem قاسم, which was the name of Muhammad's first son). Qathem means damaged or rotten, such as damaged milk. Al-Halabi explains, "After the death of Qathem Ibn Abd-Al-Mu'taleb (Muhammad's Uncle) at the age of nine, three years before Muhammad was born, his father Abd-Al-Mu'taleb felt so bad that when the prophet was born, he named him Qathem." The Prophet changed his name to Muhammad, "the praised one" either at the age of thirty or after he migrated to Medina. This information is not known to Muslims for obvious reasons. It is not flattering. However, if it were not true, it would not have been recorded by his followers.

[9] Muhammad had four daughters and two sons. His male children, Qasim and Abd al Menaf (named after deity Menaf) died in infancy. His daughters reached adulthood and married, but they all died young. The youngest daughter, Fatima, was survived by two sons. She outlived Muhammad by only six months.

mother at risk for having an episode of depression after delivery (postpartum depression).[10]

Some researchers suggest that depression in pregnant women can have direct effects on the fetus. Their babies are often irritable and lethargic. These newborns may grow into infants who become slow learners, and emotionally unresponsive, with behavior problems, such as aggression.[11]

Muhammad grew up among strangers. He was aware that he did not belong to those people. He could see that other children had parents. Why his mother, whom he visited twice a year, did not want him? Maybe other children also teased him for being an orphan. Being an orphan is a stigma in those lands, even today.

Several decades later, Halima, Muhammad's wet nurse, recounted that at first she did not want to take an orphan child of a poor widow. She accepted him because she didn't find one from a wealthier family, and she didn't want to return with no child, when her friends who had come with her to the city had all found a child to foster. Did this reflect in the way she cared for the Muhammad? Did Muhammad feel unloved in his foster family's home during those crucial formative years when a person's character is shaped?

Halima reported that Muhammad was a solitary child. He would withdraw to an imaginary world and converse with friends that no one could see. Was this a coping mechanism of a child who felt unloved in the real world and made up one in his mind in which he was loved?

Muhammad's mental health became a matter of concern to his foster parents who when he reached the age of five, took him back to Amina. Not having found a new husband yet, Amina was reluctant to take the child back, until Halima told her about his strange behavior. They had tried to return Muhammad since he was weaned at the age of two, but each time Amina insisted that they keep him longer. Ibn Ishaq has recorded Halima's words: "His [Halima's own son] father said to me, 'I am afraid that this child has had a stroke, so take him back to his family before the result appears.'... She [Muhammad's mother] asked me what happened and gave me no peace until I told her. When she asked if I feared a demon had possessed him, I replied that I did."[12]

---

[10] Studies have shown that the newborns of the mothers with prepartum and postpartum depressive symptoms had elevated cortisol and norepinephrine levels, lower dopamine levels, and greater relative right frontal EEG asymmetry. The infants in the prepartum group also showed greater relative right frontal EEG asymmetry and higher norepinephrine levels. These data suggest that effects on newborn physiology depend more on prepartum than postpartum maternal depression but may also depend on the duration of the depressive symptoms. ncbi.nlm.nih.gov

[11] www.health.harvard.edu/newsweek/Depression_during_pregnancy_and_after_0405.htm

[12] Sirat Ibn Ishaq, page 72: Ibn Ishaq (pronounced Is-haq, Arabic for Isaac) was a Muslim historian, born in Medina approximately 85 years after Hijra (704. died 768). (Hijra is

Understanding Muhammad

It is not unusual for children to have a wild imagination. Muhammad's case must have been exceptionally alarming to concern Halima and her husband. He said, "I am afraid that this child has had a stroke." Years later, Muhammad spoke of his strange childhood experiences. "Two men in white clothes came to me with a golden basin full of snow. They took me and split open my body. Then they took my heart and split it open and took out from it a black clot which they flung away. Then they washed my heart and my body with that snow until they made them pure."[13]

What is certain is that impurities of mind don't appear as a clot in the heart. Also sins cannot be removed with surgery and snow is not a good cleaner. It is clear that with these tales Muhammad was trying to impress his less than educated followers.

The child was reunited with his mother, but that did not last long. A year later, Amina died. Muhammad did not speak of her much. When he conquered Mecca, fifty five years after her death, he visited her tomb at Abwa, a place between Mecca and Medina and wept. He told his companions, "This is the grave of my mother; the Lord has permitted me to visit it. And I sought leave to pray for her, but it was not granted. So I called my mother to remembrance, and the tender memory of her overcame me, and I wept."[14]

Why would God not allow Muhammad to pray for his mother? What had she done to not deserve forgiveness? Unless we believe that God is unjust, this does not make sense. Obviously, God had nothing to do with it. It was Muhammad who could not forgive his mother, even more than half a century after her death. Did he remember her as an unloving cold woman? Was he resentful of her? Did he have deep emotional wounds that were never healed?

Muhammad's immigration to Medina and the beginning of the Islamic calendar), He was the first biographer of Muhammad and his war expeditions. His collection of stories about Muhammad was called "Sirat al-Nabi" ("Life of the Prophet"). That book is lost. However, a systematic presentation of Ibn Ishaq's material with a commentary by Ibn Hisham (d. 834) in the form of a recension is available and translated into English. Ibn Hisham, admitted that he has deliberately omitted some of the stories that were embarrassing to Muslims. Part of those embarrassing stories were salvaged by Tabari, (838–923) one of the most prominent Persian historians and a commentator of the Quran.

[13] W. Montgomery Watt: Translation of Ibn Ishaq's biography of Muhammad (p. 36)

[14] Tabaqat Ibn Sa'd v.1, p. 106. Ibn Sa'd (784-845) was a historian, student of al Waqidi. He classified his story in eight categories, hence the name Tabaqat (categories). The first is on the life of Muhammad (Vol. 1), then his wars (Vol. 2), his companions of Mecca (Vol. 3), his companions of Medina (Vol. 4), his grandchildren, Hassan and Hussein and other prominent Muslims (Vol. 5), the followers and the companions of Muhammad (Vol. 6), his later important followers (Vol. 7) and some early Muslim women (Vol. 8). The quotes from Tabaqat used in this book are taken from the Persian translation by Dr. Mahmood Mahdavi Damghani. Publisher *Entesharat-e* Farhang va Andisheh. Tehran, 1382 solar hijra (2003 A.D.).

1- Who Was Muhammad?

Muhammad had four daughters. He named Zeinab after his aunt, Fatima after Khadijah's mother, Ruqiya, after his grand aunt, but none after his mother Amina.

After the death of Amina, Muhammad spent two years in the house of his grandfather who, mindful of him being an orphan, lavished him with excessive love. Ibn Sa'd writes that Abdul Muttalib gave the child so much attention that he had not given any of his sons.[15] Muir writes in his biography of Muhammad:

> The child was treated by him with singular fondness. A rug used to be spread under the shadow of the Ka'ba, and on it, the aged chief reclined. Around the carpet, but at a respectful distance, sat his sons. The little Muhammad was wont to run close up to the patriarch, and unceremoniously take possession of his rug. His sons would seek to drive him off, but Abdul Muttalib would interpose saying: 'Let my little son alone.' He would then stroke him on the back, as he delighted in watching his childish prattle. The boy was still under the care of his nurse, Baraka, but he would ever and anon quit her, and run into the apartment of his grandfather, even when he was alone or asleep.[16]

Muhammad remembered the preferential treatment he received from Abdul Muttalib. Peppering it with his imagination, he later said that his grandfather used to say to his uncles, "Let him alone for he has a great destiny, and will be the inheritor of a kingdom;" and would tell his nurse Baraka, "Beware lest you let him fall into the hands of the Jews and Christians, for they are looking out for him, and would injure him!"[17] However, his uncles did not remember those comments and none of them accepted Islam, except Hamza, who was of his age. Abbas also joined his cause, only after his star had risen and he was at the gates of Mecca ready to invade it.

Fate was not clement to Muhammad. Only two years after living with his grandfather, the old patriarch died at the age of eighty-two and he came under the guardianship of his uncle Abu Talib.

The orphan child felt bitterly the loss of his grandfather. As he followed his bier to the cemetery, he was seen weeping; and years later, he retained a fond memory of him.

Abu Talib faithfully discharged the trust. "His fondness for the lad equaled that of Abdul Muttalib," wrote Muir. "He made him sleep by his bed, eat by his side, and go with him whenever he walked abroad. And this tender treatment he continued until Muhammad emerged from the helplessness of childhood."[18] Ibn Sa'd quotes Waqidi saying, Abu Talib, although not wealthy, took care of Muhammad and loved him more than his own children.

---

[15] Tabaqat Volume 1, page 107

[16] The Life of Muhammad by Sir. William Muir [Smith, Elder, & Co., London, 1861] Volume II Ch. 1. P. XXVIII

[17] Tabaqat v. 1, p. 107

[18] Tabaqat v. 1. p. 108

Due to the devastating psychological blows during his childhood, Muhammad feared abandonment. This becomes evident from an incident that took place when he was 12 years old. One day, Abu Talib decided to go to Syria for a business trip. When the caravan was ready to depart, Muhammad was overcome by the prospect of so long a separation and clung to his protector. Abu Talib was moved, and carried the boy along with him.[19] This degree of attachment shows that Muhammad was in constant fear of losing his loved ones.

Despite his great affection, and even though Abu Talib remained a staunch defender of him throughout his life, doting on him even more than he did on his own children, Muhammad proved to be an ungrateful nephew. He visited his aging uncle lying in his deathbed. All the sons of Abdul Muttalib were present. Thinking always of the well-being of his nephew, Abu Talib made an earnest plea to his brothers to protect Muhammad, who was now 50 years old. They promised to do so, including Abu Lahab. Taking advantage of the situation Muhammad requested Abu Talib to convert to Islam.

He knew that his followers were mostly meek and lowly and to boost his prestige he needed people of stature to embrace his cause. Ibn Ishaq narrates: "Whenever men came together at the fairs, or the apostle heard of anyone of importance coming to Mecca, he went to them with his message."[20]

Cult leaders are aware that their message per se has no validity. They try to make it attractive by wooing people of influence and win the masses through the strength of the *argumentum ad populum* fallacy. His historiographers tell us that Muhammad rejoiced immensely when Abu Bakr and then Umar enlisted in his cause. The conversion of Abu Talib would have elevated his prestige among the Quraish, the tribe that resided within Mecca and were custodians of the Ka'ba, giving him the credibility and the status he so desperately craved. Instead, the dying man smiled and said he would rather die in the faith of his forefathers. With his hopes dashed, Muhammad walked out of the room murmuring: "I wanted to pray for him, but Allah stopped me from doing so."[21]

The Quran confirms this. "It is not for the Prophet, and those who believe, to pray for the forgiveness of idolaters even though they may be near of kin (to them), after it hath become clear that they are people of hell-fire." (Q. 9:113) It is difficult to believe that God would stop his prophet praying for the man who had raised him, protected him all his life, and sacrificed so much for him. This would lower God to a level that would render him unworthy of worship. The sacrifices Abu Talib made for the sake of Muhammad were immense. He, while yet incredulous of his nephew's claim, stood like a rock against his opponents, shielding him from any

[19] The Life of Muhammad by Sir. William Muir Vol. II Ch. 1. P. XXXIII
[20] Sirat, Ibn Ishaq page. 195
[21] Life of Muhammad, Muir Vol 2 p.195

possible harm, and for 42 years remained his most stalwart supporter. Despite that when he refused to convert to his religion, Muhammad felt so rejected that he could not bring himself even to say a prayer at his deathbed. Bukhari reports: "Narrated Abu Sa'id Al-Khudri that he heard the Prophet when somebody mentioned his uncle (i.e. Abu Talib), saying, 'Perhaps my intercession will be helpful to him on the Day of Resurrection so that he may be put in a shallow fire reaching only up to his ankles. His brain will boil from it.'"[22]

On one hand he condemned his uncle to hellfire and on the other he feigned loyalty to him claiming he would intercede for him so his uncle will have reduced punishment. Yet on several occasions he said no one has the authority to intercede with God.[23]

Muhammad's youth was relatively eventless, and not noteworthy enough for him to talk about it, or for his biographers to recount. He was shy, quiet, and not sociable. Despite the fact that he was cared for, and even spoiled by his uncle, Muhammad remained sensitive to his status as an orphan. The memories of his loveless and lonely childhood haunted him for the rest of his life.

Years passed. Muhammad remained a loner, a recluse in his own world, distant, and aloof from his peers. Bukhari[24] says Muhammad was "shyer than a veiled virgin girl."[25] He remained so all his life, insecure and timid, something he tried to compensate for by puffing himself up, through self-aggrandizement.

Muhammad did not engage in any important occupation. At times he would attend a few sheep, a profession reserved for girls and deemed unmanly by the Arabs.

Marriage to Khadijah

Finally, at the age of 25, Abu Talib secured for Muhammad a job, as a trustee for a wealthy merchant woman, a relative, named Khadijah. Khadijah was a comely forty-year-old successful merchant and twice widow. Muhammad made one trip to Syria in her service, selling her merchandise and buying what she had ordered.

---

[22] Bukhari Volume 5, Book 58, Number 224:

[23] Quran 78:37-38, 2:48, 2:122-123. 2:254, 4:123, 6:5, 6:70, 32:4, 39:19.

[24] Abu Abdullah Muhammad Bukhari (c. 810-870) was a collector of hadith also known as the *sunnah*, (collection of sayings and deeds of Muhammad). His book of hadith is considered second to none. He spent sixteen years compiling it, and ended up with 2,602 hadith (9,082 with repetition). His criteria for acceptance into the collection were amongst the most stringent of all the scholars of ahadith and that is why his book is called Sahih (correct, authentic). There are other scholars, such as Abul Husain Muslim and Abu Dawood who worked as Bukhari did and collected other authentic reports. Sahih Bukhari, Sahih Muslim and Sunnan Abu Dawood are recognized by the majority of Muslims, particularly Sunnis, as complementing the Quran.

[25] Bukhari: Volume 4, Book 56, Number 762:

Upon his return, Khadijah fell in love with him and through a maid, proposed marriage to him.

Muhammad was a needy man, both financially and emotionally. The marriage with Khadijah was a blessing. In her, he could find the mother he had craved as a child, as well as the financial security that allowed him to never work again.

Khadijah was more than willing to take care of her young husband. She had her own psychological problems who found her happiness in giving, caring, and in self-sacrifice.

Muhammad was not sociable and he was not fond of work. He preferred to withdraw from the world and retreat into his own thoughts. Even as a child, he avoided the company of his peers and did not play with them. He was often seen alone, in a pensive mood. He hardly laughed, and if he did, he covered his mouth. From this, and following the tradition of their prophet, Muslims don't regard laughing out loud to be pious.

Narcissists need to be seen in a glorified light and be with people who would mirror to them their specialness. If that is not attainable they will withdraw to their shell and become a loner. They are not comfortable among peers. They want to have fans and devotees and they often form cults that may consist of their mate or a few devotee friends.

In his secluded imaginary world, Muhammad was no longer the cast-off, unwanted child that he had come to see himself during the early years of his life, but loved, respected, praised, and even feared. When reality became hard to bear and his loneliness overwhelmed him, he would escape into his fantasy world. In this pleasant world, he could be anyone he wanted to be. He must have discovered this realm at a very young age, when he was living with his foster family and spending lonesome long days in the desert. This idyllic and comforting world of fantasy was to become his refuge for the rest of his life. It became as real to him as the real world, only better. Leaving his wife at home with nine children to care for, he would retreat to a cave around Mecca and spent his days secluding himself from the world, wrapped in his own thoughts and sweet reveries.

Mystical Experience

One day, at the age of forty, after having spent many days in the cave by himself, Muhammad had a strange experience. He experienced rhythmic muscle contractions and abdominal pains, as if someone was squeezing him violently. He had fasciculation (muscle twitching), involuntary movement of head and lips, sweating, and rapid heartbeat. In this agitated state he heard voices and had a vision of a ghost.

He ran home terrified, shivering and sweating. "Cover me, cover me," he pleaded with his wife. "O Khadijah, what is wrong with me?" He told her everything and said, "I fear that something may happen to me." He thought he had become possessed by demons again. Khadijah reassured him and bade him not to be afraid, but to rejoice because the ghost must have been an angel who had brought him the glad tiding that he had been chosen as a prophet.

Khadijah was a Hanif, a monotheistic religion of Arabia based on the belief in the patriarch Abraham. Her reassurances worked, and Muhammad was convinced of his prophetic rank. This suited him well, as it also fulfilled his desire for grandiosity. And he began preaching his message.

What was his message? The message was that he had become a messenger. As the result people had to respect him, love him, and obey him. After 23 years of preaching, the core message of Muhammad remained the same. Islam's main message is that Muhammad is a messenger of God. Beyond that, there is no other message. Failure to recognize him as such entails punishment, both in this world and in the next. Even monotheism, which now is the main argument of Islam, as we shall see later, was negotiable.

With the exception of a few troubled youths and slaves, the Meccans listened to him and paid no attention. In Mecca people were free to believe in what they wanted. Muhammad wanted their attention so he began taunting and insulting their religion. They derided him at first, and then shunned him. He ordered his handful of followers to emigrate and go to Abyssinia.

When his religion stopped growing, he decided to soften his message and compromise. Ibn Sa'd writes, "One day the Prophet was in a gathering around the Ka'ba and was reading to them the sura an-Najm (53). When he came to the verses 19-20 that read, '*Have you then considered the Lat and the Uzza, and Manat, the third, the last*?' Satan placed the following two verses in the mouth of the Prophet. '*They are pretty, and there is hope in their intercession.*'"[26]

These words pleased the Quraish. They had been chanting these very words in their own prayers. The hostilities ended and the news reached the emigrants in Abyssinia who joyously returned to Mecca.

But the trick did not work, and no new person converted to Islam. Muhammad then realized that by acknowledging the daughters of Allah as deities he had undermined his position as the sole intermediary between Allah and people, making his new religion indistinguishable pagan beliefs and therefore redundant. What should he do now? By attributing those verses to God he had committed a big blunder. Could he say God had been wrong? He had a better idea. He said that those two verses that acknowledged the daughters of Allah were not revealed to him by the Angel Gabriel. They are actually satanic verses, placed in his mouth by Satan. And that he did not realize he had been fooled, until Gabriel came to him and told him, what have you done Muhammad? I did not bring those verses down to you

[26] Tabaqat Volume I, page 191

and told him to replace them with "W*hat! For you the males and for Him the females! This indeed is an unjust division!*"[27]

This incidence made the Quraish mock Muhammad even more. They said, "Muhammad has repented of what he said about the position of your gods with Allah, altered it and brought something else."[28] To justify this flip-flopping, he claimed that all prophets had beed deceived by Satan, who inspired them with demonic verses that deceptively seemed to come from God. "*And we did not send before you any messenger or prophet, but when he desired, the Satan made a suggestion respecting his desire; but Allah annuls that which Satan casts, then does Allah establish His communications, and Allah is all Knowing, Wise. So that He may make what Satan casts a trial for those in whose hearts is diseased.*" (Q.22:52-53)

There is no record of any prophet being deceived by Satan. In fact the Bible says that Job and Jesus were tempted, but were not deceived. Muhamamd is therefore the first prophet pretender, who by his own admission has been deceived. In the last verse, Muhamamd's Allah comes to his defese and says even his blunders are the fault of his detractors whose hearts is diseased.

After thirteen years of preaching, Muhammad had no more than 100 to 120 converted. His wife, who admired and idolized him, was his first convert. Her social standing convinced Abu Bakr, Othman and Umar to join his cause too. Apart from these few, the rest of his followers were slaves and disaffected youths.

The Myth of Persecution

Muhammad's call in Mecca was received with indifference. The Meccans, like most non-Muslims of today, were tolerant of all religions. Polytheistic societies are generally tolerant by their very nature. Of course they were offended when Muhammad insulted their gods, but they did not harm him. They were derisive of him and his hare-brained religion, much like the thinking people of today are derisive of Islam, but they did not persecute him.

Ibn Ishaq reports, "When the Prophet's Companions wanted to pray, they went to the glens so that their people could not see them praying, and while Sa'd ibn Abi Waqqas was with a number of the prophet's companions in one of the glens of Mecca, a band of polytheists came upon them while they were praying and rudely interrupted them. They blamed them for what they were doing until they came to blows, and it was on that occasion that Sa'd smote a polytheist with the jawbone of a camel and wounded him. This was the first blood to be shed in Islam."[29]

Note that after their faith was insulted, all the Quraish did was to mock the Muslims. In return they were assaulted and wounded. It is okay for Muslims to

[27] Quran, 53:19-22
[28] Sira p. 167
[29] Ibn Ishaq, p. 118

malign the beliefs of others, but they will become violent if the mocking is reciprocated.

Ibn Ishaq continues, "When the apostle openly displayed Islam as God ordered him, his people did not withdraw or turn against him, so far as I have heard, until he spoke disparagingly of their gods. When he did that they took great offence and revolted unanimously to treat him as an enemy."[30]

This is enough to put at rest any claim that the hostilities in Mecca against Muslims were religious persecutions. It's normal for people to become offended when their religion and their ancestors are maligned. It is also understandable if they respond to criticism with criticism and to mockery with mockery. Muslims were not accosted because of their belief in Allah or disbelief in other deities. After all, the Jews, the Christians, and the Hanifs were also monotheists and did not believe in the idols of the Quraish. Yet, they were free to practice and preach their faith. Muslims were shunned because they were abusive and insulted the religion of the Quraish.

Finally, vexed by Muhammad's affronts, the elders of the town repaired to Abu Talib and urged him to stop his insolent nephew taunting their faith. "O Abu Talib, your nephew has insulted our gods, scorned our religion, demeaned our lifestyle, and accused our ancestors of misguidance; either you must stop him or you must let us get him, for you yourself are in the same position as we are in opposition to him and we will rid you of him."[31]

This is hardly the language and approach of persecutors. This is a plea, an ultimatum to Muhammad to stop abusing their religion. Compare it to what Muslims do when their prophet is portrayed in a few cartoons. They riot and killed hundreds of innocent people. In the spirit of community cohesion, for thirteen years, the Quraish tolerated Muhammad's insults against their gods. Their tolerance emboldened him. Bullies always become more aggressive when tolerated.

For a second time the elders of the tribe came to Abu Talib, reiterating their plea and ultimatum. Abu Talib called his nephew and bade him to be more considerate of the religion and sentiment of the people. "Oh nephew," he told Muhammad, "Your people have said many derogatory statements. Spare me and yourself. Do not make me endure more than I can."

Thinking that his uncle had forsaken him, Muhammad, put up a show. He said, "If they put the sun in my right hand and the moon in my left hand on condition that I abandon this matter (i.e. preaching Islam), until Allah has made it triumphant, or I perish therein, I would not abandon it." Then this fifty years old man stood up, turned away and started crying like a baby.

---

[30] Ibn Ishaq p.118
[31] Ibn Ishaq p.119

The theatrics worked. Muhammad knew how to manipulate his uncle. The soft hearted Abu Talib called him and said, “Come back, my nephew. Go and say whatever you like for by Allah I will never give you up.” As we shall see in the next chapter, Muhammad’s emotional maturity had never developed beyond his childhood years.

When the Quraish failed to stop him and his followers insulting their faith, they did not make good on their ultimatum. Muhammad was not harmed. This is not because they were afraid of a frail impoverished man like Abu Talib. They did not harm Muhammad out of respect of his old uncle. Of course the clan of Muhammad would have been upset if one of them was murdered. But what could one family do to an entire town? It was in the name of tolerance and community cohesion that the Quraish observed self-restraint. They paid a hefty price for that and several of them were killed as the result. Eventually, their city fell and their way of life and religion were wiped out. They could have been massacred, just like many other Arab tribes. They were spared because they were the relatives of Muslims. Appeasing the bully and tolerating intolerance are mistaken policies. Many nations fell prey to Islam and lost their identity and freedom because they tolerated an intolerant religion. History should serve as a lesson to those who believe they will have peace with Muslims, if only they tolerate their bullying.

Even after Abu Talib’s death Muhammad was not harmed. There was a lot of hostility; all caused by Muhammad, but there was no persecution. Had the Quraish been more decisive, they could have uprooted Islam. But Muslims were their own kin and they did not want to harm them. On the other hand, Muslims had severed all familial ties with their non-believing relatives and were ready to kill their nearest and dearest.

One example is Abu Hudhaifa who in the battle of Badr, challenged his father Otba to single combat. His sister Hind (Abu Sufyan’s wife) retorted in satirical verses, taunting him with his squint, and with the barbarity of offering to fight his father.[32]

When asked about the worst way in which the Quraish showed their enmity to the apostle, Abdullah ibn Amr ibn As. said:

> I was with them one day when the notables had gathered in the Hijr and the apostle was mentioned. They said that they had never known anything like the trouble they had endured from this fellow; he had declared their mode of life foolish, insulted their forefathers, reviled their religion, divided the community, and cursed their gods. What they had borne was past all bearing or words to that effect. While they were thus discussing him, the apostle came towards them and kissed the black stone, then he passed them as he walked round the temple. As he passed they said some injurious things about him. This I could see from his expression. He went on and as he passed

[32] Muid, Life of Muhammad Vol 2 Page 110

> them the second time they attacked him similarly... He stopped and said, "Will you listen to me O Quriash? By him who holds my life in His hand I bring you slaughter." This word so struck the people that not one of them but stood silent and still; even one who had hitherto been most violent spoke to him in the kindest way possible, saying, "Depart, O Abul Qasim, for by God you are not violent." So the apostle went away, and on the morrow they assembled in the Hijr, I being there too, and they asked one another if they remembered what had taken place between them and the apostle so that when he openly said something unpleasant they let him alone. While they were talking thus the apostle appeared, and they encircled him saying "Are you the one who says so-and-so against our gods and our religion?" Muhammad responded, "Yes, I am the one who says that." One person then seized his clothes and Abu Bakr interposed himself weeping and saying, "Would you kill a man for saying Allah is his Lord?" Ibn Amr said, "Then they left him. This is the worst thing that I ever saw the Quraish doing to him.[33]

One person seized his clothes. That was the worst thing the Quraish did to a man who insulted their gods and vowed to slaughter them.

Muhammad was violent and abusive, and yet when someone seized his clothe, Abu Bakr engaged in the fallacy of *argumentum ad misericordiam.* He cried and portrayed his prophet as the victim, and engaging in a straw man fallacy said, "Would you kill a man for saying Allah is his Lord?" The Quraish were not about to kill Muhammad, nor they were angry at him for saying Allah is his Lord. They were angry because he had insulted their religion.

Finally, the Quraish decided to boycott Muhammad and his abusive supporters. They stopped selling goods to them and did not buy anything from them and they agreed not to intermarry with them. This boycott lasted, perhaps two years. It was hard on the Muslims, but it shouldn't be mistaken as persecution. Boycott is not the same as killing and torturing. Persecution is what Muslims do to minorities among them. Thousands of innocent Bahais were tortured and butchered with no mercy in Iran, and it continues to this day, even though the Bahais never insulted Islam, its founder, or its book.

Persecution involves an action that leads to other vexations such as deprivation of human rights, imprisonment, torture, and loss of life. Whereas boycott is inaction and it cannot be considered as persecution. It is a natural right to abandon social and economic relations with someone who is insulting one's religion.

Ibn Ishaq says "the Quraish displayed their animosity to all those who followed the Prophet. Every clan attacked their Muslims, imprisoning and torturing them by hunger and thirst, and exposing them to the burning heat of Mecca, so as to draw

---

[33] Ibn Ishaq, Sirat Rasoul Allâh p. 131

them away from their religion."[34] However, the examples that he presents are few. He talks about Bilal, a black slave who upon converting to Islam had begun insulting the religion of his master. He was chained and left lying in the heat of the sun with a stone on his chest. Abu Bakr offered Omayyah, Bilal's master, another black slave in exchange and set Bilal free. In total Abu Bakr bought seven Muslim slaves.

Do these punishments count for religious persecution? Let us put ourselves in the shoes of those masters who expected that their slaves be respectful of them and their religion, but seeing that they had converted to this new cult, they had become scornful of their faith. They could not reason with Muslims. Islam is not based on reason. It is a religion based on blind faith. All they could do was to punish the insolence rebels. Despite that, as soon as someone offered them the price of their Muslim slaves, they gladly sold them and got rid of them. Isn't this proof that these slaves were not tortured for their faith, but because they had abandoned their duty to their masters and had become disrespectful of their religion? How many employers would keep the services of an employee who insults their religion? Why should a master tolerate his slave insulting his religion?

Ibn Sa'd says, "Every clan attacked their Muslims" These Muslims were their own children who had turned against their religion and their ancestors. Their parents and relatives were upset that they had joined a cult, and since reasoning with Muslims is out of question, they tried to coerce them to make them abandon their wretched way.

Depriving one's rebellious child of pocket money, food, and even beating them to rectify them is not religious persecution. People do anything to make their rebellious children come to their senses. This was and still is considered a parental right and duty in the Middle Eastern societies.

Ibn Ishaq also narrates a story of a few Meccan youths deciding to seize a few Muslim trouble makers and admonish them. One of the Muslims was a brother of Hisham ibn Walid who was a strong man. When they told him about their plan he said, "Admonish him, but beware that you do not kill him, for I swear by God that if you kill him, I will kill the noblest of you to the last man."[35] The youths desisted pursuing their idea.

Although tension was high, which was caused by Muhammad and his followers, and although the Meccans did their best to save their children from the new cult, which included, not letting them out of the house, or in the case of slaves, beating them, they were not willing to harm them. The story of persecution of Muslims is a deception that has been rehashed for 1400 years and accepted as true. It is not supported by facts.

---

[34] Ibid p. 143

[35] Ibn Ishaq; Sirat Rasoul Allah p. 145

1- Who Was Muhammad?

Even today, Muslims claim to be victims and oppressed when their demands are not met and when their religion is criticized. From Palestine to Kashmir, from Philippines to Chechnya, from Somalia to Nigeria, and everywhere on this planet, including in western countries, Muslims are the abusers and the aggressors and at the same time they are the ones who cry victim.

A hadith narrates that Umar, prior to his conversion, had tied up his sister forcing her to leave Islam.[36] He is also reported to have savagely beaten his maid.[37] Umar was a violent man, both before and after his conversion.

In the Middle East individualism is an alien concept. What you believe and what you do is everyone's business. Women in particular cannot make their own decisions. Even today, Muslim women can be "honor-killed" if they decide to marry a man of their choice without the consent of their family or dress "wrongly".

Another case of alleged persecution is that of Othman who was seized and bonded by his uncle Hakam, who told him, "Do you prefer a new religion to that of your fathers? I swear I will not set you free until you give up this new faith you are following." Othman said; "By the Lord, I will never abandon it!" So when Hakam saw his firmness in the faith, he let him go.[38] Can we call this religious persecution?

Sometimes these pressures worked and some of the families were successful to coerce their children and make them leave Islam. This frightened Muhammad and to avoid more defection, he ordered his followers to leave Mecca. Eighty three of them migrated to Abyssinia. Their relatives dispatched two men to Negus, the king of Abyssinia, to demand their extradition. Negus refused.

The two emissaries discussed the matter. One of them said, "Tomorrow I will tell Negus something that will uproot them all." The other replied, "Do not do it, for they are still our kindred though they have gone against us."[39] This is enough to prove that Muslims were never persecuted in the sense that we understand religious persecution. The Meccans wanted their children back, but did not want Negus to become angry with them and harm them. The idea was to tell Negus, who was a Christian that Muslims insult Jesus by denying he is the son of God and called him a slave.

There is a story about a slave woman known as Summayyah. It is claimed that Summayyah, her husband Yassir, and her son Ammar were made to sit in the heat of the sun until they recant and that she was subsequently killed.

The story of Sumayyah is reported by Ibn Sa'd. He write, "Sumayyah was one of the early believers of Mecca, she used to be tortured so that she may abandon the religion of God and she showed forbearance. Until one day Abu Jahal passed in

---

[36] Sahih Bukhari *Volume 5, Book 58, Number 207*

[37] Ibn Ishaq; Sirat Rasoul Allah p. 144

[38] Tabaqat, Ibn Sa'd Vol 3 p. 46

[39] Ibn Ishaq, Sirat Rasoul Alllah p. 152

front of her and hit her chest with his javelin. She died from that wound. She, who was an old and enfeebled woman, was the first martyr in Islam."[40]

The way to understand this story, from how it is written, is that Abul Hakam passed by. Summayyahah, following the instruction of his prophet, must have insulted his religion and he hit her with his javelin. She was wounded and as the result of that wound and lack of hygiene she died some times later. This shows her death was not premeditate or intentional. Why would anyone want to kill an old woman and leave others? Her husband and son had also converted. Why no other Muslim was killed? This does not seem to be a case of intentional murder.

By telling his followers to disobey their non-Muslim masters and parents, and disparage their religion, Muhammad was disrupting the social order in Mecca. Because of that he was a *persona non grata* among his people. Yet, at no time was he or his any of followers were persecuted because of their faith.

Polytheists generally don't care about what others believe. They are pluralistic. Ka'ba housed 360 idols, each a patron of a different tribe. There were Jews, Christians, Zoroastrians, Hanifs or Sabeans and all sorts of other religions in Arabia. There were also other prophets preaching their faiths. Religious intolerance in Arabia began with Islam. It was Muhammad who insulted the faiths of others and when he came to power, slew his detractors wherever he found them.

There is also a story about a certain Abdullah Ibn Masoud who attended a religious gathering of the Quraish and started chanting the Quran. People were puzzled and wondered what he was doing. Someone said he was chanting from the verses brought by Muhammad. They slapped him and kicked him out.[41] This Muslim was a heckler. He had gone to that gathering to provoke and to agitate. He was beaten for being a nuisance. What would Muslims do if a person goes to their mosque and chants some verses from a different religious text? In Saudi Arabia one is not allowed to read the Bible even in the privacy of one's own home.

Today, Muslims build their mosques and minarets in every Western city and pollute the air with the noise of *azan*. The goal is the same. Everything they do, from how they dress to how they bring the traffic to a halt pretending to be praying in the middle of the streets in western cities, is designed to provoke.

There is no evidence of any persecution against Muhammad and Muslims in Mecca. Nonetheless, Muslims make this claim because Muhammad made it. Astonishingly, even some non-Muslim historians who are not sympathetic to Islam have fallen into this trap and have echoed this untruth.

Everywhere, it is Muslims who are killing, oppressing and persecuting. Yet they are the ones who claim to be the victims and the oppressed ones. To understand

---

[40] Tabaqat v.8, p.276

[41] Tabari V. 3, p. 877

this bizarre behavior we must understand the psychology of Muhammad and that is the scope of this book.

Muhammad preached intolerance even when he was still in Mecca. Muslims often quote Sura 109 as evidence that he preached tolerance. This Meccan sura reads:

> *Say : O ye that reject Faith!*
> *I worship not that which ye worship,*
> *Nor will ye worship that which I worship.*
> *And I will not worship that, which ye have been wont to worship,*
> *Nor will ye worship that which I worship.*
> *To you be your Way, and to me mine*

Maududi, Qutb and many other Muslim scholars knew better. They don't see this sura as an indication of tolerance. Maududi, in his interpretation of the Quran wrote:

> If the sura is read with this background in mind, one finds that it was not revealed to preach religious tolerance as some people of today seem to think, but it was revealed in order to exonerate the Muslims from the disbeliever's religion, their rites of worship, and their gods, and to express their total disgust and unconcern with them and to tell them that Islam and kufr (unbelief) had nothing in common and there was no possibility of their being combined and mixed into one entity. Although it was addressed in the beginning to the disbelieving Quraish in response to their proposals of compromise, yet it is not confined to them only, but having made it a part of the Quran, Allah gave the Muslims the eternal teaching that they should exonerate themselves by word and deed from the creed of kufr wherever and in whatever form it be, and should declare without any reservation that they cannot make any compromise with the disbelievers in the matter of Faith. That is why this Surah continued to be recited when the people to whom it was addressed as a rejoinder, had died and been forgotten, and those Muslims also continued to recite it who were disbelievers at the time it was revealed, and the Muslims still recite it centuries after they have passed away, for expression of disgust with and dissociation from kufr and its rites is a perpetual demand of Faith.[42]

Immigration to Medina

Busy with numerous children and a self-absorbed husband, Khadijah neglected her business. By the time she died, the family was impoverished. Shortly after, Muhammad's other supporter, Abu Talib, also died. Withought these two staunch allies and ignored by the Meccans, he decided to emigrate to Yathrib, where he had received pledges of allegiance by some of its inhabitants. He ordered his followers

[42] http://www.usc.edu/dept/MSA/quran/maududi/mau109.html

to go first. Some of them were reluctant. He told them that if they did not go, they would "*find their abode in Hell.*"[43] He expected compliance or he made threats.

Muhammad himself stayed behind. Then, one night, he claimed that Allah told him, his enemies were plotting to hurt him, and asked his loyal friend Abu Bakr to secretly accompany him to Yathrib. The following verse is about that intimation, "*Remember how the Unbelievers plotted against you [Muhammad], to keep you in bonds, or slay you, or get you out (of your home). They deceive, and Allah too deceives; but the best of deceivers (makerin) is Allah.*"(Q.8:30)

It appears that Allah was guessing what the Meccans were plotting. Is this verse the words of an all knowing God or the fears of a paranoid Man? Muhammad lived among the Meccans for thirteen years, taunting them and insulting their religion, and yet they had tolerated him. Except for Muhammad's own claim, there is no historical evidence that the Meccans ever tried to harm him.

One proof that Muhammad was never at risk in Mecca is the discourse of his uncle Abbas at Aqaba. When the new coverts of Yathrib came to Mecca to pledge their allegiance to Muhammad, Abbas stood up and said, "O People of Khazraj, you know what position Muhammad holds among us. We have protected him from our own people who think as we do about him. He lives in honor and safety among his people, but he will turn to you and join you. If you think that you can be faithful to what you have promised and protect him from his opponents, then assume the burden you have undertaken. But if you think that you will betray and abandon him after he has gone out with you, then leave him now, for he is safe where he is."[44] This contradicts the claim made in the Quran 8:30 that unbelievers were plotting to bond, or to slay or to exile Muhammad. How can we reconcile these contradictory statements? Truth was irrelevant for Muhammad. He said what was needed in every situation.

The night Muhammad escaped to Medina, marks the beginning of the Islamic calendar. In Medina, he found Arabs who were less sophisticated than the Meccans. An added advantage was that they were ignorant of his background and character, to which the Meccans were privy. As a result, they were more receptive to his message.

The claim that Muhammad and Muslims were persecuted in Mecca is accepted uncritically by many, if not all non-Muslim historians. However, this is a bogus claim. All that the Quraish did was to criticize Islam and to persuade those who had fallen prey to it, to leave it. For Muhammad opposition was the same as oppression. Even today, Muslims complain of being oppressed when their religion is criticized. The fact is that it was Muhammad, not the Meccans, who ordered his followers to leave their homes, first to Abyssinia and then to Yathrib. He promised. "*To those*

---

[43] Quran, 4:97: "When angels take the souls of those who die in sin against their souls, they say: 'In what (plight) were ye?' They reply: 'Weak and oppressed were we in the earth.' They say: 'Was not the earth of Allâh spacious enough for you to move yourselves away?' Such men will find their abode in Hell, - What an evil refuge!"
[44] Sirat Rasoul p. 203

who leave their homes in the cause of Allah, after suffering oppression, we will assuredly give a goodly home in this world; but truly the reward of the Hereafter will be greater. If they only realized (this)!" (Q.16:41)

In Yathrib, the immigrants had no source of income. How was Muhammad to deliver this promise and give "goodly homes" to those who, at his behest, had forsaken theirs? They had become poor and relied on the charity of the Ansar, the Medinan Muslims, for their sustenance. Muhammad had to provide for these people wor he was about to lose his credibility. His followers were whispering their discontent. Some defected from his camp. He responded to this crisis with another threat. "*They [the unbelievers] long that you should disbelieve even as they disbelieve, that you may be upon a level (with them). So choose not friends from them till they forsake their homes in the way of Allah; if they turn back (to enmity) then take them and kill them wherever you find them, and choose neither friend nor helper from among them.*" (Q.4:89)

How can we reconcile these friendship prohibitions and threats with the claim that the Meccans had driven Muslims out of their homes? In this verse, Muhammad is telling his followers to kill those Muslims who attempt to defect and return to Mecca. Cult leaders cannot tolerate defection. What Muhammad did is not different from what Jim Jones did to those who wanted to leave his compound in Guyana. He ordered his men to shoot anyone attempting to escape. Cult leaders isolate their followers. This gives them total control over them. When one is separated from family and friends and joins a cult where everyone is bewitched, it becomes difficult to think or question the leader.[45]

Why the Yathribi Arabs Converted?

Muhammad was not the first Arab prophet. Several pretenders from other parts of Arabia were his near contemporaries. The best known was Musailama, but

---

[45] Jalal al-Din al-Suyuti says: "A group of people from Mecca accepted Islam and professed their belief; as a result, the companions in Mecca wrote to them requesting that they emigrate too; for if they don't do so, they shall not be considered as those who are among the believers. In compliance, the group left, but were soon ambushed by the nonbelievers (Quraish) before reaching their destination; they were coerced into disbelief, and they professed it." [Jalal al-Din al-Suyuti "al-Durr al-Manthoor Fi al- Tafsir al-Ma-athoor," vol.2, p178;]
Suyuti writes that in one hadith Allâh's Apostle said, "There is no Hijra (i.e. migration) (from Mecca to Medina) after the Conquest (of Mecca), but Jihad and good intention remain; and if you are called (by the Muslim ruler) for fighting, go forth immediately." This shows that prior to the conquest of Mecca, emigration from that town was one of the requisites for Muslims. This is additional evidence of the fact that Muslims were coerced by Muhammad to abandon their homes, while their families did everything they could to keep their loved ones from following this man.
Jalal al-Din al-Misri al-Suyuti al-Shafi`i al-Ash`ari, also known as Ibn al-Asyuti (849-911) was the mujtahid imam and renewer of the tenth Islamic century. He was a hadith master, jurist, Sufi, philologist, and historian. He authored works in virtually every Islamic science.

unlike him, Musailama was successful in his own town and among his own people. A woman called Sijah was also a claimant to that title and she too had a sizable following among her people. Both these prophets were preaching monotheism. This is convincing evidence that prior to Islam, women in Arabia were more respected and had more rights than at any time since. None of these other prophets resorted to violence in order to expand their religion and they did not raid and rob people as Muhammad did. They did not want to conquer territories and build empires, but rather, in the tradition of the Biblical prophets, were solely interested in preaching and in inviting people to worship God. There was no rivalry among them and they often cooperated with each other. Muhammad was the only prophet-warrior of Arabia. He and his successors waged war on his competitors and their followers and killed them.

The Arabs of Yathrib accepted Muhammad readily, not because of the profundity of his teachings, which as stated above, consisted only in asserting his claim, but because of their rivalry with the Jews. The Jews, considered themselves to be "chosen people." They were also wealthier and more educated than the Arabs and, as the result, were envied by them. Most of Yathrib was owned by the Jews. This city was originally a Jewish town. The story of Yathrib should be read by all Westerners because, what happened in that town is a clear example of the failure of multiculturalism and its dire consequence.

Kitab al-Aghani traces the first settlement of the Jews in Ythrib back to the time of Moses.[46] However, in the 10th century book *Futuh al-Buldan* (*The Conquest of The Towns),* Al Baladhuri writes that, according to the Jews, a second Jewish immigration took place in 587 BC, when Nebuchadnezzar, the king of Babylon, destroyed Jerusalem and dispersed the Jews throughout the world. In Yathrib, the Jews earned their livelihood as merchants, goldsmiths, blacksmiths, artisans, and farmers, whereas the Arabs were laborers and mostly worked for them. They came to Yathrib at least a thousand years after the Jews, i.e. in 450 or 451 A.D., when a great flood in Yemen forced various Arab tribes of the Saba region to migrate to other parts of the Peninsula. They came as economic refugees. Once they converted to Islam, they banished and massacred their hosts and took over their city. The European and all non-Muslim countries would ignore the lessons of history at their own peril.

After gaining a foothold in Yathrib, the Arabs started to raid and rob the Jews. Jews in return said what any oppressed people would; that when their Messiah comes he will take their revenge from them. When the Arabs heard Muhammad was claiming to be a messenger of God and proclaiming himself to be the one

[46] A collection of poems in many volumes compiled by Abu al-Faraj Ali of Esfahan. It contains poems from the oldest epoch of Arabic literature down to the 9th cent. It is an important source of information on medieval Islamic society.

foretold by Moses, they thought that if they convert to Islam they will outrival the Jews. They did not convert because they found anything of value in Muhammad's calling, but out of political expediency. The following passage reveals the level of ignorance and gullibility of the early Muslims.

Ibn Ishaq narrates:

> Now Allah had prepared the way for Islam in that they [The Arabs] lived side by side with the Jews, who were people of the Scriptures and knowledge, while they themselves were polytheists and idolaters. They had often raided them in their district, and whenever bad feeling arose, the Jews used to say to them, 'A prophet will be sent soon. His day is at hand. We shall follow him and kill you by his aid; So when they heard the apostle's message, they said one to another: 'This is the very prophet of whom the Jews warned us. Don't let them get to him before us!'[47]

It is ironic that Judaism and its messianic belief should become the reason for the success of Islam and the basis of the first Jewish holocaust in Arabia.

Divide and Rule

Notwithstanding his frantic threats that divine punishment awaited those who would abandon him, Muhammad had to find a practical way to provide a source of livelihood for his followers. The solution is to convert his followers into bandits. He said that since the Meccans had driven them out of their homes it was lawful for them to plunder them. "*Permission (to fight) is given to those upon whom war is made because they are oppressed, and most surely Allah is well able to assist them. Those who have been expelled from their homes without a just cause except that they say: Our Lord is Allah.*" (Q.22:39-40)

The Meccans had not driven the Muslims out of their homes. They wanted them back. They even kept them bonded so they would not escape. Muhammad lied to justify his crimes. Meanwhile, he made his god issue many verses prodding his followers to fight the non-believers. "*O Prophet! Rouse the believers to the fight. If there are twenty amongst you, patient and persevering, they will vanquish two hundred: if a hundred, they will vanquish a thousand of the unbelievers: for these are a people without understanding.*" (Q.8:65)

Muhammad justified these attacks by playing the victim. He claimed that the unbelievers had been oppressing the Muslims and waging war against them. In reality, it was he who initiated the hostilities, raided the Meccans' caravans and killed them.

The contradiction is obvious. In one verse he urges his followers to emigrate and threatens those who might be thinking of staying behind with hellfire and

---

[47] Sirat Ibn Ishaq, P.197

murder, and in other verses he claims that Muslims have been expelled without just cause and refers to them as "*those against whom war is made.*"

This is what Muslims do today. They are the ones oppressing non-Muslims, terrorizing them and perpetrating systematic persecution of minorities among them. While at the same time they cry victim and portray themselves as the wronged ones. By claiming to be victims they justify more atrocities on their victims.

The Arabic proverb: *Darabani, wa baka; Sabaqani, wa'shtaka.* "He struck me, and started crying; then he preceded me and charged me with beating him!" is a perfect description of Muhammad's modus operandi. This strategy made him dazzlingly successful. He roused sons against their fathers, turned brothers against brothers, and undermined tribal alliances, and by doing so, he corroded the fabric of the society. Using this tactic, he eventually brought all of Arabia under his domination.

Do not assume that there is something about Arabs that makes them particularly susceptible to wickedness. Westerners converting to Islam become just as inimical to their own people and countries. John Walker Lindh converted to Islam and went to Afghanistan to fight for Al-Qaeda against America. Joseph Cohen was an orthodox Jew who converted to Islam; and today, he says that killing Israelis, including their children, is legitimate.[48] Yvonne Ridley, the BBC journalist who sneaked into Afghanistan in 2001 and was captured by the Taliban, converted to Islam upon her release and now she hates her own country so much that she calls it "the third most hated country of the world." She supports suicide bombings, calling them "martyrdom operations," and has called the notorious terrorist Abu Musab al-Zarqawi, the terrorist who killed thousands of Iraqis in a brutal campaign of violence and masterminded the bombing in Jordan that killed 60 and injured 115 persons in a wedding ceremony, "a hero." And the Chechen terrorist leader Shamil Basayev, the mastermind of the Moscow theatre hostage crisis and the Beslan school massacre, is for Ridley, "a martyr whose place in Paradise is assured."[49] Those who convert to Islam, lose their humanity. To the extent that they are influenced by Muhammad, they become like him, capable of murdering their own people.

Promise of Heavenly Rewards

In many places, the Quran exhorts Muslims to raid and loot for reward in this world and in the next. "*Allah promises you much booty that ye will capture.*" (Q. 48:20)

To placate the conscience of those who might have felt some guilt, he made his god say: "*Enjoy what you took in war, lawful and good.*"(Q. 8:69)

---

[48] http://www.youtube.com/watch?v=BJLsdydjSPo
[49] *Daily Muslims*, July 12, 2006

1- Who Was Muhammad?

The verse 8:74 says, "*Those who believe, and adopt exile, and fight for the Faith, in the cause of Allah as well as those who give (them) asylum and aid, - these are (all) in very truth the Believers: for them is the forgiveness of sins and a provision most generous.*"

One who is not familiar with Quran's style, may wonder how the order to loot can be reconciled with the command to fear Allah. Those who read the Quran in Arabic notice that the verses rhyme. Muhammad often added words or phrases that are out of place, such as 'fear Allah,' 'Allah is most merciful,' 'He is all knowing, all wise,' etc., to make his verses rhyme. Otherwise, it is inconceivable to fear God and at the same time pillage and murder innocent people. By doing so, i.e. by associating God with looting, genocide, and rape, Muhammad lowered the moral standards of his followers and sanctified evil. Thus, pillage became holy pillage, killing became holy killing, and iniquity was sanctioned and even glorified. He assured his men that those who fight for their Faith will be rewarded, not only with the spoils of war in this world, but also with forgiveness of their sins in the next. If you are a sinner, just kill the non-Muslims, loot them and rape them and your sins will be forgiven. Doesn't this explain why so many Muslims are so eager to kill non-Muslims all over the world? It is not about land, it is not about poverty, it is about paradise. When a Muslim kills a non-Muslim or even a Muslim whom he regards as a heretic, he is promised to go to paradise.

Many Muslim atrocities throughout the centuries were inspired by these verses. Amir Tîmûr-i-lang, a.k.a. Tamerlane (1336-1405), was a ruthless man who became emperor through banditry. In an autobiographical memoir, *The History of My Expedition against India*, he wrote:

> My principal object in coming to Hindustan (India) and in undergoing all this toil and hardship has been to accomplish two things. The first was to war with the infidels, the enemies of Islam; and by this religious warfare to acquire some claim to reward in the life to come. The other was a worldly object; that the army of Islam might gain something by plundering the wealth and valuables of the infidels: plunder in war is as lawful as their mothers' milk to Muslims who war for their faith, and the consuming of that which is lawful is a means of grace."[50]

Even if we assume that those eighty or so Muslims who emigrated were forced out by the Meccans, how can this justify the raids on the caravans? The goods in those caravans did not necessarily belong to the people who allegedly exiled the Muslims. Is anyone who thinks they are being persecuted in a city justified in taking his revenge on any citizen of that city? Muslims use the same logic when they bomb and kill innocent civilians. If they perceive a country is unfriendly to them, they

---

[50] Malfuzat-i Timuri, or Tuzak-i Timuri, by Amir Tîmûr-i-lang In the History of India as told by its own historians. The Posthumous Papers of the Late Sir H. M. Elliot. John Dowson, ed. 1st ed. 1867. 2nd ed., Calcutta: Susil Gupta, 1956, vol. 2, pp. 8-98.

think it is okay to kill anyone from that country. If their alleged oppressors are from a nominally Christian country, Christiand from all over the world become legitimate targets, including the children, because "they are from them."[51]

Everything Muslims do today that baffles the world is an imitation of what Muhammad did. In Chapter 22, Verse 39 of the Quran, Allah gives permission to fight. This is the very same verse with which Osama Bin Laden began one of his letters to America. Can we really say that Islam has nothing to do with Islamic terrorism?

Incite to Violence

In Medina, the immigrants were a mere handful. To be effective in his raids, Muhammad also needed the help of native Muslims.

However, these Arabs had not joined Islam to raid caravans. Believing in Allah is one thing. Raiding, robbing, and killing people are something else. Arabs, prior to Muhammad, were not used to religious wars. Even today, there are Muslims who do not want to fight and kill for their religion. To persuade this kind of followers, Muhammad made his Allah issue the following command: "*Fighting is good prescribed for you, and you dislike it. But it is possible that you dislike a thing which is good for you, and that you love a thing, which is bad for you. But Allah knows, and you know not.*" (Q. 2:216)

Soon, his efforts bore fruit. Goaded by greed of booty and goosed by the promises of rewards in the afterlife, the Medinan Muslims joined Muhammad in the profession of banditry. As his army grew and his ambition soared, the thug decided to graduate to potentate. He encouraged his followers, not only to wage war for him "in the way of Allah" but also to pay for the expenses of those wars. "*And spend of your wealth in the cause of Allah, and make not your own hands contribute to (your) destruction; but do good; for Allah loves those who do good.*" (Q.2:195)

Note how he linked "doing good" with looting, terror, and murder. It is by this very twisted morality that Muslims are able to sacrifice their conscience and take up a sociopathic situational ethics toward other groups, one that must always be played to their advantage. Whichever situation that benefits Muslims is considered "good." Muhammad made his followers believe that subsidizing his warfare and committing such acts of terror for Islam are the best deeds in the sight of Allah.

Muslims who cannot fight must contribute to Islamic "charities." Islamic "charities" are not established to build hospitals, orphanages, schools or senior housings. They are to expand Islam, to build mosques and madrassas, to train terrorists and to finance jihad. Islamic charities will aid the poor only to enlist them as soldiers of Islam. A good example of that is the huge amount of money that the

---

[51] Sahih Muslim Book 019, Number 4321, 4322 and 4323:

Islamic Republic of Iran pays to the Hezbollah of Lebanon. The masses of Iranians are living in poverty. They are in dire need of food, jobs, and shelter, while their wealth is given away to Lebanese Shiites. The idea is to make Islam sweet in their mouths and to enlist them in the war against Israel.

When people didn't pony up enough funds for his military campaigns, Muhammad would angrily rebuke them. "*And what reason have you that you should not spend in Allah's way? And Allah's is the inheritance of the heavens and the earth, not alike among you are, those who spent before the victory and fought (and those who did not): they are more exalted in rank than those who spent and fought afterwards.*" (Q.57:10)

He said, the money you spend warfare is like a loan you give to Allah, and he has promised you "goodly interest." "*Who is he that will Loan to Allah a beautiful loan? For (Allah) will increase it manifold to his credit.*" (Q.57:11)

While he wanted his followers to finance his wars, he did not want them to brag about their contributions. Making sacrifices was to be understood as a privilege. It was the believer who had to be grateful to him for the opportunity of serving him and giving him his money, and not the other way round. "*Those who spend their substance in the cause of Allah, and follow not up their gifts with reminders of their generosity or with injury, -for them their reward is with their Lord: on them shall be no fear, nor shall they grieve.*" (Q. 2:262)

After rousing his followers to wage war, he assured them of their rewards. "*So when you meet in battle those who disbelieve, then smite the necks until when you have overcome them, then make (them) prisoners, and afterwards either set them free as a favor or let them ransom (themselves) until the war terminates. That (shall be so); and if Allah had pleased He would certainly have exacted what is due from them, but that He may try some of you by means of others; and (as for) those who are slain in the way of Allah, He will by no means allow their deeds to perish.* (Q.47:4)

In other words, Allah does not need help to kill the unbelievers, but he wants Muslims to do it, to test their faith. Allah can be likened to a mafia godfather, who tests the loyalty of his henchmen by asking them to kill.

In Islam, the faith of the believer is ultimately tested by their bloodthirstiness and their readiness to kill and to die. He said, "*And prepare against them what force you can and horses tied at the frontier, to frighten thereby the enemy of Allah and your enemy and others besides them, whom you do not know (but) Allah knows them; and whatever thing you will spend in Allah's way, it will be paid back to you fully and you shall not be dealt with unjustly.*" (Q. 8:60)

Muhammad made empty promises that those who warred (with body or finances) against unbelievers will find rewards piled high in the afterlife. In characterizing these rewards, he was indeed most generous and extravagant. He claimed there will be all kinds of goodies and endless sensual pleasures. And he warned those who were stingy in subsidizing his raids:[52]

> *Believers! Shall I point out to you a profitable course that will save you from a woeful scourge? Have faith in Allah and His apostle, and fight for Allah's cause with your wealth and with your persons. That would be best for you, if you but knew it. He will forgive you your sins and admit you to gardens watered by running streams; He will lodge you in pleasant mansions in the gardens of Eden. That is the supreme triumph.* (Q.61:10-12)
>
> *[In Paradise] they shall recline on couches lined with thick brocade, and within reach will hang fruits of both gardens. Which of your Lord's blessings would you deny? Therein are bashful virgins whom neither man nor jinnee will have touched before. Which of your Lord's blessings would you deny? Virgins as fair as corals and rubies. Which of your Lord's blessings would you deny?* (Q.55:54-56)
>
> *[In Paradise] theirs shall be gardens and vineyards, and high-bosomed maidens for companions: a truly overflowing cup.* (Q.78:32-33)
>
> *Believe in Allah and His messenger, and spend out of the whereof He has made you heirs. For, those of you who believe and spend, - for them is a great Reward. (Q.57:7)* [53]

These and similar verses show why so many Islamic charities have been caught financing terrorist organizations.[54] One would think that charity and terrorism are contradictions, but such a distinction is not obvious to Muslims. Islamic charities are meant to promote Islam and to support jihad. To us, jihad is terrorism; to a Muslim, it is holy war, an obligation and the most meritorious act in the sight of Allah.

---

[52] Quran, Chapter 47, Verse 38: "Behold, ye are those invited to spend (of your substance) in the Way of Allâh: But among you are some that are niggardly. But any who are niggardly are so at the expense of their own souls. But Allâh is free of all wants, and it is ye that are needy. If ye turn back (from the Path), He will substitute in your stead another people; then they would not be like you!"

[53] See also Chapter 63, Verse 10.

[54] An affidavit made public in federal court in Virginia in August 19, 2003, contends that the Muslim charities gave $3.7 million to BMI Inc., a private Islamic investment company in New Jersey that may have passed the money to terrorist groups. The money was part of a $10 million endowment from unnamed donors in Jiddah, Saudi Arabia. http://pewforum.org/news/display.php?NewsID=2563
Also on July 27, 2004, the U.S. Justice Department unsealed the indictment of the nation's largest Muslim charity and seven of its top officials on charges of funneling $12.4 million over six years to individuals and groups associated with the Islamic Resistance Movement, or Hamas, the Palestinian group that the U.S. government considers to be a terrorist organization. http://www.washingtonpost.com/wp-dyn/articles/A18257-2004Jul27.html

Thus, to fight in the cause of Allah became an ordinance, binding upon all Muslims. He roused the Meccan emigrants against their own kin and called for vengeance to be taken against those who alleged persecuted them. "*Fight until there is no fitnah (mischief/dissension) and religion is wholly to Allah.*" (Q. 8:39)

When some of his followers showed reluctance to wage war on their own relatives, he warned them of their dire fate if they disobeyed. "*And those who believe say: Why has not a chapter been revealed? But when a decisive chapter is revealed and fighting is mentioned therein you see those in whose hearts is a disease look to you with the look of one fainting because of death. Woe to them then!*" (Q.47:20)

If these verses tell us one thing, it is that Islam is by definition belligerent. As long as people believe in Islam and think that the Quran is the word of God, Islamic terrorism will always win out. Those within Islam who might call for moderation, tolerance and "dialogue between civilizations," are easily silenced by the authority of the Quran, so many of its verses rouse believers to wage war against unbelievers. "*Fight then in Allah's way; this is not imposed on you except in relation to yourself, and rouse the believers to ardor maybe Allah will restrain the fighting of those who disbelieve and Allah is strongest in prowess and strongest to give an exemplary punishment.*" (Q. 4:84)

Promising his followers success, he said: "*And Allah will by no means give the unbelievers a way against the believers,*" *(Q. 4:141)* and reassuring them of heavenly rewards he said, "*Those who believed and fled (their homes), and strove hard in Allah's way with their property and their souls, are much higher in rank with Allah; and those are they who are the achievers (of their objects).* (Q. 9:20)[55]

Muslims scholars everywhere, echo this incitement to violence. Saudi Arabia's leading religious figure, its grand mufti, defended the spirit of jihad, as a God-given right. "The spread of Islam has gone through several phases, secret and then public, in Mecca and Medina," the holiest places in Islam, said Sheikh Abdel Aziz Al Sheikh in a statement carried by the state news agency SPA. "God then authorized the faithful to defend themselves and to fight against those fighting them, which amounts to a right legitimized by God, 'This... is quite reasonable, and God will not hate it,'"[56] he said.

Saudi Arabia's most senior cleric explained that war was not Muhammad's first choice: "He gave three options: either accept Islam, or surrender and pay tax, and they will be allowed to remain in their land, observing their religion under the

[55] See also Quran, 8:72, "Those who believed and those who suffered exile and fought (and strove and struggled) in the path of Allâh, - they have the hope of the Mercy of Allâh: And Allâh is Oft-forgiving, Most Merciful." and
Quran Chapter 8, Verse 74: "Those who believe, and adopt exile, and fight for the Faith, in the cause of Allâh as well as those who give (them) asylum and aid, - these are (all) in very truth the Believers: for them is the forgiveness of sins and a provision most generous."

[56] http://metimes.com/articles/normal.php?StoryID=20060918-110403-1970r

protection of Muslims."[57] The Grand Mufti is right. Few armed robbers resort to violence if their victim peacefully cooperates with their demands. Criminals only use violence if they encounter resistance.

In a debate that I conducted with Mr. Javed Ahmad Ghamidi, arguably the most prominent Pakistani Islamic scholar, through his student Dr. Khalid Zaheer, Mr. Ghamidi wrote: "The possibility of killings mentioned in the Quran are either meant for those who were guilty of murder, or causing mischief on earth, or those who were declared unworthy of living in this world any more after they had denied the clearly communicated and understood message from God." Mr. Ghamidi is a moderate Muslim. He is so moderate that he has received some death threats from the radical Muslims. However, he knows his religion well and knows that those who reject Islam are "unworthy of living in this world anymore."[58] His detractors think the same about him. Since it is natural for humans to have different understandings, every Muslim thinks he is required to kill those who don't think like him.

Raid

Muslims often speak with pride, of Muhammad's battles. It is a pride based on illusion. Muhammad avoided battles. He preferred to ambush his victims and take them by surprise. He massacred them when they were unprepared and unarmed. He was not a warrior. He preferred terrorism. It was more effective.

After he migrated to Medina and felt strong amongst his followers, he launched 74 raids.[59] Some of them amounted to little more than assassinations, while others were expeditions of thousands of men. He accompanied participated 27 of them. These expeditions are called *ghazva.* The raids he did not accompany, are called *sariyyah.* Both *ghazva* and *sariyyah* mean raid, ambush, sudden attack.

Bukhari says, "Whenever Allah's Apostle wanted to make a ghazva, he used to hide his intention by apparently referring to different ghazva."[60]

When Muhammad took part in a war, he would always stay behind his troops, protected by his special entourage and body guards. Nowhere in the authentic biographies of Muhammad, says he fought personally.

In a war known as *the Sacrilegious War,* fought in Mecca, Muhammad attended upon his uncles. Now, nearly twenty years old, his efforts were confined to gathering the arrows discharged by the enemy during the ceasefires and handing them to his uncles. In the words of Muir, "Physical courage, indeed, and martial daring are virtues which did not distinguish the prophet at any period of his career."[61]

---

[57] Ibid.
[58] http://www.faithfreedom.org/debates/Ghamidip18.htm
[59] Tabaqat, Vol. 2, pp. 1-2.
[60] Sahih *Bukhari Volume 5, Book 59, Number 702:*
[61] William Muir, Life of Muhammad Volume II, Chapter 2, Page 6.

1- Who Was Muhammad?

Muhammad and his men raided towns and villages without warning, descended upon unarmed civilians, butchered as many of them as they could and took as spoils the vanquished community's herds and livestock, their weaponry and their belongings, as well as their wives and children. The raiders sometimes ransomed the women and children for money, or sold them as slaves. The following is an account of one of these raids.

"The Prophet had suddenly attacked Banu Mustaliq without warning while they were heedless and their cattle were being watered at the places of water. Their fighting men were killed and their women and children were taken as captives; the Prophet got Juwairiya on that day. Nafi said that Ibn Umar had told him the above narration and that Ibn 'Umar was in that army."[62] In this war, says the Muslim chronicler, "600 were taken prisoners by the Muslims. Among the booty there were 2,000 camels and 5,000 goats."

When Muslim terrorists kill children, their apologists are quick to announce it and say, Muhammad prohibited that. The truth is that Muhammad allowed killing children. "It is reported on the authority of Sa'b b. Jaththama that the Prophet of Allah (may peace be upon him), when asked about the women and children of the polytheists being killed during the night raid, said: They are from them."[63]

A number of sources considered authoritative by virtually all Muslims attest that in order to win, the Prophet took advantage of the element of surprise. He would not give even an ultimatum. Ibn 'Aun reported: "I wrote to Nafi' inquiring from him whether it was necessary to extend (to the disbelievers) an invitation to accept (Islam) before meeting them in fight. He wrote (in reply) to me that it was necessary in the early days of Islam. The Messenger of Allah made a raid upon Banu Mustaliq while they were unaware and their cattle were having a drink at the water. He killed those who fought and imprisoned others. On that very day, he captured Juwairiya bint al-Harith. Nafi' said that this tradition was related to him by Abdullah b. Umar who (himself) was among the raiding troops."[64]

To justify such dastardly attacks on unarmed people, Muslim historians have often accused their victims of conspiring against Islam. However, there is no reason to believe that any Arab tribe would have benefited by invading Muslims, who were poor and had become a strong group of bandits. Contrary to this claim, many tribes adopted policies of appeasement and signed peace treaties with Muhammad in order to stay safe. Those treaties were invariably breached by Muhammad when he no longer needed those allies.

---

[62] Sahih Bukhari, Vol. 3. Book 46, Number 717

[63] Sahih Muslim Book 019, Number 4321, 4322 and 4323:

[64] Sahih Muslim Book 019, Number 4292:

Plunder

The objective of Muhammad's raids was primarily to loot. Ibn Umar reported, "The Prophet sent an expedition to Najd and I was among the troops. They got a large number of camels as booty. Eleven or twelve camels fell to the lot of every fighter and each of them also got one extra camel."[65]

The property of the victim belonged to his killer:

> Abu Qatada reported: We accompanied the Messenger of Allah on an expedition in the year of the Battle of Hunain. I turned round and attacked him from behind giving a blow between his neck and shoulder [Treachery is a hallmark of jihadis] Then the people sat down (to distribute the spoils of war). He said: One who has killed an enemy and can bring evidence to prove it will get his belongings. So I stood up... The Messenger of Allah said: What has happened to you, O Abu Qatada? Then I related the (whole) story, to him. At this, one of the people said: He has told the truth. Messenger of Allah. The belongings of the enemy killed by him are with me. Persuade him to forgo his right (in my favor). Abu Bakr said: BY Allah, this will not happen. The Messenger of Allah will not like to deprive one of the lions from among the lions of Allah who fight in the cause of Allah and His Messenger and give thee his share of the booty. So the Messenger of Allah said: Abu Bakr has told the truth, and so give the belongings to Abu Qatada. So he gave them to me. I sold the armor (which was a part of my share of the booty) and bought with the sale proceeds a garden in the street of Banu Salama. This was the first property I acquired after embracing Islam.[66]

Islam was a proposition that early believers found irresistible. They were poor, unskilled and uneducated, unable to earn a living. Islam offered them the chance to become wealthy by plundering the wealth of others. If they were killed, they were promised much more rewards in the afterlife. How could these paupers reject such an offer? The following hadith gives us a glimpse of the early Muslims attitude:

> It has been reported by Salama b. al-Akwa'. One day when we were having our breakfast with the Messenger of Allah, a man came riding a red camel. He made it kneel down, extracted a strip of leather from its girth and tethered the camel with it. Then he began to take food with the people and look (curiously around). We were in a poor condition as some of us were on foot (being without any riding animals). All of a sudden, he left us hurriedly, came to his camel, untethered it, made it kneel down, mounted it and urged the beast which ran off with him. A man on a brown camel chased him. Salama (the narrator) said: I followed on foot. I ran on until I was near the thigh of the she-camel. I advanced further until I was near the haunches of the camel. I advanced still further until I caught hold of the nose-string of the camel. I made it kneel down. As soon as it placed its knee on the ground, I drew my sword and struck at the head, of the rider who fell down. I brought the camel driving it along with the

[65] Sahih Muslim Book 019, Number 4330

[66] Sahih Muslim Book 019, Number 4340

> man's baggage and weapons. The Messenger of Allah came forward to meet me and the people were with him. He asked: Who has killed the man? The people said: Ibn Akwa'. He said: Everything of the man is for him (Ibn Akwa').[67]

The poor traveler was killed for his camel. He must have become suspicious of Muslims and decided to part their company, but was caught and slain. Muhammad approved this dastardly conduct.

He kept a fifth of all the spoils and any time he coveted something that one of his followers had stolen he claimed it for himself. A hadith has been narrated by Mus'ab b. Sa'd who heard it from his father. "My father took a sword from *khums* and brought it to the Holy Prophet and said: Grant it to me. He refused. At this Allah revealed (the Qur'anic verse): *They ask thee concerning the spoils of war. Say: The spoils of war are for Allah and the Apostle*" (Q. 8:1).[68]

I hope that Muslim readers are astute enough to know that the creator of the universe has no need for the belongings of a bunch of Arabs. Muhammad made Allah an accomplice to his thefts for legitimacy alone. I can assure you that nothing of what he plundered went to God.

Lust

The raids did not just bring wealth to Muslims; it also provided them with sex slaves. Juwairiya was a young woman whose husband was slain when Muslims raided her village. She fell to the lot of a Muslim marauder. Aisha, Muhammad's favorite and youngest wife who had accompanied Muhammad in this expedition and narrated:

> When the prophet—peace be upon him—distributed the captives of Banu Al Mustaliq, she (Juwairiya) fell to the lot of Thabit ibn Qyas. She was married to her cousin, who was killed during the battle. She gave Thabit a deed, agreeing to pay him nine okes of gold for her freedom. She was a very beautiful woman. She captivated every man who saw her. She came to the prophet - peace be upon him -, to ask for his help in the matter. As soon as I saw her at the door of my room, I took a dislike to her, for I knew that he would see her as I saw her. She went in and told him who she was, the daughter of al-Harith ibn Dhirar, the chief of his people. She said: 'You can see the state to which I have been brought. I have fallen to the lot of Thabit, and have given him a deed for ransom, and I have to come to ask your help in the matter.' He said: 'would you like something better than that? I will discharge your debt, and marry you.' She said: 'Yes.' 'O then it is Done!' the messenger of Allah replied.[69]

This account should end any argument about the real motive behind Muhammad's multiple marriages. He and his men murdered Juwairiya's husband in

[67] Sahih Muslim Book 019, Number4344
[68] Sahih Muslim Book 019, Number 4328
[69] http://66.34.76.88/alsalafiyat/juwairiyah.htm

an unprovoked raid. She was the daughter of the chief of Bani Mustaliq and a princess in her own right. She was reduced to a slave and became the possession of one of Muhammad's thugs. However, because of her beauty, the holy Prophet offered to "set her free" under the condition that she marry him. Is that freedom? What other choice did she have? Even if Muhammad did actually set her free, where could she go?

Muslim apologists insist that most of Muhammad's wives were widows. One could thus get the impression that they were old and unwanted and that he married them out of charity. What they leave out is that these "widows" were young and beautiful, and they had become widows because Muhammad had murdered their husband. Juwairiya was 20 years old at the time and Muhammad was 58. Muhammad's own biographers admit that he did not marry women unless they were young, beautiful, and childless. Except for Sauda, all Muhammad's wives were in their teens or early twenties and this is when he was in his fifties and sixties. The historian Tabari narrates[70] that Muhammad solicited Hind bint Abu Talib, his own cousin, to marry him, but when she told him that she had a child he desisted. Another woman was Zia'h bint Aamir. Muhammad asked someone to solicit her for marriage. She accepted, but when he was told of her age, he changed his mind.[71]

A Muslim named Jarir ibn Abdullah narrated that Muhammad asked him, "Have you got married?" He replied in the affirmative. Muhammad enquired, "A virgin or a matron?" He responded, "I married a matron." Then Muhammad said, "Why not a virgin? So you may play with her and she may play with you?"[72]

Ibn Sa'd also writes that when Muhammad heard of the beauty of Zaba'a, daughter of Amir, who was a widow, he sent a message with her son telling him he would like to marry his mother. The boy went home to inform her mother. When he left, Muhammad was told that although very beautiful, she is not that young anymore. So when her son returned and told Muhammad that his mother had accepted his proposal, he remained silent.[73]

Women for the messenger of Allah were only sex objects. Their function was to satisfy their husband sexually and give birth to their children. The following story will debunk any claim that Muhammad married older women for their protection.

Barra'a narrated, the Prophet sent message to Sauda informing her that he had divorced her. When Sauda heard the news, she sat in the way of the Prophet to Aisha's house. When she saw the Prophet she told him, I beseech you by the one

---

[70] Muhammad ibn Jarir al-Tabari (838–923) was one of the earliest, most prominent and famous Persian historians and exegetes of the Quran, most famous for his *Tarikh al-Tabari* and *Tafsir al-Tabari.*

[71] Persian Tabari, Vol. IV, page 1298.

[72] Bukhari *Volume 3, Book 34, Number 310:*

[73] Tabaqat V. 8 p. 157

who has revealed to you the Quran and has exalted you above all the creation to tell me why you divorced me. Have I done something wrong that has offended you? The Prophet said no! Sauda said, I then beg you for the sake of the same God to not divorce me. I am getting old; I don't need to be with a man. You can use my turn to stay with Aisha, but I wish that in the day of resurrection to be counted amongst your wives. The Prophet agreed and Sauda said that since then the Prophet spent the nights that were her turn with his favorite wife Aisha.[74]

Muhammad decided to divorce Sauda because she was old and perhaps not very attractive. His other wives were teenagers or in their early twenties. But how old was Sauda? No mention of her age is made. Ibn Sa'd writes; Sauda died during the rule of Mu'awiya in the year 54 Hijra.[75] Muhammad married her about a month after the death of Khadijah, i.e. three years before Hijra. Therefore, Sauda died 57 years after she married Muhammad. What is the normal age of a person? Sauda was a large woman. Overweigh people don't live long. But let us say she died at the age of eighty. 80-57=23. Sauda was 23 years old when she married Muhammad who was 50 years old at that time. This makes sense since even though she was previously married; she did not have a child. If Sauda died at the age of 90, which is unlikely, she could not have been older than 33 years when she married Muhammad.

As we can deduce, Sauda was about half the age of Muhammad. But she was older than his other wives who were 36 to 44 years younger than him.

Sauda was not pretty. Muhammad decided to get rid of her to "play" with his prettier and younger wives. How could she survive on her own in that kind of patriarchal society? She thought that as long as she remains a wife of the Prophet, her material needs will be taken care of – and indeed they were. The same historian tells us that the share of Sauda from the spoils of the Khaibar was 80 camel loads of dates and 20 camel loads of barley or wheat.

From every raid and pillage, the wives of Muhammad received their share of the booty, which included slaves. Umar, during his caliphate, sent to Sauda a burlap sack filled with Dirhams (Silver coins, probably the proceeds of the loot from Persia or Egypt). Sauda asked, what is this? They said it is Dirhams. She exclaimed, "SubhanAllah, they send me money in a sack of dates?"[76]

Rape

Muhammad allowed his men to rape the women captured in raids. However, Muslims faced a dilemma. They wanted to have sex with their female captives, but also wanted to return them for ransom and therefore did not want to make them pregnant. Some of these women were already married whose husbands had escaped

---

[74] Tabaqat V. 8 p. 53-54
[75] Tabaqat V.8 page 56
[76] Tabaqat V. 8 p. 55

when taken by surprise and were still alive. The raiders considered the possibility of *coitus interruptus* (withdrawing from intercourse before ejaculation). Unsure of the best course of action, they sought the counsel of their Prophet. Bukhari reports:

> Abu Saeed said: 'We went out with Allah's Apostle for the Ghazwa of Banu Al-Mustaliq and we received captives from among the Arab captives and we desired women and celibacy became hard on us and we loved to do coitus interruptus. So when we intended to do coitus interruptus, we said, 'How can we do coitus interruptus before asking Allah's Apostle who is present among us?' We asked (him) about it and he said, 'It is better for you not to do so, for if any soul (till the Day of Resurrection) is predestined to exist, it will exist.[77]

Muhammad did not forbid raping the captive women. Instead, he made an asinine claim that when Allah intends to create someone, nothing can prevent it. He told his men that coitus interruptus is ill-advised because it would be an attempt to thwart the will of Allah. He did not say a word against rape of the captives, and by discouraging *coitus interruptus*, he supported forced insemination.

He made even his god to legitimize intercourse with women captured in wars, the so-called "right hand possessions," even if they were married before their capture.[78]

---

[77] Bukhari, Volume 5, Book59, Number 459. Many other canonical hadiths recount how Muhammad approved intercourse with slave women, but said coitus interruptus was unnecessary because if Allâh willed someone to be born, that soul would be born regardless of coitus interruptus. See the following:
Bukhari 3.34.432: "Narrated Abu Saeed Al-Khudri: that while he was sitting with Allâh's Apostle he said, 'O Allâh's Apostle! We get female captives as our share of booty, and we are interested in their prices, what is your opinion about coitus interruptus?' The Prophet said, 'Do you really do that? It is better for you not to do it. No soul that which Allâh has destined to exist, but will surely come into existence.'"
Sahih Muslim is another source considered factual and accurate by Muslims. Here is Sahih Muslim 8.3381: "Allâh's Messenger (may peace be upon him) was asked about 'azl, (coitus interruptus) whereupon he said: The child does not come from all the liquid (semen) and when Allâh intends to create anything nothing can prevent it (from coming into existence)."
Muslims also consider Abu Dawood highly accurate and factual. Here is Abu Dawood, 29.29.32.100: "Yahya related to me from Malik from Humayd ibn Qays al-Makki that a man called Dhafif said that Ibn Abbas was asked about coitus interruptus. He called a slave-girl of his and said, 'Tell them.' She was embarrassed. He said, 'It is alright, and I do it myself.' Malik said, 'A man does not practise coitus interruptus with a free woman unless she gives her permission. There is no harm in practicing coitus interruptus with a slave-girl without her permission. Someone who has someone else's slave-girl as a wife does not practice coitus interruptus with her unless her people give him permission.'"
See also Bukhari 3.46.718,
5.59.459, 7.62.135, 7.62.136, 7.62.137, 8.77.600, 9.93.506 Sahih Muslim 8.3383, 8.3388, 8.3376, 8.3377, and several more.

[78] Quran, 4:24: "Also (prohibited are) women already married, except those whom your right hands possess: Thus hath Allâh ordained (Prohibitions) against you."

1- Who Was Muhammad?

Torture

Ibn Ishaq, in his narration of the conquest of Khaibar reports that Muhammad raided this fortress town and killed its unarmed Jewish inhabitants as they fled for safety. Among the captured was the youthful Kinana.

> Kinana al-Rabi, who had the custody of the treasure of Banu Nadir, was brought to the apostle who asked him about it. He denied that he knew where it was. A Jew came (Tabari says 'was brought') to the apostle and said that he had seen Kinana going to a certain ruin every morning early. When the apostle said to Kinana, 'Do you know that if we find you have it (the treasure) I shall kill you?' He said, 'Yes.' The apostle gave orders that the ruin was to be excavated and some of the treasure was found. When he asked him about the rest (of the treasure?) he refused to produce it, so the apostle gave orders to al-Zubayr Al-Awwam, 'Torture him until you extract what he has.' So he kindled a fire with flint and steel on his chest until he was nearly dead. Then the apostle delivered him to Muhammad b. Maslama and he struck off his head, in revenge for his brother Mahmud.[79]

On the same day that Muhammad tortured to death Kinana, he took his seventeen year old wife Safiya to his tent to have sex with her. Two years earlier, he had beheaded Safiyah's father and uncle, along with the adult males of the Jewish tribe Bani Quraiza.

Ibn Ishaq wrote:

> When the apostle had conquered al-Qamus the fort of B. Ab'l Huqayq, Safiya d. Huyayy b. Akhtab was brought to him along with another woman (sister of her husband Kinana). Bilal who was bringing them led them past the Jews who were slain; and when the woman who was with Safiay saw them she shrieked and slapped her face and poured dust on her head. When the apostle saw her he said, 'Take this she-devil away from me.' He gave orders that Safiyah was to be put behind him and threw his mantle over her, so that the apostle said to Bilal when he saw this Jewess behaving in that way, 'Had you no compassion, Bilal, when you brought two women past their dead husbands?' [80]

Bukhari has recorded a few hadith about Muhammad's rape of Safiya:

> Anas said, 'When Allah's Apostle invaded Khaibar, we offered the Fajr prayer there (early in the morning) when it was still dark. The Prophet rode and Abu Talha rode

---

Quran, 33:50): "O Prophet! We have made lawful to thee thy wives to whom thou hast paid their dowers; and those whom thy right hand possesses out of the prisoners of war whom Allâh has assigned to thee."
Quran, 4:3: "If ye fear that ye shall not be able to deal justly with the orphans, marry women of your choice, two or three or four; but if ye fear that ye shall not be able to deal justly (with them), then only one, or (a captive) that your right hands possess, that will be more suitable, to prevent you from doing injustice."

[79] Siral Rasul Allâh, p. 515.

[80] Ibn Ishaq Sira p. 514

> too and I was riding behind Abu Talha. The Prophet passed through the lanes of the town quickly and my knee was touching the thigh of the Prophet. He uncovered his thigh and I saw the whiteness of the thigh of the Prophet. When he entered the town, he said, 'Allahu Akbar! Khaibar is ruined. Whenever we approach near a nation then evil will be the morning of those who have been warned.' He repeated this thrice. The people came out for their jobs and some of them said, 'Muhammad (has come).' (Some of our companions added, 'With his army.') We conquered Khaibar, took the captives, and the booty was collected.
>
> Dihya came and said, 'O Allah's Prophet! Give me a slave girl from the captives.' The Prophet said, 'Go and take any slave girl.' He took Safiya bint Huyai. A man came to the Prophet and said, 'O Allah's Apostles! You gave Safiya bint Huyai to Dihya and she is the chief mistress of the tribes of Quraiza and An-Nadir and she befits none but you.' So the Prophet said, 'Bring him along with her.' So Dihya came with her and when the Prophet saw her, he said to Dihya, 'Take any slave girl other than her from the captives.' Anas added, 'The Prophet then manumitted her and married her.'
>
> Thabit asked Anas, 'O Abu Hamza! What did the Prophet pay her as mahr (dowry)?' He said, 'Her self was her mahr for he manumitted her and then married her.' Anas added, 'While on the way, Um Sulaim dressed her for marriage (ceremony) and at night she sent her as a bride to the Prophet.'[81]

There is also a hadith narrated by Anas, a companion of Muhammad, who recalled that a group of eight men from an Arab tribe came to the Prophet, but found the climate of Medina unsuitable. Muhammad prescribed to them camel urine as medicine and sent them to meet his camel attendant outside the town. The men killed the camel attendant and drove away the camels. When Muhammad was informed, he sent his men to pursue them. When captured, he had their hands and feet cut off, passed heated nails over their eyes, and left them in a rocky land to die slowly. Anas said that they asked for water, and nobody provided them with water till they died.[82]

---

[81] Sahih Bukhari, 1.8.367
In this hadith the commentator narrates how they [the Muslims] raided the city of Khaibar, during the dawn taking the population off guard. "Yakhrab Khaibar" (Khaibar is ruined) exclaimed Muhammad, as he passed from one stronghold triumphantly to another: "Great is Allâh! Truly when I light upon the coasts of any people, wretched for them is that day! After the conquest of the town, it came time to share the booty. Dihya, one of the warriors, received Safiya as his share. Safiya's father who was the chief of the Bani Nadir had been beheaded by the order of Muhammad three years earlier. After the conquest of Khaibar, her young husband Kinana was tortured and murdered by his order too. Someone informed Muhammad that the seventeen year old Safiya was very beautiful. So Muhammad offered Dihya two girls, the cousins of Safiya, in exchange and got Safiya for himself.

[82] Bukhari Volume 4, Book 52, Number 261:

These Arabs had committed murder and theft. They had to be punished, but why torture them? Wasn't Muhammad doing exactly the same things? Where did he get those camels? Weren't they stolen? Didn't he kill the owners of those camels?

This double standard is a characteristic of Muslims. The concept of the Golden Rule and fairness is absent in the psyche of Muslims. They demand all privileges in non-Muslim countries, while they deny the basic human rights to non-Muslims where they are the majority. They see nothing wrong in this. As far as they are concerned this is fair and how things should be.

The Quran says, "*Those who wage war against God and His Messenger and strive to spread corruption in the land should be punished by death, crucifixion, the amputation of an alternate hand and foot or banishment from the land: a disgrace for them in this world, and then a terrible punishment in the Hereafter*."(Q. 5:33)

Assassination

Up to this day, most Muslims believe that the only way to deal with the critics of Islam is to kill them. In 1989, Khomeini issued a fatwa (religious decree) to assassinate Author Salman Rushdie, because he had written a book, titled The Satanic Verses that some believed insulted Islam. While some people condemned Khomeini for his fatwa, amazingly, many Westerners blamed Rushdie instead, for being "insensitive" to Muslims' sensitivity. On February 14, 2006, the Iranian state news agency reported that the fatwa will remain in place permanently. Since its inception, the Islamic regime of Iran has systematically eliminated its opponents by assassinating them, whether in Iran or in exile. Hundreds of dissidents have been killed in this way, including Dr. Shapoor Bakhtiar, a true democrat and the last Prime Minister appointed by the Shah.

What most people don't know is that assassination was Muhammad's way of dealing with his opponents. Muslim terrorists such as Mohammed Bouyeri, who assassinated The Dutch filmmaker Theo Van Gogh, are merely following their prophet's example.

Only months after his arrival in Medina, Muhammad ordered the assassination of a centenarian man who had criticized him. Abu Afak, who was said to be 120 years old, had composed a poem, in which he lamented that people had become followers of Muhammad and have turned against each other. He wrote that Muhammad was a crazed man with arbitrarily rules about what is prohibited and what is allowed, and who had caused his followers to surrender their intelligence and to become hostile to their old friends and allies. Ibn Sa'd reports this story as follows:

> Then occurred the "sariyyah" [raid] of Salim Ibn Umayr al-Amri against Abu Afak, the Jew, in [the month of] Shawwal in the beginning of the twentieth month from the hijrah [immigration from Mecca to Medina in AD 622], of the Apostle of Allah. Abu Afak, was from Banu Amr Ibn Awf, and was an old man who had attained the age of one hundred and twenty years. He was a Jew, and used to instigate the people against the Apostle of Allah, and composed (satirical) verses [about Muhammad].
>
> Salim Ibn Umayr who was one of the great weepers and who had participated in Badr, said, 'I take a vow that I shall either kill Abu Afak or die before him.' He waited for an opportunity until a hot night came, and Abu Afak slept in an open place. Salim Ibn Umayr knew it, so he placed the sword on his liver and pressed it till it reached his bed. The enemy of Allah screamed and the people, who were his followers, rushed to him, took him to his house and interred him.[83]

The only "crime" this aged man had committed was to compose satirical verses critical of Muhammad.

When Asma bint Marwan, a Jewish mother of five small children heard this, she was so outraged that she composed a poem cursing the men of Medina for letting a stranger divide them and make them assassinate a venerable old man. Again, Muhammad went to his pulpit and cried out: "'Who will rid me of Marwan's daughter?' Umayr bin `Adiy al-Khatmi who was with him heard him, and that very night he went to her house and killed her. In the morning he came to the apostle and told him what he had done and he [Muhammad] said, 'You have helped Allah and His apostle, O `Umayr!' When he asked if he would have to bear any evil consequences, the apostle said, 'Two goats won't butt their heads about her.'"[84]

After receiving praise from Muhammad for the assassination of Asma, the killer went to her children, bragged about committing the murder, and taunted those little kids and their clan.

Ibn Sa'd notes:

> Now there was a great commotion among Banu Khatma that day about the affair of bint [daughter of] Marwan. She had five sons, and when `Umayr went to them from the apostle he said, 'I have killed bint Marwan, O sons of Khatma. Withstand me if you can; don't keep me waiting.' That was the first day Islam became powerful among B. Khatma; before that those who were Muslims concealed the fact. The first of them to accept Islam was `Umayr b. `Adiy who was called the 'Reader' and `Abdullah b. Aus and Khuzayma b. Thabit. The day after bint Marwan was killed the men of B. Khatma became Muslims because they saw the power of Islam.[85]

---

[83] The Kitab al Tabaqat al kabir, Vol. 2, p 31

[84] From pp. 675-676 of *The Life of Muhammad*, which is A. Guilaume's translation of *Sirat Rasul Allâh*.

[85] Ibid.

1- Who Was Muhammad?

After these assassinations, Muslims in Medina became more boastful, arrogant and imperious, as they had cast terror in the hearts of their opponents. Muhammad wanted to send the message that any opposition or criticism of him would be dealt with mercilessly.[86] That is the message Muslims want to deliver today to us, where the threat often only needs be implied. They follow the example set by their prophet, whom they regard as a greatest strategist. They want to create a boundary of fear so they may establish their supremacy through terror.

There is no doubt in the mind of Muslim that this strategy works. To them, the Quranic injunction of "*casting terror in the heart of the unbelievers*"[87] is a sure way to victory. It worked for Muhammad. He bragged, "*I have been made victorious with terror.*"[88] It worked in Spain, when the terrorists bombed a commuter train and killed 200 people on March 11, 2004. In response, the Spanish voters elected a socialist government who immediately adopted the policy of appeasement vis-à-vis the Muslims. Many people in the west and particularly in India are dreadful of Muslims. You won't believe the email I received today. An Indian man wrote, "The Bombay and recently the Kenyan attacks by Muslims have been bothering me, as they separated the Muslims from non-Muslims and asked them questions about Islam. If I am caught by in a similar situation, how can I and my family pass off as Muslims? Can you tell me how should I dress and what facts I need to know about Islam and Mohammed? Also can you tell me how to perform the Muslim prayer and can you tell 2 or 3 verses in Arabic which I can remember by heart? I would be grateful for your advice to stay alive from the jihadis."

What is the worth of the life lived with so much cowardice? This is exactly what Muslims want. This is how Islam expanded. A small group of Muslims terrorized a large number of people. The cowards then pretended to be Muslims to save their sorry lives. And in one or two generations their dependents became full-

---

[86] Ibn Sa'd narrates another version of this story: "Bint Marwan, of Banu Umayyah ibn Zayd , when five nights had remained from the month of Ramadan, in the beginning of the nineteenth month from the hijrah of the apostle of Allâh. `Asma' was the wife of Yazid ibn Zayd ibn Hisn al-Khatmi. She used to revile Islam, offend the prophet and instigate the (people) against him. She composed verses. Umayr Ibn Adi came to her in the night and entered her house. Her children were sleeping around her. There was one whom she was suckling. He searched her with his hand because he was blind, and separated the child from her. He thrust his sword in her chest till it pierced up to her back. Then he offered the morning prayers with the prophet at al-Medina. The apostle of Allâh said to him: 'Have you slain the daughter of Marwan?' He said: 'Yes. Is there something more for me to do?' He [Muhammad] said: 'No. Two goats will not butt together about her.' This was the word that was first heard from the apostle of Allâh. The apostle of Allâh called him `Umayr, 'basir' (the seeing)." -- Ibn Sa`d's in Kitab al-Tabaqat al-Kabir, translated by S. Moinul Haq, Vol. 2, p. 24.

[87] Quran 3:151 "Soon shall we cast terror into the hearts of the Unbelievers, for that they joined companions with Allâh, for which He had sent no authority: their abode will be the Fire: And evil is the home of the wrong-doers!

[88] Bukhari, 4.52.220.

fledged Muslims, joined the jihad and started oppressing others. This much cowardice is pathetic, but it proves the point that terror works. As long as cowardice exists, there will be more terrorism.

Ka'b bin Ashraf was another victim of Muhammad. He was a handsome and a poet - a chief of the Banu Nadir. After Muhammad banished the Banu Qainuqa', Ka'b became concerned about his own people. He visited Mecca to seek protection and composed poems praising the Meccans for their bravery and honor. When Muhammad heard this, he went to the mosque and after the prayer said, "'Who is willing to kill Ka'b bin Al-Ashraf who has hurt Allah and His Apostle?' Thereupon Muhammad bin Maslama got up and said, 'O Allah's Apostle! Would you like that I kill him?' The Prophet said, 'Yes.' bin Maslama said, 'then allow me to say a (false) thing (i.e. to deceive Ka'b).' The Prophet said, 'You may say it.' Then Muhammad bin Maslama went to Ka'b and said, 'that man (i.e. Muhammad) demands Sadaqa (i.e. Zakat [alms]) from us, and he has troubled us, and I have come to borrow something from you.' On that, Kab said, 'By Allah, you will get tired of him!' bin Maslama said, 'Now as we have followed him, we do not want to leave him unless and until we see how his end is going to be. Now we want you to lend us a camel load or two of food.' ...Muhammad bin Maslama and his companion promised Ka'b that they would return to him. He came to Ka'b at night along with Kab's foster brother, Abu Na'ila. Ka'b invited them to come into his fort, and then he went down to them. His wife asked him, 'Where are you going at this time?' Ka'b replied, 'None but Muhammad bin Maslama and my (foster) brother Abu Na'ila have come.' His wife said, 'I hear a voice as if blood is dripping from him.' Ka''b said, 'They are none but my brother Muhammad bin Maslama and my foster brother Abu Naila. A generous man should respond to a call at night even if invited to be killed.' ...So Muhammad bin Maslama went in together with two men, and said to them, 'When Ka'b comes, I will touch his hair and smell it, and when you see that I have got hold of his head, strike him. I will let you smell his head.' Ka'b bin Al-Ashraf came down to them wrapped in his clothes, and diffusing perfume. Muhammad bin Maslama said, 'I have never smelt a better scent than this.' Ka'b replied, 'I have got the best Arab women who know how to use the high class of perfume.' Muhammad bin Maslama requested of Ka'b, 'Will you allow me to smell your head?' Ka'b said, 'Yes.' Muhammad smelt it and made his companions smell it as well. Then he requested of Ka'b again, 'Will you let me (smell your head)?' Ka'b said, 'Yes.' When Muhammad got a strong hold of him, he said (to his companions), 'Get at him!' So they killed him and went to the Prophet and informed him.[89]

Not only Muhammad encouraged assassination, he advocated deception and treachery as well. For him, the end justified the means.

---

[89] Bukhari, 5.59.369

1- Who Was Muhammad?

Islam has advanced with terror. Muslims are convinced that terror and deception will make them victorious. They have an example in their prophet. His successes are their inspiration.

The Islamic world is sick. It would be shortsighted to deny that the cause of this sickness is Islam. Almost every crime, every abuse and inhumanity perpetrated by Muslims is inspired by the examples set by Muhammad and justified through his words and deeds. This is the inconvenient truth that so many would rather not talk about.

Genocide

There were three Jewish tribes living in and around Yathrib, the Banu Qainuqa', the Banu Nadir and the Banu Quraiza that had their fortress just outside the town. As stated above, they were the original inhabitants of Yathrib. At first Muhammad thought that because he had denounced polytheism and had embraced the Biblical prophets, the Jews will flock to his religion. The earlier chapters of the Quran are full of stories about Moses and Biblical tales. Muhammad also adopted Jerusalem as the *qibla* for his prayers. Muslim scholar W. N. Arafat writes, "It is also generally accepted that at first the Prophet Muhammad hoped that the Jews of Yathrib, as followers of a divine religion, would show understanding of the new monotheistic religion, Islam."[90] However, to his dismay, the Jews, just like the Quraish, paid little heed to him. After his hopes were dashed and his patience vexed, he grew hostile towards them. Their rejection enraged him, and he sought vengiance. The assassination of Abu Afak and Asma only marked the beginning of his animosity towards the Jews. Already emboldened by his plundering of the passing caravans, Muhammad had his eyes set on the wealth of the Jews in Yathrib and was looking for an excuse to make his move. His anger against the Jews started showing in the Quranic verses, where he accused them of being ungrateful to Allah, of killing the prophets and of breaking God's laws. He even went as far as to say that because the Jews had broken the law of Sabbath, God transformed a group of them into apes and swine.[91] To this day Muslims are convinced that that asinine tale is true. If it is in the Quran it must be true, even if it is absurd.

Invasion of Banu Qainuqa'

The first tribe of Jews to face the wrath of Muhammad was the Banu Qainuqa'. They lived in thir quarters in Yathrib. They made their living as artisans, goldsmiths, blacksmiths, making household instruments and weaponry. They were not, however, skilled in the arts of soldiering and left that aspect to the Arabs, a mistake that proved fatal to their existence. The Banu Qainuqa' were allies of the

---

90 From the Journal of the Royal Asiatic Society of Great Britain and Ireland, (1976), pp. 100-107 By W. N. Arafat

91 Quran, 2:65, 5:60, 7:166

Arab tribe of Khazraj and supported them in their conflicts with their rival Arab tribe, the Aus.

The opportunity to invade them arrived when a skirmish broke out between a handful of Jews and Muslims. A member of Banu Qainuqa' played a prank and pinned the skirt of a Muslim woman squatting in a Jeweler's shop to the ground. Upon standing, her gown tore and she was stripped naked. A Muslim, already filled with the hatred of the Jews, jumped on the Jewish prankster and killed him. The relatives of the victim then killed the Muslim in retaliation.

This was the opportunity Muhammad was looking for. Instead of trying to calm the situation, he blamed the Banu Qainuqa', all of them, and told them to submit to his religion or face war. They answered his threats with defiance and shut themselves up in their quarters. He laid siege on them, shut off the water supply to their quarter, and vowed to kill them all.

In the Quran 3:12, Muhammad reiterates this threat: "*...You will be defeated and gathered together to hell and worst indeed is that place to rest.*"

After a fortnight, the Qainuqa tried to negotiate their surrender, but Muhammad had made his mind to slay them. Abdullah ibn Ubayy the revered patriarch of the Khazraj took hold of his collar and told him that he would not allow his allies to be slain with no cause. Muhammad was aware of the respect that the Khazraj had for their chief. He pushed him away while his face was blackened with rage and agreed not to massacre the Jews provided, they leave the town. Ibn Ishaq reports:

> Banu Qainuqa' were the first of the Jews to break their agreement with the apostle and to go to war, between Badr and Ohod, and the apostle besieged them until they surrendered unconditionally. `Abdullah b. Ubayy b. Salul went to him [Muhammad] when God had put them in his power and said, 'O Muhammad, deal kindly with my clients' (now they were allies of Khazraj), but the apostle put him off. He repeated the words, and the apostle turned away from him, whereupon he thrust his hand into the collar of the apostle's robe; the apostle was so angry that his face became almost black. He said, 'Confound you, let me go.' He answered, 'No, by God, I will not let you go until you deal kindly with my clients. Four hundred men without mail (flexible armor of interlinked rings) and three hundred mailed protected me from all mine enemies; would you cut them down in one morning? By God, I am a man who fears that circumstances may change.' The apostle said, 'You can have them.'"[92]

The biographers add that Muhammad sullenly said "Let them go. God curse them, and God curse him also! So, Muhammad pardoned their lives provided they were sent into exile."[93]

---

[92] Ibn Ishaq Sirat, p. 363

[93] Ibid.

He demanded that the Banu Qainuqa' hand over their wealth and war equipage, from which he set aside one fifth for himself and distributed the rest among his followers. The Qainuqa' was then banished and Muslim historians gloat that the refugees entered Azru'a in Syria where they stayed for a while and soon perished.[94]

Invasion of Banu Nadir

Next, was the turn of the Banu Nadir. After seeing what Muhammad did to the Banu Qainuqa', Ka'b Ibn Ashraf, the chief of the Banu Nadir, sought the protection of the Quraish and as explained above, he was assassinated.

There was a retaliatory war (Ohud) between the Meccans and Muslims in which the latter had lost. Muhammad needed to compensate that loss and restore the faith of his followers. He needed a victory. This is how the Muslim mind works. Any time they manage to butcher a bunch of people they see it as divine assistance, their faith is restored and more of them join the jihad. When they lose they are disheartened and withdraw seeking reconciliation and peace, while waiting for their next opportunity to break their treaty an strike again. The Banu Nadir was an easy target.

The Pakistani Muslim historian and commentator of the Quran, and the ideologue of today's Islamic revivalism, Maududi, narrates the story as follows:

> For some time after these punitive measures [the banishment of the Qainuqa' and serial assassinations of Jewish poets] the Jews remained so terror stricken that they did not dare commit any further mischief. But later when in Shawwal, A. H. 3, the Quraish in order to avenge themselves for the defeat at Badr, marched against Medina with great preparations, and the Jews saw that only a thousand men had marched out with the Holy Prophet (upon whom be Allah's peace) as against three thousand men of the Quraish, and even they were deserted by 300 hypocrites who returned to Madina, [The followers of Abdullah ibn Ubayy, Chief of the Khazraj] they committed the first and open breach of the treaty by refusing to join the Holy Prophet in the defense of the city although they were bound to it.[95]

It is amazing that Muslims think that the Bani Nadir were bound to help Muhammad wage a religious war against the Meccans, despite the fact that he had banished one of their tribes and had assassinated their chief and their revered poets. The war between Muhammad and the Quraish had nothing to do with the Jews, and by assassinating their people and banishing the Banu Qainuqa', he had broken any agreement he may have had with them. And yet, to justify his crimes, Muslim apologists blame the Jews for being at fault with their agreement.

---

[94] AR-Raheeq Al-Makhtum by Saifur Rahman al-Mubarakpuri http://islamweb.islam.gov.qa/english/sira/raheek/PAGE-26.HTM
[95] http://www.islamicity.com/mosque/quran/maududi/mau59.html

Muhammad was now looking for an excuse to get rid of the Banu Nadir and rob their wealth. They owned the best cultivated lands in Yathrib and gardens with date trees, and employed many Arabs. Accordingly, a few Muslims killed two men from Banu Kalb. As it happened, this tribe had signed a treaty with Muhammad that his men would not rob or kill their people in exchange for their support. The killers had mistaken the victims for members of another tribe. Now, as customs dictated, Muhammad was obliged to pay blood money for this bloodshed. Despite all the wealth grabbed from the Banu Qainuqa', he went to the Banu Nadir and told them that they should pay this blood money. This was an outrageous demand. Muhammad hoped that the Banu Nadir would balk and that this would give him an excuse to do with them as he did with the Banu Qainuqa'. The Banu Nadir were too scared to argue with the rising tyrant. They agreed to pitch in and withdrew to collect the money. Muhammad and his companions sat beneath a wall, waiting. This was not what he had hoped for. He had come making the most unjust demand, expecting to get a negative response and hence act upon his devious design. Now, he needed to plot a new strategy.

Suddenly, he had flash of inspiration. He stood up and without saying anything to his companions left the place and went home. Once they saw he is not coming they went back to the mosque and upon enquiring, he told them that Angel Gabriel informed him that the Jews were plotting to drop a rock on his head from atop the wall beneath which they were sitting.

None of Muhammad's companions saw anyone climbing the wall or had any intimation about a plot against their lives. However, these men, having benefited financially from following him and believing everything he told them, had no reason or inclination to doubt what he told them.

Any rational person can see the absurdity of Muhammad's story. If the Banu Nadir wanted to kill him, they didn't need to climb a wall with a rock. Muhammad was accompanied by only a handful of his followers, Abu Bakr, Umar, Ali and perhaps one more person. It would have been easy to kill them all, if that was what they had in mind.

The Prophet who believed that God is *khairul maakereen* (the best of the deceivers, Q.3:54) was himself a cunning man. The story of Gabriel informing him of the Jews' plotting against his life is as credible as the story of his visits to hell and heaven. Nonetheless, his followers believed him and were so enraged by this fabrication that they rallied around him to shed the blood of every Jew.

Maududi finishes this narrative by saying: "Now there was no question of showing them any further concession. The Holy Prophet at once sent to them the ultimatum that the treachery they had meditated against him had come to his knowledge; therefore, they were to leave Medina within ten days; if anyone of them was found staying behind in their quarters, he would be put to the sword." Maududi demonstrates a perfect example of Islamic "logic" when he tells the story of Muhammad's treachery as if it were the natural and normal way to behave.

Abdullah ibn Ubayy did his best to help the Banu Nadir, but by then his influence had diminished and Muslims had become blinded by their zealotry and lust for the spoils. They did not allow bin Ubayy to enter Muhammad's tent as they struck him and cut his face open.

After a few days, the Banu Nadir negotiated to leave behind all their belongings for Muhammad and leave town. Some of them went to Syria and some went to Khaibar to be slain only a few years later when Muhammad raided on that prosperous and green Jewish fortress.

Even though Muhammad let these people go, his first thoughts were to massacre them. The following excerpt from Sira makes this clear:

> Concerning B. al-Nadir the Sura of Exile came down in which it is recorded how God wreaked His vengeance on them and gave His apostle power over them and how He dealt with them. God said: 'He it is who turned out those who disbelieved of the scripture people from their homes to the first exile.... 'So consider this, you who have understanding. Had not God prescribed deportation against them,' which was vengeance from God, *'He would have punished them in this world,'* (Q. 59:2-3) i.e. with the sword, 'and in the next world there would be the punishment of hell' as well.[96]

In this siege, Muhammad ordered cutting and burning the trees of the Banu Nadir. Such an act was unprecedented amongst the Arabs. All he had to do to justify his crime was to make his Allah approve of what he had done. *"When you (O Muhammad) cut down of the palm-trees, or you left them standing on their stems, it was by leave of Allah."* (Q. 59:5)

It is not difficult to understand why in the barren desert, people considered cutting trees and poisoning wells to be a capital crime. Such barbarities were against Arab morality. However, Muhammad was not bound by any norm or morality. Nothing could deter him from achieving his objectives. He was ready to sacrifice anything and anyone that stood in his way. His followers interpreted his single-mindedness and even his ruthlessness as the sign of his resolve to fulfill the divine Will. In reality he was only a sociopath, bereft of conscience.

A Muslim scholar, Al-Mubarkpouri, says:

> The Messenger of Allah (Peace be upon him) seized their weapons, land, houses, and wealth. Amongst the other booty he managed to capture, there were 50 armours, 50 helmets, and 340 swords. This booty was exclusively the Prophet's because no fighting was involved in capturing it. He divided the booty at his own discretion among the early Emigrants and two poor Helpers, Abu Dujana and Suhail bin Haneef. Anyway the Messenger of Allah (Peace be upon him) spent a portion of this wealth

[96] Ibn Ishaq Sirat, p. 438

> on his family to sustain their living the year around. The rest was expended to provide the Muslim army with equipment for further wars in the way of Allah. Almost all the verses of Sûra Al-Hashr (Chapter 59 - The Gathering) describe the banishment of the Jews and reveal the disgraceful manners of the hypocrites. The verses manifest the rules relevant to the booty. In this Chapter, Allah, the All-Mighty, praises the Emigrants and Helpers. This Chapter also shows the legitimacy of cutting down and burning the enemy's land and trees for military purposes. Such acts cannot be regarded as phenomena of corruption so long that they are in the way of Allah.[97]

Like Maududi, Al-Mubarakpouri is revealing the disturbing lack of conscience and the situational ethics that characterize the true followers of Muhammad. Muslims do what their prophet did. They consider burning and looting properties of non-Muslims legitimate. If something was practiced and sanctioned by him, it must be good even if it is evil.

Based on the actions of Muhammad, it is fair to conclude that Islamic violence is not a deviation from Islam. Murdering, plundering, raping, and assassinating are Islamic practices. Nothing is off limits when it comes to promoting the religion of Allah.

Muhammad did not share this loot with his followers. He kept all that wealth for himself. He claimed that since Muslims did not have to fight, they're not entitled to the loot. "It has been narrated on the authority of Umar, who said: The properties abandoned by Banu Nadir were the ones which Allah bestowed upon His Apostle for which no expedition was undertaken either with cavalry or camelry. These properties were particularly meant for the Holy Prophet. He would meet the annual expenditure of his family from the income thereof, and would spend what remained for purchasing horses and weapons as preparation for Jihad."[98]

The reason the Banu Nadir surrendered was because of Muhammad's followers. He cheated even from his followers. But who could argue with Allah?

Ironically, the Sura Al-Hashr ends by exhorting believers to be "pious." It is clear that piety for Muhammad had a different meaning. Muslim apologists say that the morality of today shouldn't be applied to Muhammad who lived 1400 years ago. The irony is that they uphold his morality as standard for all times.

One Muslim wrote to me, "This whole narrative has been problematic for many people because of their notions of what is morally correct and what is morally wrong. The origin of this sickness rests squarely on the Christian mentality of 'turn the other cheek,' and the 'redemptive suffering of Christ,' both of which have been sicknesses in the minds of Europe for centuries on end."

---

[97] AR-RaheeQ Al-Makhtum (THE SEALED NECTAR)- Memoirs of the Noble Prophet Saifur Rahman al-Mubarakpuri - Jamia Salafia – India http://www.al-sunnah.com/nektar/11.htm

[98] *Sahih Muslim Book 019, Number 4347*

1- Who Was Muhammad?

I don't believe that morality and kindness are sicknesses. They stem from human conscience and their compass is the Golden Rule. We know the difference between right and wrong by considering how we would like to be treated. But if tolerance is sickness, as this Muslim believes, I hope the non-Muslims get cured from it fast. If anyone is still in doubt that Islam is a threat to mankind, that person is indeed sick in the head.

Invasion of Banu Quraiza:

The last Jewish tribe of Yathrib to fall victim to Muhammad's vindictiveness was the Banu Quraiza. Soon after the Battle of the Trench (Khandaq) was over, Muhammad set his eyes on them. He claimed that the Archangel Gabriel visited him telling him to "unsheathe his sword and head for the habitation of the seditious Banu Quraiza and fight them," writes Al-Mubarakpouri. "Gabriel noted that he, with a procession of angels would go ahead to shake their forts and cast fear in their hearts. The Messenger of Allah immediately summoned the prayer caller and ordered him to announce fresh hostilities against Banu Quraiza."[99]

It is important to note that the call to prayer in Islam is also the call to war. Muslim's riots always initiate from the mosques after they offer their prayers. They are most vicious during the holy month of Ramadan and on Fridays. In a sermon commemorating the Birth of Muhammad, in 1981, Khomeini said, "Mehrab (the main niche in the Mosque) means the place of war, the place of fighting. [Mehrab derives from harb, which means war. It's an isle of a mosque where the followers of Muhammad gathered to discuss war strategies.] Out of mehrabs, wars should proceed. All the wars of Islam proceeded out of mehrabs. The Prophet had a sword to kill people. Our Holy Imams were militants. All of them were warriors. They used to wield swords. They used to kill people. We need a caliph who would chop hands, cut throats, and stone people, in the same way that the messenger of Allah chopped hands, cut throats, and stoned people."[100]

Muhammad laid siege on the fortress of the Banu Quraiza. He accused them of conspiring with the Meccans against him. The same Muslim historians deny this charge and say the Meccans withdrew without fighting because they did not receive support from the Banu Quraiza.

When Muhammad made his intentions known, Ali ibn Abu Talib, his cousin and staunch supporter, swore he would not stop until he either stormed their garrisons or was killed. This siege lasted 25 days. Finally the Banu Quraiza surrendered unconditionally. Muhammad ordered the men to be handcuffed, while the women and children were confined separately. The Aus tribe, who were allies of

[99] Ibid. www.al-sunnah.com/nektar/12.htm
[100] Ayatollah Khomeini: A speech delivered on the commemoration of the Birth of Muhammad, in 1981.

the Banu Quraiza, interceded, begging Muhammad to be lenient towards their clients. Muhammad suggested that Sa'd bin Mu'adh, a ruffian among them who had been fatally wounded, give a verdict on the Jews. Sa'd was a former ally of the Banu Quraiza, but since his conversion to Islam he had a change of heart against them. He also blamed them for the wound he had received when a Meccan threw an arrow during the Battle of Trench. He was a bodyguard of Muhammad and Muhammad knew how he felt about his old Jewsih allies.

Sa'd's verdict was that "all the able-bodied male persons belonging to the tribe should be killed, women and children taken prisoners and their wealth divided among the Muslim fighters." Muhammad beamed with joy after hearing this cruel verdict and exclaimed, "Sa'd (had) adjudged by the Command of Allah."[101]

Al-Mubarakpouri adds that "In fact, the Jews deserved that severe punitive action for the ugly treachery they had harbored against Islam, and the large arsenal they had amassed, which consisted of 1,500 swords, 2,000 spears, 300 armors and 500, all of which went into the hands of the Muslims."

What Al-Mubarakpouri forgets to mention is that the Banu-Quraiza had loaned their their shovels and picks to Muslims so they could dig the trench that saved them. Al-Waqidi reports, "Quraiza lent the besieged Muslims many tools for digging the ditch (for the defense of Medina, like shovels, baskets and axes."[102]

Muslim historians have been quick to accuse the Banu Quraiza to justify their massacre. Obviously, they saw the need for justification of this crime. They accuse them of being mischievous, causing sedition, being treacherous and plotting against Islam. However, they give no specifics as to the nature of those sins to warrant their genocide. Trenches were dug in the bazaar of Medina and between 600 to 900 men were beheaded and their bodies dumped in them.

Huyai Ibn Akhtab, the chief of the Banu Nadir, whose daughter Safiya, Muhammad took as his share of the booty when he raided Khaibar, was among the captives. He was brought to the victor with his hands tied from behind to his neck. In an audacious defiance he rejected Muhammad and preferred death to submission to this brute man. He was ordered to kneel and was beheaded on the spot.

To determine who should be killed, the youngsters were examined. Those who had grown pubic hair were bundled with the men and beheaded. Atiyyah al-Quriaz, a Jew who had survived this massacre recounted: "I was among the captives of Banu Quraiza. They (the Muslims) examined us, and those who had begun to grow hair (pubes) were killed, and those who had not were not killed. I was among those who had not grown hair."[103]

---

[101] Bukhari, *Volume 4, Book 52, Number 280:*

[102] Al-Waqidi, p. 445, and al-Samhudi, p. 1207,

[103] Sunan Abu-Dawud Book 38, Number 4390. Sunan Abu-Dawud is another collection of hadith regarded to be sahih.

After massacring the men, Muhammad ordered their women to line up. He then walked in front of them and chose the fifteen years old Rayhana as his trophy. He offered to marry her, but Rayhanah refused and preferred to remain a sex slave than marry the murderer of her father and brothers. He then sold the rest of women and children in exchange for weapons.

On his deathbed, Muhammad instructed his followers to cleanse the Arabian Peninsula of all non-believers,[104] an order that Umar, the second Caliph, carried out during his rule. He exterminated the Jews, the Christians, and the pagans forcing them to convert, to leave, or he would put them to death.

Now, enriched with the booty, Muhammad could afford to be even generous. Anas narrated: "People used to give some of their date palms to the Prophet (as a gift), till he conquered Banu Quraiza and Banu An-Nadir, whereupon he started returning their favors."[105]

There is a verse in the Quran that speaks about the massacre of the Banu Quraiza and approves Muhammad's butcheries of their men and the enslavement of their women and children. "*He caused those of the People of the Book who helped them (i.e. the Quraish) to come out of their forts. Some you killed, some you took prisoner.*"(Q. 33:26)

Did the Meccans call Muhammad Honest?

Muslims claim that Muhammad was known to be an honest man as the Meccans called him *Amin*. This claim is disingenuous. *Amin* means trustee. It was the title of those who sold and bought merchandise on behalf of others. One is called school trustee, or city trustee because of his profession. The title "*Amin*" is a label for every sort of profession. Here are some examples: *Amin El-Makataba* (Trustee of the library); *Amin El-Shortaa* (Police Trustee); and *Majlass El-Omnaa* (Council of Trustees.)

Abul Aas, husband of Zeinab, Muhammad's daughter, was also called Amin because of his profession.[106] He did not convert until he was forced to. Muhammad ordered Zeinab to leave him unless he converted.

Muhammad acted as the trustee (Amin) for Khadijah once, when he took her merchandise to Damascus and sold it on her behalf. He never engaged in that business again but kept the title. Had the Meccans believed Muhammad to be trustworthy they would not have derided him when he told them that he had received a message from God. According to Muhammad's own admission made in

[104] Bukhari Volume 4, Book 52, Number 288
[105] Bukhari Volume 4, Book 52, Number 176

[106] Tabari V. 3, p. 987

the Quran, those who knew him best called him a liar and a madman, (Q.15:6) a charge that he denied by making his Allah testify: "*Therefore continue to remind, for by the grace of your Lord, you are not a soothsayer, or a madman.*" (Q.52:29)

Taqiyah: The Holy Deception

We saw how Muhammad allowed his followers to lie, even to badmouth him, to win the trust of their victims in order to assassinate them. There are many other stories about Muslims feigning friendship with the non-believers, only to stab them in the back once they gain their trust.

At Hudaibiyyah, Muhammad signed a treaty with the Meccans, promising to return any of their youths and slaves that escaped and joined him. This treaty is evidence that the Meccan's were not persecuting the Muslims. They were concerned for their children joining the new cult as Muhammad was converting them into bandits.

Ibn Ishaq narrates the story of Abu Basir, a Meccan youth, who went to Muhammad after Hudaibiyyah's treaty was signed. His parents sent two men with a letter reminding Muhammad of his pact. Muhammad felt obliged and told Abu Basir: "Go, for Allah will bring relief and *a way of escape* for you and the helpless ones with you." Abu Basir got the hint. He returned with the emissaries. They had gone about six miles from Medina when they stopped to rest. Abu Basir said to one of his companions, "Is your sword sharp, O brother?" When he said that it was, he said that he would like to look at it. "Look at it if you want to," the man replied. Abu Basir unsheathed it and dealt him a blow that killed him. He then went back to Muhammad and said: "Your obligation is over and Allah has removed it from you. You duly handed me over to the men, and I have protected myself in my religion lest I should be seduced therein." Muhammad smiled and instructed him to go to al-Iss, a region by the shore, on the road which the Quraish were accustomed to take to Syria and rob their caravans.

Muhammad had signed a treaty not to waylay the caravans of the Quraish, so he found a way to go around it. Ibn Ishaq says, "The Muslims who were confined in Mecca heard what the apostle had said of Abu Basir, so they went out to join him in al-Iss. About seventy men attached themselves to him, and they so harried Quraish, killing everyone they could get hold of, and cutting to pieces every caravan that passed them, that Quraish wrote to the apostle begging him by the ties of kinship to take these men in, for they had no use for them. So the apostle took them in, and they came to him in Medina.[107]

The history of Islam is replete with treachery and deceit. These men were Muslims and as such they were the responsibility of Muhammad. But he send them

[107] This story is reported by Tabari, Vol 3, Page 1126

to another place with the order to rob the Meccans on their own. Despite that, Muslims claim that it was the Meccans who broke the treaty.

It is foolhardy to assume that Muslims will reciprocate kindness. Never in history, has this happened. The Emigrants severed all ties with their kin and killed them ruthlessly when they converted to Islam. On the other hand the Meccans were weakened by their love for their Muslim relatives.

When the Meccans and other Arab tribes had enough of Muhammad's raids and killings, they came together to punish him. However, unlike him, who never announced his plans and ambushed his victims with no warnings, they gave him plenty of notice to prepare himself for the battle. This gave Muhammad enough time to dig a trench around Medina. The joint army, known as the Confederates, camped outside the town wondering how to cross the trench. They asked the Banu Quraiza to assist them. Muhammad was wary of this alliance. So he devised a trick to drive a rift and distrust between the Banu Quraiza and the Confederates. A man named Nu'aym had recently converted to Islam; however he had not made his conversion known publicly. Muhammad summoned him and said, "You are only one man among us, so go and awake distrust among the enemy to draw them off us if you can, *for war is deceit*."

The following is the rest of the story reported by Ibn Ishaq:

> Nu'aym did as Muhammad told him. "He went to the B. Quraiza with whom he had been a boon companion, and reminded them of his affection for them and of the special tie between them. When they admitted that they did not suspect him, he said, 'Quraish and Ghatafan are not like you. The land is your land, your property, your wives, and your children are in it, you cannot leave it and go somewhere else. Now Quraish and Ghatafan have come to fight Muhammad and his companions, and you have aided them against him, but their land, their property, and their wives are not here, so they are not like you. If they see an opportunity they will make the most of it, but if things go badly they will go back to their own land and leave you to face the man in your country, and you will not be able to do so if you are left alone. So do not fight along with these people until you take hostages from their chiefs, who will remain in your hands as security that they will fight Muhammad with you, until you make an end of him.' The Jews said that this was excellent advice.
>
> Then he went to the Quraish and said to Abu Sufyan b. Harb and his company, 'You know my affection for you, and that I have left Muhammad. I have heard something which I think it my duty to tell you of as a warning, but regard it as confidential.' When they said that they would, he continued, 'Mark my words, the Jews have regretted their action in opposing Muhammad and have sent to tell him so, saying, 'Would you like us to get hold of some chiefs of the two tribes, Quraish and Ghatafan and hand them over to you, so that you can cut their heads off? Then we can join you in exterminating the rest of them. He has sent word back to accept their offer. So if the Jews send to you demanding hostages, don't send them a single man.'

> Then he went to Ghatafan and said, 'You are my family, the dearest of men to me, and I do not think that you can suspect me.' They agreed that he was above suspicion, and so he told the same story as he had told Quraish. [108]

The deception worked. When the Confederates asked the Banu Quraiza to join them, the Jews brought an excuse and demanded that the Quraish leave with them a few of their men as hostage, which confirmed what Nu'aym had told them. Abu Sufyan, the chief of the Confederates became disheartened and left without a fight.

This story may not be true, but it has served as a lesson to Muslims, who always incorporate deceptive strategies in their jihad. One hadith says, "Hajaj Ibn `Aalat told: 'O Prophet of Allah: I have in Mecca some excess wealth and some relatives, and I would like to have them back; am I excused if I bad-mouth you [to fool the non-Muslims]?' The Prophet excused him and said: 'Say whatever you have to say.'"[109]

Muslims come to the West and pretend to be moderates. They smile, are friendly and amiable. They even pretend to love your country and be patriotic. However, their only objective is to make Islam dominant.

Lying to advance Islam is called *taqiyah.* Taqiyah, allows a Muslim to lie and say anything to pull the wool over the eyes of non-Muslims and deceive them.

One of the major objectives, and a persistent tactic of taqiyah, is to downplay the threat of Islam. The goal is to fool potential victims that jihad is not directed at them. In his book, No god but God, Reza Aslan engages in this Islamic art of deception. He claims, "What is taking place now in the Muslim world is an internal conflict between Muslims, not an external battle between Islam and the West." He further writes: "The West is merely a bystander - an unwary yet complicit casualty of a rivalry that is raging in Islam over who will write the next chapter in its story."[110] Looks like, New York, Pentagon, London, Madrid, and Beslan are built in the crossfire between Muslims. Aslan is a Board member of the National Iranian American Council, a lobbying arm of the Islamic Republic of Iran.

A funny taqiyah often told by Muslim men to seduce western women is: "Women in Islam are treated like queen." I have yet to see a country whose queen is called deficient in intelligence, beaten, stoned, and honor-killed.

Ghazzali (1058-1111), arguably the greatest Islamic scholar noted, "Speaking is a means to achieve objectives. If praise worthy aim is attainable through both telling the truth and lying, it is unlawful to accomplish through lying because there is no

[108] Ibn Ishaq, Sirat, Battle of Trench

[109] Sirah al-Halabiyyah, v3, p61,

[110] www.nytimes.com/2005/05/04/books/04grim.html?_r=1&ex=1115784000&en=7961034fe8ef20c0&ei=5070&oref=slogin

need for it. When it is possible to achieve such an aim by lying but not by telling the truth, it is permissible to lie if attaining the goal is permissible."[111]

Needless to say that for a Muslim there is no goal loftier than promoting Islam. When a Muslim, smiles and says how much he loves your country and how he wants to be your friend, remember the words of the great commentator of the Quran, Ibn Kathir, who said, "*We smile in the face of some people although our hearts curse them.*"[112]

Jihad has two components – deception and terror. It might be of interest to note that Jesus described Devil as being a murderer and a liar. (John 8:44)

---

[111] [Ahmad Ibn Naqib al-Misri, The Reliance of the Traveler, translated by Nuh Ha Mim Keller , Amana publications, 1997, section r8.2, page 745].

[112] *Fath Al-Bārī*, 10:544, quoted in Tafsi Ibn Kathir, vol. 2, p. 141-143 comment on Q. 3:28

Chapter Two

Muhammad's Personality Profile

There are tens of thousands of short stories about Muhammad. Many of them are forgeries, others are weak and dubious. But some are believed to be *Sahih* (authentic, true) *hadith* (oral traditions). By reading these *Sahih hadiths,* a fairly consistent picture of Muhammad emerges and it is possible to make an approximate evaluation of his character and psychological make-up. The picture that emerges is that of a narcissist.

Scholarship and research on the subject is limited because Muslims have not and will not permit objective inquiry into the Quran or the life of Muhammad. However, what we know about him is not only consistent with the definition of narcissism, but also can be seen in bizarre behavior of his followers. It is as if the personality disorder of one man has been bequeathed to his followers, rendering them, in the same way, self-absorbed, pretentious and bereft of empathy.

It is through understanding the psychology of Muhammad and the situational ethics so essential to his character, that we begin to understand why Muslims are so intolerant of dissent, so violent, so paranoid, and why they see themselves as victims, when they are the aggressors and the victimizers.

What is Narcissism?

The Diagnostic and Statistical Manual of Mental Disorders (DSM- IV) describes narcissism as a personality disorder that "revolves around a pattern of grandiosity, need for admiration, and sense of entitlement. Often individuals feel overly important and will exaggerate achievements and will accept, and often demand, praise and admiration despite worthy achievements."[113]

To some extent, everyone is a narcissist. A healthy dose of narcissism allows us to build self-esteem and have a positive outlook at life. That is why it is difficult to detect it when it is a disorder.

[113] http://allpsych.com/disorders/personality/narcissism.html

To determine whether a person has narcissistic personality disorder, at least five of the following criteria must be met:

1- Feels grandiose and self-important (e.g., exaggerates achievements and talents to the point of lying, demands to be recognized as superior without commensurate achievements)
2- Is obsessed with fantasies of unlimited success, fame, fearsome power or omnipotence, unequalled brilliance (the cerebral narcissist), bodily beauty or sexual performance (the somatic narcissist), or ideal, everlasting, all-conquering love or passion
3- Is firmly convinced that he or she is unique and, being special, can only be understood by, should only be treated by, or associate with, other special, unique, or high-status people (or institutions)
4- Requires excessive admiration, adulation, attention and affirmation, or failing that, wishes to be feared and notorious (narcissistic supply)
5- Feels entitled. Expects unreasonable or special and favorable priority treatment. Demands automatic and full compliance with his or her expectations
6- Is "interpersonally exploitative" i.e., uses others to achieve his or her own ends
7- Is devoid of empathy. Is unable or unwilling to identify with or acknowledge the feelings and needs of others
8- Is constantly envious of others or believes that they feel the same about him or her
9- Is arrogant, has haughty behaviors or attitudes coupled with rage when frustrated, contradicted, or confronted [114]

ALL these criteria were present in Muhammad.

1. He claimed to be the anointed messenger of God and the Seal of the Prophets (Q.33:40),
2. He refused to provide any evidence for that claim and expected people to believe him.
3. He referred to himself *Khayru-l-Khalq* (the Best of Creation), an "excellent example" (Q.33:21), "exalted above other prophets in degrees" (Q.2:253), "the preferred one" (Q.17:55), and a "Mercy to the worlds" (Q.21:107),
4. He claimed to have been risen "to a praised estate" (Q.17:79) the station of Intercessor, advising God whom to punish and whom to forgive.

[114] The language in the criteria above is based on or summarized from:
American Psychiatric Association. (1994). Diagnostic and statistical manual of mental disorders, fourth edition (DSM IV). Washington, DC: American Psychiatric Association.
Sam Vaknin. (1999). Malignant Self Love - Narcissism Revisited, first edition. Prague and Skopje: Narcissus Publication. ("Malignant Self Love - Narcissism Revisited" http://www.geocities.com/vaksam/faq1.html)

2- Muhammad's Personality Profile

5. He exploited others promising them heavenly rewards and making them wage war, plunder and fill his coffers with booty.
6. He had no empathy neither for his victims whom he plundered, tortured, raped, enslaved and massacred, nor for those whom he sent to their death, promising them heavenly rewards.
7. He was extremely haughty and demanded total respect and obedience.
8. He had a great sense of entitlement. He thought everything belonged to the Company of Allah and his Messenger. Inc., where he was its CEO.
9. The most egregious of his claims is that God and his angels praise him constantly. "Truly, Allah and His angels send praise and blessings [forever] upon the Prophet. O you who believe! Praise and bless the Prophet with utmost laud and blessing and surrender to him a great surrender." (Q.33:56). The word used is يُصَلُّونَ. It can mean praise, exalt, glorify. So he thought that the maker of the universe praises him forever.

Here are more boasting:

- And you (stand) on an exalted standard of character. (Q.68:4)
- You [Muhammad] are a lamp with spreading light. (Q.33:46)
- You of Faith, say not (to the Prophet) words of ambiguous import like 'Listen to us,' but words of respect; and obey (him): To those who don't submit there is a grievous punishment. (Q. 2:104)
- He who obeys the Messenger obeys Allah. (Q. 4:80)
- He who disobeys the Apostle after guidance has been revealed will burn in Hell. (Q. 4:114)
- You [Muhammad] may have whomever you desire; there is no blame. (Q. 33:51)
- Allah gives his Messenger Lordship and Power over whomever He wills. (Q.59:6)
- Blessed is He who holds the reins of Kingship. (Q. 67:1)
- You [Muhammad] are an exalted character of tremendous morality. Soon you will see, and they will see, which of you is afflicted with madness. (Q. 68:4)
- Verily this is the Word (brought by) a most honorable Messenger imbued with power, the Lord of the Throne, Mighty, One to be obeyed. (Q. 81:19)

Ibn Sa'd reports Muhammad said, "Among all the people of the world God chose the Arabs. From among the Arabs he chose the Kinana. From Kinana he chose the Quraish (the tribe of Muhammad). From the Quraish he chose Bani Hashim (his clan). And from Bani Hashim he chose me."[115]

[115] Tabaqat V. 1 p. 2

The most egregious claim, in my opinion, is the claim that God promised had to forgive all his future sins. "*Lo! We have given thee (O Muhammad) a clear victory. That Allah may forgive thee of thy sin that which is past and that which is to come.*" (Q.48:1-2) Would any sane god make such an offer to anyone? Maybe that is why Muhammad lived such a despicable life of a criminal. There is hardly any sin he didn't commit. Did he really believe that he won't have to respond for all his murders, rapes and tortures?

The following are some of the claims Muhammad made about himself.

- The very first thing that Allah Almighty ever created was my soul.[116]
- First of all things, the Lord created my mind.[117]
- I am from Allah, and the believers are from me.[118]
- Just as Allah created me noble, he also gave me noble character.[119]
- Were it not for you, [O Muhammad] I would not have created the universe.[120]

Compare these pompous claims to how Jesus responded when someone called him "good master," he said, "Why do you call me good? No one is good—except God alone."[121] Jesus did not commit any of the crimes Muhammad committed and yet never said God created the universe because of him. On the contrary, he claimed to be the sacrificial lamb for the sins of othersm while Muhammad thought others must sacrifice themselves for him. Only an utterly delusional narcissist can be so cut off from reality to think the universe was created for him.

However, narcissists typically feign humility even when they brag. At-Tirmidhi quotes Muhammad saying, "I myself am the Beloved of Allah (*habibullah*) and I say this without pride, and I carry the flag of glory (*liwa ul-hamd*) on the Day of Judgment, and am the first intercessor and the first whose intercession is accepted, and the first to stir the circles of Paradise so that Allah will open it for me and I shall enter it together with the poor among my Community, and I say this without pride. I am the most honored of the First and the Last, and I say this without pride."[122]

In this passage Muhammad claims to be the first to enter paradise. In other words the paradise is not yet operational until the Day of Judgment, when he will be the first to resurrect and to enter it. This is in contradiction with his other claim that he ascended to heaven where he met the previous prophets already in paradise.

---

[116] http://www.muhammadanreality.com/creationofmuhammadanreality.htm
[117] Ibid.
[118] Ibid.
[119] Tabaqat V. 1, p. 364
[120] Ibid.
[121] Mark 10:18
[122] http://www.muhammadanreality.com/about.htm

2- Muhammad's Personality Profile

Narcissists appear to be self-confident. In reality they lack self-esteem and constantly seek an outside supply of adulation. Dr. Sam Vaknin is the author of Malignant Self-Love.[123] He's regarded as an authority on the subject. Having been diagnosed with narcissism, he understands this disorder like no other psychologist does. Narcissism, like blood pressure, comes in degrees. Vaknin is a bit more narcissistic than those who are not diagnosed with it. This gives him a much better understanding of the disorder, just as a cardiologist with heart problems may have a better understanding of his disease.

Vaknin explains, "Everyone is a narcissist, to varying degrees. Narcissism is a healthy phenomenon. It helps survival. The difference between healthy and pathological narcissism is, indeed, in measure. Pathological narcissism... is characterized by extreme lack of empathy. The narcissist regards and treats other people as objects to be exploited. He uses them to obtain narcissistic supply. He believes that he's entitled to special treatment because he harbors these grandiose fantasies about himself. The narcissist is NOT self-aware. His cognition and emotions are distorted...The narcissist lies to himself and to others, projecting 'untouchability,' emotional immunity, and invincibility... For a narcissist everything is bigger than life. If he is polite, then he is aggressively so. His promises are outlandish, his criticism violent and ominous, his generosity inane.... The narcissist is a master of disguise. He's a charmer, a talented actor, a magician and a director of both himself and his milieu. It is very difficult to expose him as such in the first encounter."[124]

The following story shows how concerned Muhammad was about his status and his preoccupation with being respected. About the year 9 A.H. (nine years after his arrival in Medina) a group of Arabs from the tribe of Bani Tamim came to visit him. In the tradition of Arabs, they called him out from outside the apartments (hujurat) of his wives. "Hey Muhammad! Here we have come from far away to see you." Muhammad did not like that. He wanted to be treated with reverence and respect, like a king. He did not respond to their calls and put the following words in the mouth of God urging everyone to be respectful to him:

> *O you who believe! Be not forward in the presence of Allah and His Messenger, and be careful of (your duty to) Allah; surely Allah is Hearing, Knowing. O you who believe! Do not raise your voices above the voice of the Prophet, and do not speak loud to him as you speak loud to one another, lest your deeds became null while you do not perceive. Surely those who lower their voices before Allah's Messenger are they whose hearts Allah has proved for guarding (against evil); they shall have forgiveness and a great reward. (As for) those who call out to you from behind the*

---

123 Sam Vaknin and Lidija Rangelovska, *Malignant Self Love – Narcissism Revisited* , Narcissus Publications, Czech Republic (January 4, 2007),

124 healthyplace.com/Communities/Personality_Disorders/Site/Transcripts/narcissism.htm

> *private chambers, surely most of them do not understand. And if they wait patiently until you come out to them, it would certainly be better for them, and Allah is Forgiving, Merciful.*" (Q.49:1-5)

These men were not being disrespectful to God. They treated Muhammad casually as one of their own. Are these verses the words of God or the petty concerns of a narcissist anxious about his status, seeking recognition and respect?

The Cult of the Narcissist

The narcissist needs admirers. He draws an imaginary circle around himself, where he is the center. He gathers his fans and followers in that circle, rewards them and encourages their sycophantism. Those who fall outside the circle are viewed as enemies. Vaknin says:

> The narcissist is the guru at the center of a cult. Like other gurus, he demands complete obedience from his flock: his spouse, his offspring, other family members, friends, and colleagues. He feels entitled to adulation and special treatment by his followers. He punishes the wayward and the straying lambs. He enforces discipline, adherence to his teachings, and common goals. The less accomplished he is in reality – the more stringent his mastery and the more pervasive the brainwashing…
>
> The narcissist's control is based on ambiguity, unpredictability, fuzziness, and ambient abuse. His ever-shifting whims exclusively define right versus wrong, desirable and unwanted, what's to be pursued and what's to be avoided. He alone determines the rights and obligations of his disciples and alters them at will.
>
> The narcissist is a micro-manager. He exerts control over the minutest details and behaviors. He punishes severely and abuses withholders of information and those who fail to conform to his wishes and goals.
>
> The narcissist doesn't respect the boundaries and privacy of his reluctant adherents. He ignores their wishes and treats them as objects or instruments of gratification. He seeks to control both situations and people compulsively.
>
> He strongly disapproves of others' personal autonomy and independence. Even innocuous activities, such as meeting a friend or visiting one's family requires his permission. Gradually, he isolates his nearest and dearest until they are fully dependent on him emotionally, sexually, financially, and socially.
>
> He acts in a patronizing and condescending manner and criticizes often. He alternates between emphasizing the minutest faults (devalues) and exaggerating the talents,

traits, and skills (idealizes) of the members of his cult. He is wildly unrealistic in his expectations, which legitimizes his subsequent abusive conduct...[125]

In the previous chapter, we saw how Muhammad separated his followers from their families and the level of control he exerted over them. This control continues to this day. I have received countless heartbreaking stories from parents who tell me their daughter or son converted to Islam and is now surrounded by Muslims who have persuaded them not to see their parents. It is by separating the new converts that Muslims can brainwash them without the interference of their loved ones. If your child has Muslims as friend, be prepared to lose them. And if you think moderate Muslims pose little danger, you are in for a crude awakening.

The Cause of the Narcissist

The Narcissist knows that direct self-promotion is repulsive and it will be rejected. So, he wears a mask of modesty and presents himself as a self-effacing servant of God, nation or humanity, whatever the case may be. Sometimes he even tells his followers not to praise him too much. There is a hadith repeated in Bukhari and Muslim that says "The Prophet said: Do not over praise me as the Christians over-praised the son of Mary. I am His slave so say: 'Allah's slave and messenger'."

Behind this facade of modesty is a clear stratagem. The narcissist bestows on his followers a cause, one so grand that the world would be at loss without it. He is a revolutionary leader, a redeemer of mankind, an advocate for change and the harbinger of hope. His cause is always more important than the lives of his followers. The narcissist encourages his followers to sacrifice themselves for the "cause". The bigger the sacrifice, the more copious will be their reward. At the center of the cause is he. The cause revolves around him. It's he alone who can make it happen and lead the world to that Promised Land. This colossal cause cannot exist without him. He therefore, becomes the most important person in the world - The One who holds the key to mankind's salvation.

The cause is a means to the narcissist's personal end. It could be anything. For Jim Jones, the man who led over 900 people to their mass suicide in Guyana, it was "social justice." He was the messiah of that cause.

Hitler did not openly glorify himself. He glorified the Arian race. To his votaries, it was not immediately clear that it was all about him. He made them thing it is about them, and that he was doing all this for their glory. However, he also made it clear that was the indispensable inspirer and the fuehrer of that cause.

---

[125] "The Cult of the Narcissist" by Dr. Sam Vaknin, published in *Malignant Self Love – Narcissism Revisited*, and at http://samvak.tripod.com/journal79.html, c. Sam Vaknin, date not given (accessed June 22, 2007).

For Stalin the cause was communism. Anyone who disagreed with him was against the proletariat. His detractors had to be killed because they were the enemies of the people.

Muhammad did not ask his followers to worship him. He claimed to be "only a warner." But demanded obedience to "Allah and his messenger." In one Quranic verse he made his god say: *"They ask you about the spoils. Say: The spoils are for Allah and the Messenger. So be careful of (your duty to) Allah and set aright matters of your difference, and obey Allah and His Messenger if you are believers."*(Q.8:1)

Since Allah had no use for things stolen from a bunch of Arabs, all those spoils had to go to his messenger. Since no one could see or hear Allah, all the obedience was to Muhammad. It was he who had to be feared because he was the only intermediary between man and this most awesome god.

Allah was an indispensible tool of domination. Without him, would anyone have sacrificed their lives, killed people, including their own kin, looted and handed everything over to him? Allah was Muhammad's alter ego.

Muhammad preached against associating partners to Allah, while at the same time he posited himself as his partner in such a way that made them logically and practically inseparable.

Narcissists hide behind their fictitious causes. The Germans did not wage the war for Hitler. They fought for the cause that he sold them.

Dr. Vaknin writes: "Narcissists use anything they can lay their hands on in the pursuit of narcissistic supply. If God, creed, church, faith, and institutionalized religion can provide them with narcissistic supply, they will become devout. They will abandon religion if it can't."[126]

Islam was Muhammad's instrument of domination. Today, Muslims use Islam to overthrow governments. Islam is a political tool. Muslims become like putty in the hands of those leaders who invoke Islam. Mirza Malkam Khan (1831-1908), an Armenian who became Muslim and together with Jamaleddin Afghani launched the "Islamic Renaissance" (*An-Nahda*), had a slogan of unrivaled cynicism: "Tell the Muslims something is in the Quran, and they will die for you."[127]

The Legacy of the Narcissist

The narcissist wants to leave a legacy. On his deathbed, Muhammad egged on his followers to continue their jihad. Genghis Khan gave a similar command to his sons on his deathbed. He told them he desired to conquer the world, but since he could no longer do it, they should fulfill his dream. For the narcissist, legacy

[126] healthyplace.com/Communities/Personality_Disorders/Site/Transcripts/narcissism.htm
[127] Amir Taheri Neo-Islam http://www.benadorassociates.com/article/19333

matters. They have no regards for the lives they destroy. They want to be remembered. What frightens the narcissist is to be forgotten.

At the age of 51, Hitler became aware of a tremor in his left hand. He usually hid it. As the disease advanced, he stayed away from the public. He realized his death was approaching. Instead of ending his madness, he became more resolute. He launched his attacks with a renewed sense of urgency, knowing he was in a race against time.

Islam is not just a religion. It is an ideology for domination. Its religious component is a thin veneer of icing on the cake. The mystical aspect of Islam was invented later by Muslim scholars and philosophers who gave esoteric interpretations to the Quran's nonsensical verses. They molded the religion according to their penchant. With the passage of time, those interpretations inherited the seal of antiquity. Without these interpretations, the Quran is an asinine book with no substance. The Salafis/Wahhabis are Muslim reformers who reject any interpretation of the Quran. They follow it literally. Hence, they promote jihad and terrorism. Theirs is the real Islam. All other interpretations are alterations and corruptions.

Islam is a political creed. Its only goal is domination. It should be compared to Nazism and communism not to other religions. If we think of religion as a philosophy of life purported to educate mankind, to bring forth it potentials, to elevate the soul, to stimulate spirituality, to unite the hearts and to enlighten the soul, Islam fails that litmus test miserably.

Narcissist wants to be important and to matter. He wants to be remembered. He doesn't care whether he is remembered for good or for bad. For him, there is no difference between good and bad. All he wants is that he is talked about. In this sense Hitler, Stalin, Charles Manson and Jim Jones succeeded as they left a legacy and will be remembered. The same is true about Muhammad. Even after Muslims come to see his deception and leave his religion, he will remain the most influential person in history - the one who brought more death and misery to this world than any other person.

Narcissist Wants To Be God

For the narcissist, what ultimately matters is power. He wants to be noticed and dreads to be ignored. He is lonely and insecure. By projecting himself as a revolutionary leader, a harbinger of hope and an ambassador of a great cause, he expects to attract votaries. The cause is a pretext. Narcissists invent fictitious gods and spurious causes and place themselves at the center of it. The more they elevate their false deities and glorify their causes the more power they can garner for themselves.

Understanding Muhammad

Through Allah, Muhammad wielded unlimited authority over his followers and became the master of their lives. There is only one God, he told them. He is as vengeful as he is forgiving, and as ruthless as compassionate. He is at once, *Al-Mutakabbir* (The Proud One), *Al-Jabbar* (The Despot), *Al-Qahhar* (The Subduer), *Al-Khafid* (The Abaser) *Al-Mudhell* (The Humiliator), *Al-Mumit* (The Death Giver) *Al-Muntaqim* (The Avenger), *Ad-Darr* (the Creator of the Harmful), as he is merciful, rightful, exalter, bestower and provider. Only through his messenger one can attain the bounties of this omnipotent and wanton god and stay away from his harm. This made Muhammad, God by proxy. To obey Allah meant to obey Muhammad and to displease him was to displease God. This is the ultimate power a narcissist can dream of.

In his article "For the Love of God – Narcissists and Religion"[128] Vaknin explains this dynamism.

> God is everything the narcissist wants to be: omnipotent, omniscient, omnipresent, admired, much discussed, and awe-inspiring. God is the narcissist's wet dream, his ultimate grandiose fantasy. But God comes handy in other ways as well. The narcissist alternately idealizes and devalues figures of authority.
>
> In the idealization phase, he strives to emulate them, he admires them, imitates them (often ludicrously), and defends them. They cannot go wrong, or be wrong. The narcissist regards them as bigger than life, infallible, perfect, whole, and brilliant. But as the narcissist's unrealistic and inflated expectations are inevitably frustrated, he begins to devalue his former idols.
>
> Now they are "human" (to the narcissist, a derogatory term). They are small, fragile, error-prone, pusillanimous, mean, dumb, and mediocre. The narcissist goes through the same cycle in his relationship with God, the quintessential authority figure.
>
> But often, even when disillusionment and iconoclastic despair have set in - the narcissist continues to pretend to love God and follow Him. The narcissist maintains this deception because his continued proximity to God confers on him authority. Priests, leaders of the congregation, preachers, evangelists, cultists, politicians, intellectuals - all derive authority from their allegedly privileged relationship with God.
>
> Religious authority allows the narcissist to indulge his sadistic urges and to exercise his misogyny freely and openly. ...The narcissist whose source of authority is religious is looking for obedient and unquestioning slaves upon whom to exercise his capricious and wicked mastery. The narcissist transforms even the most innocuous

---

[128] "For Love of God – Narcissists and Religion", by Dr. Sam Vaknin, at http://samvak.tripod.com/journal45.html (no date given) (accessed June 22, 2007), first published in "Narcissistic Personality Disorder" Topic Page on Suite 101, also appearing in *Malignant Self Love – Narcissism Revisited*, Ibid.

and pure religious sentiments into a cultish ritual and a virulent hierarchy. He preys on the gullible. His flock becomes his hostages.

Religious authority also secures the narcissist's Narcissistic Supply. His coreligionists, members of his congregation, his parish, his constituency, his audience - are transformed into loyal and stable Sources of Narcissistic Supply. They obey his commands, heed his admonitions, follow his creed, admire his personality, applaud his personal traits, satisfy his needs (sometimes even his carnal desires), revere and idolize him.

Moreover, being a part of a "bigger thing" is very gratifying narcissistically. Being a particle of God, being immersed in His grandeur, experiencing His power and blessings first hand, communing with him - are all Sources of unending Narcissistic Supply. The narcissist becomes God by observing His commandments, following His instructions, loving Him, obeying Him, succumbing to Him, merging with Him, communicating with Him - or even by defying him (the bigger the narcissist's enemy - the more grandiosely important the narcissist feels).

Like everything else in the narcissist's life, he mutates God into a kind of inverted narcissist. God becomes his dominant Source of Supply. He forms a personal relationship with this overwhelming and overpowering entity - in order to overwhelm and overpower others. He becomes God vicariously, by the proxy of his relationship with Him. He idealizes God, then devalues Him, then abuses Him. This is the classic narcissistic pattern and even God himself cannot escape it.[129]

Narcissists hide behind the veneer of modesty, while they elevate their god, ideology, cause or religion. All these are tools. While they present themselves as the instrument of God or the Cause, they are actually the objective and the ultimate goal. Behind those masks there is no one but them. Their god is their own alter ego. Their cause is self-aggrandizement.

Arkon Daraul tells a tale that elucidates the unbelievable control that narcissist cult leaders exert over their believers:

Two men in the year 1092 stood on the ramparts of a medieval castle - the Eagle's Nest - perched high upon the crags of the Persian mountains: the personal representative of the Emperor and the veiled figure who claimed to be the incarnation of God on earth. Hasan, son of Sabbah, Sheikh of the Mountains and leader of the Assassins, spoke: "You see that devotee standing guard on yonder turret-top? Watch!" He made a signal. Instantly the white-robed figure threw up his hands in salutation, and cast himself two thousand feet into the foaming torrent which surrounded the fortress.

[129] "For Love of God – Narcissists and Religion", by Dr. Sam Vaknin, Ibid.

> "I have seventy thousand men - and women - throughout Asia, each one of them ready to do my bidding. Can your master, Malik Shah, say the same? And he asks me to surrender to his sovereignty! This is your answer. Go!"
>
> Such a scene may be worthy of the most exaggerated of horror films. And yet it took place in historical fact. The only quibble made by the chronicler of the time was that Hasan's devotees numbered "only about forty thousand." How this man Sabbah came by his uncanny power, and how his devotees struck terror into the hearts of men from the Caspian to Egypt, is one of the most extraordinary of all tales of secret societies. Today, the sect of the Hashishin (druggers) still exists in the form of the Ismailis (Ishmaelites), whose undisputed chief, endowed by them with divine attributes, is the Aga Khan.[130]

Is the unconditional and consummate devotion of believers a sign of the veracity of their creed? Certainly not! In fact the reverse is true. Enlightened teachers never demand blind devotion. They encourage their disciples to "doubt everything and find your own light," as Buddha instructed his students. Akhenaten, the founder of monotheism taught, "True wisdom is less presuming than folly. The wise man doubteth often, and changeth his mind; the fool is obstinate, and doubteth not; he knoweth all things but his own ignorance."

Doubt leads to knowledge and knowledge to enlightenment. Those who demand blind faith, certitude and devotion don't enlighten, but mislead. They don't liberate, but enslave. Doubt everything and everyone, except yourself. Doubt your beliefs, but not your potential, for doubt is the beginning of wisdom. It is what makes us free.

Narcissists are ruthless, but not stupid. They are aware of the hurt that they cause. They enjoy power. They demand unwavering submission. They want to be in charge of who should be rewarded and who should be punished; who should live and who should die. This is the ultimate aphrodisiac for a sociopath narcissist. By controlling the lives of others they become godlike. Muhammad's ruthlessness, his outlandish claims of grandiosity, his eccentric generosity devised to impress and to establish his superiority, as well as his misplaced confidence and his charismatic personality are all tell tales that he suffered from severe narcissistic personality disorder, a malignant self-love.

What Causes Narcissism?

A child, who feels inferior due to real or perceived social rejection, will try to compensate his feeling of inferiority by a subconscious neurotic mechanism, which

[130] From *A History of Secret Societies* by Arkon Daraul (Citadel Press 1961/1989)

the pioneering psychiatrist Alfred Adler coined, "Superiority Complex." This involves exaggerating one's own achievements and putting down anyone he perceives as a threat.

Faulty parenting is the major contributing cause of narcissistic personality disorder. Permissive parents who give excessive praise, overindulge, spoil, fail to impose adequate discipline, and idealize the child are just as abusive to the child's character formation as those who beat them, ignore them or molest them. As a result, the child feels unprepared for adulthood. He grows up with an unrealistic view of life. Also a child who does not receive enough support and encouragement may also develop a narcissistic personality.

Muhammad was given away in infancy to be raised by a stranger. Did his mother lack interest in him? Why did he not pray at her grave even when he was over sixty years old? Was he still resentful toward her?

Halima did not want to take Muhammad because he was an orphan of a poor widow. Did this affect the way she and her family treated him? Muhammad's childhood condition was not conducive to building a healthy self-esteem.

Jon Mardi Horowitz, author of *Stress Response Syndromes* says, "When the habitual narcissistic gratifications that come from being adored, given special treatment, and admiring the self are threatened, the results may be depression, hypochondria, anxiety, shame, self-destructiveness, or rage directed toward any other person who can be blamed for the troubled situation. The child can learn to avoid these painful emotional states by acquiring a narcissistic mode of information processing."[131]

Muhammad's rage was evident from his childhood. In the raid of Hunain, a woman by the name of Shayma b. Harith was captured. Ibn Sa'd reports, "They treated her roughly as they brought her along and she told the Muslims that she was the foster-sister of the apostle, but they did not believe her until they had brought her to the apostle… When she was brought to the apostle and when asked for proof she said, 'The bite you gave me in my back when I carried you at my hip.'"[132] Muhammad recognized the mark and stretched out his robe for her to sit on and treated her kindly. Children bite when frustrated and to show their rage. It is obvious that Muhammad felt the deprivation of love at a very young age. That must have been quite a bite to last more than half a century.

There is no doubt that Muhammad had a difficult childhood. In Quran 93: 3-8 (quoted at the beginning of chapter one) he calls to mind his lonesome orphanhood and reassures himself that Allah will be kind to him and will not forsake him. This shows how much the memory of his lonesome childhood pained him. The fact that he created an imaginary world to escape from reality, so vivid that it concerned his

---

[131] Jon Mardi Horowitz – *Stress Response Syndromes: PTSD, Grief, and Adjustment Disorder*" New Jersey: Jason Aronson Inc., Third Edition, 1997, ISBN-10: 0765700255, ISBN-13: 978-0765700254.

[132] Ibn Ishaq's Sirat Rasoul translation Oxford Press p. 576

foster parents, is another clue that his early childhood was anything but pleasant. Muhammad may not have remembered the details of what happened during his first years of life, but he bore the psychological scars for the rest of his life. To him, the imaginary world he created was real. It was a safe refuge, a pleasant oasis to retreat to and to escape from the harsh reality of his loneliness. In this imaginary world, he was loved, admired, powerful, important, and feared. He could be anything he wanted to be and compensate for the lack of attention he was getting from the world outside.

Vaknin notes:

> The true cause of Narcissism is not fully understood but it does start in early childhood (before the age of five). It is believed it is caused by serious and repetitive failures on the part of the child's Primary Object (parents or other caregiver). Adult Narcissists often come from homes where one or both parents severely neglected (ignored) or abused the child… ALL children (healthy and otherwise) when they are not allowed to do something by their parents will sometimes enter into a narcissistic state where they see themselves and act as if they are all powerful. This is healthy and natural as it gives the child the confidence needed to rebound from the parental rejection with self-confidence."[133]

Neglected children internalize a feeling of inadequacy. They come to believe they are undeserving of love. They react to this feeling of inferiority and defend their egos by puffing themselves up. They see their own weakness and feel that if others come to see it, they will not like them. So they invent fantastic stories and brag about their self-importance. Their imaginary power often originates from an external source. It could be their daddy or a strong friend. This kind of narcissism in children is normal. It becomes pathological, when they retain these thoughts into adulthood. That is what causes narcissistic personality disorder.

Muhammad saw his imaginary friends as guardian agngels. He finally replaced them with Gabriel and Allah. By becoming a messenger of God and presenting himself as his sole intermediary, he incarnated all of his powers.

At the age of six, after the death of his mother, Muhammad went under the tutelage of his grandfather who spoiled him. Several hadiths show Abdul Muttalib was too permissive towards his orphaned grandson. He pitied and overindulged him. He would let him sit on his mat on his bed while his grownup sons sat reverentially on the ground around him.

Muhammad's claim that Abdul Muttalib had foreseen his greatness can be attributed to his wild imagination. In one place he recounted that when his uncles wanted to remove him from the mat occupied by Abdul Muttalib, he bade them, "Let him alone for he has a great destiny, and will be the inheritor of a kingdom"[134] In another place he crowed hearing the old patriarch tell his nurse, "Beware lest you

---

133 www.faqfarm.com/Q/Can_you_be_responsible_for_your_spouse's_narcissism

134 Tabaqat Vol 1 p. 107

let him fall into the hands of the Jews and Christians, for they are looking out for him, and would injure him!"[135] These are typical fantasies of narcissists who think of themselves as so important that they believe everyone is after them to harm them out of jealousy. Jews and Christians are not looking for any messenger to injure. The claim is preposterous and can only be understood as an indication that Muhammad suffered from paranoia and narcissism.

It is clear that Abdul Muttalib made Muhammad feel special. He pampered and loved his orphaned grandchild. Muhammad interpreted that extra attention as the confirmation of his grandeur. The image he cast about himself in his fantasy world during his childhood was thus bolstered by his grandfather's overindulgence. He was reconfirmed to be unique, special, and exceptional.

After the death of Abdul Muttalib, his uncle Abu Talib, also treated him differently from other children. His status as an orphan, with no siblings, evoked pity. Both his grandfather and uncle showed excessive compassion and failed to impose discipline on him. These extremes contributed to Muhammad's narcissistic personality disorder. Psychologists J. D. Levine and Rona H. Weiss write:

> Just as we know, from the point of view of the physiologist, that a child needs to be given certain foods, that he needs to be protected against extreme temperatures, and that the atmosphere he breathes has to contain sufficient oxygen, if his body is to become strong and resilient, so do we also know, from the point of view of the depth-psychologist, that he requires an empathic environment, specifically, an environment that responds (a) to his need to have his presence confirmed by the glow of parental pleasure and (b) to his need to merge into the reassuring calmness of the powerful adult, if he is to acquire a firm and resilient self.[136]

Muhammad first experienced neglect and abandonment and then excessive permissiveness. His circumstances were conducive for him to become a narcissist.

There is no record that Muhammad ever spoke of his mother. He visited her tomb after he conquered Mecca, but he refused to pray for her. What was the point of that visit? Was this a way to prove to her that despite her neglect, he had made it?

Psychologists tell us that the first five years of a child's life are the years that either make him or break him. Muhammad's emotional needs during the first five years of his life were not met. He carried the painful memories of those lonesome years into his adulthood and old age. He grew up insecure and had a fluctuating sense of self-worth, a weakness he tried to hide with overwhelming haughtiness, by growing a sense of entitlement, grandiosity, and an illusion of superiority.

---

[135] Ibid.

[136] J. D. Levine and Rona H. Weiss. The Dynamics and Treatment of Alcoholism. Jason Aronson, 1994

He positioned himself as the partner of God and to make sure that no one would ever usurp that rank, he claimed to be the last messenger. His power was thus absolute and everlasting.

Khadijah's Influence on Muhammad

Khadijah's role in Islam has not yet been fully appreciated. But her influence on Muhammad cannot be overemphasized. Khadijah should be regarded as Muhammad's partner in giving birth to Islam. Without her, there would be no Islam.

Khadijah adored her young husband. There is no report that Muhammad ever worked after marrying her. After the marriage, her business went down the tubes. By her death, the family had become impoverished. Dejected by the world and unable to interact with others as equal, Muhammad spent most of his time recluse, in his affable chimerical world.

In Vaknin's words, "To avoid such intolerable pain, some patients with Narcissistic Personality Disorder (NPD) socially withdraw and feign false modesty and humility to mask their underlying grandiosity. Dysthymic and depressive disorders are common reactions to isolation and feelings of shame and inadequacy."[137]

Muhammad would take enough food for several days, returning only when his provisions were finished to procure more and go back to his contemplative cave.

Khadijah remained at home. She took care of her nine children, but also of her husband who acted like an irresponsible child. She did not complain. She was happy to sacrifice. Why?

This is an important question. It suggests that Khadijah may have had her own personality disorder. She was what we would call today, a co-dependent. This crucial piece of puzzle will help us understand why she stood by her self-absorbed husband and when he told her of his bizarre hallucination and expressed that he may have been demon possessed, instead of becoming alarmed and calling an exorcist, she persuaded him that what he had seen was an angel and that he had become a prophet.

The National Mental Health Association defines co-dependency as:

> A learned behavior that can be passed down from one generation to another. It is an emotional and behavioral condition that affects an individual's ability to have a healthy, mutually satisfying relationship. It is also known as 'relationship addiction' because people with codependency often form or maintain relationships that are one-sided, emotionally destructive and/or abusive. The disorder was first identified about ten years ago as the result of years of studying interpersonal relationships in families of alcoholics.

[137] http://www.globalpolitician.com/25109-barack-obama-elections

2- Muhammad's Personality Profile

> Codependent behavior is learned by watching and imitating other family members who display this type of behavior.[138]

Khadijah was a dainty accomplished woman. She was the favorite daughter of her father Khuwaylid who, relied on her more than he did on his sons. She was, what in today's parlance we'd call, a "daddy's girl." She had rejected the hands of the powerful men of Mecca. But when she saw the youthful and dispossessed Muhammad, she fell in love with him and sent a maid to propose marriage.

On the surface it seems that Muhammad was so attractive that he mesmerized this powerful woman. This, however, is a superficial understanding of a complex dynamism. Prior to Khadijah, no woman had ever shown interest in him.

The historian Tabari writes: "Khadijah sent a message to Muhammad inviting him to take her. She called her father to her house, plied him with wine until he was drunk, anointed him with perfume, clothed him in a striped robe and slaughtered a cow. Then she sent for Muhammad and his uncles. When they came in, her father married him to her. When he recovered from his intoxication, he said, 'What is this meat, this perfume, and this garment?' She replied, 'You have married me to Muhammad bin Abdullah.' 'I have not done so,' he said. 'Would I do this when the greatest men of Mecca have asked for you and I have not agreed, why would I give you to a bum?'"[139]

The party of Muhammad replied indignantly that the alliance had been arranged by Khuwaylid's own daughter. The old man drew his sword in anger and the relatives of Muhammad drew theirs. Blood was to be shed when Khadijah intervened and made her love for Muhammad known and confessed to having masterminded the whole proceeding. Khuwaylid was thus pacified, resigned to the *fait accompli* and reconciliation ensued.

How can one explain a seemingly levelheaded and successful woman suddenly fall in love with an indigent youth 15 years her junior? This erratic behavior belies a certain personality disorder.

Evidence suggests that Khadijah's father was an alcoholic. Khadijah must have known her father's weakness for the intoxicant to devise such an intricate and audacious plan. Non-alcoholic people often drink in moderation and hardly alone. Khuwaylid became drunk before the arrival of the guests.

Now, why should this matter? Because it's another piece of the puzzle in support of the theory that Khadijah was a co-dependent. Children of alcoholics often develop co-dependency.

Khadijah's father was overly protective of her and had high expectations for her. From his reaction to the marriage of his 40-year-old daughter to an ordinary man and his saying, "the greatest men of Mecca have asked for you and I have not

[138] http://www.nmha.org/infoctr/factsheets/43.cfm
[139] Persian Tabari v. 3 p.832

agreed," we can deduce that Khadijah was the apple of her father's eyes. Khuwaylid had other children too, including a few sons, but this daughter was his pride and joy. At this time Khadijah is said to be the wealthiest woman in Mecca.

Children who are placed on a pedestal by their emotionally needy parents grow in their shadow. They often develop co-dependency personality disorder. They become obsessed with their needy father (or mother) and see their own function in making them look good in the eyes of the outsiders. They are expected to be the "*wunderkind.*" They strive to live up to that expectation and not to disappoint their parents.

Under the constant demand for better performance, the child becomes unable to develop her own independent personality. She seeks her fulfillment in satisfying the needs of her perfectionist/narcissistic parent. She does not feel loved for *who* she is, but rather for *how* she performs. The alcoholic parent unloads his own emotional baggage on his children, especially on the one with more potential. He expects her to excel in everything and to make up for his own failures.

Co-dependents cannot find fulfillment and happiness in normal and emotionally healthy relationships that can happen among equals. Only in the capacity of *caregivers* and *pleasers* can they find their equilibrium. The "perfect" match for a co-dependent is therefor, a needy narcissist.

Khadijah rejected her powerful suitors and fell in love with a poor young man who was both emotionally and financially needy. Co-dependents confuse love with pity. They have the tendency to love people they should pity and rescue.

Vaknin uses the term "inverted narcissism" instead of co-dependency. Here is what he says about the co-dependent-narcissist relationship. "The inverted narcissist can only truly FEEL anything when he is in relationship with another narcissist. The inverted narcissist is conditioned and programmed from the very beginning to be the perfect companion to the narcissist - to feed their Ego, to be purely their extension, to seek only praise and adulation if it brings greater praise and adulation to the narcissist."[140]

This explains why a successful and beautiful woman like Khadijah would become interested in a needy young man like Muhammad. Although inverted narcissists tend to be successful in their careers, their relationships are often unhealthy. Vaknin explains:

> In a primary relationship, the inverted narcissist attempts to re-create the parent-child relationship. The invert thrives on mirroring to the narcissist his own grandiosity and in so doing the invert obtains his OWN Narcissistic Supply (the dependence of the narcissist upon the invert for their Secondary Narcissistic Supply). The invert must have this form of relationship with a narcissist in order to feel complete and whole. The invert will go as far as he

[140] http://samvak.tripod.com/faq66.html

> needs to ensure that the narcissist is happy, cared for, properly adored, as he feels is the narcissist's right. The invert glorifies his narcissist, places him on a pedestal, endures any and all narcissistic devaluation with calm equanimity, impervious to the overt slights of the narcissist.[141]

The marriage of Muhammad and Khadijah was made in heaven (no pun intended). Muhammad was a narcissist who craved for constant praise. He was poor and emotionally needy - an adult, with an inner child still yearning for attention. He needed someone to take care of him, to provide for him and to exploit and abuse, the way an infant exploits and abuses his mother.

The relationship between a mother and her infant is narcissistic-co-dependent relationship. A mother is emotionally co-dependent on her child, and the child is by nature a narcissist. She endures all his abuses joyfully. This mother-child sadomasochistic relationship is absolutely healthy, normal and even necessary. But it is not normal or healthy when happens between two adults.

The emotional maturity of the narcissist is frozen at childhood. His infantile needs have never been satisfied. He is constantly trying to procure for those childish needs. If the narcissistic needs of children are not satisfied, their emotional maturity halts. In their adulthood, they seek the attention that they missed during their childhood. They become emotionally dependent on others, their mates and even their children.

Muhammad expressed his craving for love on many occasions. Ibn Sa'd quotes him saying, the families of Quraish are all related to me and even if they don't love me for the message I am bringing them, they should love me because of my kinship to them.[142] Of course as a narcissist he did not think that he also owed them the same love that he demanded from them. It was okay for him to hate them and to threaten to slaughter them. In the Quran he said: "No reward do I ask of you for this except the love of those near of kin."[143] These words are desperate cries of one dire need for love and attention.

Bukhari says, "The Prophet was holding Umar's hand, who said, 'O Allah's Apostle! You are **dearer** to me than everything except my own self.' The Prophet said, 'No, by Him in Whose Hand my soul is, you will not have faith till I am dearer to you than your own self.' Then Umar said, 'However, now, by Allah, you are dearer to me than my own self.' The Prophet said, 'Now, Umar, you are a believer.'[144]

---

141 http://www.toddlertime.com/sam/66.htm

142 "I do not ask of you any reward for it but love for my near relatives" Tabaqat vol.1 page.3

143 Quran Sura 42: verse 23

144 Bukhari 8.628

Khadijah, on the other hand, was an inverted narcissist who needed someone to fulfill her own fantasies as a caregiver. Not only does the co-dependent not mind being taken advantage of, she actually enjoys it.

Vaknin writes: "The inverted narcissist feeds on the primary narcissist and this is his narcissistic supply. So these two typologies can, in essence become a self-supporting, symbiotic system. In reality though, both the narcissist and the inverted narcissist need to be well aware of the dynamics of this relationship in order to make this work as a successful long-term arrangement."[145]

Psychologist Florence W. Kaslow, explaining this symbiosis, says that both parties have personality disorders (PDs) – but on opposite ends of the spectrum. "They seem to have a fatal attraction for each other in that their personality patterns are complementary and reciprocal – which is one reason why, if they get divorced, they are likely to be attracted over and over to someone similar to their former partner."[146]

The symbiotic relationship between Muhammad and Khadijah worked to perfection. He no longer needed to be preoccupied with work or money and spent his days wandering in the caves and wilderness of his fertile fantasies, in the affable realm where he was loved, admired, and respected. Khadijah became engulfed in him and in attending to his needs to such an extent that she neglected her commerce and her thriving business dwindled and her wealth evaporated. She must have been around fifty years old when her youngest child was born. She stayed home while her husband was away most of the time, a recluse in his mental and physical caves.

According to Vaknin, "the inverted narcissist is extinguishingly selfless, sacrificial even unctuous in his interpersonal relationships and will avoid the assistance of others at all costs. He can only interact with others when he can be seen to be giving, supportive, and expending an unusual effort to assist."[147]

Vaknin defines co-dependents as "people who depend on others for their emotional gratification and the performance of Ego or daily functions. They are needy, demanding, submissive, fear abandonment, cling, and display immature behaviours in their effort to maintain the 'relationship' with their companion or mate upon whom they depend."[148]

Melody Beattie, author of *Codependent No More*, says that co-dependents unconsciously pick troubled partners in order to have purpose, be needed and feel fulfilled.

---

[145] http://samvak.tripod.com/faq66.html

[146] Quoted from "Mixing oil and water" by Bridget Murray, APA Online Monitor On Psychology, Vol. 35, No. 3, March 2004, (online version), Print version: page 52, online version found at http://www.apa.org/monitor/mar04/mixing.html (accessed June 22, 2007www.apa.org/monitor/mar04/mixing.html

[147] www.toddlertime.com/sam/66.htm

[148] "The Inverted Narcissist" Sam Vaknin, HealthyPlace.com Personality Disorders Community, at www.healthyplace.com/communities/Personality_Disorders/narcissism/faq66.html (date not given) (accessed June 22, 2007)

2- Muhammad's Personality Profile

A sensible person would have interpreted Muhammad's bizarre experience as psychosis or "demon possession," as they used to call it then. Muhammad himself thought he had become a *kahin* (sorcerer) or demon-possessed. The wise people of Mecca thought he had become a *majnoon* (possessed by jinns / insane). But such a thought was too much to bear for Khadijah, who sought her fulfillment in the fulfillment of her husband and her glory in his glory. She had to cling to her narcissist at any cost. As a co-dependent, she felt the urge to step in, be helpful, give advice, and salvage her narcissist, the source of her own narcissistic supply.

Khadijah can be classified as 'vicarious co-dependent.' Vaknin says, "Vicarious co-dependents live through others. They 'sacrifice' themselves in order to glory in the accomplishments of their chosen targets. They subsist on reflected light, on second-hand applause, and on derivative achievements. They have no personal history, having suspended their wishes, preferences, and dreams in favor of another's."[149]

The narcissist often demands sacrifices from people around him and expects them to become his co-dependents. He also lives above the moral code. He feels too important to abide by any morality or rule. The co-deponent is more than eager to comply.

The Case of a Narcissist

John de Ruiter is a self-proclaimed messiah from Alberta, Canada. His followers worship him like God. "One day we were sitting around the kitchen smoking cigarettes," says Joyce, de Ruiter's estranged wife of 18 years, in an interview. "He was talking about my 'death.' He acknowledged that I had gone through a lot of dying, which was a good thing. I had let go of ninety-five percent of the life that I had to let go of. But he said I wasn't letting myself go completely. He suggested that my ultimate death would be if he took on two more wives." Joyce said she thought he was joking. He wasn't. He brought up the matter a second time, and asked Joyce if she thought his three wives could live in the same house.[150]

Fortunately, Joyce was not co-dependent enough to agree to this much humiliation and left her degenerate narcissist husband. A true co-dependent would do anything to appease her narcissist. The relationship of a co-dependent and her narcissist is sadomasochism.

Unfortunately for mankind, Khadijah was a real co-dependent who was willing to sacrifice everything for her adored narcissist. It was she who encouraged Muhammad to pursue his prophetic ambition and spurred him in that direction.

---

149 http://samvak.tripod.com/personalitydisorders22.html

150 "The Gospel According to John," by Brian Hutchison, Saturday Night Magazine, May 5, 2001, at http://www.rickross.com/reference/ruiter/ruiter3.html (accessed June 22, 2007

When his epileptic seizures ceased, she was disappointed. Ibn Ishaq writes: "After this, Gabriel did not come to him for a while and Khadijah said, 'I think that your Lord must hate you.'"[151] This demonstrates her eagerness for her narcissist to become a prophet so she can bask in his glory and share his prestige.

Muhammad did not take other wives when Khadijah was still alive. He was living off her money and in her house. Furthermore, the majority of Meccans derided him. He was called a lunatic. No one would have married him even if he had money of his own and Khadijah had not been an issue. In Mecca, his followers were a handful of teenagers and slaves with only a few women among them. None was eligible for him to marry. Had Khadijah survived to see his rise to power, she probably would have had to put up with her husband's vagaries and the humiliation of sharing him with younger and prettier women.

After her death, Muhammad never found another co-dependent to take care of his emotional needs like she did. Instead, he became a sexual butterfly. A month after his wife's death, he convinced his loyal follower, Abu Bakr, to betroth to him his six-year-old daughter. Abu Bakr tried to dissuade him, saying, "But we are brothers." Muhammad reassured him they were only brothers in faith and that his marriage to that little girl was okay.[152]

He further told Abu Bakr that Aisha had been shown to him twice in dreams in which he saw an angel carrying her wrapped in a silken piece of cloth. "I said (to myself), 'If this is from Allah, then it must happen.'"[153]

Now Abu Bakr was left with two options: To Leave Muhammad, for whom he had made so many sacrifices, denounce him, call him a liar and go back to his people and acknowledge he had been a fool, or to do whatever he asked of him. This is often the difficult choice cultists must make. Abu Bakr had even built a mosque in the backyard of his house. He would often cry when reciting Muhammad's allegedly revealed verses. Denouncing him at this stage was not easy. Cultists are trapped. They sacrifice so much that going back is impossible.

Vaknin describes the hold that narcissists have on their cultists from their own perspective: "I lie to your face, without a twitch or a twitter, and there is absolutely nothing you can do about it. In fact, my lies are not lies at all. They are the truth, my truth. And you believe them, because you do, because they do not sound or feel like lies, because to do otherwise would make you question your own sanity, which you have a tendency to do anyway, because from the very beginning of our relationship you placed your trust and hopes in me, derived your energy, direction, stability, and

---

[151] Sira Ibn Ishaq, p. 108

[152] Sahih Bukhari 7.62.18 Narrated 'Ursa: The Prophet asked Abu Bakr for 'Aisha's hand in marriage. Abu Bakr said "But I am your brother." The Prophet said, "You are my brother in Allâh's religion and His Book, but she (Aisha) is lawful for me to marry."

[153] Sahih Bukhari, Volume 9, Book 87, Number 140

confidence from me and from your association with me. So what's the problem if the safe haven I provide comes with a price? Surely I am worth it and then some."[154]

Bob Larson writes: "Cult leaders know that once an initiate has been reconditioned to accept their particular worldview and as soon as he feels a sense of meaningful belonging, his mind will be ready to accept any teaching, including a belief that the leader represents God."[155]

Abu Bakr pleaded with Muhammad to wait three more years before consummating the marriage. Muhammad agreed and meanwhile, he married Sauda, the widowed wife of one of his followers, a few days later.

Muhammad created a harem with a score of women. He tried to compensate the loss of Khadijah with an abundance of young women. He kept adding to the collection of his wives and concubines, but none could meet his emotional needs the way Khadijah did. He needed a mother to take care of his inner child, something, his teenager wives could hardly be, to a man who could be their grandfather.

Muhammad's Belief in His Own Cause

From his early youth, Muhammad attended the annual fair in Okaz, where people from all over Arabia met for commerce and fun. Christian preachers read stories of the Biblical prophets to their captivated audiences and other storytellers narrated the legends of kings. Muhammad was fascinated by those stories. Being loved and respected were the only thoughts that occupied his young mind. "How great it would be to be a prophet and maybe also a king, to be loved, respected and feared!" he must have thought while listening to those stories. Now, his wife was reassuring him that he had become a prophet and his fantasy has been fulfilled. It seemed that God had finally looked upon him mercifully, had chosen him from amongst all the people and had raised him to enviable stator of prophethoood.

You cannot attract followers if you have the slightest shadow of doubt. Muhammad was convinced of his mission. His thoughts were so grand and his faith so unwavering that they kindled his followers to rise and to champion his cause, to wage war and murder, even their own brothers and father.

Muhammad built his empire without fighting a single battle personally. By promising heavenly rewards, he made others to fight for him, and to sacrifice their lives for his cause. Narcissists are masters of lies. Ironically, they themselves are the first victims of their own deception. They compensate their intolerably poor self-images by inflating their egos with grandiosity. They turn themselves into glittering images of immense grandeur surrounded by walls of denial. Through this self-deception they become impervious to external criticism and to their roiling sea of

---

[154] http://samvak.tripod.com/kenintro.html
[155] Larson's New Book of Cults 1989, pp. 14-15

doubts. Narcissists are pathological liars. So precarious is their house of cards that they cannot tolerate any dissention.

Vaknin says, "The narcissist is ever in the pursuit of excitement and drama intended to alleviate his all-pervasive boredom and melancholy. Needless to say, both the pursuit itself and its goals must conform to the grandiose vision that the narcissist has of his (False) Self. They must be commensurate with his vision of his uniqueness and entitlement."[156]

This explains Muhammad's constant warfare. The drama, the rush of adrenaline and excitement were his narcissistic supplies. However, in a sense he was "honest." The narcissist believes in his own malarkey.

Vaknin says: "Granted, the narcissist's hold on reality is tenuous (narcissists sometimes fail the reality test). Admittedly, narcissists often seem to believe in their own confabulations. They are unaware of the pathological nature and origin of their self-delusions and are, thus, technically delusional (though they rarely suffer from hallucinations, disorganized speech, or disorganized or catatonic behaviour). In the strictest sense of the word, narcissists appear to be psychotic."[157]

He says however, that narcissists, while masters of self-deception or even malignant con-artistry, "are usually fully aware of the difference between true and false, real and make-believe, the invented and the extant, right and wrong. The narcissist consciously chooses to adopt one version of the events, an aggrandizing narrative, a fairy-tale existence, a 'what-if' counter-factual life. He is emotionally invested in his personal myth. The narcissist feels better as fiction, than as fact – but he never loses sight of the fact that it is all just fiction. The narcissist is in full control of his faculties, cognizant of his choices, and goal-oriented. His behavior is intentional and directional. He is a manipulator, and his delusions are in the service of his stratagems. Hence his chameleon-like ability to change guises, his conduct, and his convictions on a dime…The narcissist attempts to condition his nearest and dearest to positively reinforce his delusional False Self."[158] In the case of Muhammad, that role was played by Khadijah.

This is somewhat difficult to understand. On the one hand, Vaknin says the narcissist never loses sight of the fact that it is all his fiction, and on the other, he says that the narcissist's hold on reality is tenuous and that often he believes in his confabulations. Although these two statements present a logical dilemma for normal people, they are both true in the case of narcissists, who lie and then go on to convince themselves of those lies, as if they were absolute truth. While at the same time they will change their narrative whenever it suits them.

---

[156] Dr. Sam Vaknin Narcissism FAQ #57

[157] "Pathological Narcissism, Psychosis, and Delusions" by Sam Vaknin, at Sam Vaknin Sites, http://samvak.tripod.com/journal91.html (accessed June 22, 2007)

[158] ibid.

2- Muhammad's Personality Profile

We tend to believe that either a person is insane or he is a liar and that the two are mutually exclusive. This is not true. Often criminals plead insanity to escape punishment. Courts and even many mental health professionals have fallen for this deception. This folly has reached the absurd. James Pacenza, a 58-year-old man who was fired for spending his time visiting adult Internet chat-rooms at work, sued his employer (IBM) for wrongful dismissal, claiming that he was addicted to online chat-rooms and IBM should have offered him sympathy and treatment instead of firing him. He was awarded $5,000,000 compensation.[159] I can't stop thinking that the Judge who passed that ruling must have been a sex pervert himself.

The truth is that narcissists are fully aware of their actions. New York serial killer David Berkowitz, who called himself "Son of Sam," escaped capital punishment because his crimes were so horrendous and senseless that everyone thought he was insane and therefore not responsible for his actions. Actually he knew what he was doing. As a narcissist, he craved attention and left clues to be found. The exhilaration of reclaiming all the celebrity status that surrounded the case was more impelling than his freedom. He could not pass the opportunity of basking in the glory of his 15 minutes of fame, even as a serial killer. What Berkowitz did was consistent with psychopathic narcissism. When he was caught and locked in prison, he decided to become a born-again Christian. Why did he not do this before? Did he undergo a brain surgery in prison? No! He just decided to change tactic to gain the attention that he so intensely craved. In prison, the only way to do that was to become a holy man. The narcissist is a chameleon. He carefully monitors others to see what elicits more attention and then acts accordingly.

Narcissists know the difference between right and wrong. They seek attention. If for that they have to become a serial killer, they become a serial killer; if they have to become religious, they become religious.

The serial killer is addicted to the "high" that he gets by exerting power over his victims. Compare him to a smoker. They both know that what they do is wrong. Yet their urges are stronger than their willpower. The smoker kills himself, one cigarette at a time, and the serial killer kills others one person at a time. Why doesn't a smoker quit? Because he is addicted! Likewise, the narcissist psychopath is addicted to the adrenaline rush and the excitement of playing god.

Narcissists know what they do is wrong because they don't like to be on the receiving end of it. Muhammad raided villages; and after massacring unarmed men, he looted their belongings. Yet, he tortured to death eight men who had killed one of his shepherds and stole his stolen camels. He raped women captured in his raids, even if they were married; yet he could not stand anyone looking at his wives and ordered them to cover themselves. He prohibited killing and stealing, but justified his own mass murders and loots. As a narcissist, he believed to be entitled to

159 http://news.bbc.co.uk/2/hi/americas/6682827.stm

special rights and at liberty to do anything his whims dictated. Muhammad was both insane *and* liar. This is possible only if you are a psychopathic narcissist.

More on the Policy of Divide and Rule

As stated in the previous chapter, Muhammad severed his followers' ties to their families in order to secure his absolute control over them. He ordered the Emigrants, not to contact their relatives back home. Despite his warnings, some of them did, probably because they needed money. To stop this, he dictated the following verse.[160]

"O you who believe! Take not my enemies and yours as friends (or protectors), - offering them (your) love, even though they have rejected the Truth that has come to you, and have (on the contrary) driven out the Prophet and yourselves (from your homes), (simply) because you believe in Allah your Lord! If you have come out to strive in My Way and to seek My Good Pleasure, (take them not as friends), holding secret converse of love (and friendship) with them: for I know full well all that you conceal and all that you reveal. And any of you that do this has strayed from the Straight Path. (Q.60:1)

We see this urge to alienate in a later verse too. *"O you who believe! Take not for protectors your fathers and your brothers if they love infidelity above Faith: if any of you do so, they do wrong.* (Q. 9:23)

Why was Muhammad so keen to isolate his followers? Vaknin explains: "The narcissist is the guru at the centre of a cult. Like other gurus, he demands complete obedience from his flock: his spouse, his offspring, other family members, friends, and colleagues. He feels entitled to adulation and special treatment by his followers. He punishes the wayward and the straying lambs. He enforces discipline, adherence to his teachings, and common goals. The less accomplished he is in reality – the more stringent his mastery and the more pervasive the brainwashing."[161]

This was something Muhammad could not accomplish while his followers still lived in Mecca, where they could, if things got tough, return to their families. To isolate their followers, cult leaders often enclose them in compounds where they can brainwash and control them. At first, Muhammad sent the early believers to Abyssinia, but later, when he made a pact with the Arabs of Yathrib, he chose that town as his compound. He even changed the name of Yathrib and called it *Medinatul Nabi*, Prophet's Town.

---

[160] The Quran can be tedious, and that is mainly why few Muslims have read it. However, at the risk of boring my readers, in this chapter I will have to quote several Quranic verses as evidence to support my portrait of Muhammad.

[161] http://samvak.tripod.com/journal79.html

2- Muhammad's Personality Profile

Vaknin says: "The – often involuntary – members of the narcissist's mini-cult inhabit a twilight zone of his own construction. He imposes on them a shared psychosis, replete with persecutory delusions, 'enemies,' mythical narratives, and apocalyptic scenarios if he is flouted."[162]

Note how accurately the above description applies to Muhammad and Muslims, who to this day have persecutory delusions and see enemies everywhere. They believe in mythical narratives such as jinns, and fairy tales like Mi'raj, Doomsday, and more.

According to Vaknin, "the narcissist's deep-rooted conviction that he is being persecuted by his inferiors, detractors, or powerful ill-wishers, serves two psychodynamic purposes. It upholds the narcissist's grandiosity and it fends off intimacy."[163]

Vaknin writes:

> The narcissist claims to be infallible, superior, talented, skilful, omnipotent, and omniscient. He often lies and confabulates to support these unfounded claims. Within his cult, he expects awe, admiration, adulation, and constant attention commensurate with his outlandish stories and assertions. He reinterprets reality to fit his fantasies. His thinking is dogmatic, rigid, and doctrinaire. He does not welcome free thought, pluralism, or free speech, and doesn't brook criticism and disagreement. He demands – and often gets – complete trust and the relegation to his capable hands of all decision-making. He forces the participants in his cult to be hostile to critics, the authorities, institutions, his personal enemies, or the media – if they try to uncover his actions and reveal the truth. He closely monitors and censors information from the outside, exposing his captive audience only to selective data and analyses."[164]

By elucidating the characteristics of the narcissist, Vaknin, unintentionally and yet with astounding accuracy describes Muhammad's mind and the Muslim mind-set. Muslims are narcissists to the extent that they emulate their prophet.

A Comparison between Islam and the Cult of the Narcissist

First, let us see what Vaknin says about the cult of the narcissist:

> The narcissist's cult is "missionary" and "imperialistic." He is always on the lookout for new recruits – his spouse's friends, his daughter's girlfriends, his neighbors, new colleagues at work. He immediately attempts to 'convert' them to his 'creed' – to convince them how wonderful and admirable he is. In other words, he tries to render them Sources of Narcissistic Supply.

162 ibid.
163 www.suite101.com/article.cfm/6514/95897
164 http://samvak.tripod.com/journal79.html

> Often, his behavior on these 'recruiting missions' is different to his conduct within the 'cult'. In the first phases of wooing new admirers and proselytizing to potential 'conscripts' – the narcissist is attentive, compassionate, empathic, flexible, self-effacing, and helpful. At home, among the "veterans" he is tyrannical, demanding, willful, opinionated, aggressive, and exploitative.
>
> As the leader of his congregation, the narcissist feels entitled to special amenities and benefits not accorded the "rank and file." He expects to be waited on hand and foot, to make free use of everyone's money and dispose of their assets liberally, and to be cynically exempt from the rules that he himself established (if such violation is pleasurable or gainful).
>
> In extreme cases, the narcissist feels above the law – any kind of law. This grandiose and haughty conviction leads to criminal acts, incestuous or polygamous relationships, and recurrent friction with the authorities.
>
> Hence the narcissist's panicky and sometimes violent reactions to "dropouts" from his cult. There's a lot going on that the narcissist wants kept under wraps. Moreover, the narcissist stabilizes his fluctuating sense of self-worth by deriving Narcissistic Supply from his victims. Abandonment threatens the narcissist's precariously balanced personality.
>
> Add to that the narcissist's paranoid and schizoid tendencies, his lack of introspective self-awareness, and his stunted sense of humor (lack of self-deprecation) and the risks to the grudging members of his cult are clear.
>
> The narcissist sees enemies and conspiracies everywhere. He often casts himself as the heroic victim (martyr) of dark and stupendous forces. In every deviation from his tenets he espies malevolent and ominous subversion. He, therefore, is bent on disempowering his devotees – by any and all means.
> The narcissist is dangerous.[165]

Now let us see if there are similarities between this description and what we know about Muhammad and his religion.

Islam is both missionary and imperialistic. Muhammad's main objective was to conquer and to dominate. He tried to force everyone to convert to his cult, starting with his family and relatives. He asked Abu Talib, his uncle and guardian, to convert to Islam while the old man was on his deathbed. When he declined, Muhammad refused to pray for him and condemned him to hell. In consideration for what Abu Talib had done for him, he conceded to place him in a shallow hell where fire would reach only to his ankles, but would boil his brain. He managed to convert his uncle's children and many younger members of his clan.

---

[165] The Cult of Narcissist http://samvak.tripod.com/journal79.html

2- Muhammad's Personality Profile

When he was still weak with few followers, he was courteous, attentive, compassionate, flexible, helpful and even feigned humility. There is a sharp contrast between the Quranic verses written during this period and those written in Medina when he became powerful. In Medina, he became demanding, tyrannical, willful, aggressive, and exploitative. There he raided villages and towns and after killing unarmed men and looting them, demanded the survivors to submit to him, pay jizyah, or face death.

The following are a few examples of the Meccan verses:

1. Be patient with what they say, and part from them courteously. (Q.73:10)
2. To you be your religion, and to me my religion. (Q. 109:6)
3. Therefore be patient with what they say, and celebrate (constantly) the praises of your Lord. (Q.50:39)
4. Speak well to men. (Q.2:83)
5. We well know what the infidels say: but you are not to compel them. (Q.50:45)
6. Hold to forgiveness; command what is right; but turn away from the ignorant. (Q.7:199)
7. Pardon thou, with a gracious pardoning. (Q.15:85)
8. Tell those who believe, to forgive those who do not look forward to the Days of Allah. (Q.45:14)
9. Those who follow the Jewish (scriptures), and the Christians - any who believe in Allah and the Last Day, and work righteousness, shall have their reward with their Lord; on them shall be no fear, nor shall they grieve. (Q.2:62)
10. And do not dispute with the followers of the Book except by what is best. (Q.29:46)

Compare the above to verses written in Medina, after he became powerful.

1. Oh you who believe! Murder those of the disbelievers and let them find harshness in you. (Q.9:123)
2. I will instill terror into the hearts of the unbelievers: smite above their necks and smite all their finger-tips off. (Q.8:12)
3. Whoso desires another religion than Islam, it shall not be accepted of him. (Q.3:85)
4. Slay the idolaters wherever you find them. (Q.9:5)
5. Kill them wherever you find them, and drive them out from wherever they drove you out. (Q.2:191)
6. Fight them on until there is no more dissension and religion becomes that of Allah. (Q.8:39)
7. Fight them, and Allah will punish them by your hands, cover them with shame. (Q.9:14)
8. Make no excuses: you have rejected Faith after you had accepted it. If we pardon some of you, we will punish others amongst you, for that they are in sin. (Q.9:66)
9. You who believe! Verily, the Mushrikûn (unbelievers) are Najasun (impure). So let them not come near Al-Masjid-al-Harâm (the grand mosque at Mecca) after this year. (Q.9:28)
10. Fight those who do not believe in Allah and the last day... and fight People of the Book, who do not accept the religion of truth (Islam) until they pay tribute by hand, being inferior. (Q.9:29)

This much should suffice as evidence that Muhammad changed drastically after he came to power. The gentle, attentive, compassionate, and empathic preacher was transformed into a tyrannical, ruthless, and willful despot.

However, it was after the battle of Badr that the cruel and vindictive spirit of Muhammad began to display itself. Muir narrates:

> The prisoners were brought up before him. As he scrutinized each, his eye fell fiercely on Nadr, the son of Harith (Muhammad's own cousin who was a poet and critical of him). 'There was death in that glance,' whispered Nadr, trembling, to a bystander. 'Not so,' replied the other; 'it is but your own imagination.'
>
> The unfortunate prisoner thought otherwise, and besought Mus'ab (a friend of him who had converted to Islam) to intercede for him. Mus'ab reminded him that he had denied the faith and ridiculed Muhammad. 'Ah!' said Nadr, 'had the Quraish made you a prisoner, they would never have put you to death!' 'Even were it so,' Mus'ab scornfully replied, 'I am not as you are; Islam has rent all bonds asunder.' (Emphasis added) Mus'ab the captor, seeing that the captive, and with him the chance of a rich ransom, was about to slip from his hands, cried out, 'The prisoner is mine!' At this moment, the command to "strike off his head!' was interposed by Muhammad, who had been watching all that passed. 'And, O Lord!' he added, 'do thou of thy bounty grant unto Mus'ab better prey than this?' Nadr was forthwith beheaded by Ali.
>
> Two days afterwards, about half-way to Medina, Oqba, another prisoner, was ordered out for execution. He ventured to expostulate, and demand why he should be treated more vigorously than the other captives. 'Because of your enmity to God and to his Prophet,' replied Muhammad. 'And my little girl!' cried Oqba, in the bitterness of his soul, 'Who will take care of her?' – 'Hellfire!' exclaimed the heartless conqueror; and on the instant his victim was hewn to the ground. 'Wretch that he was!' continued Muhammad, 'and persecutor! Unbeliever in God, in his Prophet, and in his Book! I give thanks unto the Lord that has slain you, and comforted mine eyes thereby.'[166]

There is a tender love story in all these tales of murder that highlights even more the ruthlessness of Muhammad. After some of the prisoners captured in the battle of Badr were put to death, because they had insulted Muhammad years earlier in Mecca, an offence a narcissist is incapable of forgiving, the rest were kept for ransom. Among them was Abul Aas, the above mentioned husband of Muhammad's daughter, Zeinab. The families of the prisoners procured what the bandit demanded to rescue their loved ones from death. Zeinab sent a necklace with precious stones, which she had received from her mother Khadijah at her wedding. Upon seeing that necklace and recognizing it as once worn by Khadijah, Muhammad was moved. He agreed to release Abul Aas without ransom, provided

---

[166] Sir William Muir: The Life of Mohamet, Vol. 3 Ch. XII Page 115-116

that Zeinab abandon him and come to Medina. Other captives had to pay ransom for their release.

The self-proclaimed mercy to all worlds was incapable of any act of kindness or of giving anything up without demanding something in exchange. Even his largesse was designed to impress the recipients and win them over to his side.

To save her husband, Zeinab joined his father in Medina and Abul Aus was released. In the sixth year of Hijra, Muhammad sent 170 armed men to raid a merchant caravan that was coming back to Mecca from Syria. Abul Aus, who was the trustee of that caravan was captured again and was brought to Medina along with the survivors and the loot. Upon hearing of her husband's capture, Zeinab went to the mosque and announced in loud voice that she has given protection to Abul Aus. Muhammad then accepted that protection and declared "Believers are protectors of one another and they can grant protection to any one they choose. I too grant protection to anyone that Zeinab protects."[167]

Nonetheless, he said that as long as Abul Aas remains an infidel his marriage with his wife is null. Abul Aus returned to Mecca, but could not bear the separation from his beloved wife and agreed to convert to Islam in order to be with her. Muhammad ordered him to remarry his wife as his original marriage had become automatically void upon her conversion to Islam. Shortly after his reunion with his wife, she became ill and died.

To this day, Muslims use this kind of blackmail to coerce their fiancés or spouses to convert to Islam. Unfortunately, many give in under the pressure. Such marriages are often nightmarish. The person who is forced to convert feels abused and cheated and they lose the respect of their Muslim spouse. Spineless people neither deserve nor will have respect. The right thing is to leave the Muslim partner. Never submit to bullying in your marriage because it reduces your standing. Never get involved romantically with a Muslim unless you are after trouble.

Muslims claim Islam is a religion of peace and tolerance, and will assume a smiling countenance to proselytize potential recruits. They are extremely helpful, loving and charming to those whom they want to woo. They particularly wear a big smile in front of the media. Among themselves, however, they act very differently. They are tyrannical and demanding. Once you convert and the honeymoon is over, they will drop the smiling mask and become high-handed, aggressive, and abusive. They expect the convert's questioning of Islam to end. After conversion any possibility of going back is considered terminated. This is consistent with cultic behaviour.

Muhammad felt entitled to special benefits and treatments not accorded to his followers. Not only he did things that were ethically wrong, even in the primitive society in which he lived, but, he also went against his own stated rules. He did whatever he pleased and when that shocked his followers, he brought a verse from

---

[167] Tabaqat Volume VIII page 31-32

Allah to justify his actions and silence the critics. With a verse from Allah under his belt, anyone whispering a word against his indecency would be denying God. The punishment of one who disputes with God is beating, death, or both. What Muhammad said was *faslul-khitab* (the end of discussion). Examples abound. Here are a few:

License to Lie

The Quran limits believers to four wives. However, Muhammad thought that he should not be restricted by his own rules and therefore, made God reveal the Quran 33:49-50 telling him that he is exempt and can have any number of women as he pleases, as wives, concubines or sex slaves. Lest other Muslims decide to emulate him, he added "*This only for you, [O Muhammad] and not for the Believers…in order that there should be no difficulty for you. And Allah is Oft-Forgiving, Most Merciful.*"

What difficulty? The difficulty to control his lustfulness! Why God was not concerned of Muhammad's sexual needs in Mecca when he was younger and had to content himself with an older woman? Why suddenly so much largesse when the prophet had become old and impotent? Or was this another sign of an aging man gone wild with his newfound power, who, like a child left unchecked in a candy store, was unable to set limits for himself?

One day Muhammad visited his wife Hafsa, daughter of Umar and upon meeting her maid Mariyah, lusted after her. Mariyah was a beautiful Coptic girl sent as a gift by Muqaqis (Patriarch) of Egypt to Muhammad. To get rid of Hafsa he lied to her and told her that her father wanted to see her. As soon as she left, Muhammad took Mariyah to Hafsa's bed and had sex with her. Hafsa who went to her father and had found out that he had not sent for her, returned home and found her illustrious husband, with his pants down enjoying her maid. She became upset and started making a scene. (Ah, women will be always women!) To placate her, Muhammad promised to prohibit Mariyah to himself. But that did not last long as he realized that he still lusted after that pretty girl. How could he break his oath? Well, that is easy when you have God up in your sleeve. The "maker of the universe" came to the aid of his prophet and revealed to him the sura Tahrim, in which he said it is okay to break your oath [oh Muhammad] and have sex with that cute girl. After all she is your "right hand possession." The almighty God, now acting as a pimp for his beloved prophet, was even angry at him and rebuked him for prohibiting himself carnal pleasures just to appease his wives. (Hence the name of the sura given for this incident is *Tahrim,* Prohibition.) "*O Prophet! Why do you ban (for yourself) that which Allah has made lawful to you, seeking to please your wives? And Allah is Oft-Forgiving, Most Merciful. Allah has already ordained for you (O men), the dissolution of your oaths. And Allah is your Maula (Lord, or Master, or Protector, etc.) and He is the All-Knower, the All-Wise.*" (Q.66:1-5)

2- Muhammad's Personality Profile

Ibn Sa'd writes:

> Abu Bakr has narrated that the messenger of Allah (PBUH) had sexual intercourse with Mariyah in the house of Hafsa. When the messenger came out of the house, Hafsa was sitting at the gate (behind the locked door). She told the prophet, 'O Messenger of Allah, do you do this in my house and during my turn? The Prophet said, control yourself and let me go for I make her haram to me. Hafsa said, I do not accept, unless you swear for me. The Prophet said, by Allah I will not touch her again.'[168]

As usual, Muslims have justified Muhammad for the breach of his oath. No matter what he did, Muslims will always justify his actions. Ibn Sa'd continues:

"Qasim ibn Muhammad has said that this promise of the Prophet that had forbidden Mariyah to himself is invalid – it does not become a violation (*hormat*).[169]

If that oath was invalid, why did he make it; and if it was valid, why did he break it? There are countless examples of Muhammad breaking his own promises and oaths. Muslims do the same. Muhammad had sworn to God to not touch Mariyah and not even that was an impediment to him. His god was his invention and he was not as stupid as to let his imagination stop him from having sex with that beautiful girl. The whole idea of inventing Allah was to empower him to do as he pleased, not to put restrictions on him. That would defeat the whole purpose of inventing a religion, wouldn't it?

My copy of the Quran contains the following *tafseer* (commentary) side by side with the Sura Tahrim:

> Also it is reported that the Prophet had divided his days among his wives. And when it was the turn of Hafsa, he sent her for an errand to the house of her father Umar Khattab. When she took this order and went, the prophet called his slave girl Mariyah the Copt who (later) bore his son Ibrahim, and who was a gift from Najashi, and had sexual intercourse with her. When Hafsa returned, she found the door locked from inside. She sat there behind the locked door until the prophet finished the business and came out of the house while sweat was dripping from his face. When Hafsa found him in that state she rebuked him saying, you did not respect my honor; you sent me out of my house with an excuse so you could sleep with the slave girl. And in the day that was my turn you had intercourse with someone else. Then the Prophet said, be quiet for although she is my slave and halal to me, for your contentment I, at this moment, make her haram to myself. But Hafsa did not do this and when the Prophet went out of her house she knocked at the wall that separated her quarter from that of Aisha and told her everything.[170]

---

[168] Ibn Sa'd, Tabaqat Vol 8: p 195

[169] Ibid

[170] Published by Entesharat-e Elmiyyeh Eslami Tehran 1377 lunar H. Tafseer and translation into Farsi by Mohammad Kazem Mo'refi

For Muslims oaths have no meaning. They promise something and then renege when they can. Bukhari reports a hadith where Muhammad said: “By Allah, and Allah willing, if I take an oath and later find something better than that, then I do what is better and expiate my oath.”[171]

And he advised his followers to do the same: "If you ever take an oath to do something and later on you find that something else is better, then you should expiate your oath and do what is better."[172]

This explains the behavior of Muslims. They promise something only to break it. Their words mean nothing; their promises are not binding and even their oaths are worthless. Narcissists believe they are entitled to break their words and that their promises and obligations are not binding on them. Like a while animal, the only time you can trust a Muslim is when he is caged. Those who are offended by the above statement are fools and will pay the price of their naiveté. All you have to do to know this is the truth is look at reality. Muslims oppression towards non-Muslims is proportional to their number and strength. In America Muslims are far more peaceful than in UK and the Muslims in UK are a lot more peaceful than those in France. This has nothing to do with their indoctrination, but everything to do with their numbers. In America, Muslims are about 1% of the total population. In UK they are about 4% and in France they are 10%. At about half of the population, as in Bosnia, Chad and Lebanon, widespread massacres, terror attacks and ongoing militia warfare will become the norm. The more they have the power the more violent they become. The only peaceful Muslim is the one under your boot.

License to Violate Moral Codes

One day Muhammad went to see his adopted son Zayd. He was not home. He entered the house and had a glimpse of Zayd’s semi naked wife Zeinab (not to be confused with Muhammad’s daughter with the same name). His heart was suddenly transformed. He became aroused by her beauty and overwhelmed by desire. “Praised be Allah, the best of all creators, who transforms hearts,” he murmured lustfully as he left the house.

When Zayd learned this, he told Muhammad that he will divorce Zeinab so he could have her. Feigning modesty Muhamamd responded, *"Keep your wife to yourself, and fear Allah."* (Q.33:37) However, soon after Zayd left, the remembrance of Zeinab’s soft skin, her firm breasts and disheveled hair awoke his lust and his Allah rushed to reveal a verse admonishing him for fearing criticism of the people, instead of fearing God. “*You did hide in yourself that which Allah will make manifest, you did fear the people whereas Allah had a better right that you should fear Him. So when Zayd had accomplished his desire from her (i.e. divorced*

---

[171] Sahih Bukhari Vol.7 Book 67, No.424
[172] Sahih Bukhari Vol.9 Book 89, No.260

her), we gave her to you in marriage, so that (in future) there may be no difficulty to the believers in respect of (the marriage of) the wives of their adopted sons when the latter have no desire to keep them. And Allah's Command must be fulfilled." (Q.33: 37)

A few years earlier, when Muhammad claimed to have ascended to heaven, he told Zayd an anachronistic story about meeting Zeinab there with dark ruby lips and being told that she belongs to Zayd. Thinking that his marriage with Zeinab had been arranged in heaven, Zayd married her. Nonetheless, when Muhammad saw her semi-nude, he forgot all about his heavenly fable. After all, he knew that the whole story of Mi'raj was a fib.

Muhammad's marriage to his daughter-in-law confounded his followers. But who could argue with Allah? To silence any gossiper, the maker of the universe sent down a verse and said the prophet is not the father of anyone, but the messenger of God and the Seal of the prophets. (Q.33:40) He claimed God ordered him to marry Zeinab so that people know that adoption is an abomination. Thanks to Muhammad's inability to control his sexual urge, adoption in Islam is prohibited. God knows how many orphans lost the chance of finding a loving family because of this ruling.

Special Privileges

Muhammad reintroduced the pagan tradition of fasting. However, he found it difficult to observe it, so he ate whenever he pleased. Ibn Sa'd writes: "The Messenger of Allah used to say 'We the prophets are required to eat our morning food later than others and hurry in breaking our fast in the evening.'"[173]

These are just a few examples of how Muhammad did as he pleased and made his Allah approve whatever he did. The young and perceptive Aisha noticed this and said "I feel that your Lord hastens in fulfilling your wishes and desires."[174] She uttered the above when Muhammad made his Allah order him to take his daughter-in-law, Zeinab, as a bride.

In none of the wars that Muhammad fought did he put his own life in danger. He stood behind his troops, wearing often two coats of chain-link mail, one on top of the other.[175] The double armouring made him so heavy that he needed assistance to stand or walk. While in that state, he would shout toward the front row and goad his men to be valiant and not fear death, promising them high-bosomed virgins and celestial food in the other world. For himself, he preferred these goodies in this world. Sometimes he would grab a handful of dust, throw it in the direction of the

[173] Tabaqat, Volume 1, page 369
[174] Sahih al-Bukhari, 6: 60: 311
[175] Flexible armor of interlinked rings. Dawud: 14: 2584

enemy and curse them. That was the extent of his bravery and contribution to his wars.

His actions must have bewildered some of his followers. To dispel their doubts he made his Allah say, *"It is not ye who slew them; it was Allah: when thou threw (a handful of dust), it was not thy act, but Allah's; in order that He might test the Believers by a gracious trial from Himself: for Allah is He Who heareth and knoweth (all things)."* (Q.8:17)

Any time he did something that baffled his follower or prophesied something that did not come true, he would reveal a verse saying, Allah wanted to test your faith by a gracious trial.

While still living in Mecca, whenever he met a group of people and invited them to accept Islam the first thing he asked them was protect him like their women and children. In his secret meeting in Aqaba, where he met the Arabs of Medina and conspired with them against Mecca his protection was the first thing in his mind. Ibn Ishaq says, "'The apostle spoke and recited the Quran and invited men to God and commended Islam and then said: "I invite your allegiance on the basis that you protect me as you would your women and children."[176]

Although protecting his own life was his priority, he would tell his followers about the greatness of martyrdom. He would tell them, "By Him in Whose Hands my life is! I would love to be martyred in Allah's Cause and then come back to life and get martyred, and then come back again and get martyred and then come back again and get martyred.[177]

To finance his military expeditions, he exhorted his followers to contribute their wealth. He urged them to serve him and wait upon him. He encouraged their adulation of him and strongly frowned on dissent and criticism. Orwa, the negotiator of the Quraish who visited him among his men in Hudaibiyyah, witnessed that his followers "rushed to save the water in which he had performed his ablutions, to catch up his spittle, or seize a hair of his if it chanced to fall."[178]

This degree of zealotry should not be interpreted or dismissed as an exaggeration of later years, as the historian Sir Willam Muir believed. Muhammad, like all cult leaders, had created a personality worship of himself that has endured to this day. We can see this kind of personality worship in modern cults even today.

Muhammad thought himself to be above the law. He broke every moral and ethical code whenever it suited him, and then made his Allah reveal a verse or two to approve what he had done.

Arabs were simple people, but they had dignity and prided themselves on their chivalry. They had designated four months in a year as sacred, during which they

---

176 Sira, p. 203
177 Bukhari Book 52: #54
178 Sirat Ibn Ishaq, p.823.

did not fight. During these months people travelled freely and went on pilgrimage. Fighting and killing at such a time of the year was a sacrilege. In one such month, Muhammad sent a raiding expedition to Nakhlah, a place known for its palm trees, to lay siege and ambush a caravan carrying raisins, butter, wine, and other goods from Taif to Mecca. He sent eight men without revealing their mission. He gave a sealed letter to his cousin Abdullah, the leader of the expedition with the instruction to read it to his companions after arriving at the destination. Abdullah was the only person who knew about the mission. When the men opened the letter, they realized Muhammad was asking them to do a sacrilege and to kill in sacred months. The men discussed the situation and finally convinced themselves that the orders of the prophet should be obeyed even if they went against their consciences and seemed wrong. To set up the ambush, they shaved their heads and pretended to be preparing themselves for pilgrimage. When the merchants lowered their guard, the Muslims leapt upon them, killed one and took two as hostages. The fourth person escaped. This killing sent a shockwave through the Quraish who realized that their opponent, in his quest for power, is willing to kill and would not respect any law.

There are countless cases in which Muhammad broke the laws of the land and disregarded the codes of ethics and morality. Laying siege to merchant caravans or raiding villages and seizing their wealth is theft and is against the law in any society. From incest to polygamy, from rape to paedophilia, from assassination to genocide, the Prophet of Allah did them all. He was disdainful of authorities, and so are Muslims. He was deceitful and violent and so are his followers.

Total Control

Islam means submission. The Quran says: "*No believing man and no believing woman has a choice in their own affairs when Allah and His Messenger have decided on an issue.*"(Q.33:36) Even non-believing people have no choice. They must submit or be killed. Muhammad interpreted dissent as betrayal. For narcissists, dissent is intolerable. It threatens the wobbly position of their authority. Painful childhood memories of abandonment shake their precariously balanced personality. They feel hurt and seek revenge.

Muhammad thought everyone was conspiring against him and had spies everywhere. He even encouraged his followers to spy on each other. Muslims do this to this day. As the result, an ambience of terror is created in all Islamic countries, where no one dares to raise the slightest question about Islam. Your own kin may report you.

Muhammad's Sacred Secretions

Despite his pretense of modesty, Muhammad encouraged the cult of personality around himself. Islam has nothing to do with God. It is all about worshipping Muhammad as the following story demonstrate.

In his book, *Religion and Life - Modern Everyday Fatwas*, Egyptian Mufti Dr. Ali Gum'a wrote that the companions of the Prophet Muhammad would bless themselves by drinking his urine, and described an incident of urine-drinking from a hadith: "Umm Ayman drank the urine of the Prophet, and the prophet told her: 'This stomach will not be dragged through the fire of Hell, because it contains something of our Lord the Messenger of Allah.'" [179]

"This blessing," Al-Gum'a added, "[can also] be done with the honorable saliva, sweat, hair, urine or blood of the Prophet. This is because anyone who knows the love of the Messenger of Allah is not repulsed [by these]; just as a mother is not repulsed by the feces of her son, this is even more so [in the case of] our Lord the Messenger of Allah, whom we love more than our fathers, sons, and wives. Anyone who was or is repulsed by the Messenger of Allah must recant his faith."[180]

Following the ensuing uproar, Dr. Gum'a came to the defense of his fatwa, saying: "The entire body of the Prophet, whether exposed or hidden, is pure, and there is nothing in it- including his secretions - that [can] repulse anyone. Umm Haram would collect this sweat and distribute it to the people of Al-Madina."[181]

He added: "the hadith of Suhail bin Umar at Al-Hudaybiya says: 'Oh Lord, I was with Kisra [the ruler of Persia] and with Kaisar [the ruler of Byzantium] and I saw no instance in which the leader was glorified like the Companions of the Prophet glorified Muhammad. The second Muhammad spat, one of them would immediately hasten [to grab his saliva] and smear it upon his face.' Hence, the ulema, including Ibn Hajar Al-Askalani, Al-Baihaqi, Al-Daraqutni and Al-Haythami, determined that the Prophet's entire body was pure.'"[182]

Dr. Gum'a's ruling outraged Many Muslims. Egyptian Religious Endowments Minister said: "Fatwas such as these damage Islam, serve its enemies, and push the people towards backwardness and ignorance.'[183] There were many condemnations.

---

[179] Baraka Umm Ayman was a servant of the Prophet Muhammad as well as his nursemaid.

[180] *Al-Masri Al-Yawm* (Egypt) May 20, 2007.

[181] Umm Haram bint Milhan was a cousin of the prophet on his mother's side, and one of the first to embrace Islam and immigrate to Mecca.

[182] *Al-Masri Al-Yawm* (Egypt) May 23, 2007. Dr. Gum'a made similar statements to the Egyptian weekly *Al-Liwa Al-Islami*, May 26, 2007.

[183] *Al-Masri Al-Yawm* (Egypt) May 22, 2007.

2- Muhammad's Personality Profile

However, the story is true. Muhammad suggested that anyone who drinks his urine will be saved from hellfire. He also claimed that his saliva had miraculous curing power. His pretenses of modesty were eclipsed by his boastfulness and covert display of holiness and superiority.

A similar incident took place when Dr. Izzat Atiya of Egypt's al-Azhar University, offered a way around segregation of the sexes at work places. He suggested that women should breast feed their male colleagues directly, for at least five times, so they become *mahram* and can work together without having to cover themselves from their make colleagues. "Breast feeding an adult puts an end to the problem of the private meeting, and does not ban marriage," he ruled. "A woman at work can take off the veil or reveal her hair in front of someone whom she has breastfed."[184]

This ruling is based on a hadith. According to Muhammad, breast-feeding establishes a degree of maternal relation, even if a woman nurses a child who is not biologically hers.

After he annulled the institution of adoption, Abu Hudhaifa and his wife Sahla, who had an adopted son called Salim, came to him for advice. "Messenger of Allah, Salim is living with us in our house," said Sahla. "He has attained (puberty) as men attain it and has acquired knowledge (of the sex problems) as men acquire." In response to her Muhammad improvised an ingenious solution. "Suckle him," he told her. "How can I suckle him as he is a grown-up man?" She asked perplexed. Muhammad laughed and said: "I know that he is a young man." In fact Salim was old enough (over fifteen) to have participated in the Battle of Badr.[185] The hadith says that he then laughed.

Again, the majority of Muslims was outraged and Dr. Atiya was forced to retract his fatwa. Here is where I see a glimmer of hope. These episodes show that there is a limit to which Muslims are willing to be fooled, beyond which they will not go. Therein lies my conviction that once the naked truth about Islam is exposed, the thinking Muslims will see the light and will leave it. Muslims must leave Islam. Humanity cannot survive with this insanity. Threre can be no compromise. The choice is between Islam and human civilization. The two can't coexist.

[184] http://news.bbc.co.uk/2/hi/middle_east/6681511.stm

[185] Sahih Muslim 8.3424, 3425, 3426, 3427, 3428

Chapter Three

Muhammad's Ecstatic Experiences

New understanding of the human mind sheds light on Muhammad's mystical experiences, which he described in striking language. As usual the words are placed in the mouth of Allah.

And he is in the highest part of the horizon. Then he drew near, then he bowed. So he was the measure of two bows or closer still. And He revealed to His servant what He revealed. The heart was not untrue in what he saw. What! Do you then dispute with him as to what he saw? And certainly he saw him in another descent. At the farthest lote-tree; near which is the garden, the place to be resorted to. When that which covers covered the lote tree. The eye did not turn aside, nor did it exceed the limit. Certainly he saw of the greatest signs of his Lord. (Q.53:6-18)

In another passage he emphatically affirmed his visual experience: "*And of a truth he saw himself on the clear horizon.*" (Q.81:23)

A hadith reports him recounting, "While I was walking I heard a voice from the sky. I looked up towards the sky, and behold! I saw the same Angel who came to me in the Cave of Hira', sitting on a chair between the sky and the earth. I was so terrified by him that I fell down on the ground. Then I went to my wife and said, 'Wrap me in garments! Wrap me in garments!' They wrapped me."[186]

When someone asked, "How does the divine inspiration come to you?" Muhammad replied, "Sometimes it is *like the ringing of a bell*, this form of Inspiration is the hardest of all and then this state passes, off after I have grasped what is inspired. Sometimes the Angel comes in the form of a man and talks to me and I grasp whatever he says.' 'Aisha added: Verily I saw the Prophet being inspired divinely *on a very cold day and noticed the sweat dropping from his forehead* (as the Inspiration was over)."[187]

---

[186] Sahih al-Bukhari, Volume 6, Book 60, Number 448:
[187] Sahih al-Bukhari Volume 1, Book 1, Number 2

Zayd Ibn Thabit narrated: "I used to write down the words of *wahy* (revelation) for him. When wahy came to him he felt burning with heat and drops of perspiration would start rolling down on his body like pearls." [188]

Ibn Sa'd wrote, "At the moment of inspiration, *anxiety* pressed upon the Prophet, and his *countenance was troubled.*"[189] He further wrote, "When the revelation descended on the Prophet, for some hours he used to become *drowsy like a sleepy person.*"[190] Bukhari says: "The commencement of divine inspiration to Allah's Messenger was in the form of dreams that came true *like a bright light.*"[191]

A hadith in Sahih Muslim reads: "A'isha, the wife of the Apostle of Allah, reported: The first (form) with which was started the revelation to the Messenger of Allah was the true vision in sleep. And *he did not see any vision but it came like the bright gleam of dawn.*"[192]

Tabari reports: "The Prophet said, 'I had been standing, but *fell to my knees; and crawled away, my shoulders trembling.* '"[193]

Bukhari has also recorded a long hadith that describes the entire episode of how Muhammad received his revelations.

Narrated 'Aisha:

> The commencement of the Divine Inspiration to Allah's Apostle was in the form of good righteous (true) dreams in his sleep. He never had a dream but that it came true like bright daylight. He used to go in seclusion (the cave of) Hira' where he used to worship (Allah Alone) continuously for many (days) nights. He used to take with him the journey food for that (stay) and then come back to (his wife) Khadijah to take his food likewise again for another period to stay, till suddenly the Truth descended upon him while he was in the cave of Hira. The angel came to him in it and asked him (the illiterate Muhammad) to read. The Prophet replied, 'I do not know how to read.' The angel caught me (forcefully) and pressed me so hard that I could not bear it anymore. He then released me and again asked me to read, and I replied, 'I do not know how to read,' whereupon he caught me again and pressed me a second time till I could not bear it anymore. He then released me and asked me again to read, but again I replied, 'I do not know how to read (or, what shall I read?)' Thereupon he caught me for the third time and pressed me and then released me and said, 'Read: In the Name of your Lord, Who has created (all that exists). Has created man from a clot. Read and Your Lord is Most Generous...up to...that which he knew not.' (Q.96:15)
>
> Then Allah's Apostle returned with the inspiration, his neck muscles twitching with terror till he entered upon Khadijah and said, 'Cover me! Cover me!' They covered him till his fear was over and then he said, 'O Khadijah, what is wrong with me?'

---

[188] Majma'uz Zawaa'id with reference to Tabraani
[189] Tabaqat Volume 1 page 184 Persian translation
[190] Ibid.
[191] Bukhari Volume 1, Book 1, Number 3:
[192] Sahih Muslim *Book 001, Number 0301:*
[193] *Tabari VI:67*

3- Muhammad's Ecstatic Experiences

Then he told her everything that had happened and said, 'I fear that something may happen to me.' Khadijah said, 'Never! But have the glad tidings, for Allah will never disgrace you as you keep good reactions with your kith and kin, speak the truth, help the poor and the destitute, serve your guests generously and assist the deserving, calamity-afflicted ones.'

Khadijah then accompanied him to (her cousin) Waraqa bin Naufal bin Asad bin 'Abdul 'Uzza bin Qusai. Waraqa was the son of her paternal uncle, i.e., her father's brother, who during the Pre-Islamic Period became a Christian and used to write the Arabic script and used to write of the Gospels in Arabic as much as Allah wished him to write. He was an old man and had lost his eyesight. Khadijah said to him, "O my cousin! Listen to the story of your nephew." Waraqa asked, 'O my nephew! What have you seen?' The Prophet described whatever he had seen.

Waraqa said, 'This is the same Namus (i.e., Gabriel, the Angel who keeps the secrets) whom Allah had sent to Moses. I wish I were young and could live up to the time when your people would turn you out.' Allah's Apostle asked, "Will they turn me out?" Waraqa replied in the affirmative and said: 'Never did a man come with something similar to what you have brought but was treated with hostility. If I should remain alive till the day when you will be turned out then I would support you strongly.' But after a few days Waraqa died and the Divine Inspiration was also paused for a while and the Prophet became so sad as we have heard that *he intended several times to throw himself from the tops of high mountains* and every time he went up the top of a mountain in order to throw himself down, Gabriel would appear before him and say, 'O Muhammad! You are indeed Allah's Apostle in truth!' whereupon his heart would become quiet and he would calm down and would return home. And whenever the period of the coming of the inspiration used to become long, he would do as before, but when he used to reach the top of a mountain, Gabriel would appear before him and say to him what he had said before.[194]

The claim that Waraqa, based on his studies of the scriptures recognized Muhammad as a prophet is balderdash. There is nothing in any scripture that points to Muhammad. Waraqa was dead and Muhammad felt free to make wild claims just as he claimed that his grandfather predicted his great destiny. It is not unlikely that Khadijah, as his co-dependent corroborated his lies, unless this claim is entirely a later fabrication. There is a similar claim made by Muhammad pertaining to the time he went to Busra. He said that as caravans entered the outskirts of Busra, he sat beneath the shade of a tree and was spotted by a Nestor monk. "Who is the man beneath that tree?" the monk reportedly inquired of Maysarah, the young servant of Khadijah who was accompanying Muhammad in this trade expedition. "A man of Quraish," the lad responded. "None other than a Prophet is sitting beneath that tree," said the monk. According to this story, the monk noticed his rank by observing two

---

[194] *Sahih Bukhari Volume 9, Book 87,* Number *111*

small clouds shading him from the oppressive heat of the sun. "Is there a glow, a slight redness, around his eyes that never parts with him?" asked the monk. When Maysarah answered in the affirmative, he said, "He most surely is the very last Prophet; congratulations to whoever believes in him."[195]

In another place he claimed that the big mole that he had between his shoulders was the sign of his prophethood. I have not yet come across any scripture confirming that a mole between shoulders and redness around eyes are signs of prophethood. Chronic redness of the eye is a medical condition called blepharitis caused by inflammation of the eyelids. In one kind of blepharitis, meibomian gland dysfunction (MGD) patients frequently have a co-existing skin disorder known as rosacea and seborrheic dermatitis. Rosacea is also characterized by redness of the face. Ali ibn Abu Talib described Muhammad's face as reddish-white.[196]

Relying on the credulity of his followers, Muhammad told them anything he fancied. Even the symptoms of his diseases were claimed as signs of his prophethood. Had the story of the Busra Monk been true, Maysarah should have been the first to believe, but there is no mention of him again accepting Islam.

The above hadith shows the important role that Khadijah played in Islam. When Muhammad had his vision, he thought that he had become demon-possessed. It was Khadijah who reassured him that he had been chosen to be a prophet and encouraged, what otherwise should have been dismissed as hallucination.

Some of Muhammad's hallucinations were visual, some were somatic and others were auditory. Ibn Ishaq writes: "The apostle, at the time when Allah willed to bestow His grace upon him and endow him with prophethood, would go forth for his affair and travel far afield, until he reached the glens of Mecca and the beds of its valleys, where no house was in sight, and not a stone or tree that he passed by, but would say, 'Peace unto thee, O apostle of Allah.' And the apostle would turn to his right and left and look behind him, and he would see nothing but trees and stones."[197] Muhammad had several other hallucinations:

> The Prophet once offered the prayer and said, 'Satan came in front of me and tried to interrupt my prayer, but Allah gave me an upper hand on him and I choked him. No doubt, I thought of tying him to one of the pillars of the mosque till you get up in the morning and see him. Then I remembered the statement of Prophet Solomon, 'My Lord! Bestow on me a kingdom such as shall not belong to any other after me.' Then Allah made him (Satan) return with his head down."[198]

It is important to note that Muhammad was ignorant of the Bible. Solomon was a king, not a prophet, and he never made such a statement or prayer as stated by

[195] Tabaqat Vol. 1. p. 119
[196] *Tirmidhi Hadith,* Number *1524*
[197] Sira Ibn Ishaq, p. 105
[198] Sahih Bukhari Volume 2, Book 22, Number 301

Muhammad. He did, however, ask God for wisdom rather than riches. Muhammad here reveals his own craving for kingdom and power

A symptom of mental illness is that one often cannot tell the difference between reality and fantasy.

> Narrated Aisha: Magic was worked on Allah's Apostle so that he used to think that he had sexual relations with his wives while he actually had not (Sufyan said: That is the hardest kind of magic as it has such an effect). Then one day he said, 'O 'Aisha do you know that Allah has instructed me concerning the matter I asked Him about? Two men came to me and one of them sat near my head and the other sat near my feet. The one near my head asked the other. What is wrong with this man?' The latter replied "he is under the effect of magic.' The first one asked, 'Who has worked magic on him?' The other replied 'Labid bin Al-A'sam, a man from Bani Zuraiq who was an ally of the Jews and was a hypocrite.' The first one asked, 'What material did he use?' The other replied, 'A comb and the hair stuck to it.' The first one asked, 'Where (is that)?' The other replied. 'In a skin of pollen of a male date palm tree kept under a stone in the well of Dharwan.' So the Prophet went to that well and took out those things and said 'That was the well which was shown to me (in a dream). Its water looked like the infusion of henna leaves and its date-palm trees looked like the heads of devils.' The Prophet added, 'Then that thing was taken out.' I said (to the Prophet) 'Why do you not treat yourself with Nashra?' He said, 'Allah has cured me; I dislike to let evil spread among my people.'[199]

In another hadith we read, "Revelation came to the Apostle of Allah and he was covered with a cloth, and Ya'la said: Would that I see revelation coming to the Apostle of Allah. He (Umar) said: Would it please you to see the Apostle of Allah receiving the revelations? 'Umar lifted a corner of the cloth and I looked at him and he was *emitting a sound of snorting.* He (the narrator) said: I thought it was the sound of a camel."[200]

Bukhari reports, "When Gabriel revealed the Divine Inspiration in Allah's Apostle, he (Allah's Apostle) moved his tongue and lips, and that state used to be very hard for him, and that movement indicated that revelation was taking place.[201]

Here is a list of psychological and physical effects of "revelation" on Muhammad reported in various hadiths.

1. visions (hallucinations) of seeing an angel or a light and of hearing voices
2. bodily spasms and excruciating abdominal pain and discomfort
3. overwhelmed by sudden emotions of anxiety and fear
4. twitching in neck muscles
5. uncontrollable lip movement, lip smacking

---

[199] Sahih Bukhari Volume *7, Book 71, Number 660:*

[200] Sahih Muslim Book 007, Number 2654:

[201] Sahih Bukhari Volume 6, Book 60, Number 451:

6. sweating even during cold days
7. face flushed
8. countenance was troubled
9. rapid heart palpitation
10. snorting like a camel
11. drowsiness
12. suicidal thoughts

These are also symptoms of Temporal Lobe Epilepsy. TLE happens unexpectedly with no prior warning to the patient. This too was true in the case in Muhammad.

Bukhari reports, "While Allah's Apostle was talking about the period of pause in revelation, he said in his narration, 'Once while I was walking, all of a sudden I heard a voice from the sky. I looked up and saw to my surprise, the same Angel as had visited me in the cave of Hira'. He was sitting on a chair between the sky and the earth. I got afraid of him and came back home and said, wrap me! Wrap me!"[202]

Suicidal Thoughts

The chroniclers say that Muhammad attempted suicide on several occasions, only to be stopped by Gabriel every time.

> I have never abhorred anyone more than a poet or a *kahin*. I cannot stand looking at either of them. I will never tell anyone of Quraish of my Revelation. I will climb a mountain and throw myself down and die. That will relieve me. I went to do that, but halfway up the mountain I heard a voice from the sky saying 'O Muhammad! You are the Messenger of Allah and I am Gabriel.' I looked upwards and saw Gabriel in the form of a man putting his legs on the horizon. He said: 'O Muhammad! You are the Messenger of Allah and I am Gabriel.' I stopped and looked at him. His sight distracted my attention from what I had intended to do. I stood in my place transfixed. I tried to shift my eyes away from him, but towards whatever region of the sky I looked, I saw him as before.[203]

The only way one can make sense of this vision is that the image that Muhammad saw was in his head. That is why in whichever direction he turned his head it always appeared in front of him. Visual hallucinations occur in various non-psychiatric conditions including cerebral lesions, sensory deprivation, the administration of psychedelic drugs and migraine. Some hallucinations are elementary, (i.e. the patient sees light, colors or simple geometrical forms). These kinds of hallucinations often occur in occipital lobe epilepsy. Complex visual hallucination and delusions, such as those experienced by Muhammad, occur in temporal lobe seizures and other neurological disorders like Parkinson's disease and

---

[202] Bukhari Volume 6, Book 60, Number 478

[203] Sira Ibn Ishaq p. 106

Creutzfeldt–Jakob disease. These hallucinations are usually vivid images of animals, humans or mythical creatures such as angels and jinns.[204] They can be accompanied by auditory, gustatory, olfactory and somatosensory hallucinations. The somatosensory and kinesthetic hallucinations are mostly associated with temporal lobe seizures. This explains Muhammad's experience in the cave Hira where he felt that Angel Gabriel squeezed him so hard until he felt an excruciating pain in his abdomen and thought that he would die. Unless you believe that Archangel Gabriel is a bit crazy, TLE, satisfactorily explains what happened to Muhammad in that cave.

The research scientist Scott Atran explains:

> Sudden alterations of activity in the hippocampus and amygdala can affect auditory, vestibular, gustatory, tactile, and olfactory perceptions and lead to hallucinations involving voices or music, feelings of sway, or physical suspension, the tastes of elixirs, burning or caressing, the fragrance of Heaven or the stench of Hell. For example, because the middle part of the amygdala receives fibers from the olfactory tract, direct stimulation of that part of the amygdala will flood co-occurring events with strong smells. In religious rituals, incense and fragrances stimulate the amygdala so that scent can be used to focus attention and interpretation on the surrounding events. In temporal-lobe epilepsy, the sudden electrical spiking of the area infuses other aspects of the epileptic experience with an odorous aura.[205]

Muhammad described Gabriel as having 600 wings.[206] This is hard to envision. Buraq, the steed upon which he took his night-flight to Jerusalem and to the heavens, had a human head and the wings of an eagle. Unless one decides to believe in absurdities, it is clear that Muhammad was hallucinating.

The Egyptian Muslim scholar and historian, Haykal describes the angel as seen by Muhammad.

> The first heaven was of pure silver and the stars suspended from its vault by chains of gold;" [This shows that Muhammad had no understanding of what stars are. He envisioned them something like Christmas lights hanging from the 'vault of the sky.' This is consistent with Ptolemy's cosmology and was commonly believed in Muhammad's time.] "and in each one an angel lay awake to prevent the demons from climbing into the holy dwelling places and the spirits from listening indiscreetly to celestial secrets." [This absurdity is stated also in the Quran, where it says the jinns used to stand on each other's shoulders to listen to the conversation of the 'Exalted Assembly,' until they were shot down by stars that were fired at them like missiles. In the old days people used to think meteorites were shooting stars.][207]

---

[204] Often mischievous form of spirits in Arab mythology, capable of appearing in human and animal forms.

[205] Scott Atran, NeuroTheology: Brain, Science, Spirituality, Religious Experience by Chapter 10 http://jeannicod.ccsd.cnrs.fr/docs/00/05/32/82/RTF/ijn_00000110_00.rtf

[206] Bukhari:Volumne 4, Book 54, Number 455

[207] Quran, 72:8; 37:6-10; 63:5.

> There, Muhammad greeted Adam. And in the six other heavens the Prophet met Noah, Aaron, Moses, Abraham, David, Solomon, Idris (Enoch), Yahya (John the Baptist) and Jesus. He saw the Angel of Death, Azrail, so huge that his eyes were separated by 70,000 marching days. [This is roughly ten times longer than the distance between the Moon and the Earth] He commanded 100,000 battalions and passed his time in writing in an immense book the names of those dying or being born. [Can't someone donate a computer to Azrail and relieve him of his burden?] He saw the Angel of Tears who wept for the sins of the world; the Angel of Vengeance with brazen face, covered with warts, who presides over the elements of fire and sits on a throne of flames; and another immense angel made up half of snow and half of fire surrounded by a heavenly choir continually crying: `O God, Thou hast united snow and fire, united all Thy servants in obedience to Thy Laws. In the seventh heaven where the souls of the just resided was an angel larger than the entire world, with 70,000 heads; each head had 70,000 mouths, each mouth had 70,000 tongues and each tongue spoke in 70,000 different idioms singing endlessly the praises of the Most High.'[208]

Muhammad had an extraordinary imaginative power. However, his thinking was warped. Such a creature cannot be envisioned by sane people, let alone exist.

- Muhammad sees an angel larger than the world, which logically absurd.
- He has 70,000 heads; each head has 70,000 faces. (He has 4.9 billion faces)
- Each face has 70,000 mouths (He has 343 trillion mouths)
- Each mouth has 70,000 tongues (He has over 24, million trillion, or 24 quintillion tongues)
- Each tongue speaks 70,000 idioms (He speaks 1.68 trillion trillion, or 1.68 septillion idioms.)

Why would Allah need to create such a monstrosity, only to praise him endlessly in that many languages? Imagine someone filling his house with numerous computers and tape recorders and program them to praise him incessangly in all the languages. Wouldn't you say he is insane? Allah is the personification of Muhammad's alter ego. His psychology reflects that of his prophet. As a narcissist, Muhammad had an insatiable craving for praise and so does his imaginary god.

Muhammad was a loner. He had married an important woman, but he was not an important person in his own right. His hallucinatory experiences, interpreted by his wife as the sign of his prophethood, were his biggest narcissistic supplies. They made him feel important. When those experiences stopped, he felt depressed.

[208] Muhammad Husayn Haykal (1888, 1956): The Life of Muhammad, translated by Isma'il Razi A. al-Faruqi. ISBN: 0892591374 Chapter 8: From the Violation of the Boycott to al Isra'.

Vaknin says. "Depression is a big component in the narcissist's emotional make-up. But it mostly has to do with the absence of narcissistic supply. It mostly has to do with nostalgia to more plentiful days, full of adoration and attention and applause… Depression is a form of aggression. Transformed, this aggression is directed at the depressed person rather than at his human environment. This regime of repressed and mutated aggression is a characteristic of both narcissism and depression… However, the narcissist, even when depressed, never forgoes his narcissism: his grandiosity, sense of entitlement, haughtiness, and lack of empathy.[209]

This explains, the cause of Muhammad's depression, as well as his suicidal thoughts, and also why he never carried those thoughts to culmination. Narcissists hardly ever commit suicide. Isn't it strange that Muhammad, repeatedly thought of suicide and each time Gabriel would come to reassure him that he is a prophet, ane yet he would attempt the suicide again? Narcissists don't commit suicide, but they talk about it to garner attention and sympathy.

"How could a narcissist who thinks of himself as a Colossus, as an immensely important person, as the center of the universe commit suicide?" asks Agatha Christie in *Dead Man's Mirror* "He is far more likely to destroy someone else - some miserable crawling ant of a human being who had dared to cause him annoyance.... Such an act may be regarded as necessary - as sanctified! But self-destruction? The destruction of such a Self?"[210]

To the question, "Why are narcissists not prone to suicide?" Vaknin responds, "Because they died a long time ago. Narcissists are the true zombies of the world. Many scholars and therapists tried to grapple with the void at the core of the narcissist. The common view is that the remnants of the True Self are so ossified, shredded, cowed into submission, and repressed – that, for all practical purposes, the True Self is dysfunctional and useless."[211]

Unlike bipolar patients who need medication to get out of their depression, all a narcissist needs is "one dose of narcissistic supply to elevate from the depth of misery, to the heights of manic euphoria," says Vaknin.[212]

Temporal Lobe Epilepsy

The first to suspect that Muhammad had epilepsy was Halima, or her husband, when Muhammad was just five years old. Theophanous, (752-817) a Byzantine

[209] /www.mental-health-matters.com/articles/article.php?artID=92
[210] *Dead Man's Mirror* by Agatha Christie - in "Hercule Poirot The Complete Short Stories" - Great Britain, HarperCollins Publishers, 1999
[211] http://samvak.tripod.com/faq48.html
[212] http://samvak.tripod.com/journal71.html

historian was the first recorded scholar to claim that Muhammad suffered from epilepsy.[213] Today, we can confirm that claim.

Temporal lobe epilepsy (TLE) was defined in 1985 by the International League Against Epilepsy (ILAE) as a condition characterized by recurrent unprovoked seizures originating from the medial or lateral temporal lobe. The seizures associated with TLE consist of simple partial seizures without loss of awareness (with or without aura) and complex partial seizures (i.e., with loss of awareness). The individual loses awareness during a complex partial seizure because the seizure spreads to involve both temporal lobes, which in turn causes impairment of memory.[214]

Muhammad's seizures were of both kinds. Sometimes he fell and lost consciousness and at other times he did not. One hadith reports that during the construction of the Ka'ba, before he received his prophetic intimation, Muhammad fell unconscious on the ground with both his eyes towards the sky. At that time he lost his senses.[215] This is very much an epileptic seizure.

According to the website emedicine.com, "90% of patients with temporal interictal epileptiform abnormalities on their EEG have a history of seizures." Muhammad had seizures since his childhood. He saw two men in white opening his chest and washing his heart with snow. American neurosurgeon and a pioneer of brain surgery, Harvey Cushing, reports of a boy with a cystic glioma in the right temporal lobe resulted in a vivid three dimensional vision of a man dressed in white.[216] The Irish-American neurologist Robert Foster Kennedy (1884-1952) was one of the first to identify vividly real hallucinations of an audio-visual nature, localized outside of the body as being temporal lobe in origin.[217]

Talking about his youth, Muhammad said, "I found myself among the boys of Quraish, carrying stones such as boys play with. We had all uncovered ourselves, each taking his shirt [a cloth wrap] and putting it round his neck as he carried the stones. I was going to and fro in the same way, when an unseen figure slapped me painfully saying, 'Put your shirt on' so I took it and fastened it on me, then began to carry the stones upon my neck, wearing my shirt, alone among my fellows."[218]

It is interesting to note that Muhammad's imaginary friends were just as rough and violent as he was. However, science gives us a better explanation. Emotional pain can exacerbate physical pain. Sadness, unexpressed anger, anxiety, shame and guilt can cause physical pain. Anger releases adrenalin, which increases muscle tension and speeds up breathing. Without being expressed, it can cause long-term tension. Anxiety, worry and fear also release adrenalin. This generally results in jumpiness, a

---

[213] Theophanes, 1007, Chronographia, vol. 1, p334
[214] www.emedicine.com/NEURO/topic365.htm
[215] Sahih Bukhari, Volume, Book 26, Number 652
[216] Cushing: Brain 1921-1922 xliv p341
[217] Kennedy: Arch Int Med 1911 viii p317.
[218] Sirat Rasoul p. 81

tendency to startle easily and the inability to relax. Shame and guilt often result in a feeling of "butterflies" or weight in the stomach. Muhammad was an emotional wreck.

Symptoms of Temporal Lobe Seizure

A seizure originating in the temporal lobe may be preceded by an aura or warning symptom, such as abnormal sensations, epigastric sensations (a funny feeling in the stomach), hallucinations or illusions (vision, smells, tastes, or other sensory illusions), sensation of déjà vu, recalled emotions or memories, or sudden and intense emotion not related to anything occurring at the time. All these symptoms were present during Muhammad's seizures.

The epileptic experience can be partial, during which consciousness is maintained or partial complex, resulting in the loss or reduction of consciousness during the seizure or spell. Other symptoms include abnormal head movements and forced turning of the eyes. This kind of seizure happened to Muhammad during the construction of Ka'ba.

Repetitive movements and rhythmic muscle contraction affecting one side of the body, one arm, one leg, part of the face, or other isolated area are also symptoms of TLE. Other symptoms include, abdominal pain or discomfort, nausea, sweating, flushed face, rapid heart rate/pulse and changes in vision, speech, thought, awareness and personality. Of course, sensory hallucinations (visual, hearing, touch, etc.) are major symptoms.[219]

Dr. Mogens Dam, an internationally noted Danish epileptologist and the author of many books on the subject, defines simple partial seizures as follows: "Simple partial seizures with mental symptoms, which can be remembered, afterwards, have from ancient times been known as 'aura'. They are often followed by a convulsion. They are often dream-like… He thinks that he is going mad."[220] Muhammad actually did think that he was going mad. It was Khadijah who persuaded him otherwise.

Dr. Dam writes, "It has long been debated as to whether persons with epilepsy have particular personality traits, which are different from other peoples. It has particularly been singled out that people with temporal lobe epilepsy are more emotionally unstable than others, perhaps with a tendency towards aggression. Some people were said to be self-centered, they could be sensitive to the point of paranoia, and took every chance remark as a personal slight. They were described as being given to brooding over things, and were particularly interested in religious, mystic, philosophical and moral issues."[221]

---

219 www.nlm.nih.gov/medlineplus/ency/article/001399.htm

220 www.epilepsy.dk/Handbook/Mental-complications-uk.asp

221 Ibid.

Dam further explains that people suffering from TLE are more likely to become depressed, have suicidal thoughts, and hallucinate. The person gets the feeling that he is being persecuted. His emotional contact with other people, however, is always much better than in cases of true schizophrenia. Unlike schizophrenia, TLE often resolves on its own. This must have happened to Muhammad as in later years of his life there were fewer fits of seizure. However, this did not stop him from "revealing" verses as situations dictated and the needs arose.

There is a difference in tone, language, and the structure between the early Meccan verses and the later Medinan ones. The suras written during the early phase of Muhammad's prophetic career are poetic in style. They rhyme. They are short and striking. They are filled with exhortations to be pious and charitable, to feed the orphans and to free the slaves, to be patient, kind and compassionate, and plenty of warnings and promises of hell for those who would not heed to his call.

Sura 91, "The Sun," is a typical sura pertaining to this period. It talks about a fable known to Arabs, that Allah had sent a she-camel to warn people of Samood, who in their waywardness slaughtered this animal prophetess. In the early verses, the influence of Paganism and moon and sun worship on Muhammad, are still apparent.

> *I swear by the sun and its brilliance, And the moon when it follows the sun,*
> *And the day when it shows it, And the night when it draws a veil over it,*
> *And the heaven and Him Who made it, And the earth and Him Who extended it,*
> *And the soul and Him Who made it perfect, Then He inspired it to understand what is right and wrong for it; He will indeed be successful who purifies it,*
> *And he will indeed fail who corrupts it. Samood gave the lie (to the truth) in their inordinacy, when the most unfortunate of them broke forth with. So Allah's messenger said to them (Leave alone) Allah's she-camel, and (give) her (to) drink. But they called him a liar and slaughtered her; therefore their Lord crushed them for their sin and leveled them (with the ground).*
> *And He fears not its consequence.*

Sura 113, "The Dawn," is another example of this period.

> *In the name of Allah, the Beneficent, the Merciful.*
> *Say: I seek refuge in the Lord of the dawn,*
> *From the evil of what He has created,*
> *And from the evil of the utterly dark night when it comes,*
> *And from the evil of those who blow on knots,*
> *And from the evil of the envious when he envies.*

3- Muhammad's Ecstatic Experiences

While still in Mecca, Muhammad's ambition was limited to that town and its surroundings. He wrote, "*Thus have we sent by inspiration to you an Arabic Quran: that you may warn the Mother of Cities and all around her*."(Q.42:7)[222] The Mother of Cities, *Umul Qura,* is Mecca. In other verses[223] he said that he came specifically for those who had not yet received a revelation from God. According to these verses, the Jews, the Christians, and the Zoroastrians were not his addressees. .

In other verses he said:

> *And never have We sent forth any apostle otherwise than [with a message] in his own people's tongue, so that he might make [the truth] clear unto them.* (Q.14:4)
>
> *And indeed, within every community have We raised up an apostle.* (Q16:36)
>
> *To every people (was sent) a messenger.* (Q.10:47)

These and several other verses show that at first, Muhammad did not have ambitions to spread his message outside Mecca. As time passed and the Meccans showed little interest in his religion, he turned his attention to other tribes and eventually demanded that everyone must submit to him or be killed.

The language in later suras is legalistic. It is the language of a despot setting laws and ordinances and inciting his subjects to conquer new lands. In regards to the Medinan verses, A. S. Tritton says, "The sentences are long and unwieldy so that the hearer has to listen carefully or he will miss the rhyme altogether; the language has become prose with rhyming words at intervals. The subject matter is laws, comments on public events, statements of policy, rebukes to those who did not see eye-to-eye with the prophet, Jews especially, and references to his domestic troubles. Here imagination is weak and stock phrases are dragged in to conceal the poverty of ideas, though occasionally the earlier enthusiasm bursts out."[224]

In several hadiths Muhammad narrated his encounters with jinns. In one story he claimed to have spent a night in their town converting many of them to Islam. In the Quran there are at least 30 references to jinns.

Other Symptoms of TLE

People with TLE tend to demonstrate some of these five interictal traits (*between* rather than *during* seizures).

---

[222] The same claim is made in *Quran, 6:92*

[223] "Nay, it is the Truth from thy Lord, that thou mayest admonish a people to whom no warner has come before thee: in order that they may receive guidance."(Quran 32:3) and In order that thou mayest admonish a people, whose fathers had received no admonition, and who therefore remain heedless (of the Signs of Allâh). (Qura'an, 36:6)

[224] A.S. Tritton, *Islam: Belief and Practice 1951, p. 16.*

1. **Hypergraphia**: Hypergraphia is an obsession phenomenon manifested by writing extensive notes and diaries. Even though apparently illiterate, Muhammad composed the Quran, asking others to write it down for him.
2. **Hyper religiosity**: Religious beliefs not only are intense, but may also be associated with elaborate theological or cosmological theories. Patients may believe that they have special divine guidance. Muhammad obviously had an unusual degree of concern with philosophy and mysticism, which led him to invent a new religion.
3. **Clingingness**: From the stories that talk about Muhammad's attachment to his uncle, when he was a boy and from other stories we can determine that Muhammad was emotionally needy and that he was very offended when rejected or abandoned.
4. **Altered interest in sex**: Muhammad's obsession with women indicates that his interest in sex was heightened even though, as we shall see later, his abilities may have diminished or entirely disappeared in his later years.
5. **Aggressiveness**: Intense emotions are often labile, so that the patient may exhibit great warmth at one time, whereas at another time, anger and irritability may evolve into rage and aggressive behavior. Muhammad was at times friendly, particularly to his companions, but extremely short-tempered and irritable to those whom he perceived as resisting his demands. Bukhari says: "If the Prophet disliked something, the sign of aversion would appear on his face."[225]

The Heavenly Night Journey

There are various versions of the story of Muhammad's *Mi'raj,* his alleged night journey to heaven. Ibn Ishaq has woven together these traditions stemming from stories told by his companions, particularly his wife Aisha. According to the narrative, Muhammad reported:

> While I was asleep in the hijr, Gabriel came and stirred me with his foot. I sat up, but saw nothing and lay down again. He came a second time and stirred me with his foot. I sat up, but saw nothing and lay down again. He came to me a third time, and stirred me with his foot. I sat up, and he took hold of my arm and I stood beside him. He brought me out to the door of the mosque, and there was a white animal, half mule, half donkey, with wings on its sides with which it propelled its feet, putting down each forefoot at the limit of its sight. He mounted me on it. Then he went out with me, keeping close to me. When I came up to mount him, he shied. Gabriel placed his hand on its mane and said, are you not ashamed, O Buraq, to behave in this way? By Allah, none more honorable before Allah than Muhammad has ever ridden you before. The animal was so ashamed that he broke out into a sweat, and stood so that I could mount him.

[225] Bukhari, Volume 4, Book 56, Number 763.

3- Muhammad's Ecstatic Experiences

> The apostle and Gabriel went their way, until they arrived at the temple at Jerusalem. There he found Abraham, Moses, and Jesus among a company of the prophets. The apostle acted as their imam in prayer. Then he was brought two vessels, one containing wine and the other milk. The apostle took the milk and drank it, leaving the wine. Gabriel said, 'You have been rightly guided to the way of nature, the true primeval religion, and so will your people be, Muhammad. Wine is forbidden to you.' Then the apostle returned to Mecca, and in the morning he told Quraish what had happened. Most of them said, 'By Allah, this is a plain absurdity! A caravan takes a month to go to Syria and a month to return. How can Muhammad do the return journey in one night? [226]

Ibn Sa'd says; "Upon hearing this story many who had prayed and joined Islam became renegades and left Islam." And this Quranic verse was revealed in response: "*We made the vision which we showed you only for a test to men.*"[227]

Muslim chroniclers have gone out of their way to embellish this story and give it credibility. Ibn Ishaq added that people asked for proof and Muhammad replied that he had passed the caravan of so-and-so in such-and-such a valley, and the animal he rode scared them and a camel bolted. Then Muhammad is quoted as saying:

> And I showed them where it was, as I was on the way to Syria. I carried on until, in Dajanan, a mountain near Tihama, some 25 miles from Mecca. I passed by a caravan of the Banu so-and-so. I found the people asleep. They had a jar of water covered with something. I took the covering off and drank the water, replacing the cover. The proof of that is that their caravan is this moment coming down from al-Baida' by the pass of al-Tan'im, led by a dusky camel loaded with two sacks, one black and the other multihued.' Baida is a hill near Mecca, on the Medina side. Tan'im is on the high ground near Mecca. The people hurried to the pass, and the first camel they met was as he had described. They asked the men about the vessel, and they told them that they had left it full of water and covered it, and that when they woke, it was covered but empty. They asked the others too, who were in Mecca and they said that it was quite right, they had been scared, and a camel had bolted. They had heard a man calling them to it, so that they were able to recover it."[228]

These traditions were written down more than a hundred years after the death of Muhammad. There was no way to prove the authenticity of such claims after the lapse of this much time. However, what Muslims in general have missed is that at the time that Muhammad allegedly visited the Temple in Jerusalem, there was no temple in Jerusalem. Six centuries before al-Buraq took his flight, the Romans had destroyed it. By 70 A.D. not one stone stood upon another. The Temple of

---

226 Sira: Ibn Ishaq:182
227 Quran: Sura 17, Verse 60
228 Sirat; Ibn Ishaq. p. 184

Solomon was built around 10th century BC, according to the Bible. The Dome of the Rock was raised on the foundations of the Roman Temple of Jupiter in 691 A.D. Al-Aqsa mosque was constructed over a Roman basilica on the southern end of the Temple Mount by the Umayyads in 710 AD. It is ironic that Muhammad saw the caravan of the tribe of so-and-so on his way, but failed to see that the temple, in which he claimed to have prayed, did not exist. The fact that some of his followers left him on this account and he said this happened *only for a test to men* is evidence that the veracity of his claim could not be proven. If it could have been verified, people's faith would have been reconfirmed, not lost.

Another hadith says that to test the truth of Muhammad's claim Abu Bakr asked him to describe Jerusalem and when he did, Abu Bakr said "That's true. I testify that you are the apostle of Allah." Jerusalem was a city in ruins and not a commercial destination for Meccans to visit. Assuming Abu Bakr had been there, it is surprising that he did not notice that the temple in which Muhammad claimed to have led the prophets in prayer did not exist.

There is another version of this story that is probably more reliable, as it is ratified in the Quran. In this version Muhammad says:

> After the completion of my business in Jerusalem, a ladder was brought to me, finer than any I have ever seen. It was that to which the dying man looks when death approaches. My companion mounted it with me, until we came to one of the gates of heaven, called the Gate of the Watchers. An angel called Isma'il was in charge of it, and under his command were twelve thousand angels, each of them having twelve thousand angels under his command.
>
> When Gabriel brought me in, Isma'il asked who I was, and when he was told that I was Muhammad, he asked if I had been given a mission, or sent for, and on being assured of this, he wished me well.
> All the angels who met me when I entered the lowest heaven smiled welcomingly and wished me well, except one who said the same things, but did not smile or show that joyful expression which the others had. And when I asked Gabriel the reason, he told me that if he had ever smiled on anyone before, or would smile on anyone hereafter, he would have smiled on me. He does not smile, because he is Malik, the Keeper of Hell. I said to Gabriel, he holding the position with regard to Allah, which he has described to you 'obeyed there, trustworthy.' (Surah 81:21) 'Will you not order him to show me hell?' And he said, 'Certainly! O Malik, show Muhammad Hell.' Thereupon he removed its covering, and the flames blazed high into the air, until I thought that they would consume everything. So I asked Gabriel to order him to send them back to their place, which he did.
>
> I can only compare the effect of their withdrawal to the falling of a shadow, until, when the flames retreated whence they had come, Malik placed their cover on them.

3- Muhammad's Ecstatic Experiences

When I entered the lowest heaven, I saw a man sitting there, with the spirits of men passing before him. To one he would speak well and rejoice in him, saying, 'A good spirit from a good body.' Of another, he would say 'Faugh' and frown, saying: 'An evil spirit from an evil body.'

In answer to my question, Gabriel told me that this was our father Adam, reviewing the spirits of his offspring. The spirit of a believer excited his pleasure, and the spirit of an infidel excited his disgust. 'Then I saw men with lips like camels. In their hands were pieces of fire, like stones, which they used to thrust into their mouths, and they would come out of their posteriors. I was told that these were those who sinfully devoured the wealth of orphans.[229] Then I saw men in the way of the family of Pharaoh, with such bellies as I have never seen, there were passing over them, camels maddened by thirst when they were cast into hell, treading them down, they being unable to move out of the way. These were the usurers.[230]

Then I saw women hanging by their breasts. These were those who had fathered bastards on their husbands.[231]

Then I was taken to the second heaven, and there were the two maternal cousins, Jesus, son of Mary, and John, son of Zakariah. Then to the third heaven, and there was a man whose face was as the moon at the full. This was my brother Joseph, son of Jacob. Then to the fourth heaven, and there as a man called Idris. 'And we have exalted him to a lofty place.' Surah 19:58 Then to the fifth heaven, and there was a man with white hair and a long beard, never have I seen a more handsome man than he. This was the beloved among his people, Aaron, son of 'Imran. Then to the sixth heaven, and there was a dark man with a hooked nose, like the Shanu'a. This was my brother Moses, son of 'Imran. Then to the seventh heaven, and there was a man sitting on a throne at the gate of the immortal mansion, Paradise. Every day, seventy thousand angels went in, not to come back until the resurrection day. Never have I seen a man more like myself. This was my father, Abraham. Then he took me into Paradise, and there I saw a damsel with dark red lips and asked her to whom she

[229] Some years later, when Muhammad came to power, he reduced children to orphans by killing their fathers, enslaving their mothers and taking their belongings.

[230] The allusion is to Surah 40:46, 'Cast the family of Pharaoh into the worst of all punishments

[231] Sahih Bukhari *Volume 1, Book 6, Number 301 reports Muhammad saying* "I have seen that the majority of the dwellers of Hell-fire were you (women)." They asked, "Why is it so, O Allâh's Apostle?" He replied, "You curse frequently and are ungrateful to your husbands. I have not seen anyone more deficient in intelligence and religion than you. A cautious sensible man could be led astray by some of you." The women asked, "O Allâh's Apostle! What is deficient in our intelligence and religion?" He said, "Is not the evidence of two women equal to the witness of one man?" They replied in the affirmative. He said, "This is the deficiency in her intelligence. Isn't it true that a woman can neither pray nor fast during her menses?" The women replied in the affirmative. He said, "This is the deficiency in her religion."

> belonged, for she pleased me much when I saw her, and she told me 'Zayd b. Haritha.' The apostle gave Zayd the good news about her.[232]

One tradition says that when Gabriel took Muhammad up to each heaven and asked permission to enter, he was asked to introduce his companion, and whether his guest had received a mission or had been sent for, after which the gatekeepers would respond "Allah grant him life, brother and friend!" and let them pass, until they reached the seventh heaven and there Muhammad met Allah. During his interview with the Creator, the duty of fifty prayers per day was laid upon his followers. On his return he met Moses and this is what he said happened:

> On my return, I passed by Moses, and what a fine friend of yours he was! He asked me how many prayers had been laid upon me, and when I told him fifty, he said, 'Prayer is a weighty matter, and your people are weak, so go back to your Lord and ask him to reduce the number for you and your community.' I did so, and He took off ten prayers. Again I passed by Moses, and he said the same again, and so it went on, until only five prayers for the whole day and night were left. Moses again gave me same advice. I replied that I had been back to my Lord and asked him to reduce the number until I was ashamed, and I would not do it again. He of you who performs them in faith and trust will have the reward of fifty prayers.[233]

Muhammad Was Not Lying

The Russian existential writer Fyodor Dostoyevsky thought that Muhammad was telling the truth. He believed that Muhammad's experiences were real, at least to him. Dostoyevsky himself suffered from temporal lobe epilepsy. He revealed, via one of his characters, that when he had a seizure the gates of Heaven would open and he could see row upon row of angels blowing on great golden trumpets. Then two great golden doors would open and he could see a golden stairway that would lead right up to the throne of God.[234]

In an article titled "Religion and the Brain" published in *Newsweek*, on May 7, 2001, a Canadian neuropsychology researcher explained:

> When the image of a cross, or a Torah crowned in silver, triggers a sense of religious awe, it is because the brain's visual-association area, which interprets what the eyes see and connects images to emotions and memories, has learned to link those images to that feeling. Visions that arise during prayer or ritual are also generated in the

---

[232] This story is also repeated in Sira of Ibn Ishaq p. 186. Some years later in Medina Muhammad fell in love with Zayd 's wife and made his lust known. Zayd felt compelled to divorce his wife so Muhammad could marry her.
[233] Bukhari *Volume 9, Book 93, Number 608:*
[234] www.emedicine.com/neuro/topic658.htm

association area: electrical stimulation of the temporal lobes (which nestle along the sides of the head and house the circuits responsible for language, conceptual thinking and associations) produces visions.

Temporal-lobe epilepsy—abnormal bursts of electrical activity in these regions — takes this to extremes. Although some studies have cast doubt on the connection between temporal-lobe epilepsy and religiosity, others find that the condition seems to trigger vivid, Joan of Arc-type religious visions and voices.

Although temporal-lobe epilepsy is rare, researchers suspect that focused bursts of electrical activity called "temporal-lobe transients" may yield mystical experiences. To test this idea, Michael Persinger of Laurentian University in Canada fits a helmet jury-rigged with electromagnets onto a volunteer's head. The helmet creates a weak magnetic field, no stronger than that produced by a computer monitor. The field triggers bursts of electrical activity in the temporal lobes, Persinger finds, producing sensations that volunteers describe as supernatural or spiritual: an out-of-body experience, a sense of the divine. He suspects that religious experiences are evoked by mini electrical storms in the temporal lobes, and that such storms can be triggered by anxiety, personal crisis, lack of oxygen, low blood sugar and simple fatigue—suggesting a reason that some people "find God" in such moments.[235]

The Origin of Muhammad's Mystical Experiences

Is it possible to tickle the temporal lobe and induce mystical experiences such as sensing a "presence," hearing sounds, seeing lights, or even ghosts?

Michael Persinger, the neuropsychologist at Canada's Laurentian University cited above, thinks so. He has been able to demonstrate that the sensation described as "having a religious experience" is merely a side effect of our bicameral brain's feverish activities. In simple words: When the right hemisphere of the brain, the seat of emotion, is stimulated in the cerebral region presumed to control notions of self, and then the left hemisphere, the seat of language, is called upon to make sense of this nonexistent entity, the mind generates a "sensed presence."[236]

Ken Hollings, in an article titled "The Exorcism" writes: "Persinger… argues that religious experience is created within the brain. Current studies suggest that our sense of self is produced by the left temporal lobe, located in the logical and precise hemisphere of our brains, which helps maintain the boundary between individual consciousness and the outside world. Shut that lobe down, and you feel at one with the Universe – a prime form of religious experience. Stimulate the right temporal

[235] Newsweek May 7, 2001, U.S. Edition; Section: SCIENCE AND TECHNOLOGY; Religion And The Brain By Sharon Begley With Anne Underwood

[236] http://web.ionsys.com/~remedy/Persinger,%20Michael.htm

lobe, on the creative and more emotional side of our brains, and a right hemispheric sense of self is invoked, which we tend to experience as a 'separate' entity."[237]

Persinger fitted a motorcycle helmet with solenoids emitting mild electromagnetic fields around the volunteers' temples. The volunteers were made to sit blindfolded in an empty room – "the chamber of heaven and hell" as it was jokingly called. By alternating the electrical charges, 80% of the subjects that took part in this experiment sensed "presence" of a ghostly being in the room, sometimes touching or grabbing them. Some of them said that they smelled the fragrance of paradise or the stench of hell. They heard voices, saw dark tunnels, lights, and had profound religious experiences.

Ed Conroy, also reporting on Michael Persinger's experiments writes: "The personalities of normal people who display enhanced temporal lobe activity... display enhanced: creativity, suggestibility, memory capacity, and intuitive processing. Most of them experience a rich fantasy or subjective world that fosters their adaptability. Many of them are prone to bouts of physical and mental activity followed by mild depression. These people have more frequent experiences of a sense of presence during which time 'an entity is felt and sometimes seen'; exotic beliefs rather than traditional religious concepts are endorsed."[238]

Persinger has found out that different subjects label this ghostly perception with the names that are familiar to them. Religious people experience the holy personalities of their faith - Elijah, Jesus, the Virgin Mary, Mohammad, the Sky Spirit, etc. Some subjects have emerged with Freudian interpretations - describing the presence as one's grandfather, for instance.

This method has been used also to induce near-death experiences (NDEs). Hollings writes, "In 1933 Montreal neurosurgeon Wilder Penfield discovered that when he electrically stimulated certain nerve cells in the temporal lobe, the patient would 'relive' previous experiences in convincing sensory detail. In his controversial 1976 publication, *The Origin of Consciousness in the Breakdown of the Bicameral Mind*, Princeton psychologist Julian Jaynes argued that the sensation commonly described as 'having a religious experience' is merely a side effect of the feverish interactivity between the right and left halves of our brain. Our ancient ancestors, he suggested, lacked a strong enough sense of individual identity to explain such exchanges as anything but voices and visions from the gods on high."[239]

---

[237] Ken Hollings
http://www.channel4.com/science/microsites/S/science/body/exorcism.html
[238] Michael Persinger in Report on Communion by Ed Conroy
http://www.futurepundit.com/archives/000721.html
[239] Ken Hollings
http://www.channel4.com/science/microsites/S/science/body/exorcism.html

3- Muhammad's Ecstatic Experiences

What exactly happens in that moment of intense spiritual awareness? Hollings says, "Activity in the brain's amygdala, which monitors the environment for threats and registers fear, is dampened. Parietal lobe circuits, which orient you, go quiet, while circuits in the frontal and temporal lobes, which mark time and generate self-awareness, become disengaged. Using brain-imaging data collected from Tibetan Buddhists during meditation and Franciscan nuns at prayer, Dr. Andrew Newberg of the University of Pennsylvania observed that a bundle of neurons in the superior parietal lobe, toward the top and back of the brain, had shut down. This region also helps processes information about orientation and time."[240]

Persinger has shown that "spiritual" and "supernatural" experiences are the result of the lack of proper communication and coordination between the left and right temporal lobes. The sense of a presence in the room, an out-of-body experience, bizarre distortion of body parts, and even religious feelings are all caused in the brain. Persinger calls these experiences 'temporal lobe transients', or increases and instabilities in neuronal firing patterns in the temporal lobe.

How do these experiences produce religious states? Our "sense of self," says Persinger "is maintained by the left hemisphere temporal cortex. Under normal brain functioning this is matched by the corresponding systems in the right hemisphere temporal cortex. When these two systems become uncoordinated, such as during a seizure or a transient event, the left hemisphere interprets the uncoordinated activity as 'another self', or a 'sensed presence', thus accounting for subjects' experiences of a 'presence' in the room (which might be interpreted as angels, demons, aliens, or ghosts), or leaving their bodies (as in near-death experiences), or even 'God'. When the amygdala (deep-seated region of the brain involved with emotion) is involved in the transient events, emotional factors significantly enhance the experience which, when connected to spiritual themes, can be a powerful force for intense religious feelings."[241]

Brain Stimulation Creates Shadow Person

Swiss scientists have found that electrical stimulation of the brain can create the sensation of a "shadow person" mimicking one's bodily movements, according to a brief report in the journal *Nature* and in an article titled "Brain stimulation creates shadow person" appearing in the on-line science journal Physorg.com:

> Olaf Blanke and colleagues at the Federal Polytechnic School of Lausanne say their discovery might help shed light on brain processes that contribute to the symptoms of

---

240 *Ibid*

241 *How We Believe*, 2000, Michael Shermer p.66

> schizophrenia, which can include the sensation that one's own actions are being performed by someone else.
>
> Doctors evaluating a woman with no history of psychiatric problems found stimulation of an area of her brain called the left temporoparietal junction caused her to believe a person was standing behind her.
>
> The patient reported that "person" adopted the same bodily positions as her, although she didn't recognize the effect as an illusion. At one point in the investigation, the patient was asked to lean forward and clasp her knees: this led to a sensation that the shadow figure was embracing her, which she described as unpleasant.
>
> The finding could be a step towards understanding psychiatric affects such as feelings of paranoia, persecution and alien control, say neuroscientists.
>
> The discovery is reported in a Brief Communication in this week's issue of the journal Nature.[242]

Could these findings explain what Muhammad heard, saw, and felt during his epiphanic experiences? Muhammad came from a culture that believed in jinns, angels, ghouls and demons and these were the creatures that he saw in his hallucinations. The dispute about whether there is one God, as Jews and Christians believed, or whether there are many gods, as Muhammad's clan thought, was an ongoing debate. Muhammad sided with the more "exotic" belief of monotheism, instead of the traditional religious concept endorsed by his own people. We must also not undermine the influence that Khadijah exerted on him in interpreting his hallucinatory experiences. She was a monotheist.

What Muhammad experienced was real to him, yet it was only mental. When he relayed his story to Khadijah, all she could think of was that her beloved husband had either gone mad or had been touched by angels. So when he told her "I fear that something may happen to me", she replied, "Never! Allah will never disgrace you."[243] Since she could not accept that her narcissist had lost it was she opted to believe in the alternative. If it had not been for Khadijah's unconditional support and encouragement, Muhammad might have continued thinking that he had become possessed, and perhaps sought some help to get rid of his condition.

---

[242] www.physorg.com/news77992285.html, published 17:31 EST, September 20, 2006, copyright 2006 by United Press International, accessed June 21, 2007

[243] Bukhari *Volume 1, Book 1, Number 3*

3- Muhammad's Ecstatic Experiences

Camel Kneeling Under the Power of Revelation

Muslims often exaggerate and attribute miracles to their prophet. This is quite normal for cultists. A hadith claims that one day, when Muhammad was on a camel, a revelation descended on him so intensely that the beast knelt down on the ground.

If this story is true it could be another indication that Muhammad was epileptic. Bonnie Beaver, an expert in animal behavior at the College of Veterinary Medicine at Texas A&M University says, "Dogs and cats have been known to alert some people when a seizure is about to begin. It's common for animals to sense a seizure in their owners, and some dogs can even be trained to warn a person of an impending seizure."[244]

The University of Florida study conducted by Ms. Dalziel and Dr. Reep surveyed a pool of patients experiencing at least one epileptic seizure per month. Of this pool, 30 owned dogs, and five percent of these 30 individuals "reliably" reported that their dogs demonstrated distinct behavior signifying the onset of a seizure. "They reported defined and unusual behavior that the dog didn't usually exhibit," Dr. Reep explained. He said that of all the theories, it is most plausible that some dogs can smell a seizure coming. He added that patients with epilepsy have reported that their dogs were able to detect seizures from other rooms in the house—behavior that could not, of course, depend upon visual or electrical cues.[245]

Today, dogs are trained to warn their owner when they are about to have a seizure. Animals seem to have sensory perceptions that we humans don't possess or may have lost. They seem to sense the advent of an earthquake, hours before it happens. Many animals - especially horses and cattle - can sense a thunderstorm before it occurs.

On January 4, 2005, The National Geographic News wrote: "Before giant waves slammed into Sri Lanka and India coastlines ten days ago, wild and domestic animals seemed to know what was about to happen and fled to safety. According to eyewitness accounts, elephants screamed and ran for higher ground, dogs refused to go outdoors, flamingos abandoned their low-lying breeding areas and zoo animals rushed into their shelters and could not be enticed to come back out. The belief that wild and domestic animals possess a sixth sense—and know in advance when the earth is going to shake—has been around for centuries."[246]

The point is that animals are known to perceive events, especially pending epilepsy in their owners. It is not unusual for an animal to become distressed and behave erratically when his owner is about to have a fit of seizure. We know that neither Muhammad's wives nor his companions were affected or sensed anything

---

[244] http://www.tamu.edu/univrel/aggiedaily/news/stories/04/070104-3.html

[245] http://www.workingdogs.com/vcepilepsy.htm

[246] National Geographic: "Did Animals Sense Tsunami Was Coming?" http://news.nationalgeographic.com/news/2005/01/0104_050104_tsunami_animals.html

when he was receiving "revelations." During one of his hallucinatory experiences Muhammad told Aisha, "This is Gabriel. He sends his greetings and salutations to you. Aisha replied, 'Salutations and greetings to him.' Then addressing the Prophet she said, 'You see what I don't see.'"[247] If only camels could feel what was happening to Muhammad, it is another clue that what he was experiencing was a seizure.

The Case of Phil K. Dick

Case studies of other epileptic sufferers can give us a better understanding of what may have happened to Muhammad. The similarities are often astounding.

The American science fiction writer Philip Kindred Dick (1928-1982), speaking of his own strange visions to Charles Platt said, "I experienced an invasion of my mind by a transcendentally rational mind, as if I had been insane all my life and suddenly I had become sane."[248] All Dick's works start with the basic assumption that there cannot be one single, objective reality. Charles Platt describes Dick's novels. "Everything is a matter of perception. The ground is liable to shift under your feet. A protagonist may find himself living out another person's dream, or he may enter a drug-induced state that actually makes better sense than the real world, or he may cross into a different universe completely."[249]

Like Muhammad, Dick was also paranoid, emotionally infantile, was narcissistic, had suicidal thoughts, and was resentful of his parents. He imagined that plots against him were being perpetrated by the KGB or FBI, and that they were constantly laying traps for him. We see the same kind of paranoia in the writings of Muhammad, who constantly talked about the unbelievers and how they were plotting against him, opposing his religion, and persecuting him and his followers. VALIS, the first of Dick's three final autobiographical novels,[250] is a fool's search for God, who turns out to be a virus, a joke, and a mental hologram transmitted from an orbiting satellite.

The proponent of the novel is thrust into a theological quest when he receives communion in a burst of pink laser light and turns out to have a direct link with God. In this work, Dick examines his own supposed encounters with a divine presence.

VALIS is an acronym for *Vast Active Living Intelligence System*. He theorizes that VALIS is both a "reality generator" and a means of extraterrestrial communication.

---

[247] Bukhari:Volume4, Book 54, Number 440

[248] [248] Platt, Charles. (1980). *Dream Makers: The Uncommon People Who Write Science Fiction*. Berkley Publishing. ISBN 0-425-04668-0

[249] Ibid

[250] The others are *Divine Invasion* and *The Transmigration of Timothy Archer*.

3- Muhammad's Ecstatic Experiences

Lawrence Sutin, in *Divine Invasions: A Life of Philip K. Dick* writes about one of Dick's mystical experiences that eerily resemble those of Muhammad.

> Monday night he called me and said that the night before, he'd been smoking some marijuana that a visitor had left, and felt himself entering that by-now-familiar state in which he had visions (generally not dope-related), and he said, 'I want to see God. Let me see you.' And then instantly, he told me, he was flattened by the most extreme terror he'd ever felt, and he saw the Ark of the Covenant, and a voice said, 'You wouldn't come to me through logical evidence or faith or anything else, so I must convince you this way.' The curtain of the Ark was drawn back, and he saw, apparently, a void and a triangle with an eye in it, staring straight at him. Phil said he was on his hands and knees, in absolute terror, enduring the Beatific Vision from nine o'clock Sunday evening until five o'clock Monday morning. He said he was certain he was dying, and if he could have reached the telephone he'd have called the paramedics. The Voice told him, in effect, 'You've managed to talk yourself into disbelieving everything else. I let you see, but this you'll never be able to forget or adapt or misrepresent.'[251]

Dick, who died prematurely at the age of 54, wrote millions of words. His biographer Sutin quotes one of his writings in which he explains his mystical experience:

> God manifested himself to me as the infinite void; but it was not the abyss, it was the vault of heaven, with blue sky and wisps of white clouds. He was not some foreign God but the God of my fathers. He was loving and kind and he had personality. He said, 'You suffer a little now in life; it is little compared with the great joys, the bliss that awaits you. Do you think I in my theodicy would allow you to suffer greatly in proportion to your reward?' He made me aware, then of the bliss that would come; it was infinite and sweet. He said, 'I am the infinite. I will show you. Where I am, infinity is; where infinity is, there I am… They reckon ill who leave me out; With me they fly I am the wings. I am the doubter and the doubt.'[252]

Other Cases of TLE

On October 23, 2001 PBS television aired a documentary on TLE. One of the persons interviewed was a man with temporal lobe epilepsy, John Sharon. Also present at the interview were Sharon's father and V. S. Ramachandran, a neurologist with the University of California-San Diego. It is interesting to read his case and compare it to what we know about Muhammad. This could shed more light on the Prophet's state of mind and his illness.

---

251 *Divine Invasion , A Life of Philip K. Dick* by Lawrence Sutin, p.264, published _____

252 Ibid. p.269

***John Sharon**:* The seizures involve my person and my soul and my spirit, all of it. When I get one of those feelings my whole body just tingles and I just, oh...that's that.
***Narrator**:* John's epileptic seizures are essentially an electrical storm in his temporal lobes when a group of neurons starts firing at random, out of sync with rest of his brain.
Recently John experienced one of his worst episodes to date. He'd gone out to the desert with a girlfriend, and they'd both got very drunk, with disastrous results. John was suddenly hit by a volley of seizures; each one lasted about five minutes and involved violent convulsions that left him unconscious. Eventually, John managed to get a call through to his father who drove out to the desert to bring him home.
***John**:* On the way home, he and I got just into some philosophical questions about everything. And I just would not shut up once I...on the way home I was going and going. It was like I was wired.
***Mr Sharon, Sr**.:* It's basically an earthquake within the body, and like any earthquake there are aftershocks. And like any earthquake that does damage, things have to be rebuilt. Things have to subside. Mainly what I deal with is the aftermath, particularly with this last episode. It was very much like stepping into a Salvador Dali painting. Instantly everything was surreal. And that's, in essence, what his seizures are all about – the aftermath – where it puts his brain, where it puts his memory, where it puts his mind, his thinking ability, everything else.
Narrator: When John's seizures came to an end he was exhausted but he felt omnipotent.
***John**:* I went running down the streets screaming that I was God. And then this guy came out and I just, like, pelvic thrust at him and his wife and I was like, "You want to f–ing bet, I ain't God?"
***Mr. Sharon Sr**.:* And I said, literally, 'you asshole, get back in here! What do you think you're doing? You're disturbing the neighbors. They're gonna call the cops. What is this all about?'
***John**:* I kind of just looked at him, cool and calm, and apologized to him, and like, 'No. No one's going to call the police.' Like, I didn't say this last part, but I'm thinking to myself, 'No one's going to call the police on God!'
Narrator: John had never been religious, yet the onset of his seizures brought on overwhelming spiritual feelings. Vilayanur S. Ramachandran is Director of the Center for Brain and Cognition and professor with the Psychology Department and the Neurosciences Program at the University of California, San Diego. He has done extensive studies on Temporal Lobe Epilepsy.
***V.S. Ramachandran**:* It has been known for a long time that some patients with seizures originating in the temporal lobes have intense religious auras, intense experience of God visiting them. Sometimes it's a personal god, sometimes it's a more diffuse feeling of being one with the cosmos. Everything seems suffused with meaning. The patient will say, "Finally I see what it's really about, Doctor. I really understand God. I understand my place in the universe, in the cosmic scheme." Why does this happen and why does it happen so often in patients with temporal lobe seizures?
***John**:* Oh my God. And you know what? I am so right in my own head; I know I could go out there and get people to follow me. Not like these whackos with sheets on

their heads, not like those idiots...but now it's just the new generation of the prophets. And were all the prophets' people who were flopping around on the ground; is that what this whole message was, the gift from the gods, this whole time?

V.S. Ramachandran: That's possible, isn't it? Yes?

John: I've never been religious, ever. People say, "No, you can't see into the future...unh unh." That's what that gift is, but you've got to pay for it by getting slammed around.

V.S. Ramachandran: Now, why do these patients have intense religious experiences when they have these seizures? And why do they become preoccupied with theological and religious matters even in between seizures?

One possibility is that the seizure activity in the temporal lobes somehow creates all kinds of odd, strange emotions in the person's mind...in the person's brain. And this welling up of bizarre emotions may be interpreted by the patient as visits from another world, or as, "God is visiting me." Maybe that's the only way he can make sense of this welter of strange emotions going on in his brain. Another possibility is that this is something to do with the way in which the temporal lobes are wired up to deal with the world emotionally. As we walk around and interact with the world, you need some way of determining what's important, what's emotionally salient and what's relevant to you versus something trivial and unimportant.

How does this come about? We think what's critical is the connection between the sensory areas in the temporal lobes and the amygdala, which is the gateway to the emotional centers in the brain. The strength of these connections is what determines how emotionally salient something is. And therefore, you could speak of a sort of emotional salience landscape, with hills and valleys corresponding to what's important and what's not important. And each of us has a slightly different emotional salience landscape. Now, consider what happens in temporal lobe epilepsy when you have repeated seizures. What might be going on is an indiscriminate strengthening of all these pathways. It's a bit like water flowing down rivulets along the cliff surface. When it rains repeatedly there's an increasing tendency for the water to make furrows along one pathway and this progressive deepening of the furrows artificially raises the emotional significance of some categories of inputs. So instead of just finding lions and tigers and mothers emotionally salient, he finds everything deeply salient. For example, a grain of sand, a piece of driftwood, seaweed, all of this becomes imbued with deep significance. Now, this tendency to ascribe cosmic significance to everything around you might be akin to what we call a mystical experience or a religious experience.

There is no specific area in the temporal lobe concerned with God. But it's possible there are parts of the temporal lobes whose activity is somehow conducive to religious belief. Now this seems unlikely, but it might be true. Now, why might we have neural machinery in the temporal lobes for belief in religion? Well, belief in religion is widespread. Every tribe, every society has some form of religious worship. And maybe the reason it evolved, if it did evolve, is that it's conducive to the stability of

> society, and this may be easiest if you believe in some sort of Supreme Being. And that may be one reason why religious sentiments evolved in the brain.[253]

History is full of charismatic religious figures who suffered from TLE. Psychologist William James (1842 – 1910) believed Apostle Paul's vision on his way to Damascus may have been "a physiological nerve storm or discharging lesion like that of epilepsy." Paul saw lights and heard a voice asking him "Saul, Saul, why do you persecute me?"[254] He was then temporarily blinded and consequently he converted to Christianity. Paul talked about his visions in these words. "To keep me from becoming conceited because of these surpassingly great revelations, there was given me a thorn in my flesh, a messenger of Satan, to torment me. Three times I pleaded with the Lord to take it away from me. But he said to me, 'My grace is sufficient for you, for my power is made perfect in weakness.'"[255]

Another famous case concerns a16th century nun known as Santa Teresa of Avila (1515 -1582). She experienced vivid visions, intense headaches and fainting spells, followed by "such peace, calm, and good fruits in the soul, and ... a perception of the greatness of God"[256] Her biographers suggest that she may well have experienced epileptic seizures.[257]

LaPlante says that painters and writers like Vincent van Gogh, Gustave Flaubert, Lewis Carroll, Marcel Proust, Tennyson, and Fyodor Dostoyevsky all had TLE. The TLE sufferers often undergo patterns of personality changes, typically including compulsive writing or drawing and hyper-religiosity.

LaPlante believed that Muhammad also suffered from TLE. More recent examples are *Joseph Smith*, the founder of Mormonism, and *Ellen White,* the founder of the Seventh Day Adventist Movement, who at the age of 9 suffered a brain injury that totally changed her personality. She also began to have powerful religious visions.

Helen Schucman, the atheist Jewish psychologist who claimed receiving messages from Jesus Christ in the form of "readings" that she called *A Course in Miracles*, was most certainly a sufferer of TLE. Reportedly, Schucman spent the last two years of her life in a terrible, paranoid depression.

Syed Ali Muhammad Bab the founder of the Babi religion may also have been an epileptic sufferer. Bab's *Persian Bayan* (translated into English and available online) is a classical epileptic writing – loquacious, verbose, stylish, yet short in content.

---

253 www.pbs.org/wgbh/nova/transcripts/2812mind.html
254 Acts 9:1-9.
255 2 Corinthians 12:7-9
256 Theresa, Saint of Avila (1930) Interior castle. London: Thomas Baker p. 171.
257 Sackville-West 1943, The Eagle and the Dove : a Study in Contrasts - St Teresa of Avila, St Therese of Lisieux

Other Famous People with Epilepsy

Heidi Hansen and Leif Bork Hansen allege Søren Kierkegaard wrote in his journal that he suffered from TLE and had kept it a secret all his life, They quote him saying: "Of all sufferings there is perhaps none so martyring as to become an object of pity, nothing which so tempts one to rebel against God. People usually regard such a person as stupid and shallow, but it would not be difficult to show that precisely this is the hidden secret in the lives of many of the most eminent world-historical figures."[258]

The Danish philosopher was right. Far from being stupid, the TLE sufferers are among the geniuses. TLE can well be defined as the disease of creativity. Many famous and talented people in the history suffered from TLE and arguably, they owed their creativity to this condition. Between five to ten persons in every 1,000 people have TLE. Not all of them, of course, reach fame.

Steven C. Schechter, M.D., professor of neurology at Harvard Medical School and author of several books on epilepsy, has compiled a list of prominent people in history who possibly suffered from TLE. This list comprises philosophers, writers, world leaders, religious figures, painters, poets, composers, actors, and other celebrities.

"Ancient people" writes Schachter, "thought epileptic seizures were caused by evil spirits or demons that had invaded a person's body. Priests attempted to cure people with epilepsy by driving the demons out of them with magic and prayers. This superstition was challenged by ancient physicians like Atreya of India and later Hippocrates of Greece, both of whom recognized seizure as a dysfunction of the brain and not a supernatural event." He further says, "Epileptic seizures have a power and symbolism which, historically, have suggested a relationship with creativity or unusual leadership abilities. Scholars have long been fascinated by evidence that prominent prophets and other holy men, political leaders, philosophers, and many who achieved greatness in the arts and sciences, suffered from epilepsy."[259]

Aristotle, who was the first to connect epilepsy to genius, claimed that Socrates had epilepsy. Schachter notes that Dr. Jerome Engel, professor of neurology at the University of California, School of Medicine, considers the co-existence of epilepsy and genius to be a coincidence.[260]

However, Schachter continues: "Others disagree, claiming to have found an association between epilepsy and giftedness in some people. Eve LaPlante in her

---

[258] www.utas.edu.au/docs/humsoc/kierkegaard/docs/Kierkepilepsy.pdf

[259] Epilepsy.com, "Famous People with Epilepsy", at www.epilepsy.com/epilepsy/famous.html , Topic Editor: Steven C. Schachter, M.D., Last Reviewed 12/15/06, accessed June 21, 2007

[260] Dr. Jerome Engel, *Seizures and Epilepsy*:, F. A. Davis Co., Philadelphia, 1989.

book *Seized,* writes that the abnormal brain activity found in temporal lobe (complex partial) epilepsy plays a role in creative thinking and the making of art. Neuropsychologist Dr. Paul Spiers maintains: 'Sometimes the same things that cause epilepsy result in giftedness. If you damage an area [of the brain] early enough in life, the corresponding area on the other side has a chance to overdevelop.'"[261]

This is an interesting theory. If Spiers is right, it is not the TLE that brings forth genius and creativity but the reaction of the brain to compensate for what is damaged.

The following is a short list of some of the geniuses who Schachter believes may have had epileptic seizures.

Harriet Tubman: the black woman who led hundreds of her fellow slaves from the American South to freedom in Canada. She came to be known as the "Moses" of her people.

Saint Paul: the greatest Christian evangelist without whom Christianity would probably never have reached Europe to become a World Religion.

Joan of Arc: the young uneducated farmer's daughter in a remote village of medieval France who altered the course of history through her amazing military victories. From age thirteen Joan reported ecstatic moments in which she saw flashes of light, heard voices of saints and saw visions of angels.

Alfred Nobel: the Swedish chemist and industrialist who invented dynamite and financed the Nobel Prize.

Dante: the author of *La Divina Comedia*;

Sir Walter Scott: one of the foremost literary figures of the romantic period; the 18th century.

Jonathan Swift: English satirist, author of *Gulliver's Travels.*

Edgar Allan Poe: the nineteenth century American author.

Lord Byron, Percy Bysshe Shelley, and *Alfred Lord Tennyson:* three of the greatest English Romantic poets,

Charles Dickens: the Victorian author of such classic books as *A Christmas Carol* and *Oliver Twist.*

Lewis Carroll: author of *Alice's Adventures in Wonderland* who may have been writing about his own temporal lobe seizures. The sensation initiating Alice's adventures - that of falling down a hole is a typical one to many people with seizures.

Fyodor Dostoyevsky, the great Russian novelist, author of such classics as *Crime and Punishment* and *The Brothers Karamazov,* who is considered by many to have brought the Western novel to the peak of its possibilities.

---

[261] www.epilepsy.com/epilepsy/famous.html

3- Muhammad's Ecstatic Experiences

Muhammad had his first seizure at age five. Dostoyevsky had his first seizure at nine. After a remission, which lasted up to age 25, he had seizures every few days or months, fluctuating between good and bad periods. His ecstatic auras occurring seconds before his bigger seizures were moments of transcendent happiness, which then changed to an anguished feeling of dread. His experiences were similar to those of Muhammad, whose vision of hell was dreadful, filled with doom and horrendous scenes of torture. Here are a couple of examples of what Muhammad saw:

> *But those who deny for them will be cut out a garment of Fire: over their heads will be poured out boiling water. With it will be scalded what is within their bodies as well as (their) skins. In addition there will be maces of iron (to punish) them. Every time they wish to get away from anguish they will be forced back therein and (it will be said), 'Taste ye the Penalty of Burning*!' (Q. 22: 19-22)

> *But those, whose balance is light, will be those who have lost their souls; in Hell will they abide. The fire will burn their faces, and they will therein grin, with their lips displaced.* (Q. 23: 103-104)

Dostoyevsky also saw a blinding flash of light. Then he would cry out and lose consciousness for a second or two. Sometimes the epileptic discharge generalized across his brain, producing a secondary tonic-clonic (grand mal) seizure. Afterward he could not recall events and conversations that had occurred during the seizure, and he often felt depressed, guilty, and irritable for days.

Count Leo Tolstoy: The great nineteenth century Russian author of *Anna Karenina* and *War and Peace*, also may have had epilepsy.

Gustave Flaubert: is another great name in literature. This nineteenth century French literary genius wrote such masterpieces as *Madame Bovary* and *A Sentimental Education.* According to Schachter, "Flaubert's typical seizure began with a feeling of impending doom, after which he felt his sense of self grow insecure, as if he had been transported into another dimension. He wrote that his seizures arrived as 'a whirlpool of ideas and images in my poor brain, during which it seemed that my consciousness sank like a vessel in a storm.' He moaned, had a rush of memories, saw fiery hallucinations, foamed at the mouth, moved his right arm automatically, fell into a trance of about ten minutes, and vomited."

Dame Agatha Christie: the leading British writer of mystery novels is also reported to have had epilepsy.

Truman Capote: American author of *In Cold Blood* and *Breakfast at Tiffany's.*

George Frederick Handel: the famous baroque composer of the *Messiah.*

Niccolo Paganini: one of the greatest violinists.

Peter Tchaikovsky: The eminent Russian composer of the ballets *Sleeping Beauty* and *The Nutcracker*.

Ludwig van Beethoven: One of the greatest classical composers ever.

Schachter says, this is just a sampling of the many, many famous people whose epilepsy has been recorded by historians. In fact the list of famous people diagnosed or suspected for having epilepsy is long. Muhammad is not among bad company. His imaginative power, his depression, his suicidal thoughts, his irritability, his interest in religion, his vision of the Doomsday and the afterlife, his visual and auditory hallucinations and many of his physical and psychological characteristics can all be explained by TLE.

However, epilepsy does not explain Muhammad's ruthlessness, his lack of empathy, his mass murders, and his dogged determination. Those were the results of his narcissistic personality disorder. It was this combination of personality and mental disorders that made him the phenomenon that he became. Muhammad harbored thoughts of grandiosity and omnipotence. His epileptic visions reaffirmed his megalomania and gave him the confirmation that he was indeed the chosen prophet of God. As if that were not enough, he married a co-dependent woman who sought her own greatness in lionizing her husband and encouraging his madness.

Muhammad was convinced of his prophetic mission. It was this self-assurance that inspired those who were close to him and confirmed their faith. This does not mean that all the verses of the Quran have been "revealed" to him during his epileptic trances. The seizures probably stopped after a few years. However, convinced of his righteousness, he kept reciting verses as situation dictated. As a narcissist, he received his confirmation from his followers. It is difficult to say who was fooling whom. Muhammad was convinced of his claim – even though he freely lied, making up verses as he needed them – and yet, when people believed in him he was reconfirmed. As a result, he's thought that he was vested with divine authority to exact punishment on those who disagreed with him. He was the voice of God and opposition to him meant opposition to the Almighty. He felt entitled to lie. It was for a good cause and therefore justified. When he looted and massacred, he did it with a clear conscience. The end was so august that he deemed all means to achieve it are legitimate. He was so convinced that it felt right to kill anyone who stood in his way. The following Qura'nic verses are self-explanatory.

> *And whoever disobeys Allah and His Messenger and goes beyond His limits, He will cause him to enter fire to abide in it, and he shall have an abasing chastisement.* (Q.4:14)

> *On that day will those who disbelieve and disobey the Messenger desire that the earth were leveled with them, and they shall not hide any word from Allah.* (Q.4:42)

> *Whoever disobeys Allah and His Messenger surely he shall have the fire of hell to abide therein for a long time.* (Q. 72:23)

3- Muhammad's Ecstatic Experiences

Sexuality, Religious Experience and Temporal Lobe Hyper Activation

The collections of hadiths shed a lot of light into Muhammad's sexual conduct. Does TLE affect sexuality as well? If it does and if it can explain Muhammad's sexual habits, then we have one more piece of evidence that he suffered from TLE. Neuroscientist Rhawn Joseph thinks it does. He writes:

> A not uncommon characteristic of high levels of limbic system and inferior temporal lobe activity are changes in sexuality as well as a deepening of religious fervor. It is noteworthy that not just modern day evangelists, but many ancient religious leaders, including Abraham, Jacob, and Muhammad, tended to be highly sexual and partook of many partners, or had sex with other men's wives, or killed other men in order to steal their wives (Muhammad, King David)... Many of the prophets and other religious figures also displayed evidence of the Kluver-Bucy syndrome, such as eating dung (Ezekiel),262 as well as temporal lobe, limbic hyper activation and epilepsy, coupled with hallucinations, catalepsy, insanity, or language disorders.
>
> Whereas Moses suffered from a severe speech impediment, Muhammad, Allah's messenger, was apparently dyslexic and agraphic. [A cerebral disorder characterized by total or partial inability to write] Moreover, in order to receive the word of God, Muhammad would typically lose consciousness and enter into trance states (Armstrong 1994; Lings 1983). In fact, he had his first truly spiritual-religious conversion when he was torn from his sleep by the archangel Gabriel who enveloped him in a terrifying embrace so overpowering that Muhammad's breath was squeezed from his lungs. After squeezing and suffocating him repeatedly Gabriel ordered Muhammad to speak the word of God, i.e. the Quran. This was the first of many such episodes with the archangel Gabriel who sometimes appeared to Muhammad in a titanic kaleidoscopic panoramic form.
>
> In accordance with the voice of 'God' or his angels, Muhammad not only spoke but he began reciting and chanting various themes of God in a random order over the course of the following 23 years; an experience he found quite painful and wrenching (Armstrong 1994; Lings 1983). In addition to his religious zest, Muhammad was reported to have the sexual prowess of forty men, and to have bedded at least 9 wives and numerous concubines including even one young girl (Lings 1983). On one occasion, after being rebuffed, he went into a trance, and then claimed 'God' had commanded that another man's wife become his wife.
>
> He [Muhammad] was also known to fly into extreme rages and to kill (or at least order killed) infidels and merchants and those who opposed him. These behaviors when coupled with his increased sexuality, heightened religious fervor, trance states,

[262] Muhammad prescribed camel urine for stomachache. He certainly must have drauk it himself. Camel urine is sold in Islamic countries as remedy, even today.

mood swings, and possible auditory and visual hallucinations of a titanic angel, certainly point to the limbic system and inferior temporal lobe as the possible neurological foundation for these experiences. Indeed, Muhammad also suffered from horrible depressions and on one occasion sought to throw himself from a cliff – only to be stopped by the archangel Gabriel.[263]

[263] The Limbic System And The Soul From: Zygon, the Journal of Religon and Science (in press, March, 2001) by Rhawn Joseph, Ph.D. http://brainmind.com/BrainReligion.html

Chapter Four

Other Mental Disorders

Narcissism is frequently accompanied by a series of co-morbidities. Likewise, clinically, the sufferer of TLE is commonly diagnosed as having a variety of psychiatric illnesses. In psychiatry, psychology and mental health counseling, co-morbidity refers to the presence of more than one diagnosis occurring in an individual at the same time. In this chapter we'll explore the presence of several co-morbidities in Muhammad starting with the most obvious.

Obsessive-Compulsive Disorder (OCD)

According to Canadian Mental Health Association, Obsessive-Compulsive Disorder is an anxiety disorder - one of a group of medical disorders, which affects the thoughts, behavior, emotions, and sensations.

> Collectively, these disorders are among the most common of mental health problems. It is estimated that 1 in 10 people suffers from an anxiety disorder sometime in their life... For people with obsessive-compulsive disorder, obsession creates a maze of persistent thoughts. Those thoughts lead them to act out rituals (compulsions), sometimes for hours a day... Worries and doubts, superstitions and rituals are common to most everyone. OCD occurs when worries become obsessions and the compulsive rituals so excessive that they dominate a person's life. It's as if the brain is a scratched vinyl record, forever skipping at the same groove and repeating one fragment of song.
>
> Obsessions are persistent ideas, thoughts, impulses or images; they are intrusive and illogical. Common OCD obsessions revolve around contamination, doubts, and disturbing sexual or religious thoughts... Often, a person's obsessions are accompanied by feelings of fear, disgust and doubt, or the belief that certain activities have to be done just so... People with OCD try to relieve their obsessions by performing compulsive rituals, over and over again, and often according to certain "rules."
>
> Children with OCD appear to be more likely to have additional psychiatric problems. They may suffer from conditions such as panic disorder or social phobia, depression,

> learning disorders, tic disorders, disruptive behavior disorders, and body dysmorphic disorder (imagined ugliness).[264]

Based on the above definition it is very likely that Muhammad may have suffered from OCD. Prayer is conversation with God. There are no rules to follow when conversing with God. All we need is to direct our attention to Him. But that is not what Muhammad thought. He was obsessed with rituals, such as how to perform ablution; how many times to stand pray and how they should be executed. He explained in minute details how to wash one's hands, face, nose, ears, etc., and in which order. All these rituals, including the various positions that the worshipper should assume while praying, are meaningless. Communication with God does not require rituals. Yet to Muhammad, they were crucial, to the extent that he thought if a detail of these rituals is missed, the prayer would not be accepted.

Prayer is conversation with God. To Muhammad it was a chore that the individuals had to perform in order to collect reward points and then cash them in the Day of Judgment. The quality of prayer is not important; it is the quantity that matters. Every prayer fetches a point and every prayer lost makes you lose several points. The personal relationship between God and man that is so pivotal in Christianity is complexly absent in Islam. The relationship is not that of father and child, but that of a slave master and his slaves. Instead of love, the emphasis is placed on obedience and fear of God. There is not a word about God's love for humans. The reason Allah created people is so that they worship him and server him, and to use them a fuels in hell if they fail to do so.

Muhammad's obsession with rituals can only be understood through Obsessive Compulsive Disorder. OCD sufferers are obsessed with patterns, rituals, and numbers. Mohammad was fixated with number three. There are many rituals that Muslims are required to perform three times. There is no logical explanation for it except for the fact that it is a *sunnah* (tradition) of Muhammad. The following are the rituals that the believer must perform before praying:

- Declare the intention that the act is for the purpose of worship.
- Rinse out the mouth with water three times
- Cleanse the nostrils by sniffing water in to them three times.
- Wash the whole face three times.
- Wash the right arm three times up to the far end of the elbow and then do the same with the left arm.
- Wipe the whole head or any part of it with a wet hand once.
- Wipe the inner sides of the ears with the forefingers and their outer sides with the thumbs. This should be done with wet fingers.

---

[264] http://www.cmha.ca/bins/content_page.asp?cid=3-94-95

- Wipe around the neck with wet hands.
- Wash the two feet up to the ankles three times beginning with the right foot.

What is the meaning of washing three times? What is the point of wiping one's head, neck or feet with wet hand? Why wash the right hand first? These and countless other rituals like these have nothing to do with cleanliness or spirituality.

Muhammad's obsession with rituals becomes further evident through what is known as *tayammum*. When water is not available, or for any reason it cannot be used, he prescribed *tayammum*. It is performed as follows:

- Strike both hands slightly on earth or sand or stone.
- Shake the hands off and wipe the face with them once in the same way as done in the ablution.
- Strike the hands again and wipe the right arm to the elbow with the left hand and the left arm with the right hand.

These rituals are absurd. The same can be said about positions for performing prayer, such as *qiyaam* (standing), *sujud* (prostrating), *ruku'* (bowing) and *jalsa* (sitting). Islam is full of rituals that make no sense. They reveal Muhammad's obsession with patterns and numbers and makes us conclude that he suffered from OCD.

The following are a few rituals considered to be the sunnah of Muhammad that Muslims follow meticulously. They have no meaning whatsoever. Yet, Muhammad thought that disregarding them will bring punishment upon the offender while their observance will bring reward. Pious is one who observes these rules.

- To sit and eat on the floor.
- To eat with the right hand.
- To eat from the side that is in front of you.
- To remove your shoes before eating.
- When eating, to sit with either both knees on the ground or one knee raised or both knees raised.
- Whilst eating one should not remain completely silent.
- To eat with three fingers.
- One should not eat very hot food.
- Do not blow on the food.
- After eating one should lick his fingers.
- A Muslim should drink with the right hand. Satan drinks with the left hand.
- To sit and drink.
- To drink in 3 breaths removing the utensil from the mouth after each sip.
- To make the bed yourself.
- To dust the bed thrice before retiring to bed.
- To sleep on the right hand side.

- To sleep with the right palm under the right cheek.
- To keep the knees slightly bent when sleeping.
- To face Qiblah.
- To recite Surah Ikhlaas, Surah Falaq, and Surah Naas before sleeping 3 times and thereafter blow over the entire body thrice.
- On awakening to rub the face and the eyes with the palms of the hands.
- When putting on any garment RasulAllah (the messenger of Allah) always began with the right limb.
- When removing a garment RasullAllah always removed the left limb first.
- Males must wear the pants above the ankles. Females should ensure that their lower garment covers their ankles.
- Males should wear a turban. Females must wear scarves at all times.
- When wearing shoes, first wear the right shoe then the left.
- When removing them first remove the left and then the right.
- To enter the toilet with your head covered.
- To recite the dua (prayer) before entering the toilet.
- To enter with the left foot.
- To sit and urinate. One should never urinate whilst standing.
- To leave the toilet with the right foot.
- To recite the dua after coming out of the toilet.
- One should not face Qiblah or show his back towards the Qiblah.
- Do not speak in the toilet.
- Be very careful of the splashes of urine (being unmindful in this regard causes one to be punished in the grave).
- Using a miswaak (wooden tooth brush) is a great sunnah of Rasulullah. One who makes miswaak when making wuzu and thereafter performs salaah will receive 70 times more reward. To take a Ghusl bath on a Friday.
- To keep a beard that is one fist in length.
- To carry ones shoes in the left hand.
- To enter the masjid (mosque) with the right foot.
- To leave the masjid with the left foot.[265]

Aisha narrated a story about Muhammad that is further evidence of his OCD.

> When it was my turn for Allah's Messenger (may peace be upon him) to spend the night with me, he turned his side, put on his mantle and took off his shoes and placed them near his feet, and spread the corner of his shawl on his bed and then lay down

---

[265] http://www.scribd.com/doc/2252573/sunnahs-of-ap-s-a-w Available all over the Internet.

> till he thought that I had gone to sleep. He took hold of his mantle slowly and put on the shoes slowly, and opened the door and went out and then closed it lightly. I covered my head, put on my veil and tightened my waist wrapper, and then went out following his steps till he reached Baqi' (cemetery). He stood there and he stood for a long time. He then lifted his hands three times, and then returned and I also returned. He hastened his steps and I also hastened my steps. He ran and I too ran. He came (to the house) and I also came (to the house). I, however, preceded him and I entered (the house), and as I lay down in the bed, he (the Holy Prophet) entered the (house), and said: Why is it, O 'A'isha, that you are out of breath? I said: There is nothing. He said: Tell me or the Subtle and the Aware would inform me. I said: Messenger of Allah, may my father and mother be ransom for you, and then I told him (the whole story). He said: Was it the darkness (of your shadow) that I saw in front of me? I said: Yes. He struck me on the chest which caused me pain, and then said: Did you think that Allah and His Apostle would deal unjustly with you? She said: Whatsoever the people conceal, Allah will know it. He said: Gabriel came to me when you saw me. He called me and he concealed it from you. I responded to his call, but I too concealed it from you (for he did not come to you), as you were not fully dressed. I thought that you had gone to sleep, and I did not like to awaken you, fearing that you may be frightened. He (Gabriel) said: Your Lord has commanded you to go to the inhabitants of Baqi' (to those lying in the graves) and beg pardon for them. I said: Messenger of Allah, how should I pray for them (How should I beg forgiveness for them)? He said: Say, Peace be upon the inhabitants of this city (graveyard) from among the Believers and the Muslims, and may Allah have mercy on those who have gone ahead of us, and those who come later on, and we shall, God willing, join you.[266]

Why would God order his prophet to go to the cemetery in the middle of the night to ask Him for forgiveness for the dead? Can't He forgive them without inconveniencing His prophet in such odd hours? If he has decided to forgive those dead people, why does he need that Muhammad lobby for them? Ironically, his strange behavior was interpreted by his followers as evidence of his prophethood. He was odd. He did things that no one else did or could understand, so he must be a prophet, they reasoned.

He admonished his followers, "Save your heels from the fire"[267] by wiping them with wet hand. It was not cleanliness that concerned Muhammad, but the ritual itself. He thought one can save himself from hellfire by passing wet hand over one's feet or even socks. Bukhari says Muhammad wiped his feet while wearing leather socks. "Narrated Al-Mughira bin Shu'ba: 'I was in the company of Allah's Apostle on one of the journeys… I poured water and he performed ablution; he washed his face, forearms and passed his wet hand over his head and over the two Khuff, (leather socks).'"[268]

---

[266] Sahih Muslim Book 4, Number 2127

[267] Bukhari Volume 1, Book 3, Number 57

[268] Bukhari Volume 1, Book 4, Number 182

In another hadith Bukhari quotes Humran, (the slave of 'Othman):

> I saw 'Othman bin 'Affan asking for a tumbler of water (and when it was brought) he poured water over his hands and washed them thrice and then put his right hand in the water container and rinsed his mouth, washed his nose by putting water in it and then blowing it out. Then he washed his face and forearms up to the elbows thrice, passed his wet hands over his head and washed his feet up to the ankles thrice. Then he said, "Allah's Apostle said 'If anyone Performs ablution like that of mine and offers a two-rak'at prayer during which he does not think of anything else (not related to the present prayer) then his past sins will be forgiven.'" [Then he added] "I heard the Prophet saying, 'If a man performs ablution perfectly and then offers the compulsory congregational prayer, Allah will forgive his sins committed between that (prayer) and the (next) prayer till he offers it.[269]

This is unreasonable. Only one suffering from OCD can think that one's sins can be forgiven by performing certain rituals.

Compulsions are defined by repetitive behaviors or mental acts that the person is driven to perform according to rules that must be applied rigidly, and by behaviors or mental acts that are aimed at preventing or reducing distress or preventing some dreaded event or situation, such as hell.

Islam is full of meaningless rules and rituals. The rules of *wudu* (ablusion), *ghosl* (bathing), *salat* (obligatory prayer) and the very fact that it is obligatory, *hajj,* fasting, etc., show that Muhammad was obsessed with rituals. He even said how many pebbles one must use to clean one's private part after excreting. (They must be odd numbers, if you must know, and preferably three. Three pebbles clean better than four.)

In one hadith he said, "When one of you passes urine, he should empty his penis three times." The Ayatollahs of Iran have concluded that any urine dripping on the cloths after the penis is squeezed three times is clean and it does not annul the prayer.

Schizophrenia

Schizophrenia is the disease of thought disorder of inappropriate emotions and of inappropriate attribution of things. It is a disease of cognitive abnormalities and abnormal sequential thoughts.

Auditory hallucinations, paranoid or bizarre delusions, or disorganized speech and thinking are some of the symptoms of Schizophrenia. There are also signs of and symptoms associated with impaired occupational or social function. The symptoms typically occur in young adulthood and last a lifetime.

Apart from one trip Muhammad made to Syria as the *amin* (trustee) of Khadijah, he did not engage in any occupation. He was also withdrawn and used to

[269] Bukhari Volume 1, Book 4, Number 161:

spend his days in a cave alone. This satisfies the criterion of impaired occupational and social function. Prior to his prophetic enterprise, Muhammad was a loner. His only occupation before marrying Khadijah was herding family goats, where interaction with others was kept to minimum. At one point, when he tried to act like a normal youth and sneaked into a wedding party, he felt dizzy and was weighed down by excruciating spasms.

The same Muhammad who became a sexual butterfly at his old age, during his youth was unable to establish normal relationships with members of the opposite sex and remained a virgin until Khadijah proposed to him. Schizoid personality disorder can explain this behavior. The Diagnostic and Statistics Manual of Mental Health IV explains,

> Schizophrenia falls in two broad categories: positive and negative. The positive symptoms appear to reflect an excess or distortion of normal functions, whereas the negative symptoms appear to reflect diminution or loss of normal functions. The positive symptoms involve distortion of thoughts (delusions), perception (hallucinations), language and thought process (disorganized speech), and grossly disorganized or catatonic behavior. Negative symptoms include restrictions in range and intensity of emotional expression, (affective, flattening), in the fluency and productivity of thought and speech, and in the initiation of goal-directed behavior. Delusions are erroneous beliefs. Their content may include a variety of themes (e.g. persecutory, referential, somatic, religious or grandiose). Persecutory delusions are most common; the person believes he or she is being tormented, followed, tricked, spied on, or ridiculed. Referential delusions are also common; the person believes that certain gestures, comments, passages from books, newspapers, song lyrics, or other environmental cues are specifically directed at him or her. The distinction between a delusion and a strongly held idea is sometimes difficult to make and depends in part on the degree of conviction with which the belief is held despite clear contradictory evidence regarding its veracity. Although bizarre delusions are considered to be especially characteristic of Schizophrenia, "bizarreness" may be difficult to judge, especially across different cultures. Delusions are deemed bizarre if they are clearly implausible and not understandable and do not derive from ordinary life experiences. An example of a bizarre delusion is a person's belief that a stranger has removed his or her internal organs and has replaced them with someone else's organs without leaving any wounds or scars. An example of a non-bizarre delusion is a person's false belief that he or she is under surveillance by the police. Delusions that express a loss of control over mind or body are generally considered to be bizarre; these include a person's belief that his or her thoughts have been taken away by some outside force ("thought withdrawal"), that alien thoughts have been put into his or her mind ("thought insertion"), or that his or her body or actions are being acted on or manipulated by some outside force ("delusions of control"). If the delusions are judged to be bizarre, only this single symptom is needed to satisfy Criterion A for Schizophrenia."[270]

[270] Diagnostic and Statistics Manual of Mental Disorder IV, p. 299

As per above, the story of magic being worked out on Muhammad making him believe he had sexual intercourse with his wives when he did not, and his claim that he saw two men standing over him and discussing his condition as narrated by Aisha (quoted in the previous chapter), are enough to diagnose Muhammad with Schizophrenia. Another clue to his delusional thinking is his claim that two men in white threw him on the ground, pulled out his heart and after washing it with snow replaced it without leaving any scar.

Muhammad's strange belief that Jews and Christians had found out that he was their promised prophet foretold in their sacred books and consequently were after him to kill him is another sign of his schizophrenia. The absurdity of such claim is enough to diagnose Muhammad with persecutory delusion, which is a criterion of Schizophrenia.

During his youth, up to the time he launched his prophetic carrier and surrounded himself with, not peers, but votaries and adulators, Muhammad was a loner. Only as a superior being he felt at ease in the company of other people. Until then he appeared aloof, dull, and humorless. He was ignored in social settings. During his formative years he showed a flattened and restricted range of emotions and appeared indifferent to what was going on around him. At the same time his inner life was rife with deep emotional needs, sensitivity, and confusion about the world around him. People with schizoid personality are either incapable of initiating and maintaining personal relationships or find themselves suffocated and anxious in the company of others. They retreat into their inner worlds. If they seek relationship it's for security.[271]

SPD is considered part of the "schizophrenic spectrum" of disorders, which includes schizotypal and schizophrenia. These conditions have similar symptoms, such as an incapacity for social relations and emotional inexpressiveness. The main distinction is that people with schizoid personality don't usually experience the perceptual distortions or illusions characteristic of schizotypal personality or the psychotic episodes of schizophrenia.[272] Muhammad had strange supernatural beliefs, and visions of ghosts, angels, demons, and jinns. He claimed to have visited the city of jinns and spend a night in their midst.

Signs of schizotypal personality disorder in adolescence may begin as gravitation towards solitary activity or high level of social anxiety. The child may be an underperformer or appear socially out-of-step with peers. This is very much true in the case of Muhammad had no childhood friends, did not play with other kids, did not frequent feasts and despite belonging to nobility, did not attend school and remained illiterate. All his uncles and even aunts could read and write, but not him.

---

[271] http://www.mayoclinic.com/health/schizoid-personality-DS00865/DSECTION=symptomsdisorder/
[272] Ibid.

4- Other Mental Disorders

Paranoid schizophrenia

With paranoid schizophrenia, the ability to think and function in daily life is better than with other types of schizophrenia. The patient may not have as many problems with memory, concentration, or dulled emotions. Still, paranoid schizophrenia is a serious, lifelong condition that can lead to many complications, including suicidal behavior.

Signs and symptoms of paranoid schizophrenia may include:

- Auditory hallucinations, such as hearing voices
- Delusions, such as believing a co-worker wants to poison you
- Anxiety
- Anger
- Aloofness
- Violence
- Verbal confrontations
- Patronizing manner
- Suicidal thoughts and behavior

With paranoid schizophrenia, the patient is less likely to be affected by mood problems or problems with thinking, concentration, and attention. Instead, he is most affected by what are known as positive symptoms.

Positive symptoms are symptoms that indicate the presence of unusual thoughts and perceptions that often involve a loss of contact with reality. Delusions and hallucinations are considered positive symptoms of paranoid schizophrenia.

- **Delusions:** In paranoid schizophrenia, delusions are often focused on the perception that you're being singled out for harm. Your brain misinterprets experiences and you hold on to these false beliefs despite evidence to the contrary. For instance, you may believe that the government is monitoring every move you make or that a co-worker is poisoning your lunch. (Remember Muhammad's comments about his grandfather recommending his wet nurse to not let Jews and Christians find him lest they may injure him? Or suddenly leaving the quarter of the Banu Nadir and later claiming that Gabriel informed him the Jews were plotting to throw a stone on his head? He might have actually thought so.) The patient may also have delusions of grandeur — for example, the belief that he can fly, that he is famous, or that has a relationship with a famous person. This explains Muhammad's delusion about being the chosen prophet of Allah or that his saliva having miraculous curative effect. Delusions can result in aggression or violence. The patient believes he must act in self-defense against those who want to harm him.
- **Auditory hallucinations:** An auditory hallucination is the perception of sound — usually voices — that no one else hears. The sounds may be a single voice or many voices. These voices may talk either to the patient or to each other. The voices are usually unpleasant. They may give a running critique of what you're thinking or doing, or they may harass you about real or imagined faults. Voices may also command you to

do things that can be harmful to yourself or to others. When you have paranoid schizophrenia, these voices seem real. You may talk to or shout at the voices.[273]

Muhammad thought magic was worked on him so that he thought that he had sexual relations with his wives when he did not. He heard two men standing over him discussing his condition and in childhood, he saw two men pulling his heart out and washing it. These were all hallucinations. Of course his ascension to heaven and Gabriel were also hallucination.

Apart from false beliefs, held with conviction in spite of reason, hallucinations, disorganized thoughts, restlessness, and violent/aggressive behavior, there is one particular syndrome that also characterizes schizophrenia: 'catatonic behavior,' in which the affected person's body becomes rigid and the person may be unresponsive.[274]

Muhammad's disorganized thoughts can be ascertained through the Quran. He was violent and restless. In just ten years, he launched over seventy raids. As for his catatonic behavior, a syndrome characterized by muscular rigidity and mental stupor, it is enough to quote his cousin Ali, who grew up in his house and spent more time with him than any of his companions. Ali said, "When he [Muhammad] walked he would lift his feet with vigor, as if walking up a slope. When he turned towards a person he would turn with his entire body."[275]

Muhammad's childhood, visual and auditory hallucinations, are also telltales that he may have had childhood schizophrenia, a type of chronic mental illness in that reality is interpreted abnormally (psychosis), with a profound impact on a child's ability to function. Childhood schizophrenia includes hallucinations, delusions, irrational behavior, and thinking.

Paranoid Personality Disorder

Paranoia does not always involve hallucination. Muhammad's constant persecutory delusions and his violent reaction to his perceived enemies strongly suggest that he suffered from paranoia. Paranoid patient becomes a prey to premature delusion. The cause of delusion may be internal, with no hallucination involved.

The main symptom is permanent delusion. There is delusion in schizophrenia also, but in the case of paranoia it is organized and permanent. In paranoia the symptoms of delusion appear gradually, and the patient is suspicious, irritable, introverted, depressed, obstinate, jealous, selfish, unsocial and bitter. The

---

[273] http://www.mayoclinic.com/health/schizoid-personality-DS00865/DSECTION=symptomsdisorder/
[274] www.emedicinehealth.com/schizophrenia/article_em.htm
[275] The Book of Merits (manaqib) in Sunan Imam at-Tirmidhi. www.naqshbandi.asn.au/description.htm

4- Other Mental Disorders

"Diagnostic and Statistical Manual of Mental Disorders", fourth edition (DSM-IV), lists the following symptoms for paranoid personality disorder:

- preoccupied with unsupported doubts about friends or associates
- suspicious; unfounded suspicions; believes others are plotting against him/her
- perceives attacks on his/her reputation that are not clear to others, and is quick to counterattack
- maintains unfounded suspicions regarding the fidelity of a spouse or significant other
- reads negative meanings into innocuous remarks
- secrecy and reluctant to confide in others.

Many of these symptoms were present in Muhammad. His delusions about Jews and Christians wanting to kill him because they had found that he is their promised prophet, his paranoia about men looking at his wives, his secretiveness and his inability to trust even his companions, can be explained with PPD.

There are several types of paranoia:

1. **Persecutory paranoia** - This is the most prevalent type of paranoia, and in this patient makes himself believe that all those around him are his enemies, bent on harming him or even taking his life. In this delusion people of an aggressive temperament often turns dangerous killers.
2. **Delusion of Grandeur** - In this patient believes himself to be, a great individual, and according to Bleuler, this delusion of grandeur accompanies a persecutory delusion.
3. **Religious paranoia** - Here the patients suffer from a permanent delusion of a primarily religious nature. He for example believes that he is the messenger of God who has been sent to the world to propagate some religion.
4. **Reformatory paranoia** - In this the patient turns to considering himself a great reformer. He accordingly looks upon all those around him as suffering from dangerous disease, and believes that he is their reformer and curator.
5. **Erotic paranoia** - Here the patient often tends to believe that some members of the family of the opposite sex, belonging to an illustrious family, want to marry him. Such people even write love letters and thereby, cause much botheration to other people.
6. **Litigious paranoia** - In this kind the patient takes to feeling meaningless cases against other people and feels that people are linked together to bother him. Sometimes he even tries to murder.
7. **Hypochondrical paranoia** - In this kind the patients believes that he is suffering from all kind of ridiculous diseases, and also that some other people are to blame for his suffering.[276]

---

[276] http://www.depression-guide.com/paranoia.htm

Bipolar Disorder:

As if all the above is not enough, Muhammad may have also been a manic-depressive (a more popular name for bipolar disorder). Bipolar disorder causes dramatic mood swings—from overly "high" and/or irritable to sad and hopeless, and then back again, often with periods of normal mood in between. The periods of highs and lows are called episodes of mania and depression. Extreme mood swings punctuated by periods of even-keeled behavior characterize this disorder.

The symptoms of BD in the manic phase are irritability, inflated self-esteem, decreased need for sleep, increased energy, racing thoughts, feelings of invulnerability, poor judgment, heightened sex drive, and denial that anything is wrong. In the depressed phase, feelings of hopelessness or worthlessness, or melancholy, fatigue, thoughts of death or suicide, and suicide attempts.

Ibn Sa'd reports a hadith that fits the bill. He writes: "Sometimes the Prophet used to fast so much, as if he did not want to end it, and sometimes he would not fast for so long that one thought he did not want to fast at all."[277]

Muhammad was most likely suffering from a variety of disorders. My objective is not to prescribe medication. I may have misdiagnosed him in some cases. My goal is to provide an alternative explanation to his eccentric behavior that his followers thought is the sign of his prophethood. According to Occam's razor, one should not make more assumptions than the minimum needed to explain anything. If mental illnesses explain the mystique of Muhammad, why resort to metaphysics, and unsubstantiated mystical claims? Evidence suggests that Muhammad was most likely, mentally infirm. His contemporaries knew that. Even though they could not diagnose him, they suspected that he was a mad man.

It is no wonder that Islamic countries are in such a deplorable state of misery. To the extent that they follow Muhammad they are more wretched. When sane people follow an insane man they act insanely.

The Mystery of the Cave Hira

One friend, while proof reading this book made an interesting observation about the Oracles of Delphi that may explain why Muhammad received his prophetic intimation in a cave.

The Oracle of Delphi was an ancient Greek temple site. People came from all over Europe to call on the Pythia at Mount Parnassus to have their questions about the future answered. The Pythia, a role filled by different women, was the medium through whom the god Apollo spoke.

---

[277] Tabaqat, Volume 1, Page 371

4- Other Mental Disorders

Plutarch, a priest at the Temple of Apollo, attributed Pythia's prophetic powers to vapors that came from a chasm in the ground. A recent study of the area in the vicinity of the shrine is causing archaeologists to revisit the notion that intoxicating fumes loosened the lips of the Pythia.[278]

The study, reported in the August 2001 issue of *National Geology,* reveals that two faults intersect directly below the Delphic temple. The study also found evidence of hallucinogenic gases rising from a nearby spring and preserved within the temple rock.

"Plutarch made the right observation. Indeed there were gases that came through the fractures," says Jelle De Boer, a geologist at Wesleyan University in Middletown, Connecticut, and co-author of the study. One of the gases was ethylene that he found in the spring water near the site of the Delphi temple. Ethylene has a sweet smell and produces a narcotic effect described as a floating or disembodied euphoria.

Diane Harris-Cline, a classics professor at The George Washington University in Washington, D.C. believes that Ethylene is a serious contender for explaining the trance and behavior of Pythia. "Combined with social expectations, a woman in a confined space could be induced to spout off oracles," she said. [279]

According to traditions, the Pythia derived her prophecies in a small, enclosed chamber in the basement of the temple. De Boer believes that if the Pythia went to the chamber once a month, as tradition says, she could have been exposed to concentrations of the narcotic gas that were strong enough to induce a trance-like state.

It is likely that the cave Hira may have contained euphoric gasses, which made Muhammad want to spend most of his time there. Although he had several epileptic trances, since his childhood, we must not discard the possibility that Cave Hira may have trapped hallucinogenic vapors that triggered his visions. If ethylene in mild doses causes euphoria, this could explain why Muhammad was so keen to spend days on end in that cave. It certainly is peculiar behavior, especially for a family man, to take off with several days' provision of food, just to stay in a cave! If something in the caves made him feel euphoric, his retreats seem a little less mysterious.

Cave Hira is about 3.5 meter by 1.5 – the size of a small bathroom. If God is omnipresent, why would Muhammad be so interested in this particular cave?

Apart from toxic gases, fungi, and microbial agents present in caves and other enclosed spaces can also affect the brain. The "curse of the Pharaohs," turned out to be largely caused by a deadly fungus growing in the pyramids.

Concentration of vapors in caves fluctuates. It depends on earthquakes that keep Earth's narcotic juices flowing. The possibility that Cave Hira may have been contaminated when Muhammad used to spend days therein alone should not be discarded.

---

[278] John Roach for National Geographic News August 14, 2001 http://news.nationalgeographic.com/news/2001/08/0814_delphioracle.html

[279] ibid.

Chapter Five

Physical Ailments

hysically, Muhammad was also a sick man. From his descriptions in the hadith, we can detect at least two of them: acromegaly, the disease that killed him and impotence.

Acromegaly

Acromegaly is a rare disease with a reported annual incidence of 3 per million population. The clinical presentation of acromegaly consists of both physical features, which are characteristic and psychological symptoms.

In his youth, Muhammad must have been handsome enough, at least for Khadijah, a becoming woman herself, to become attracted to. However, in the last years of his life he acquired odd features that his companions found strange. Anas narrated, "The Prophet had big hands and feet, and I have not seen anybody like him, neither before nor after him, and his palms were soft."[280]

In addition to his extremities, his facial features also grew out of proportion. Imam at-Tirmidhi, in the *Book of Merits* (manaqib) has collected several hadiths that describe Muhammad's physical characteristics.[281] A review of them provide us with clues about his state of health and ailments.

His followers have gone out of their way to describe their prophet superlatively – praising his radiance, describing how his beauty surpassed that of the moon, and

[280] Bukhari Volume 7, Book 72, Number 793

[281] Abū ʿĪsā Muħammad ibn ʿĪsā ibn Mūsā ibn ad-Dahhāk as-Sulamī at-Tirmidhī (824-892) was a collector of hadith. His collection, Sunan al-Tirmidhi, is one of the six canonical hadith compilations used in Sunni Islam. The following hadiths are from his collections.

how everyone stood in awe of his moon-like beauty and awe inspiring presence, etc. These are subjective descriptions and of little use to us.

The following are some of his followers' more objective descriptions of him, taken from Tabaqat.[282]

> Ali narrates: "The Prophet was neither tall nor short. He has thick-set fingers and toes. He had a large head and joints. He had a long line of thin chest-to-lower-navel hair. When he walked he would literally lean forward, as if descending a slope. I never saw anyone like him before or after him. He was large of head and beard."
>
> In another hadith the same narrator says: "He was of medium stature. His hair was slightly waved. There was roundness in his face. He was fair with redness in his complexion. His eyes were very black and his eyelashes very long. He had a large back and shoulder-joints. He had thick-set fingers and toes. When he walked he would lift his feet with vigor, as if walking up a slope. When he turned towards a person he would turn with his entire body. His neck seemed (smooth and shiny) like that of a statue molded in silver. His body was stout and muscular, of equal belly and chest (barbell like). He was wide-shouldered, big- jointed. When he disrobed his limbs emanated light (oily skin). There was hair on his arms, shoulders, and upper torso. His forearms were long, his palms wide, his fingers and toes thick-set and extended. His feet were so smooth that water rolled off them."
>
> Hind ibn Abi Hala, has also reported: "The Prophet… had a large head. His hair was wavy. He had a rosy complexion, a wide forehead, arched dense eyebrows that did not meet in the middle. Between them there was a vein which thickened when he was angry. He had an aquiline nose touched with a light that raised it so that at first sight it seemed higher than it was. He had a thick, dense beard, expanded, not elevated cheeks, a strong mouth with a gap between his front teeth. His neck seemed smooth and shiny like that of a statue molded in silver. His body was well-proportioned, stout and muscular, of equal belly and chest. He was wide-shouldered, big- jointed. His forearms were long, his palms wide, his fingers and toes thick-set and extended. The middle of his soles rose moderately from the ground. His feet were so smooth that water rolled off them.
>
> When he walked he lifted his feet with vigor, leaned slightly forward, and tread gently on the ground. When he turned (to look), he turned his whole body. His gaze was lowered and he looked at the ground more often than he looked at the sky. He glanced at things rather than stared."
>
> A hadith from another companion of Muhammad, Jabir ibn Samura reports: The Prophet had a wide mouth and wide eyes.

---

[282] Ibn Sa'd, Persian Tabaqat, v.1, p. 391

5- Physical Ailments

> Ibn Abbas, a cousin of Muhammad has claimed: "The Prophet's two front teeth were spaced in between."
>
> Again Ali said: "His hands and feet were heavy and thick [but not calloused]. He had a large head, large bones. When he walked, he leant forward as if going up a slope. He was white skinned, having a reddish tinge. His joints were large as was his upper back.

Bukhari also says that Muhammad's feet and legs were swollen.[283]

The following is a list of what we can learn from the hadiths about Muhammad's physical appearances.

- heavy and thick fleshy hands and feet
- wide and dough like palms
- large head
- large bones and joints
- wide chest, large upper back, and shoulder-joints
- long forearms
- long thick fingers and toes
- long, aquiline fleshy nose that looked upturned
- wide mouth and thick lips
- large eyes
- spaced teeth
- long silvery neck
- luster on his skin (looked oily)
- thick beard and hair, dense protruding eyebrows
- walked leaning forward as if ascending a slope (stiffness)
- walked briskly (restlessness)
- difficulty moving the neck and turned with full torso (catatonic behavior)
- had white skin with a reddish tinge
- sweating
- peculiar smell that he masked with excessive perfume
- snored like a camel
- suffered from head-ache (performed cupping to alleviate it)
- In later years he was impotent
- lips moved involuntarily
- was shy and prudish

---

[283] Bukhari Volume 2, Book 21, Number 230

These are all symptoms of acromegaly. Acromegaly is a rare endocrine syndrome characterized by mesenchymal hyperplasia (abnormal multiplication of cells that are capable of developing into connective tissues) caused by excessive secretion of pituitary gland. Its manifestation is usually extremely insidious, as it precociously develops with coetaneous alterations, (changes occurring at the same time), making the skin shiny and soft to the touch like dough. Overactive pituitary glands in children sometimes results in gigantism. The most common age at diagnosis for acromegaly is 40-45 years. If untreated, it can lead to severe illness and death that often occurs around the age of 60.

The main clinical aspect of this affliction is the elongation or intumescences of the cartilaginous tissue and acral bone ('*acro*' means extremity, while '*megaly*' refers to huge or gigantic). Fingers, hands and feet show an increase in size, as soft tissue begins to swell. A very characteristic case is Acromegaloid facial appearance syndrome, featuring a prominent forehead, mandibular protrusion, enlarged nose, large ears, enlargement of the tongue, and abnormal largeness of the lips. Overgrowth of bone and cartilage often leads to arthritis. When tissue thickens, it may trap nerves, causing carpal tunnel syndrome, characterized by numbness and weakness of the hands. Enlargement of the jaw, increases the spacing between teeth.[284]

Other symptoms are a deepening of the voice due to enlarged sinuses and vocal cords, snoring due to upper airway obstruction, excessive sweating, and skin odor, fatigue and weakness, headaches, impaired vision, and impotence in men. There may be enlargement of body organs, including the liver, spleen, kidneys and heart.[285]

In the description of Muhammad, we read that he had a rosy complexion. However, several other hadiths say that when he raised his hands showing his armpits, or when riding a horse exposing a thigh, his companions noticed the whiteness of his skin. Hyper pigmentation occurs in roughly 40% of cases of acromegaly and almost always in photo exposed areas (exposed to sunrays). That is why his face was reddish while the parts of his body not exposed to light were white.

Another symptom of acromegaly is the elevation of the dorsal-to-sole transition of the foot.[286] This too was reported in a hadith, quoted above.

Muhammad sweated excessively and had an unpleasant smell that he tried to camouflage with an abundance of perfume. Haykal quotes a hadith that says the scent that Muhammad used was so strong that its lingering smell would make people in the streets know that he had been there.

---

284 www.scielo.br/scielo.php?pid=S0365-05962004000400010&script=sci_arttext&tlng=en
285 http://endocrine.niddk.nih.gov/pubs/acro/acro.htm
286 www.scielo.br/scielo.php?pid=S0365-05962004000400010&script=sci_arttext&tlng=en

5- Physical Ailments

Jabir said: "Whoever pursues a road that has been trodden by the Messenger of Allah, will certainly scent his smell and will be quite sure that the Messenger of Allah has already passed it."[287]

Muhammad was also canny to use perfume prior to visiting his wives. In several hadiths Aisha says: "I applied perfume to the Messenger of Allah and he then went round his wives."[288] He so exaggerated in the use of perfume that Aisha commented, "I used to perfume Allah's Apostle with the best scent available till I saw the shine of the scent on his head and beard."[289]

Muhammad said, "Made beloved to me from your world are women and perfume."[290] One of his companions, Al-Hasan al-Basri, also wrote: "The Messenger of God said, "The only two things I cherish of the life of this world are women and perfume."[291]

Another version of this tradition narrated by Aisha says, "The Prophet of God liked three things of this world: Perfume, women, and food; he had the [first] two, but missed food."[292] It is not that Muhammad could not afford food. He had the wealth of thousands of people whom he had vanquished. The fact is that excessive appetite is yet another symptom of acromegaly.[293] Sometimes he ate so much that he could no eat more and sometimes he had no interest in food.

This excessive preoccupation with perfume suggests that Muhammad was wary of his bad odor and did his best to mask it. Another symptom of acromegaly is headache, which Muhammad tried to relieve with cupping.[294] Bukari reports, "The Prophet was cupped on his head for an ailment he was suffering from while he was in a state of Ihram (dresses for hajj) at a water place called Lahl Jamal. Ibn 'Abbas further said: Allah's Apostle was cupped on his head for unilateral headache while he was in a state of Ihram."[295]

Acromegaly causes high blood pressure and poor blood circulation in extremities. This results in cold hands and feet.

---

[287] Muhammad Husayn Haykal (1888, 1956): The Life of Muhammad, http://www.witness-pioneer.org/vil/Books/SM_tsn/ch7s12.html

[288] Sahih Muslim Book 007, Number 2700

[289] Volume 7, Book 72, Number 806

[290] Ahmad and Nasaa`i

[291] Tabaqat, Volume 1, Page 380

[292] Ibid.

[293] Several ahadith say that Muhammad often slept hungry. These are exaggerations to portray him as a long-suffering prophet. How could he go hungry when he had confiscated the wealth thousands of Jews of Arabia and had hundreds of slaves, is a question that only Muslim forgerers of hadith could answer. When Muhammad migrated to Medina, he was poor. However, he soon accumulated a lot of wealth through pillaging.

[294] The ancient process of drawing blood from the body by scarification and the application of a cupping glass, or by the application of a cupping glass without scarification, as for relieving internal congestion. (*Random House Unabridged Dictionary, © Random House, Inc. 2006.*)

[295] Bukhari Volume 7, Book 71, Number 602

Abu Juhaifa said: "I took his hand and put it on my head and I found that it was colder than ice and better scented than the musk perfume."[296]

Haykal also quotes the following hadith:

Jabir bin Samurah — who was a little child then — said: "When he wiped my cheek, I felt it was cold and scented as if it had been taken out of a shop of a perfume workshop."[297]

Some people with acromegaly may have abnormal curvature of the spine from side to side and from front to back (*kyphoscoliosis*). This may have been the reason why Muhammad leaned forward when walking. Additionally, abnormal enlargement of the pituitary gland, located deep within the brain, may cause headaches, fatigue, visual abnormalities, and/or hormonal imbalances.

Muhammad was stout, of equal belly and chest. Patients with acromegaly develop barrel chest, due to changes in vertebral and costal morphology. Vertebral bodies become enlarged and elongated, whereas the inter-vertebral discs thicken at the cervical and lumbar levels and become thin in the thoracic region, thus resulting in development of kyphosis, an abnormal, convex curvature of the spine, with a resultant bulge at the upper back. This is why he had a large back and shoulder joints.

The costochondral junctions may become prominent and enlarged, thus giving a typical rosary aspect. These anatomical rearrangements alter the elastic chest mechanics and markedly impair the respiratory muscle activation, which is further aggravated by muscle weakness/wasting associated with acromegaly. The difficulty in breathing causes inadequate oxygenation of the blood or hypoxemia. The patient needs to take long breaths.

Ibn Sa'd quotes a hadith from Anas, who said: "The Messenger of God used to breathe three times when he wanted to drink something and used to say, this is better, easier, and tastier. Anas said that since I learned this, I too breathe three times when drinking." Anas thought deep breathing before drinking is part of piety and tried to imitate his prophet to again access to paradise. Muhammad had shortness of breath. This tells us how mindlessly Muslims emulate their prophet.

There are other hadiths that reveal Muhammad had shortness of breath. He spoke slowly, and breathed in between his words. Ibn Sa'd quotes Aisha, "The Messenger of Allah did not speak as continuous and fast as you speak. His speech was intermittent and slow so anyone who listened could understand."[298] And, "The speech of the Prophet was not like singing, but he lengthened the words and pronounced forcefully."[299]

Acromegaly may increase metabolic rate, which results in excessive sweating (hyperhidrosis), an abnormal intolerance to heat and/or an increase in the production

[296] Bukhari Volume 4, Book 56, Number 753
[297] Sahih Muslim 2/256
[298] Tabaqat Volume 1 page 361
[299] Ibid. page 362

of oil (sebum) by the sebaceous glands in the skin, resulting in abnormally oily skin. According to hadith, Muhammad washed frequently, partly to get rid of the excessive oil and his odor and partly because of his OCD.

Five days before he died, his temperature rose so high and he suffered from so much pain that he fainted. "Pour out on me seven *qirab* (water skin pot) of various water wells so that I may go out to meet people and talk to them," he bid one of his wives.

It is not unlikely that the reason Muhammad prohibited drawing his picture was because he was conscious of his facial and bodily deformities.

Various psychiatric symptoms have been reported in patients with acromegaly characterized by personality changes. There are a few case reports of the presence of auditory and visual hallucinations, and delusions in patients with acromegaly. Describing the Psychotic symptoms in acromegaly, Denzil Pinto, A.T. Safeekh, and Mohit Trivedi write:

> Bleuler was the first to study psychiatric symptoms in patients with acromegaly. He described personality changes characterized by brief periods of impulsive behavior and, at times, cheerfulness and self-satisfaction. He also observed brief mood swings with spells of anxiety along with bradyphrenia (slowness of mental processes), egocentricity, and lack of concern. The presence of depressive symptoms was reported by Avery and Margo. Sivakumar and Williams reported a case of acromegaly with depression and pathological gambling. The presence of psychotic symptoms in a patient with acromegaly was described by Pye and Abbott in 1983. Their patient had delusions of reference, persecution, and visual and second-person auditory hallucinations. Spence reported the presence of delusions of persecution, visual and auditory hallucinations with depression in a patient with acromegaly.[300]

Muhammad died a painful death. Aisha said, "I never saw anyone suffer more pain than the messenger of Allah."[301] In the end he could not walk and his followers had to carry him around. Aisha said, "When the Prophet became seriously ill and his disease became aggravated he asked for permission from his wives to be nursed in my house and he was allowed. He came out with the help of two men and his legs were dragging on the ground."[302]

Muhammad thought that his pains were caused by the poison he took in Khaybar. But that was three years before his death. His companion, Bishr, who swallowed the morcel in his mouth, died instantly. Muhammad's death was caused by his achromegaly and his excruciating pains prove the point.

---

300 http://www.ncbi.nlm.nih.gov/pmc/articles/PMC2918321/
301 Sunan Ibn Majah 1622
302 Sahih Bukhari, 11:634

Acromegaly

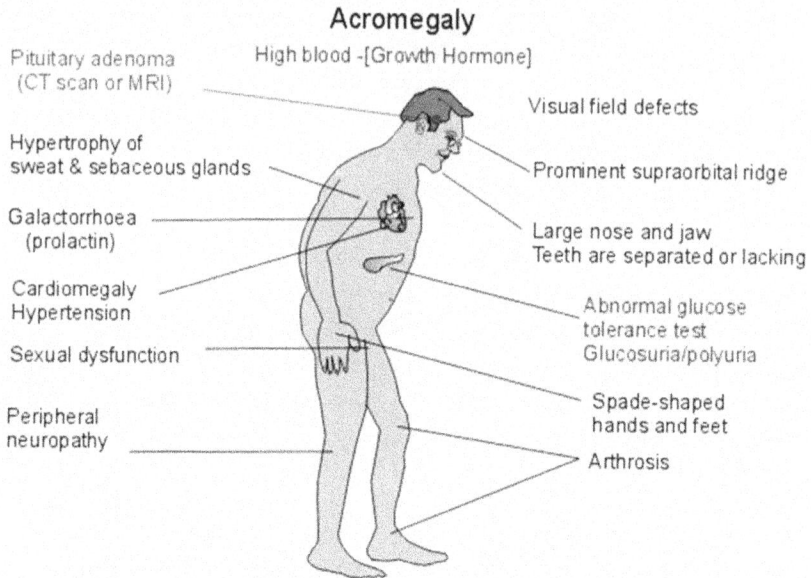

High blood -[Growth Hormone]

Pituitary adenoma
(CT scan or MRI)

Visual field defects

Hypertrophy of
sweat & sebaceous glands

Prominent supraorbital ridge

Galactorrhoea
(prolactin)

Large nose and jaw
Teeth are separated or lacking

Cardiomegaly
Hypertension

Abnormal glucose
tolerance test
Glucosuria/polyuria

Sexual dysfunction

Spade-shaped
hands and feet

Peripheral
neuropathy

Arthrosis

Source: http://healthkut.com/blog/2010/02/acromegaly-symptoms/

A picture is worth a thousand words. On the left is a print of a normal foot. On the right is Muhammad's heavy and thick fleshy footprint. Not only hadiths show that he suffered from acromegaly, we have also solid evidence cast in bronze.

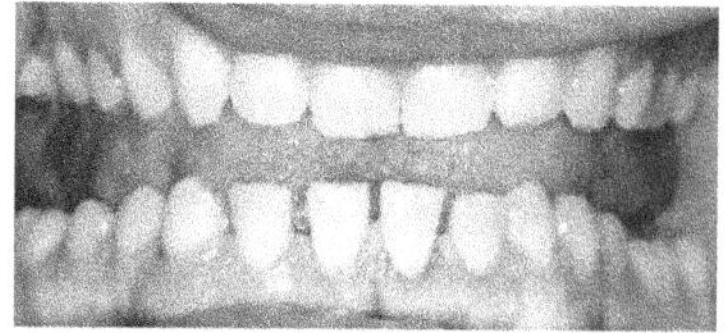

Photo of teeth showing classic teeth gapping due to acromegaly on lower jaw.

5- Physical Ailments

Maurice Tillet (1903-1955), an acromegaly sufferer, was a professional wrestler. Born in France, he was highly intelligent and could speak 14 languages.

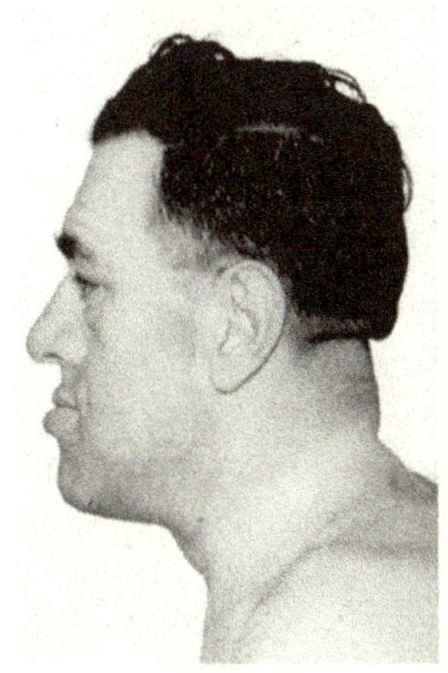

A man with acromegaly showing the characteristic changes of enlargement of the jaw, nose and frontal bones, and coarse facial features.

Impotence

Muslims believe that Muhammad had the sexual strength of fourty men. This belief is based on various hadiths. One hadith is attributed to Salma, a maid of Muhammad who said: "One night all nine wives of the Prophet (pbuh) who were with him until his death (Muhammad had other wives whom he divorced) were in his presence. The Prophet slept with all of them. When he finished with each one, he used to ask me to bring water so he could perform ablution. I asked, oh messenger of Allah, isn't one ablution enough? He responded this is better and cleaner."[303]

However, my research had led me to conclude that the claim of Muhammad's virility is hogwash, and that in fact in the last decade or two of his life he was actually impotent. Muhammad had an insatiable libido, which he tried to satisfy by fondling his women, without being able to engage in complete intercourse.

Research in the University of Utrecht, in the Netherlands suggests that endogenous opioids, the so-called feel-good chemicals produced by the brain, may increase sexual appetite and diminish sexual performance.[304] In another study,

303 Tabaqat Volume 8, Page 201

304 W. R. Van Furth, I. G. Wolterink-Donselaar and J. M. van Ree. Department of Pharmacology, Rudolf Magnus Institute, University of Utrecht, The Netherlands http://ajpregu.physiology.org/cgi/content/abstract/266/2/R606

researchers observed higher opioid activity during the mania phase in unmediated bipolar patients.[305] Muhammad was subject to huge mood swings. Sometimes he was euphoric and full of energy, while at other times he suffered from severe depression to the point of contemplating suicide. These findings explain why he had such a high libido, yet, despite numerous young and fertile sexual partners, remained childless. This suggests he was unable to perform sexually.

Nonetheless, there was a hole in my theory. If Muhammad was impotent in his later years, as evidence suggested, how could he father Ibrahim when he was already sixty? Ibrahim was born to Mariyah, a beautiful Coptic slave girl with curly hairs whom Muhammad's Arab wives were jelous of. I suspected that Ibrahim may have been fathered by someone else, but I had no evidence. You can't say something based on wild guesses. Then I found the smoking gun.

I came across a story reported by Ibn Sa'd who said there was a Coptic man in Medina that used to visit Mariyah. His name was Mabur, the person who accompanied Mariyah and her sister Sirin from Egypt to Medina. Rumor circulated that he was Mariyah's lover. Because of the ensuing brauhuha about the Prophet's sex with Mariyah, he relocated her to a garden to the North of Medina. Thus, away from the eyes of the public, Mabur had a good chance to pay regular visits to Mriyah.

The rumor reached Muhammad. According to Ibn Sa'd, he dispatched Ali to kill Mabur. Upon seeing Ali coming towards him with a sword in his hand, Mabur lifted up his garment and Ali saw that he had no awrat (genital) and spared his life.[306]

Tabari writes:

> The Messenger of God also had a eunuch called Mabur, who was presented to him by al-Muqaqis with two slave girls, one of them was called Mariyah, whom he took as a concubine, and the other [was called] Sirin, whom he gave to Hasaan ibn Thabit after Safwan ibn al-Mu'attal had committed an offense against him. Sirin gave birth to a son called 'Abd al-Rahman ibn Hasaan. Al-Muqaqis had sent this eunuch with the two slave girls in order to escort them and guard them on their way [to Medina]. He presented them to the Messenger of God when they arrived. It is said that he was the one [with whom] Mariyah was accused of [wrongdoing], and that the Messenger of God sent 'Ali to kill him. When he saw 'Ali and what he intended to do with him, he uncovered himself until it became evident to 'Ali that he was completely castrated, not having anything left at all of what men [normally] have, so [Ali] refrained from killing him."[307]

---

[305]www.ncbi.nlm.nih.gov/entrez/query.fcgi?cmd=Retrieve&db=PubMed&list_uids=627101 9&dopt=Abstract

[306] Tabaqat,. Volume 8, Page 224

[307] The History of Al-Tabari: The Last years of the Prophet, translated and annotated by Ismail K. Poonawala [State University of New York Press (SUNY), Albany 1990], Volume IX, p. 147

5- Physical Ailments

How reliable is this story? Aisha was also accused of having an affair with a young man named Safwan, which resulted in a huge scandal and was finally settled through God's intervention. Again the traditions claimed that Safwan was a eunuch. Why would a free young man be casterated? This was of course a convenient way to put an end to the rumor.

Another tradition says that Mabur was "extremely old." Mabur was a gift of al-Muqaqis to Muhammad. He accompanied Mariyah and her sister Sirin to protect them during the long journey. Why would the governor or Egypt send an extremely old man as gift or as protecter? Slave owners manumitted their old slaves so they won't have to take care of them in their old age. Wouldn't sending an extremely old slave as a gift be an insult? How could an extremely old man protect these two young women? It is cleare that the claims that Mabur as old and castrated were made up to end the rumors. Muhammad also claimed that when Ibrahim was born, Angel Gabriel gave him the confirmation that he was the father of the infant by saluting him "*Assalamo Alaikum ya aba Ibrahim*," (Peace to you o father of Ibrahim). Why the need for such confirmation?

Despite the fact that Mariyah was the only woman who bore Muhammad a son in his old age, and even though she was very beautiful, Muhammad did not marry her. Why?

Ibn Sa'd narrates that when Ibrahim was born; Muhammad took him to Aisha and said, "look how he looks like me." Aisha responded, "I see no resemblance in him." Muhammad said, "Don't you see his white and chubby cheeks?" She replied, "All babies have chubby cheeks."[308] It does not seem that Muhamamd was convinced that Ibrahim was his and sought confirmation from someone a bit more real than his imaginary friend from the sky.

The claim that Muhammad had the sexual strength of forty men is another fake story to disguise the fact that he was impotent. Muhammad had six children by Khadijah, who was already forty when he married her. These children were conceived when he was between 25 to 35 years old. And yet, with the exception of Mariyah, none of his young and fertile wives and concubines bore him any child in the last ten years of his life.

One side effect of achromegaly is impotence. Also "erectile dysfunction with intact libido in men with epilepsy has been known to researchers since the 1950s," says French neurologist Henri Jean Pascal Gastaut (1915-1995).[309] And the psychiatrist Pritchard P. postulates that hyperprolactinemia resulting from CP seizures contributes to male sexual dysfunction in epilepsy.[310]

---

[308] Tabaqat Volume I, page 125

[309] Gastaut H: So-called psychomotor and temporal epilepsy: a critical study. Epilepsia 1953; 2: 59-76.

[310] Pritchard PB. Hyposexuality: a complication of complex partial epilepsy. Trans Am Neurol Assoc 1980; 105: 193-5.

The traditions tell us that Muhammad imagined having sex when he didn't. There is also a hadith that shows he did not have intercourse with his wives, but only "fondled" them. He would visit them, sometimes all nine of them, in one night and would engage in foreplay with them, but not in intercourse. Aisha said, "None of you have the self-control of the Prophet for he could fondle his wives, but not have intercourse"[311] Aisha was only a child. She probably did not know that her illustrious aging husband was not exercising self-control; he simply couldn't do it. The fact that he would go from one wife to another touching and fondeling them is evidence enough that he was sex starved. In another place she said, "I never looked or saw the *awrat* (genitalia) of the Prophet."[312] I leave it to the reader to decide why.

This does not mean that Muhammad did not have an insaciable sexual craving. He would not miss any opportunity to solicit sex. His apetite for sex only reveals that despite so many women in his harem, he could not get released.

There is a hadith that says when he raided the town of Bani Jaun, a young girl called Jauniyya, was brought to him, accompanied by her wet nurse. The Prophet said to her, "Give yourself to me." (In today's parlance: Let me have sex with you.) The girl retorted, "Can a princess give herself to an ordinary man?" Muhammad then raised his hand to strike her. She exclaimed, "I seek refuge with Allah from you."[313]

Upon this Muhammad did not beat her and while overcomed by momentary guilt, he ordered a follower to give the girl two white linen dresses. Obviously he had not brought those dresses along as gifts for his victims. They were the dresses he had stolen from this very girl or perhaps another girl of her tribe.

Jauniyya was accompanied by a wet nurse. This tells us that she was just a child. The fact that she responded, in such an audacious way, "would a princess give herself to an ordinary man?" to a man who had the power to kill her is another clue that was only a child.

The English translator of this hadith inserted the word (in marriage) in parenthesis. "Give yourself to me (in marriage)." This word does not exist in the original text. The Arabic text reads *habba nafsika li.* The word '*habba*' is never used for marriage.

The hadith says Muhammad raised his hand to strike her so that she might become tranquil. The translator notices the inappropriateness of Muhammad's action and translates the word strike as "pat." The Arabic word used is *ahwa.* It derives from *hawa.* It means to pounce down, to swoop down suddenly, not patting.

Why did Jauniyya exclaim "I seek refuge with Allah from you" if all Muhammad was doing was gently patting her?

---

[311] Sahih Bukhari *Volume 1, Book 6, Number 299.*
[312] Tabaqat Volume 1, page 368
[313] Bukhari Volume 7: 63: 182:

5- Physical Ailments

It is almost impossible to fully grasp the violence of the Quran and the hadith relying only on their English translations. The translators have done their best to substitute harsh words with mild ones to camouflage their violence. When reading the stories of Muhammad, written by his followers, one has to read between the lines to get at the truth.

All this talk about Muhammad's impotence is speculation, you say. Here is one hadith that leaves no doubt about it. Ibn Sa'd quotes his teacher al Waqidi: "The prophet of Allah used to say that I was among those who have little strength for intercourse. Then Allah sent me a pot with cooked meat. After I ate from it, I found strength any time I wanted to do the work."[314]

You heard it from the mouth of the horse. It is up to you now to decide whether to believe the fairy tale that Allah was so concerned about his favorite prophet's sexual vagaries that he sent him a pot of meat to cure his impotence, or to conclude that our megalomaniac male chauvinist prophet, like most Arabs who consider sexual power to be the symbol of their manhood and constantly boast about it, was merely gasconading to hide his impotence. Why Allah did not send a cure for his migraines? Aisha said she never saw anyone suffer more pain than the Messenger of Allah. Allah could not care less about his prophet's headaches, but he would cook a special dish and rush it to him via his Archangel to cure his impotence? Was Muhammad's sex life more important then his health? Did Allah care more about his prophet's erection than he did for his head?

He told his followers, "Gabriel brought me a small pot of food. I ate from that food and gained the sexual strength of forty men."[315] He gained the strength of forty men but all he could do was to fondle his wives. Looks like all that strength went to his fingers.

I think it is more logical to assume that Muhammad fabricated these stories to conceal his impotence. A narcissist, with such a monumental ego, could not possibly be seen as impotent, especially in a society were virility was regarded as man's highest virtue.

Curiously, on the day that Ibrahim died, Muhammad went to the mosque and after praying, delivered a sermon on, of all topics, adultery and the punishment that awaits the adulterers.

He bellowed from the pulpit, "O followers of Muhammad! By Allah! There is none who has more *ghaira* than Allah as He has forbidden that His slaves, male or female commit adultery. O followers of Muhammad! By Allah! If you knew that which I know you would laugh little and weep much."[316]

---

314 Tabaqat Volume 8, Page 200
315 Ibid.
316 Bukhari, *2: 18: 154*

Ghaira is sense of shame and honor. Your *ghaira* can be injured when your property or your *mahram* (sacred, a close kin) is violated. If you touch, look at or flirt with a Muslim's wife, sister, or daughter, his *ghaira* is injured. To restore it, he must take revenge. If he has a lot of *ghaira*, he may kill you and also kill his female kin. Only then his honor can be restored. One who does not retaliate, is one who has no *ghaira* or shame.

Note that Muhammad is talking about Allah's *ghaira.* If Allah does not have a female relative, then how can his *ghaira* become injured? It's not hard to see that Muhammad identified himself with Allah. He was talking about his own *ghaira.* He was suspicious of Mariyah and it is for her that he was delivering this fiery and completely inappropriate sermon about the chastisement of adulterers, in her child's funeral. Allah was Muhammad's alter ego. He said, "I have been shown the Hellfire and I never saw a worse and horrible sight than the sight I have seen today."[317]

Was he uttering this sermon for the ears of Mariyah? Why in the funeral of his son should he talk about adultery and hellfire?

[317] Bukhari, *1: 8: 423*

Chapter Six

Muhammad's Cult

e are often taken aback by the level of fanaticism of Muslims. Millions of them riot, burn churches, and temples of other faiths, and kill innocent people because a newspaper has published a few cartoons of Muhammad or because the Pope has quoted a medieval emperor who said violence is not compatible with the nature of God.

People generally are biased in favor of a belief system that has so many followers. They think that the sheer size of Islam qualifies it as a religion. This is the fallacy of *argumentum ad numerum*. Can 1.5 billion people be wrong? Yes they can. History shows that often all mankind has been wrong. In the words of Bertrand Russell, "The fact that an opinion has been widely held is no evidence whatever that it is not utterly absurd; indeed in view of the silliness of the majority of mankind, a widespread belief is more likely to be foolish than sensible." The truth of a proposition is not determined by the number of its proponents, but by the validity of its arguments. Is Islam really a religion like others?

Some say that all religions have started as cult until, with the passage of time, they gained acceptance and the status of religion. However, there are certain characteristics that distinguish a cult from religion.

Carole Wade in "Psychology 101 says," studies of religious, political, and other cults have identified a number of key steps in this type of coercive persuasion:

1 People are put in physically or emotionally distressing situations;
2 Their problems are reduced to one simple explanation, which is repeatedly emphasized;
3 They receive unconditional love, acceptance, and attention from a charismatic leader;
4 They get a new identity based on the group;
5 They are subject to entrapment (isolation from friends, relatives, and the mainstream culture) and their access to information is severely controlled.[318]

---

[318] Psychology 101, Carole Wade et al., 2005

All these traits characterized Islam during its formative stage. Dr. Janja Lalich and Dr. Michael D. Langone have created a list of such traits, later published in a book co-authored by Lalich[319] that describes cults fairly well.[320] The more a group or a doctrine has these characteristics, the more it should be defined and labeled as cult. I am going to quote these cultic characteristics and compare them to Islam to see whether they fits the description.

1 The group displays excessively zealous and unquestioning commitment to its leader and (whether he is alive or dead) regards his belief system, ideology, and practices as the Truth, as Law.

Muslims are extremely zealous about their faith and have an unquestioning commitment to their prophet, whose book, the Quran, to them is Truth and Law. You may find some of these characteristics apply also to other faiths. However, this is generally an exception and not the norm. In Islam cultic mentality is the norm.

2 Questioning, doubt, and dissent are discouraged or even punished.

Muslims are prohibited to question or doubt the basic tenets of their faith, and dissent is punishable by death. The Quran 5:101-102 says "*O ye who believe! Ask not questions about things which, if made plain to you, may cause you trouble. Some people before you did ask such questions, and on that account lost their faith.*" Cults are based on irrational beliefs. The cult leader discourages questions that may expose his lies.

3 Mind-altering practices (such as meditation, chanting, speaking in tongues, denunciation sessions, and debilitating work routines) are used in excess and serve to suppress doubts about the group and its leader(s).

Muslims stop whatever they do and stand for a repetitive and ritualistic prayer, five times per day. They chant the Quran in Arabic that most of them don't understand. For one month in the year they fast, which means total abstinence from eating and drinking, from dawn to dusk, a practice that can be particularly taxing in summertime, leading to sever kidney and liver diseases. The preoccupation with performing these rituals and the fear of failing them or doubting their relevance is intense. Anyone caught eating or drinking in public will be severely punished.

---

[319] Lalich, Janja and Tobias, Madeleine, Take Back Your Life: Recovering from Cults and Abusive Relationships, Bay Tree Publishing (2006), ISBN10 0972002154, ISBN 13 9780972002158.

[320] Published at ICSA (International Cultic Studies Association) website, Janja Lalich, PH.D. & Michael D. Langone, Ph.D., www.csj.org/infoserv_cult101/checklis.htm, accessed June 21, 2007.

4 The leadership dictates, sometimes in great detail, how members should think, act, and feel. For example, members must get permission to date, change jobs, marry—or leaders prescribe what types of clothes to wear, where to live, whether or not to have children, how to discipline children, and so forth.

Every detail of the life of a Muslim is prescribed. He is told what is *haram* (forbidden) and what is *halal* (permitted), what foods to eat, with what hand eat it and which fingers to lick after eating, how to dress, which shoe to wear first and which one to take off first, how to shave, what should be the length of one's beard, how to brush one's teeth, what rituals to perform when praying, how to respond to the call of nature and how to squeeze out the urine after peeing. A Muslim is not allowed to date. Marriages are arranged. Corporal punishment, including torture such as flogging for violating the above codes is prescribed, both for children and for adults.

5 The group is elitist, claiming a special, exalted status for itself, its leader(s) and members For example, the leader is considered the Messiah, a special being, an avatar—or the group and/or the leader is on a special mission to save humanity.

Muslims claim special status for themselves and their prophet, while they vilify all other religions, including Christianity and Judaism that they claim to respect. The Isa and the Musa of the Quran are not the same Jesus and Moses of the Bible. Isla is a nephew of Moses, not the Son of God and he was not crucified and did not ascend to heaven. The gods of Hindus are of course all idols and the statues of Buddha can be destroyed. At the same time Muslims can be extremely violent if Muhammad is slighted. They constantly lobby for concessions and demand preferential treatments. They push that public institutions in non-Muslim countries cater to their religious needs, such as serve halal food and reserve a special room for their prayers. Meanwhile, they destroy the churches and temples in Islamic countries and persecute and kill the followers of other faiths.

6 The group has a polarized us-versus-them mentality, which may cause conflict with the wider society.

Muslims have a very strong us-versus-them mentality. They call all non-Muslims, *kafir*, a derogatory term which means one who covers the truth. For them, the world is divided into *Dar al Islam* (House of Islam) and *Dar al Harb* (House of War). Non-Muslim countries are House of War. It is the duty of every Muslim to wage jihad in the House of War, to fight, to kill, and to subdue the non-Muslims. As thousands of terrorist attacks show the objective is to kill the non-Muslims. The goal is not to convert them, but to force them into submition. Peace, according to Islam, can only be attained when non-Muslims submit to Muslims and accept their supremacy. Non-Muslims can practice their religion, but only as *dhimmis*, (bonded people). This provision is given to the people of the Book. Christians and Jews will not be massacred, provided they pay the protection tax, *jizyah* (fine), and feel themselves humiliated and subdued, as prescribed in the Quran.[321] If they fail to pay the *jizyah*, they must be exiled or put to death. In fact Islam has been the inspiration for the Mafia. If you want to live and be left alone you must pay a protection fee. As for other unbelievers (pagans, polytheists, atheists, animists, etc.), they must either convert or be killed.

7 The leader is not accountable to any authority.

For Muslims, the words and actions of Muhammad constitute law. He cannot be held accountable. He was entitled to marry or have sex out of marriage with as many women as he wished. He could raid civilians, kill unarmed men, loot them, and take their women and children as slaves. He could assassinate his critics and torture them. He could have sex with children. He could lie and deceive. He could massacre his prisoners of war cold-bloodedly. He could rape his captives. None of these bother his followers. At first they deny these charges vehemently. They take offence and accuse you of bigotry and libel. You are only a hate monger and an ignorant "Islamophobe," even a racist. But once the irrefutable evidence is presented, they suddenly change tactic and defend their prophet rationalize and justify the very things they had indignantly denied earlier. This dramatic 180 degrees shift, from utter denial to complete acceptance and justification is baffling. It is comical and tragic at once and it happens every time with every Muslim. Don't take me for my words. Try it for yourself. Find the most open minded and educated Muslim and ask them about one of the many crimes of Muhammad. Take note how they deny that charge in the strongest way. Then show them the hadith or the quranic verse and watch how they start defending Muhammad and explain away the very crime that he had denied.

For Muslims, Muhammad's actions should not be measured by the standards of the Golden Rule. Rather, he is the standard and the measure of right and wrong. If he committed a crime, that crime is a holy deed. Muslims will commit the most hideous deeds with a clear conscience, as long as it is the *Sunna* of their prophet. If Muhammad did it, it must be right. Man must not question the wisdom of God. Allah knows best.

---

[321] Quran 9:29 Fight those who believe not in Allâh nor the Last Day, nor hold that forbidden which hath been forbidden by Allâh and His Messenger, nor acknowledge the religion of Truth, (even if they are) of the People of the Book, until they pay the Jizya with willing submission, and feel themselves subdued.

8 The group teaches or implies that its supposedly exalted ends justify whatever means it deems necessary. This may result in members' participating in behaviors or activities they would have considered reprehensible or unethical before joining the group (for example, lying to family or friends, or collecting money for bogus charities).

For Muslims, the end always justifies the means. All laws, even the laws of Islam can be broken, if the intention is justifiable. A Muslim is allowed to denounce Muhammad and Allah, if necessary, in order to deceive non-Muslims and advance Islam.

Abdullah Hassan al-Asiri, a suicide bomber who was killed by detonating explosives hidden in his rectum in a failed attempt to kill a Saudi Prince, had religious justification to commit sodomy in order to widen his anus and make room for the explosives.

On 27 August 2009, Fadak TV, a London-based Arabic television read a fatwa that appeared on the Lions of Sunna Internet forum. One Wahhabi informed fellow jihadis of "an innovative and unprecedented way to execute martyrdom operations by placing explosive capsules in your anus. However, to undertake this jihadi approach" wrote this Muslim, "you must agree to be sodomized for a while to widen your anus so it can hold the explosives."

Others inquired further by asking for formal fatwas. Citing his desire for "martyrdom and the virgins of paradise," one jihadi asked another sheikh, "Is it permissible for me to let one of the jihadi brothers sodomize me to widen my anus if the intention is good?"

'Yes' was the answer of the cleric, as he gave the following fatwa: "In principle, sodomy is forbidden. However, Jihad is more important. It is the pinnacle of Islam. If sodomy is the only way to reach this pinnacle of Islam, then there is no harm in it. The rule is that necessity makes the forbidden permissible. Something that is required in order to perform a duty becomes a duty in and of itself. No duty takes precedence over Jihad. Therefore, you must be sodomized... After you have been sodomized, you must ask Allah for forgiveness. Know, my son, that Allah resurrects the mujahideen on Judgment Day on the basis of their intentions. Allah willing, your intention is to support Islam. May Allah include you among those who heed His call."

In Islam, killing is prohibited, but if it is enjoined and becomes the noblest deed, which will have the highest reward when it is done to promote Islam. Suicide is prohibited. But suicide bombing with the intent to cause the death of non-Muslims is *ghazwa* (holy raid). Stealing from fellow Muslims is prohibited. Your hand can be chopped off if you steal a loaf of bread. But raiding and looting the non-believers is prescribed in the Quran and was practiced by Muhammad. Sexual intercourse out of marriage is a grave sin, punishable by stoning. However, rape of unbelieving women, even if they are married, is allowed in the Quran. Lying in Islam is prohibited, except when the intent is to deceive the non-Muslims, which is then elevated as *taqiyah,* one of the twin wings of jihad. The goal of advancing Islam is so lofty that there is nothing that a Muslim would not do in order to achieve it. The early Muslims waged war against their own people and even murdered their father and brothers. These crimes are praised as the sign of faith and devotion of the believer. Thousands of young women and girls are murdered in the hands of their parents and brothers every year in the name of "honor." There is no crime that a Muslim would not commit, when ends justify the means. If you are a Muslim and offended by these words, just think. Will you not consider killing your daughter if, for example, she appears in a porn movie?" Of course you would. To the extent that one believes in Islam, to that very extend, he loses his humanity. Since Muslims are generally devout believers, there is little humanity left in them.

9 The leadership induces feelings of shame and/or guilt in order to influence and/or control members. Often, this is done through peer pressure and subtle forms of persuasion.

Muslims' thoughts tend to be overridden with guilt. There is no sense of guilt in hurting others. The guilt is in relation to the observation of the Law. If a Muslim does something contrary to what is permitted, other Muslims are required to remind him of the Law, induce shame in him, and demand compliance. In countries that are more Islamic, particularly in Iran and in Saudi Arabia, it is the state that makes sure the individual follows the religious laws. In March 2002 Saudi Arabia's religious police stopped schoolgirls from leaving a blazing building because their hairs were not covered.[322] As a result, fifteen girls were burned alive. The observance of the dress code was deemed more important than the lives of these girls.

10 Subservience to the leader or group requires members to cut ties with family and friends, and radically alter the personal goals and activities they had before joining the group.

Muslim converts are encouraged to sever their ties with their non-Muslim family and friends. I have received countless heart-rending stories from non-Muslim parents, whose children have converted to Islam and as a result they have lost touch with them completely. Occasionally, they may receive a call or a cold visit; but the visit may be so restricted, so bereft of any love, that the outcome further saddens the already heartbroken parents. The purpose of these visits is usually to ask the non-Muslim parents or siblings to convert to Islam. They leave, as soon as resistance is encountered. Once a person converts to Islam, they become someone else, as if they are

[322] http://news.bbc.co.uk/1/hi/world/middle_east/1874471.stm

possessed. Their heart is transformed, into stone. Their soul seems to be snatched and their body is occupied by a stranger.

11 The group is preoccupied with bringing in new members.

Muslims' main goal is to promote Islam. This practice is called *da'wa.* It is the duty of every Muslim to make new converts, starting with their own family and friends. Expanding Islam is the obsession of every Muslim, particularly the newcomers. Through *da'wa* (Islamic version of evangelization) their own faith is also strengthened. That's when they learn to lie in order to promote their faith. They will only reveal the parts of Islam that are less objectionable and gloss over its more unsavory parts. People, who never thought they would lie, engage in the most brazen deceptions to fool others, including their loved ones, to convince them that Islam is beautiful.

12 The group is preoccupied with making money.

Raising funds for jihad is one of the main objectives of all Muslims. Today, this is done through what are known as Islamic "charities". Muslims pay huge amount of money to Islamic "charities." None of that is spent on charity. Islamic charity is to finance jihad.

In Muhammad's time and throughout the course of history, raising money for jihad was done by looting. Spoils of war provided funding for other wars. Islam's main goal is to establish itself as the pre-eminent earthly power. Muhammad exhorted his followers to give money and support his warfare. "*Of their goods take alms so that thou mightiest purify and sanctify them...*" (Q.9:103)

13 Members are expected to devote inordinate amounts of time to the group and group-related activities.

Muslims' main preoccupation is Islam. They are required to regularly go to the mosque, attend obligatory prayers five times a day, and listen to the sermons. So enwrapped they become about how to perform their religious duties, what to wear, what to eat, etc., that they have very little time left for thinking of anything else. They are even told what to think. As Muslims say, Islam is not a religion; it is a way of life. It permeates every aspect of the life of the believer. So involved they become that life without Islam becomes inconceivable to them.

14 Members are encouraged or required to live and/or socialize only with other group members.

Muslims are taught to shun *kafirs* and to socialize only with fellow Muslims. The Quran prohibits taking friends from among unbelievers (Q.3:28). It calls them *najis* (filthy, impure) (Q.9:28) and orders harshness against them (Q.9:123). According to Muhammad, unbelievers are the "vilest animals" in the sight of God. (Q.8:55). One Islamic site writes, "One of the aspects of iman (faith) is *al wala wal bara,* loving and hating for the sake of Allah Alone. It is one of the most important beliefs of Islam after Tawheed (Oneness of God). Allah says in His Book: Let not the believers take disbelievers for their friends in preference to believers. Whoever does this has no connection with Allah unless you are guarding yourselves against them as a precaution. Allah bids you to beware of Himself. And to Allah is the journeying. (Q.3:28)"[323]

The doctrine of *al wala wal bara,* is Islam in a nutshell. It embodies the core message of this faith. It is undisguised and unadulterated hate. Muslims must hate all non-Muslims and be harsh to them, "*unless you are guarding yourselves against them as a precaution,* (to deceive them)" (Q. 3:28) i.e., unless it is to deceive them.

15 The most loyal members ("the true believers") feel there can be no life outside the context of the group. They believe there is no other way to be, and often fear reprisals to themselves or others if they leave (or even consider leaving) the group.

The thought of leaving Islam is so unbearable for true Muslims that they can't entertain it. Despite the fact that millions have left this faith in recent years, hardcore Muslims remain adamant in their belief that nobody ever really leaves Islam, and that such claims are all fabrications and part of the conspiracy to shake the faith of the believers. Emails that I have received from Muslims share one common theme. They all warn me of hell. Between the fear of hell and fear of reprisal, Muslims are trapped in a web of terror of their own making.

Islam is not to teach spirituality, nor is it for enlightenment. The spiritual message in Islam is nonexistent. Piety in Islam means emulating Muhammad, a man who was far from pious by our standard. Rituals like prayers and fasting are to numb the mind of the believer.

Therefore as you see, all the characteristics of a cult are present in Islam. Islam is an overgrown cult.

A Comparison of Muhammad with a Few Cult Leaders

The personality of Muhammad is an enigma to many scholars. Even those who don't accept his claim admit that he had an impressive and charismatic personality. He could mesmerize those around him to such an extent that they would kill at his

[323] http://quranicverse99.tripod.com/islamicways/id15.html. This article can be found in many other sites.

bidding. How did he summon up so much determination, aspired so high, thought so grandiose, and became so powerful in such a short time?

What drove Muhammad to success was his need to be loved. This is the secret behind history's great narcissists. It is this need that drives them so incessantly and tirelessly.

There is no shortage of people who proclaim to be messengers of God or messiahs. Likewise, there is no dearth of fools who would follow them and kill or die for them, to demonstrate their loyalty.

The craving for respect and power are what drives the narcissist. Narcissists are con artists. They are driven by their need for recognition. They are stubborn, manipulative and determined. They are also smart, cunning and resourceful. All these are keys to success. Some famous narcissist sociopaths are: Napoleon, Hitler, Stalin, Mussolini, Pol Pot, Mao, Saddam Hussein, Idi Amin, Jim Jones, David Koresh, Shoko Asahara, and Charles Manson.

The narcissist is emotionally disturbed. He seeks validation in power, and to achieve that he stops at nothing. He lies convincingly, inspires confidence and appears self-assured. These are masks he wears to hide his insecurity and his inner fears. He pretends to be concerned about you and claims to love you when in reality he uses you like a pawn and will discards you when you are no longer needed. Your life means nothing to him. He will sacrifice those whom he claims to love when his interests so dictate.

Let us take a closer look at a few narcissists and compare them to Muhammad. This will also help us understand Muslims, as we compare them to other cultists.

Jim Jones

Jim Jones convinced normal decent people that he was the Messiah (of socialism of all things). He persuaded them to leave their families and follow him to his "Medina" in the middle of the jungle. He charmed the Government of Guyana to give him 300 acres of land for free. He convinced his followers to let him sleep with their wives. He encouraged them to carry gun and to kill anyone who dissented. His followers became so blinded by their faith in him that they shot and killed a senator and his bodyguards when Jones told them to do it. Then he persuaded everyone in his compound, to drink a cyanide potion and commit mass suicide. Over 900 people willingly did what he told them and died. Before killing themselves they made their children drink the poison. I have dedicated an entire chapter comparing this cult with Islam.

David Koresh

David Koresh gathered his followers in a compound named after himself outside of Waco, Texas. He told them he was the Son of God and they believed him. His first announcement was made to the Seventh Day Adventists Church in southern California, which read in part: "I have seven eyes and seven horns. My Name is the Word of God...Prepare to Meet Thy God."

Marc Breault, a former member of Koresh's cult wrote that Vernon (the real name of David Koresh) confided to him early in his ministry: "I'll have women begging me to make love to 'em. Just imagine; virgins without number." A couple of years later he would be attended by at least twenty young women, including two that were just 14 years old, and one who was age 12. Like Allah who was attentive to his apostle's sexual needs, David's god was also concerned about his carnal desires. Starting as a preacher, he soon rose to the position of the Son of God and began demanding sex from the wives of his followers – women who he believed had married their husband without his permission and who belonged to him. "All you men are just fuckers. That's all you are," David told his followers. "You married without getting God's permission. Even worse, you married my wives. God gave them to me first. So now I'm taking them back." According to Marc Breault, everybody was shocked by these statements, but they did not react, while Koresh kept saying things like: "So Scott; how does it feel to know you're not married anymore?" According to Breault, in 1989 David "began having sex with the other men's wives... and directed the women to inform him when they had reached the fertile part of their cycle to maximize the chance of pregnancy." As per the men, he informed them that it was their job to "defend King Solomon's bed." He not only had sex with and impregnated their wives—fathering over 20 children— but began having sex with their children as well. "Children were spanked for any reason; crying during a sixteen-hour Bible study, refusing to sit on David's lap, or daring to defy the Prophet's wishes…Some women thought the best way to please their Son of God lover was to be especially severe when dishing out discipline. But sometimes it wasn't easy for the adults to spank the children. They couldn't find a spot on the child's buttocks that wasn't black and blue or bleeding." The women were sometimes subjected to the same treatment. One 29-year-old woman who announced that she was hearing voices was imprisoned in one of the small cottages on their property. She was beaten, and repeatedly raped by her guards. [324]

Like Muhammad, Koresh was also a prophet of doom. His followers armed themselves. When raided by police, they shot and killed four ATF agents and booby-trapped the compound, blowing it apart, causing their own deaths and the deaths of their families, rather than surrender. Ninety people died as the result.

This story is beyond belief. How can anyone let himself to be fooled to this extent? And yet, aren't Muslims more foolish to think that they will go to paradise if they kill non-Muslims. Albert Einstein was not joking when he said, "Two things are infinite: the universe and human stupidity; and I'm not sure about the universe."

---

[324] *Inside the Cult: A Member's Chilling, Exclusive Account of Madness and Depravity in David Koresh's Compound* Breault & King, 1993

6- Muhammad's Cult

Order of the Solar Temple:

This apocalyptic cult claimed 74 victims in three bizarre mass suicide rituals. Most of the members of the sect were highly educated and well-to-do individuals. They were much more intelligent than Abu Bakr, Umar, and Ali, and all companions of Muhammad combined.

The cult gave great importance to the Sun. Their fiery ritual murder-suicides were meant to take members of the sect to a new world on the star "Sirius." To assist with the trip, several of the victims, including some children, were shot in the head, asphyxiated with black plastic bags and/or poisoned.

The two known leaders of the group were Luc Jouret, a Belgian homeopathic doctor, and Joseph di Mambro, a wealthy businessman. They were Muhammad and Abu Bakr of this cult. They believed in their own insanity so much that along with their followers they too committed suicide. This is something Muhammad was not willing to do. Muhammad never put his life in the way of harm. He surrounded himself with bodyguards at all times and never confronted the enemy in person.

In a letter delivered after their deaths, Jouret and di Mambro wrote that they were *"leaving this earth to find a new dimension of truth and absolution, far from the hypocrisies of this world."*[325] Cults have an infatuation with death. This sounds eerily familiar to Muhammad's preaching, except that he was more attached to this world and its lustful pleasures. He had no intention of leaving this world. He praised martyrdom, but that was for others. He did not advocate suicide. That was of no use to him. Instead, he goaded his followers to wage jihad, kill and readily die. He told them to love death more than life, to loot and to bring booty, women and slaves for "Allah and his messenger." He was more pragmatic, more this worldly than other cult leaders.

Heaven's Gate

On March 26, 1997, 39 members of the cult known as "Heaven's Gate" decided to "*shed their containers*" and get on a companion craft "hiding in the tail of the Hale-Bopp comet".

The Heaven's Gaters died in three shifts over a three-day period after celebrating their last meal on earth. As one set of cultists ingested the poison, a lethal dose of phenobarbital mixed in with pudding and/or applesauce and chased with a shot of vodka, they would lie down while other cultists would use a plastic bag on their head to speed up the death. Then the cultists would clean up after each round of killing. Before the last two killed themselves, they took out the trash leaving the rented mansion in perfect order. Wanting to be helpful even after death, all bodies had some sort of identification. Strangely though, they also had five-

---

[325] http://www-tech.mit.edu/V114/N47/swiss.47w.html

dollar bills and change in their pockets and small suitcases neatly tucked under their cots and beds. Like Muslim suicide bombers who shave their bodies and some even wrap their penis in aluminum foil, supposedly to keep it intact from the blast of the bomb in preparation for their nuptial encounter with the celestial houris, the Heaven's Gaters must have thought they will take their bodies and suitcases along on their celestial voyage.

Charles Manson

This infamous psychopath of the late sixties at one point had nearly 100 young men and women among his followers (roughly the same number of followers Muhammad had gathered in Mecca and somewhat of the same caliber), known as the "Family." He was seen as their Messiah. He had made these rebel kids believe that civilization was about to end in a racial war in which the blacks would fight the whites and would win, but since they don't know how to run the world, they would come to him for help, and he and his followers will rule the world. He was so convincing that his followers did not question his sanity. They did everything he told them to do, including engage in prostitution, theft, and murder. This is not unlike what Muhammad urged his followers to do.

When the promised racial war did not happen in 1969 as he had prophesied, Manson thought he should kick start it himself. He ordered his followers to enter the houses of rich people randomly, kill them and make it look as if it has been done by blacks. His young followers did exactly what he ordered them. They were eager to please him and vied with each other to obey his orders. They had come to believe Manson had special divine powers and was endowed with hidden knowledge.

The influence of Manson on his followers was such that in 1975, Lynette Fromme, one of his "girls" known as Squeaky, attempted to assassinate President Gerald Ford and was sentenced to life in prison. "She's very bright, an intelligent, pleasant woman," Fromme's attorney said of her. "She's anything but crazy. When you talk with her, everything is fine until you mention Manson." This can be said of all cultists. They are normal, intelligent people, until you mention their cult leader. Muslims are generally affable people until you mention Muhammad. Then suddenly, blood rushes to their heads, insanity overtakes them and they may kill you. Cultists are all alike. They derive their insanity from a psychopath narcissist leader.

Another of Manson's girls, Sandra Good, was convicted for sending death threats through mail in 1976 and served ten years in jail. Following her release, she moved to an area close to Corcoran prison, where Manson is held, and tended his website until 2001. That is the power of brainwashing. Sandra Good was interviewed by CBC radio about a week after Fromme's attempted assassination. She said, "People all over the world are due to be assassinated. This is just the beginning. This is just the beginning of many assassinations that are about to take place." When asked, how could she talk about the trees that she wants to protect when she does not care about men? Good responded: "Men that kill life, that kill harp seals, that kill trees, that poison oceans, rivers and life are killing all of us."[326]

Cultists justify their terrorist deeds. This is the same apologetic given by Muslims to justify Islamic terrorism. They first build a straw-man of the West accusing it of killing Muslim children and then based on that lie they justify their heinous crimes. How many times have we heard "respectable" and prominent Muslims appear on TV to say, "We condemn terrorism BUT (yes there is always a but) this is a reaction to what Israel, America, the West, etc. are doing to Muslims?" And this is blatant lie. What had the innocent victims in Kenya's Westgate mall had done to deserve massacre. What is the fault of the Christians in Nigeria, Egypt and Pakistan?

Manson still receives a large amount of mail, more than any other prisoner in the United States prison system, much of it from young people who want to join the "Family." Can this possibly explain why the cult of Islam is still thriving? Foolish people and evil people will always gravitate towards evil doctrines. Those who find Islam attractive are either fool or evil. No sane person, no good human, can find Islam appealing.

Like all cults, Manson also had a cause. His cause was preservation of Air, Trees, Water, Animals (ATWA) He made his cause look so important that it justified murder. After spending more than three decades in prison, Fromme was still faithful to Manson: "Manson told me he could give me a natural world," said Fromme in an interview. "Almost forty years ago he told me that money should work as hard for people as people work for money. He was talking about air and water, land and life. I don't know how it can be done, so I'm just waiting. I would work hard for and invest in a world like that because it would support not just me but the continuum of generations to come." This is an eloquent testimony to the power of brainwashing. That is why Muslims are not leaving Islam despite the fact that they know Muhammad led a despicable and shameful life. Belief is a potent drug that destroys the thinking ability of the believer. The American philosopher Elbert Hubbard said, "Genius may have its limitations, but stupidity is not thus handicapped."

In one of their killing raids, Manson, peeping through the window of the house of his victims, saw pictures of children on the wall. At first he thought this house should be spared, but then he changed his mind and said, the cause is so important that children should not come in the way.

Joseph Cohen, A.K.A. Yusuf Khattab, a Jewish man who converted to Islam, in an interview available on Youtube said, every Israeli is a legitimate target and

---

[326] http://archives.cbc.ca/IDC-1-68-368-2086/arts_entertainment/frum/

should be killed. When asked about children, he said that their killing would be a blessing to them because they will die before having the chance to commit sin.

Shoko Asahara

In March of 1995 a Japanese cult called "Aum Supreme Truth" released deadly Sarin gas within the subways of Tokyo. Four people died immediately and thousands were rushed to hospitals. This unprovoked attack shocked the world.

Later, it was learned that this was not the first violent act of the cult. In 1989 Aum's leader Shoko Asahara ordered the abduction and murder of an anti Aum lawyer, his wife and infant son. Less than a year before the Tokyo gas attack (June 1994) Aum members released Sarin gas in Matsumoto killing seven residents.

Shoko Asahara was born into a poor family. Visually impaired, he went to a special school for the blind. Like other cult leaders, from childhood, Asahara saw himself as a great leader and later had political ambitions. Tokyo University rejected him. In his late twenties Asahara became spiritual and wandered in India, supposedly seeking and then receiving enlightenment while in the Himalayas. At 35 he returned to Japan and in 1984 founded his religious society called "Aum."

Aum is a composite belief system, which incorporated Asahara's own idiosyncratic interpretations of Yoga along with facets of Buddhism, Christianity, and even the writings of Nostradamus. In 1992 Asahara published a book, within which he declared himself "Christ," Japan's only fully enlightened master and the "Lamb of God." His purported mission was to take upon himself the sins of the world. Asahara said, he could transfer to his followers' spiritual power and ultimately take away their sins and bad Karma. He also saw dark conspiracies everywhere promulgated by Jews, Freemasons, and rival Japanese religions.

Ultimately, Asahara outlined a doomsday prophecy, which included a Third World War. This scenario foretold the eruption of Mt. Fuji and also what would later prove to be a self-fulfilling prediction--the gas attack upon Tokyo. Asahara's final conflict would culminate in a nuclear Armageddon. Humanity would end, except for an elite few. Aum's mission was not only to spread the word of "salvation," but also to survive these "End Times."

Aum's efforts to fulfill Shoko Asahara's vision of Armageddon led to a vast recruitment effort. This often included proselytizing professionals from the Japanese scientific community. According to court testimony the expertise of these Aum professionals led to the development of the cult's chemical and biological weapons. Aum's search for new weapons included a "medical mission" in 1992 to Zaire, supposedly to help fight an outbreak of the Ebola virus, but actually devised to obtain a strain of that virus for use in biological warfare. Aum also purchased gas masks in the United States to strategically develop defensive equipment that complemented its growing offensive arsenal.

Aum's radio broadcasts became both increasingly paranoid and virulent. Asahara incessantly attacked the Jews and even the British Royal Family as principals in conspiracies. He named the United States as the Beast from the Book of Revelations predicting America would eventually attack Japan.

Aum's Tokyo gas attack was supposedly the spark that would set off Asahara's prophetic vision of a final conflict. However, members of the cult later confessed this was also seen as a means to delay and/or prevent anticipated government action against the group. It was a brutal demonstration of their power and a warning of their willingness to use it. Asahara's last taped broadcast to his followers called upon them to rise up and carry out his plan for salvation and to "meet death without regrets."

Imprisoned cult leader Shoko Asahara received a death sentence in February of 2004 regarding 13 criminal cases. His lawyer filed an appeal. Asahara remains in prison and his lawyers claim the cult leader is "mentally incompetent." Despite this, the guru continues to garner the devotion of many remaining followers that insist he is a "spiritual being."[327]

Joseph Kony

Joseph Kony is a madman who claims to be a "spirit medium." He founded the Lord's Resistance Army (LRA), a guerrilla group that was until 2006, engaged in a violent campaign to establish a theocratic government in Uganda, allegedly based on the Ten Commandments. He abducted an estimated 20,000 children since 1987 and turned them into killing machines. The unfortunate children were then forcefully indoctrinated, much like Muslim children in madrassas. Savage beatings were meted out to the rebellious and the nonbelievers.

Like Muhammad and most cult leaders, Kony was also a polygamist. He prayed to the God of the Christians on Sundays, reciting the Rosary and quoting the Bible; but on Fridays, he performed the Islamic *Al-Jumm'ah* prayer. He celebrated Christmas, but also fasted for 30 days during Ramadan and prohibited the consumption of pork.

Joseph Kony had convinced his young warriors that with faith and recitation of the proper prayers, the Holy Spirit will shield them in battle. He promised the fighters that a magical power will render them victorious and made them believe that bullets fired at them will turn around in midair to hit the soldiers who were firing them. Similar malarkeys were promised by Muhammad to his followers who told them that angels will come to their help and twenty believers can vanquish two hundred and a hundred believers can vanquish a thousand of the unbelievers (Q. 8:65). But Muhammad was not stupid enough to believe in his own lies. Instead of

[327] www.culteducation.com/asahara.html

relying on angels he relied on espionage, sudden ambush, and terrorism to overcome his hapless victims.

Kony gave a bottle of water to his boys for protection against the Ugandan army. He told them that if they empty the bottle's contents, a river will be created that would drown the enemy soldiers. Muhammad used to throw a handful of sand in the direction of his enemies and cursed them. Both Kony and Muhammad stayed safely in the rear, while encouraging their followers to be courageous and not fear death. Another similarity of Kony and Muhammad is their common belief in evil spirits.

In 2005 the International Criminal Court (ICC) issued arrest warrants for Joseph Kony for crimes against humanity. The charges against him included murder, enslavement, sexual enslavement, cruel treatment of civilians, intentionally directing attacks against civilian populations, pillaging, rape, and forced enlisting of children into the rebel ranks. These are the very charges that Muhammad should have been indicted for.

Like Muhammad, Kony had very little tolerance for dissent. Anyone who resisted LRA indoctrination, or who attempted to escape was executed – often savagely beaten to death by those newly abducted into Kony's "Spirit Army."

Muhammad's success is due to the fact that he came in a place where there was no central government to stop him. He raided, looted and conquered, unchecked, starting as a robber and making his way up to become an emperor. He combined the seductiveness of a cult leader with the ruthlessness of a conqueror.

Narcissists often succeed because of their tremendous drive and a dogged determination. They seek to satiate their feelings of loneliness and lack of love with quest for power and domination.

The Cult Leader's Sexual Appetite

As narcissists, vested with unlimited authority, cult leaders develop a sense of entitlement to sexual vagaries that they do not allow their followers. One more characteristic of Muhammad that places him in the league of other infamous cult leaders is his abuse of his authority to obtain sexual gratification from his female followers. He had a predilection for younger and prettier women. The following is a short list of some of the contemporary cult leaders with similar appetite.

- Jim Jones (1931-1978) had sex with several women, and fathered children with some.
- David Koresh (1959-1993) restricted the sexual activity of his followers, while marrying wives as young as twelve because puberty was an accepted age for marriage in Old Testament times.
- Charles Manson (1934-) had sex with many of his female followers. He fathered children with three of them.

- Raël (1946-) founded Raelism and had sex with hundreds of women, "...a new one every day, all pretty young devotees who thought he was some kind of god." His ex-wife of 15 years said, "...over the years I began to think the whole Raelian movement was a trick to have more sex.[328]
- Bhagwan Shree Rajneesh (1931-1990) had sexual relationships with some of his female followers.[329] According to Tim Guest, whose mother joined the cult when he was 4 years old, group leaders in the Osho movement often initiated fourteen and fifteen-year-old girls into sex.[330]
- Sathya Sai Baba (1926-2011) Was a conman but according to Salon.com, "...the growing number of ex-devotees who decry their former master as a sexual harasser, ... and even a pedophile has hardly put a dent in his following." I personally saw an altar dedicated to this charlatan in the biggest minstream Hindu temple in London. The world is full of stupid people.
- Kenneth Emanuel Dyers (1922-2007) of Kenja Communication was charged with multiple counts of child sex molestation. As well there were a significant number of allegations relating to women within the group. He committed suicide amidst these charges.

The Harder the Better

Muslims often ask: If Muhammad was such a liar, why would he create a religion that is so hard with so many restrictions? If all he wanted was to have followers, why did he not make his religion easier? In fact, Islam is one of the hardest religions to practice. It is very demanding, with too many prohibitions, rituals, and obligations. Isn't difficulty in following a religion an indication that it is true?

A basic axiom of faith is one that also contains a paradox, which can be stated as follows: The more difficult a doctrine is, the more appealing it becomes. It is part of our psyche that we appreciate things for which we strive harder. On the other hand, we value less and give less importance to things we obtain easily or freely. Cults praise hardship and disdain the easy life. It's precisely this hardship that makes them attractive.

All cults are difficult to follow. The followers of Warren Jeffs, the Mormon polygamist cult, known as the Fundamentalist Church of Jesus Christ of Latter Day Saints, FLDS, worked for him for free or if they worked for someone else, handed

---

328 http://www.rickross.com/reference/raelians/raelians68.html

329 297James S. Gordon, The Golden Guru, p. 79

330 Bedell, Geraldine (January 11, 2004). "The future was orange: Tim Guest's upbringing as a child of the Bhagwan Shree Rajneesh 'free love' movement in the Sixties left him anything but spiritually enlightened", The Observer, Guardian News and Media Limited

over to him all their earnings. He made in excess of two million dollars per month, while his followers depended on welfare for their sustenance. Jeffs had absolute control over his followers. He prohibited them from watching TV, listening to radio or any music, except to his own songs. He assigned them houses to live in and told them not to intermingle with non-believers. He chose for them their spouses, and if he was unhappy with someone, he would order that person's wives to leave him, and they obeyed. Cults demand total submission and great sacrifices.

Cults are not easy to practice. Members are often asked to hand over their worldly possessions to the leader and to leave their jobs, friends and relatives behind. They are expected to live austere lives and in some cases, to abstain from sex. Meanwhile, the cult leader has everything. David Koresh slept with his followers' wives and prescribed celibacy for them. All cult leaders severely punish those who disobey them. Despite these abuses and hardships, the worst punishment for the members is excommunication. Some cultists commit suicide after being excommunicated.

Cult leaders separate the cultists from their family. They take away their money, their individuality and their identity. Stripped from everything they have nowhere to go and can easily be controlled. Excommunication means devastation.

This tactic is used, not only to keep the believers on a short leash, but also to expand the membership of the cult. Wherever Muslims are the majority, they isolate, harass, and ostracize the non-Muslims to coerce them into conversion.

In Pakistan, the religious minorities live in constant fear. Anyone can accuse you of blasphemy and whether guilty or not your freedom is ended. The hapless accused will almost never get out of prison alive. The non-Muslims are segregated, denied equal opportunities, and given menial jobs. There is one way out of this oppression and that is to convert to Islam. As the result, at least two dozen of Pakistani Christians convert to Islam each week by pledging an oath and signing a green and white document in which they accept Islam as "the most beautiful religion" and promise to "remain in the religion of Islam for the rest of my life, acknowledging that blessings are only from Allah."[331]

Cults demand sacrifice. Through sacrifice, believers can prove their faith and loyalty to God or the leader and gain their pleasure and acceptance. The more one sacrifices for something, the more one values it. No sacrifice is too great when your eternal salvation is at stake. Muhammad offered eternal life in Paradise, a bevy of celestial virgins and the sexual strength of 80 men, to those who sacrificed their lives for his cause in this world. As the reward is increased, the sacrifice must be proportionately bigger. To encourage his followers to do more he said:

---

[331] http://www.thestar.com/news/world/article/925715--some-christians-in-pakistan-convert-fear-into-safety

6- Muhammad's Cult

Not equal are those believers who sit (at home) and receive no hurt, and those who strive and fight in the cause of Allah with their goods and their persons. Allah has granted a grade higher to those who strive and fight with their goods and persons than to those who sit (at home). Unto all (in Faith) has Allah promised good, but those who strive and fight has He distinguished above those who sit (at home) by a special reward. (Q. 4:95)

In simple language, if you believe, you will be rewarded, but your reward will not be equal to the reward of those who wage jihad, who sacrifice their wealth and lives.

People's lives really don't matter to cult leaders. Muhammad gave all sorts of promises that the believers would reap after their death, if only they made him powerful and rich in this world.

The more dangerous a cult, the more stringent are its requirements. Some cults won't even accept you as a full member until you prove your loyalty by making a huge sacrifice. Muhammad made his followers believe that sacrifice was necessary and part of faith.

Cult leaders are master manipulators. They love to see people do strenuous tasks for them, so they can feel the power and savor their own omnipotence. They get their narcissistic supply by observing the servitude and the sacrifices of their followers. The believers will do anything, including kill, assassinate, and commit suicide to gain the approval of the leader. This servile attitude feeds their narcissistic craving for power. The cultist then mistakes the single-mindedness and intransigence of the leader with the truth of his cause.

Cults typically apply rigorous rituals. By observing these rituals meticulously, the followers are led to believe they will attain salvation. They become obsessed with rituals. They feel guilty when they fail them. These senseless rituals are to be performed, to please God or to become enlightened. The true intent is to keep them hooked and on their leash. The shorter the leash the better they can be controlled. Rituals have nothing to do with God or spirituality. They are designed to give the leader maximum power.

In Islam there is a whole list of things that are "unclean" that believers must avoid, such as dog, pig, urine, and kafirs. Believers must be aware of these unclean things and wash each time they come in contact with them. For women, there are more restrictions. As the result the majority of the converts to Islam are women. Going shopping, wrapped in Islamic hijab on a hot day, is nothing short of torture. All these ordeals increase the faith of the believer and make Islam sweeter in their mouth. More suffering means more rewards. Women must be obedient, docile, and respectful. They can be insulted, battered, and killed, with little legal protection. It is because of these that women find Islam attractive. Islam is precious to its believers, precisely because it is difficult.

The psychology of this phenomenon is explained by Osherow:[332] "Consider the prospective member's initial visit to the People's Temple (Jim Jones cult), for example. When a person undergoes a severe initiation in order to gain entrance into a group, he or she is apt to judge that group as being more attractive, in order to justify expending the effort or enduring the pain.

In a psychology test, Aronson and Mills[333] demonstrated that students who suffered a greater embarrassment as a prerequisite for being allowed to participate in a discussion group rated its conversation (which actually was quite boring), to be significantly more interesting than did those students who experienced little or no embarrassment in order to be admitted. Not only is there a tendency to justify undergoing the experience by raising ones estimation of the goal in some circumstances. Choosing to experience a hardship can go so far as to affect a person's perception of the discomfort or pain he or she felt.

Zimbardo[334] and his colleagues also showed that when subjects volunteered for a procedure that involved their being given electric shocks, those thinking that they had more choice in the matter reported feeling less pain from the shocks. More specifically, those who experienced greater dissonance, having little external justification to account for their choosing to endure the pain, described it as being less intense. This extended beyond their impressions and verbal reports; their performance on a task was hindered less, and they even recorded somewhat lower readings on a physiological instrument measuring galvanic skin responses. Thus the dissonance-reducing process can be double-edged: Under proper guidance, a person who voluntarily experiences a severe initiation not only comes to regard its ends more positively, but may also begin to see the means as less aversive: "We began to appreciate the long meetings, because we were told that spiritual growth comes from self-sacrifice," wrote Jeanne Mills an ex-member of Jim Jones cult (Mills, 1979).

This explains why Muslims are grateful for the tortures they endure voluntarily and consider them to be a blessing. All these hardships are seen as little sacrifices for achieving a bigger reward. An extreme form of this devotion can be seen during the month of Ashura, when the Shiite Muslims beat themselves on the chest, lacerate their backs with a bundle of chains, and cut their foreheads with machetes to bleed. Covered in their blood, they march in processions that bring to mind Dante's description of hell.

The belief that there is no gain without pain is so entrenched in human psyche that in some cultures people sacrificed humans and even their own children to please their gods.

---

[332] More on him chapter 7

[333] Aronson, E., AND Mills, J. The effects of severity of initiation on liking for a group. *Journal of Abnormal and Social Psychology.* 1959, 59, 177-18 1.

[334] Zimbardo, P. *The cognitive control of motivation.* Glenview, Ill.: Scott Foreman, 1969.

6- Muhammad's Cult

The Power of the Big Lie

Adolf Hitler, in his *Mein Kampf*, (1925) wrote: "The broad mass of a nation will more easily fall victim to a big lie than to a small one." As a master liar, Hitler was an expert on this subject. He added:

> In the big lie there is always a certain force of credibility; because the broad masses of a nation are always more easily corrupted in the deeper strata of their emotional nature than consciously or voluntarily; and thus in the primitive simplicity of their minds they more readily fall victims to the big lie than the small lie, since they themselves often tell small lies in little matters but would be ashamed to resort to large-scale falsehoods. It would never come into their heads to fabricate colossal untruths, and they would not believe that others could have the impudence to distort the truth so infamously. Even though the facts which prove this to be so may be brought clearly to their minds, they will still doubt and waver and will continue to think that there may be some other explanation. For the grossly impudent lie always leaves traces behind it, even after it has been nailed down, a fact which is known to all expert liars in this world and to all who conspire together in the art of lying.

Let not your dislike of Hitler obfuscate the truth of these words. We must give credit where credit is due. Hitler explains the power of the big lie and how it can fool millions like a true philosopher.

Another good statement is that of George Orwell, author of *Politics and the English Language*. He wrote: "Political language ... is designed to make lies sound truthful and murder respectable and to give an appearance of solidity to pure wind."[335]

Big lies are so outlandish that they often startle the listener. Most people are not equipped to process them. When the lie is colossal, the average person is left to wonder how anyone can have the audacity, the impudence to say such a thing with straight face. You are left with the difficult decision between three extremes: The person, who is saying this, must be either insane, a charlatan, or he must be telling the truth. Now, what if for any reason, such as your reverence for this person, his charisma, or your commitment to him, you can't bear the thought of repudiating him and accepting the fact that he maybe indeed insane or a quack? Then you are left with one choice and that is to believe in whatever he tells you even if what he says sounds crazy.

The big lie offsets the scale of our common-sense. It's like loading a scale made to weigh *kilos* with *tons*. It stops showing the correct weight. The indicator may break and stop at zero. Hence, the big lie can be more believable than a small lie.

---

[335] Politics and the English Language 1946
http://www.resort.com/~prime8/Orwell/patee.html

When Muhammad recounted his tale of ascending to heaven, Abu Bakr was at first taken aback. This sounded nuts. He had three choices: admit that the man whom he had accepted as a prophet and revered, and for whom he had sacrificed his wealth and endured ridicules, was indeed either insane or a liar, or believe in his fantastical tales and whatever else he might say. There was no middle ground.

Ibn Ishaq says when Muhammad made his vision known, "many Muslims gave up their faith. Some people went to Abu Bakr and said, 'What do you think of your friend? He alleges that he went to Jerusalem last night and prayed there, and came back to Mecca!' He replied that they were lying about the apostle, but they said that he was in the mosque at that very moment, telling people about it. Abu Bakr said, 'If he says so, then it is true. And what is so surprising in that? He tells me that communication from Allah, from heaven to earth, comes to him in an hour of a day or night, and I believe him. That is more extraordinary than that at which you boggle!'"[336]

The logic is flawless. What Abu Bakr was saying is that once you give up your rational faculty and believe in an absurdity, you might as well believe in anything. Once you let yourself to be fooled, you should be prepared to be fooled *ad infinitum,* because there is no end to the foolishness. Stupidity is a bottomless abyss. How many people would let a 53-year-old man rape their nine-year-old daughter? Abu Bakr did. This requires extreme foolishness.

Abu Bakr, by now had spent most of his wealth on Muhammad and his cause. This man had a lot at stake. At this stage, he had no other choice but to go along with whatever Muhammad told him. Admitting that he had been conned was too painful and embarassing. How could he explain this to his wife? What could he say to the wise men of Mecca who had laughed at him and told him he was a fool? The doors of going back for Abu Bakr were shut. He had to protect his pride and that meant he had to dispel any doubt. All he could do was to dig in deeper and blindly follow Muhammad to wherever he took him – to willfully suspend thinking and believe in anything his guru fancied. When you put your entire faith in someone and sacrifice so much for him, you give up your thinking faculty to him and become putty in his hand. This is what cult leaders want. Only this kind of devotion satiates their narcissistic craving and that is why they make their cults difficult and demanding. The more sacrifice you make the more hooked you become. When you have nothing left, you are theirs for good.

Hitler, Stalin and many other despotic leaders were insane. Those who saw their insanity could not whisper it to others. The "superior wisdom" of the despotic leader is the invisible cloak of the emperor. Those around him pretend to see it and extol its beauty. Those who are not in the immediate circle are convinced by the

---

[336] Sira Ibn Ishaq:P 183

conviction of others. Thus the big lie is perpetuated and no criticism of it is tolerated.

Use of Violence

Apart from believing in his own lies, the psychopath is ever ready to use violence to defend it. Appealing to force, in order to support a claim has often been successfully applied throughout history. It is called *Argumentum ad baculum*. It happens when someone resorts to force or the threat of force to push others to accept a conclusion.

The threat can be direct, like:

- *Slay the idolaters wherever you find them.* (Q. 9:5)
- *I will instill terror into the hearts of the unbelievers: smite ye above their necks and smite all their finger-tips off them.* (Q.8:12)

Or it can be indirect like:

- *And as for those who disbelieve and reject Our Signs, they are the people of Hell.* (Q.5:10)
- *For him [the disbeliever] there is disgrace in this life, and on the Day of Judgment We shall make him taste the Penalty of burning (Fire).* (Q.22:9)
- *(As for) those who disbelieve in Our communications, We shall make them enter fire; so oft as their skins are thoroughly burned, We will change them for other skins, that they may taste the chastisement; surely Allah is Mighty, Wise.* (Q.4:56)

The threat gives the big lie a dramatic sense of awe. The impact is so intense that the feeble mind can't remain indifferent. "How can one be so certain that God will punish those who disbelieve in him?" or "How can one kill someone for the mere fact that they disbelieve?" The threat gives more weight to the lie and makes it appear more credible. As I said before, virtually all the emails that Muslims send me contain the threat that I will go to hell. To them this is a valid argument. Take that threat away and none of them will know why they believe. Here is one example of how threat can be a convincing argument.

> The apostle said, 'Kill any Jew that falls into your power.' Thereupon Muhayyisa b. Mas`ud leapt upon Ibn Sunayna, a Jewish merchant with whom they had social and business relations, and killed him. Huwayyisa was not a Muslim at the time, though he was the elder brother. When Muhayyisa killed him, Huwayyisa began to beat him, saying, 'You enemy of God, did you kill him when much of the fat on your belly comes from his wealth?' Muhayyisa answered, 'Had the one who ordered me to kill him ordered me to kill you I would have cut your head off.' He said that this was the beginning of Huwayyisa's acceptance of Islam. The other replied, 'By God, if

> Muhammad had ordered you to kill me would you have killed me?' He said, 'Yes, by God, had he ordered me to cut off your head I would have done so.' He exclaimed, 'By God, a religion which can bring you to this is marvellous!' and he became a Muslim.[337]

Huwayyisa converted because he saw his brother had been transformed to such an extent that he was ready to kill, even his own brother. Zealotry is not the proof of the validity of a faith. But to people with feeble minds that distinction is not obvious. For them, extreme violence is extremely convincing. Most people have feeble minds. Rational thinkers are rare, especially in societies where there has been no tradition of rational thinking. The North Koreans, literally worship their mad leaders. This certainty comes to them through the dictators use of extreme violence and their zero tolerance for dissent. When your life depends on believing, you will believe in anything.

When the followers of Shoko Asahara were ordered to release sarin gas in the subways of Tokyo, they did not question the abhorrence of that order. They silenced their conscience and accepted it as the sign of the greater wisdom of their guru. They were faced with two choices: accept that their enlightened messiah is insane, that they have been fooled and all their sacrifices have been in vain, or convince themselves that his wisdom is vastly superior to theirs and therefore, they should not question him. These people had given up everything to be part of the cult of Asahara. They had burned all bridges to their personal lives. They had nothing left to fall back on and nowhere to go. Since questioning Asahara or dissenting would not have been tolerated, they had no choice but to believe that whatever he said was right. They banished their doubts and trusted their guru. The fact that he had come up with such an outrageous plan, not only did not dissuade them, it actually confirmed their faith in him even further. No ordinary person dares to do such a thing. Since they did not want to accept that their beloved leader was crazy, they submitted their intelligence to him and did the unthinkable. Highly educated people, who had joined the group for enlightenment, were transformed into mindless and heartless murderers.

Dr. Ikuo Hayashi was a respected and renowned doctor who had become one of Asahara's zealous followers. He was one of five persons who were ordered to plant the toxic sarin gas in the subways of Tokyo. Hayashi was a trained physician and had taken the Hippocratic Oath to save lives. In his trial he said that before puncturing the packages containing the deadly liquid, he looked at the woman sitting in front of him and for a moment had misgivings. He knew that he was about to cause that woman's death. But he immediately silenced his conscience and

---

[337] This story is recorded in by Ibn Ishaq in his Sirat Rasul Allâh as translated by A. Guillaume, The Life of Muhammad, page 369 and also in Sunnan Abu Dawud 19:2996.

convinced himself that Asahara knew best, and that it would not be right for him to question his master's wisdom.

Blind faith is lethal. Umayr was a 14 year old lad who accompanied Muhammad in one of his battles. Muhammad spoke so glowingly of martyrdom that Omeir was kindled with zealotry. Throwing away a handful of dates, which he was eating, he exclaimed "Is it these that hold me back from Paradise? Verily, I will taste no more of them, until I meet my Lord!" With such words, he drew his sword, and casting himself upon enemy's ranks, soon obtained the fate he coveted.

Once you become a believer, you dismiss the thought that your beloved leader may be a liar or insane. Psychopaths don't have a conscience. They are indifferent if millions of people, including those who believe in them and love them, are sacrificed for their selfish ambitions. They see others as tools. They develop the same kind of attachment to people around them that you may have to your pawns in a game of chess. In a game of chess, you don't develop love and attachment to your pawns. Your goal is to win and if you have to sacrifice them in order to win you will, without having any feelings for your pawns. For narcissists, people are mere objects. They are dispensable. The cultist, on the other hand, adulates and reveres his leader. He is under the delusion that his unbounded love is reciprocated. The cult leader professes to care, but nothing is further from truth. The narcissist cannot love people; he uses them. Paradoxically, his emotional detachment and his readiness to sacrifice anyone, including his nearest and dearest, are interpreted by his votaries as proof of his superiority. Normal people are incapable of such a thing. Therefore, they conclude that there must be something special about him.

Ayatollah Montazeri, the man who was to succeed Khomeini, until he fell from grace because of his disagreements with him, in his memoir wrote, when Khomeini ordered the massacre of more than 3,000 dissident boys and girls, he objected. Khomeini retorted that he will respond to God for his actions and that Montazeri should mind his own business. Khomeini believed in God. However, as a narcissist psychopath he was convinced that he was doing God's work. Those who have laid their faith in insane men see their proneness to kill as a portent of their greatness.

Narcissists are convinced and convincing. In one of his most revealing statements Hitler wrote. "Hence today I believe that I am acting in accordance with the will of the Almighty Creator: by defending myself against the Jew, I am fighting for the work of the Lord."[338] It was his conviction that attracted the support of so many Germans. He was a spellbinding speaker. When he spoke, he became louder and louder, as he vented his rage at the perceived enemies of Germany. He aroused the patriotism of Germans. His belief that bigger lies are more believable proved

[338] Adolf Hitler, Mein Kampf, Ralph Mannheim, ed., New York: Mariner Books, 1999, p. 65.

true. Millions of Germans believed him. They loved him and were moved to tears by his fiery speeches.

Ibn Sa'd reveals more similarities between Muhammad and Hitler. He wrote, "During his sermons, the eyes of the Prophet would turn red as he would raise his voice and speak angrily, as if he was the commander of an army warning his men. He would say 'the resurrection and I are like these two fingers (showing his index and middle finger). He would say 'the best of guidance is the guidance of Muhammad and the worst thing is innovation and any innovation will result in perdition."[339]

In the same place Ibn Sa'd says: "During his sermons, the Prophet used to wield a stick." Obviously, to symbolize his dominance!

You can't easily master the art of manipulation, unless you are a narcissist. Your biggest deterrent is your conscience. To become a master manipulator you have to be bereft of conscience. You must be willing to kill and destroy other people's lives without hesitation and not have any remorse. You can't do that unless you are a narcissist or a sociopath.

He Frowned

Islamic societies are dysfunctional, patriarchal, misogynous, and dictatorial. Children are abused, beaten and humiliated. Consequently, they grow up scarred, have low self-esteem, fancy grandiosity, and evince symptoms of pathological narcissism. Islamic countries cannot become democracies because their "demos" (common people) are damaged psychologically and emotionally.

During my teen years in Pakistan, I had an Afghani friend who had all these characteristics. One day he told me he wanted to "become a Hitler." Hitler is a popular figure in Islamic countries. I was annoyed with that stupid remark and after giving him a piece of my mind, I walked away from him. Fearing to lose my friendship, the next day he came to me and said that the night before he dreamt the Prophet scolding him and telling him that he should become a "spiritual Hitler". This is how a pathological narcissist thinks. Instead of confessing that what he had said was foolish, he invented a ridiculous lie to fool me. There is a sura in the Quran titled *'Abasa* (He Frowned) that shows its author's similar pathetic mindset.

Early Muslims were mostly slaves or rebellious youths with no social standing. Muhammad was very eager to enlist some influential men in his religion. One day, he was sitting among the dignitaries of Mecca trying to convert them. One of his followers, a blind poor man named Ibn Umm Maktum, approached him with a question. Muhammad disliked this interruption and frowned. Those sitting around

---

[339] Ibn Sa'd Tabaqat, v. 1, p. 362

him noticed his contempt. They criticized him for his hypocrisy for smiling at the wealthy and frowning at the poor. There was no way for Muhammad to get out of this embarrassing situation. He could not possibly make God approve his snobbishness, as he was wont of doing any time he found himself in difficulty. Instead of acknowledging his mistake and apologizing for his poor judgment, like a mature person, the next day he claimed to have received a sura in which Allah rebuked him for ignoring the poor blind man, while trying to impress the rich.

He frowned and turned (his) back,
Because there came to him the blind man.
And what would make you know that he would purify himself,
Or become reminded so that the reminder should profit him?
As for him who considers himself free from need (of you),
To him do you address yourself.
And no blame is on you if he would not purify himself
And as to him who comes to you striving hard,
And he fears,
From him will you divert yourself.
Nay! Surely it is an admonishment.
So let him who pleases mind it.
In honored books,
Exalted, purified,
In the hands of scribes. (Q. 80: 1-15)

In these verses Muhammad makes Allah admonish him for his condescendence. He plays the same silly game of my hypocrite Afghani friend. To benighted Muslims however, these verses are proof of his sincerity.

Why Did Everyone Praise Muhammad?

A question that boggles Muslims is why, if Muhammad was so evil, his companions failed to see it and why did they praise him so much? Why no one spoke opprobriously of him, even after his death?

In a cultic society, speaking one's mind is not safe. Telling the truth could bring you ostracism or worse. Most people have sheep mentality. They go with the flow. This is more so in cults. Those who think differently are wise enough to keep their mouths shut so they can keep their heads on their shoulders.

Where critics are silenced, sycophants and bootlickers will try to endear themselves by eulogizing the leader with flattery and exaggerated adulation. Saddam was hated by most of the Iraqis, and yet all you could hear about him in Iraq, while he was still in power, were his praises. The narcissist is so cut off from reality that he believes in those praises and in a sense becomes a victim of his own deception. Because Muhammad is believed to be a prophet, his reign of terror did not end with his death. Those who had fallen for his Big Lie perpetuated it through terror and silenced those who disagreed, just as they do today. Once those who knew him personally died, subsequent generations had no way of knowing the truth and believed in what they were told. Thus, the lie passed from one generation to another. After his death, sycophants continued fawning over him, praising him to the skies, even attributing miracles to him. This added to their prestige and made them look pious.

Fourteen hundred years later, millions of Muslims behave in the same way they did at the time of Muhammad in Medina. The dissenters are afraid to talk, and if they do, they are swiftly silenced. Meanwhile, the sycophants and fawners are honored for extolling the Prophet's "virtues." How can truth triumph in an atmosphere so fraught with terror, hypocrisy and sycophancy?

There are several stories about Umar, Muhammad's right hand man, drawing his sword and threatening to strike the head of anyone who dared to defy the authority of his master or slightly disagreed with him. Muhammad encouraged this sycophantism and punished independent thinking. Those trapped in such an oppressive climate, eventually come to believe in the superhuman qualities of the leader. The Big Lie, propped with violence, is far more believable.

A few years ago, a team of eye surgeons went to North Korea to help people with cataracts. Thousands of young and old lined up for help. After they recovered their sights, the doctors were stupefied to see that the first thing the patients did was to go to the large portraits of their dictator Kim Jong Il and his father hanging on the wall, to prostrate and thank THEM. They did not thank the doctors who helped them, but the tyrants who had kept them poor and blind. The North Koreans love their despots for the same reason Muslims love their prophet. They are brainwashed victims of cultism. Where oppression rules and questioning is banned, truth is always the casualty.

Muhammad succeeded because he preached to a largely ignorant, superstitious and chauvinistic people. The qualities he needed to bolster his marauding religion were already present in his early followers. Chauvinism, bigotry, haughtiness, arrogance, megalomania, stupidity, boastfulness, lustfulness, greed, disdain for life, and other ignoble character traits that are the hallmarks of Islam were already the *materia prima* of Arabs. These attributes were then imposed on other nations who fell under the domination of Islam. Anyone with these base qualities found in Islam a common ground and the "divine" validation for their deviant criminal penchant. Even today, Islam is the favorite religion of prison inmates, fools and criminally minded people, while good humand born in Islam are leaving it in droves.

Chapter Seven

When Sane People Follow Insane People

Muslims seem perfectly normal people. They work and raise their families like anyone else. They are regular people, employees, colleagues, bosses, neighbors and citizens. And they have the same dreams, hopes and fears that others have. However, they also have a dark side. To the extent that they believe in Islam they are cultists. Under the influence of Islam they can be transformed from Dr. Jekyll to Mr. Hyde. This transformation can happen instantly and with no prior notice.

Fanaticism is defined as excessive enthusiasm, unreasoning zeal, or wild and extravagant notions on any subject, especially religion. People don't embrace a religion to become murderers and terrorists. So what makes some disregard commonsense, engage in despicable acts and murder their fellow beings in the name of religion?

In the previous chapter, I showed that Islam has many cultic features. In this chapter, I will go in more detail and will compare Islam to the cult of the People's Temple. All cults share similar characteristics. We can compare Islam to any cult and the result would be the same.

Stirred by their insane leader, the members of People's Temple, administered a poison-laced drink to their children and drank it themselves. Their bodies were found lying together, arm in arm; over 900 perished. How could such a tragedy happen? What drove these sane people commit such insanity? This article will explore how mind control works and will show the frightening similarities between Islam and People's Temple.

Jim Jones started his preaching in Indiana twenty years before the mass suicide, in 1965, with a handful of followers. He stressed the need for racial equality and integration. His group helped feed the poor and find them job. He was charismatic and persuasive. Soon, his followers began to multiply; new congregations were formed and a headquarters was established in San Francisco.

Absolute Obedience

Jones was to his followers, a beloved leader. They affectionately called him "Father," or simply "Dad." As time went on, he gradually assumed the role of messiah. As his influence grew, he demanded more obedience and loyalty. His followers were more than eager to comply. He persuaded them that the world is about to be destroyed in a nuclear holocaust and if they followed him, they would emerge as the only survivors. Dooms day threat is common theme in all cults. They use fear as a tool to manipulate and control.

Neal Osherow has studied People's Temple and in an article titled *An Analysis of Jonestown: Making Sense of the Nonsensical,* he explains the anatomy of cults. He writes, "Many of his harangues attacked racism and capitalism, but his most vehement anger focused on the 'enemies' of the People's Temple - its detractors and especially its defectors."[340]

The same can be said about Muhammad. At first, he was only a "warner," who called people to believe in God and fear the Day of Judgment. He said that he had come to call the polytheists of Mecca and its surrounding to tell them to worship one God and to take care of the poor. As his influence grew, his ambitions also became more menacing. He asked his followers to abandon their homes and threatened them with divine chastisement and murder if they didn't. Many of his early harangues attacked polytheism (*shirk*), but his most vehement anger was directed at the "enemies" of Islam, his detractors, and his defectors.

Jim Jones took his people to a jungle in Guyana. He wanted to isolate them and separated them from their families. Cut off from all external influences, and under his total control, he could easily brainwash and indoctrinate them. This was also the reason why Muhammad was so insistent that his followers leave Mecca. He told them, "*As to those who believed but came not into exile, you owe no duty of protection to them until they come into exile.*" (Q. 8:72)

This verse says that the believers should not give protection to those Muslims who did not emigrate. In 4:89 he advised them to kill their pals of they decide to defect and return to Mecca. And to make them perish, even the thought of defecting, he reminded them that "*Allah is the All-Seer of what you do.*"

---

340 Osherow, Neal. "Making Sense of the Nonsensical: An Analysis of Jonestown." In *Readings about the Social Animal*, 7th edition, ed. Elliot Aronson. New York: W. H. Freeman. Available online. [URL=http://www.academicarmageddon.co.uk/library/OSHER.htm] All Osherow's quotes in this chapter are taken from this source.

7- When Sane People Follow Insane People

Muhammad's Allah has an uncanny resemblance to George Orwell's enigmatic dictator of Oceania, "*Big Brother,"* in his novel, *Nineteen Eighty-Four*. In Orwell's fictional society everybody is under complete surveillance through telescreens. People are constantly reminded of this by the phrase "Big Brother is watching you," which is the core "truth" of the propaganda system in this state.

In the novel, it is not clear if the Big Brother actually exists as a person, or is an image crafted by the state. Since Inner Party torturer O'Brien points out that Big Brother can never die, the apparent implication is that Big Brother is the personification of the party. Nobody has ever seen him. He is a face on the hoardings, a voice on the telescreen.... Big Brother is the guise in which the Party chooses to exhibit itself to the world. His function is to act as a focusing point for love, fear, and reverence, emotions which are more easily felt towards an individual than towards an organization. The loyal citizens of Oceania don't fear Big Brother, but in fact love and revere him. They feel he protects them from the evils out there.[341]

Muhammad's Allah fulfills has the same characteristics and attributes. He is invisible and yet ever-present. He is loved and simultaneously feared, and he watches your every move and monitors your thought. Allah keeps a record of everything people do to punish them or to reward them after they die.

Indeed, your Lord is ever watchful (Q. 89:14), *Who sees you when you stand up and sees your every movement!* (Q. 26: 218-219).

Death as the Proof of Faith

Osherow says: "But when in 1978 the concerned relatives of People's Temple persuaded the Congressman Leo Ryan to investigate the cult, he and the journalists that accompanied him heard most residents praise the settlement, expressing their joy at being there and their desire to stay. Two families, however, slipped messages to Ryan that they wanted to leave with him. But when the visiting party and these defectors tried to board planes, they were ambushed and fired at until five of them including Ryan, were murdered. Then Jim Jones gathered his followers and told them to drink from the poison-laced beverage and '*die with dignity*'".

Excerpts from a tape, recorded as the final ritual was being enacted reveal the believers, with few exceptions, voluntarily drank the poison and fed it to their children. The talks and assurances of Jim Jones are eerily recognizable to those who are familiar with the Quran. A woman protests, but the crowd silences her and everyone expresses their readiness to die.

---

[341] Wikipedia.com

The following is the transcript of the tape recording (available on Youtube). It is truly shocking, but a testimony of the total hold that cult leaders have on their followers.

Jim Jones: I've tried my best to give you a good life. In spite of all I've tried, a handful of people, with their lies, have made our life impossible. If we can't live in peace then let's die in peace. (Applause) … We have been so terribly betrayed… What's going to happen here in the matter of a few minutes is that one of the people on that plane is going to shoot the pilot - I know that. I didn't plan it, but I know its going to happen … So my opinion is that you used to in ancient Greece, and step over quietly, because we are not committing suicide-it's a revolutionary act …We can't go back

First Woman: I feel like that as there's life; there's hope.

Jones: Well, someday everybody dies.

Crowd: That's right, that's right!

Jones: What those people gone and done, and what they get through will make our lives worse than hell... But to me, death is not a fearful thing. It's living that's cursed. Not worth living like this.

First Woman: But I'm afraid to die.

Jones: I don't think you are. I don't think you are.

First Woman: I think there were too few who left for 1,200 people to give them their lives for those people who left... I look at all the babies and I think they deserve to live.

Jones: But don't they deserve much more? They deserve peace. The best testimony we can give is to leave this goddam world. (Applause)

First Man: It's over, sister... We've made a beautiful day. (Applause)

Second Man: If you tell us we have to give our lives now, we're ready. (Applause) [Baltimore Sun, 1979]

Above the cries of babies wailing, the tape continues, with Jones insisting upon the need for suicide and urging the people to complete the act:

Jones: Please get some medication. Simple! It's simple There's no convulsions with it... Don't be afraid to die. You'll see people out here. They'll torture our people...

Second Woman: There's nothing to worry about. Everybody keep calm and try to keep your children calm... They're not crying from pain; it's just a little bitter tasting...

Third Woman: This is nothing to cry about. This is something we could all rejoice about. (Applause)

Jones: Please, for God's sake, let's get on with it... This is a revolutionary suicide. This is not a self-destructive suicide. (Voices praising, "Dad." Applause)

Third Man: Dad has brought us this far. My vote is to go with Dad...

Jones: We must die with dignity. Hurry, hurry, hurry! We must hurry... Stop this hysterics. Death is a million times more preferable to spending more days in this life... If you knew what was ahead, you'd be glad to be stepping over tonight...

7- When Sane People Follow Insane People

Fourth Woman: It's been a pleasure walking with all of you in this revolutionary struggle... No other way I would rather go than to give my life for socialism, Communism, and I thank Dad very much.

Jones: Take our life from us... We didn't commit suicide. We committed an act of revolutionary suicide protesting against the conditions of an inhuman world.[342]

The release of this tape shocked the world. Yet, this mindless obedience is also a characteristic of Islam. No other religion reduces its followers into such zombies as Islam does. To Muslims, their zealotry is the proof of the truth of their faith. Tales of mindless devotion and readiness to die abound the annals of the Islamic history. Islam means submission. Believers must relinquish their will and disregard everything, including their family and their life to prove their loyalty to Allah and his messenger. The Quran says: "*...then seek for death, if you are sincere.*"(Q.2:94) In another place Muhammad challenged the Jews to desire death in order to prove that they are truthful. *Say: "O ye that stand on Judaism! If ye think that ye are friends to Allah, to the exclusion of (other) men, then express your desire for Death, if ye are truthful."* (Q.62:6)

To a narcissist cult leader, the ultimate test of devotion is death. The Palestinian televisions often show mothers of suicide bombers proudly speaking of the sacrifice of their children and expressing their hope that their other children will follow suit. This irreverence for life is a characteristic of cults.

Punishment and Coercion

Osherow explains: "If you hold a gun at someone's head, you can get that person to do just about anything. The Temple lived in constant fear of severe punishment, brutal beatings coupled with public humiliation for committing trivial or even accidental offenses. Jim Jones used the threat of severe punishment to impose the strict discipline and absolute devotion that he demanded, and he also took measures to eliminate those factors that might encourage resistance or rebellion among his followers."

Muslims live constantly under the threat of punishment. They don't write to challenge my views. They write to threaten me with the punishment in hell. The most recurring theme in the Quran is 'hell,' repeated over 200 times, followed by the 'Day of Judgment,' repeated 163 times and in third place, 'Resurrection,' repeated 117 times.

The threat is not just of hell but also of physical punishment. In Islamic madrassas, (religious schools) children are beaten as the norm and in some instances they chained. The beating is not limited to children; adults are also corporally

[342] Newsweek, 1978, 1979

punished, flogged publicly, humiliated, maimed, or stoned to death. The offences can be a trivial as eating in public during Ramadan, or for a woman, revealing too much hair.

The Sharia bans any form of independence. Critics, freethinkers, reformers and apostates are to be killed.

Bukhari reports two hadiths where Muhammad said "Allah has forbidden for you to ask too many questions."[343] Ignorance is the only way to maintain the illusion of Islam. With its compulsory blind faith, Islam can only be enforced through fear.

Osherow writes, "But the power of an authority need not be so explicitly threatening in order to induce compliance with its demands, as demonstrated by social psychological research. In Milgram's experiments,[344] a surprisingly high proportion of subjects obeyed the instructions of an experimenter to administer what they thought were very strong electric shocks to another person."

Elimination of Dissention

Cult leaders know that absolute obedience will be noticeably reduced if there is a small minority of dissenters. "Research showed," Osherow writes, "that the presence of a 'disobedient' partner greatly reduced the extent to which most subjects in the Milgram situation[345] obeyed the instructions to shock the person designated the 'learner.' Similarly, by including just one confederate who expressed an opinion different from the majority's, Asch[346] showed that the subject would also agree far less, even when the 'other dissenters' judgment was also incorrect and differed from the subjects."

Muhammad and Jim Jones could not tolerate dissent. They demanded exclusive and absolute allegiance and made the thought of questioning and criticizing them an unthinkable option. Muhammad forgave those who fought against him, if they accepted Islam and his hegemony, but he did not forgive those who deserted him.

Jeanne Mills, who spent six years as a high-ranking member of People's Temple, before becoming one of the few who left it, wrote: "There was an unwritten but perfectly understood law in the church that was very important: No one is to criticize Father, wife, or his children."[347]

---

[343] Bukhari *3:.41:591and 2:.24: 555:*

[344] Milgram, S. Behavioural study of obedience. *Journal of Abnormal and Social Psychology,* 1963, 67, 371-378.

[345] Milgram S. Liberating effects of group pressure. *Journal of personality and Social Psychology,* 1965, 1, 127-134.

[346] Asch, S. Opinions and social pressure. *Scientific American,* 1955, 193.

[347] Mills, J. *Six years with God.* New York: A & W Publishers, 1979.

7- When Sane People Follow Insane People

Muhammad said his wives are the mother of believers and claimed that his close companions have a special rank. Dr. Yunis Sheikh, a college professor in Pakistan, commented that the parents of Muhammad were not Muslims. This seems obvious since they died when Muhammad was only a child, and is confirmed by Muhammad who refused to pray at their graves, “revealing” a verse for it. "*It is not for the Prophet, and those who believe, to pray for the forgiveness of idolaters even though they may be near of kin (to them) after it hath become clear that they are people of hell-fire.*" (Q. 9:113)

Yet, Dr. Sheikh’s comment angered his students who thought he had insulted the parents of their prophet. They complained to the clerics, who took Dr. Sheikh to a court, accused him of blasphemy and the court condemned him to death. Dr. Sheikh was released after a few years when many from around the world protested.

In September 2006, Mohammed Taha Mohammed Ahmed, the editor-in-chief of the Sudanese independent daily, Al-Wifaq, was kidnapped by a group of Muslims who put him through a mock trial before slitting his throat in a style used to slaughter camels, and then decapitated him. He was accused of blasphemy after his paper republished an article from the Internet that questioned the parentage of Muhammad. All that Taha did was to quote small excerpts of the offending article in order to and write his own rebuttal.[348]

If you criticize Islam, Muhammad, or his companions, there is a chance that you could be killed even if you live in a non-Muslim country. The Dutch filmmaker, Theo Van Gogh, learned this lesson too late. He was stabbed by a Muslim for assisting the Muslim dissident Ayan Hisi Ali in making a movie about women in Islam.

Ettore Caprioli, the Italian translator of *The Satanic Verses* was grievously injured, Hitoshi Igarishi, the translator of that book into Japanese, was assassinated, amd William Nygaard, its Norwegian translator was knifed.

The idea is to instill terror so no one dares to speak against Islam. Deborah Blakey, another long-time member of the cult of People’s Temple who managed to defect, testified: “Any disagreement with Jim Jones’s dictates came to be regarded as ‘treason.’... Although I felt terrible about what was happening, I was afraid to say anything because I knew that anyone with a differing opinion gained the wrath of Jones and other members.”[349]

Inconsistencies

Many early Muslims, just as some members of the People’s Temple, realized that the stated aim of their belief and the practices of their respective leader were inconsistent. Jim Jones slept with many women in his congregation and he was not

[348] http://www.news24.com/News24/Africa/News/0,,2-11-1447_2034654,00.html
[349] Blakey, D. Affidavit: San Francisco. June 15, 1978.

coy about it. Muhammad also did a lot of things that raised eyebrows, even among the Arabs with such a lax morality.

In one hadith Aisha narrates: "I used to look down upon those ladies who had given themselves to Allah's Apostle and I used to say, 'Can a princess give herself (to a man)?' But when Allah revealed: '*You (O Muhammad) can postpone (the turn of) whom you will of them (your wives), and you may receive any of them whom you will; and there is no blame on you if you invite one whose turn you have set aside,*' (Q.33:51) I said (to the Prophet), 'I feel that your Lord hastens in fulfilling your wishes and desires.'"[350]

Aisha was not only a pretty girl, but also a witty one. Indeed we see on many occasions Muhammad's god coming to his help and licensing him to do whatever he pleased.

Muhammad broke several social norms such as marrying his daughter-in-law, and having sex with Mariyah, one of his wives' maids. He was 50 years old when he married the 6 year old Aisha and slept with her when she was only nine and still playing with dolls. He claimed to have received most of his inspirations under the blanket with Aisha.

> 'Aisha said, "My companions (i.e. the other wives of the Prophet) gathered in the house of Um Salama and said, "0 Um Salama! By Allah, the people choose to send presents on the day of 'Aisha's turn and we too, love the good (i.e. presents etc.) as 'Aisha does. You should tell Allah's Apostle to tell the people to send their presents to him wherever he may be, or wherever his turn may be." Um Salama said that to the Prophet and he turned away from her, and when the Prophet returned to her (i.e. Um Salama), she repeated the same, and the Prophet again turned away, and when she told him the same for the third time, the Prophet said, "O Um Salama! Don't trouble me by harming 'Aisha, for by Allah, the Divine Inspiration never came to me while I was under the blanket of any woman amongst you except her."[351]

A narrative of Yunus Ibn Ishaq records that the apostle saw Ummu'l-Fadl when she was a baby, crawling before him and said, "If she grows up and I am still alive I will marry her."[352] Another hadith says, Muhammad saw Um Habiba daughter of Abbas when she was fatim (age of nursing) and he said, "If she grows up while I am still alive, I will marry her."[353] Fortunately for both these babies, he died shortly after that. Abbas lived in Mecca. So Muhammad must have seen his baby when he invaded that town. At that time he was 61 years old. At that age he lusted after one or two years old babies.

---

[350] Bukhari, 6: 60: 311
[351] Bukhari, 5: 57: 119:
[352] Ibn Ishaq: Suhayli, 2.79 p. 311
[353] Musnad Ahmad, Number 25636

7- When Sane People Follow Insane People

Of course, many early believers must have wondered why, if Muhammad is a messenger of God, he is so ungodly. We cannot assume that all his followers were completely bereft of conscience and did not know what he was doing was wrong. However, if they had any doubts, they were unable to express them. They feared ostracism and punishment. If you live among cultists you can't criticize the leader. Detractors were quickly silenced.

Ubn Ishaq reports, on one occasion, the Meccan companions of Muhammad, the Immigrants, got into fight with his Medinan followers while they were out of town raiding and robbing. Abdullah ibn Ubayy, the man who had stopped Muhammad massacring the Banu Nadir, was enraged. He said, "Have they [the Immigrants] actually done this? They dispute our priority, they outnumber us in our own country, and nothing so fits us and the vagabonds of Quraish as the ancient saying 'Feed a dog and it will devour you.' By Allah, when we return to Medina, the stronger will drive out the weaker." Then he went to his people who were there and said, "This is what you have done to yourselves. You have let them occupy your country, and you have divided your property among them. Had you but kept your property from them they would have gone elsewhere." When this news reached Muhammad he decided to kill Ibn Ubayy. Upon hearing this, his son who had converted to Islam came to Muhammad and told him, "I have heard that you want to kill 'Abdullah b. Ubayy for what you have heard about him. If you must do it, then order me to do it and I will bring you his head, for al-Khazraj knows that they have no man more dutiful to his father than I. I am afraid that if you order someone else to kill him, my soul will not permit me to see his slayer walking among men and I shall kill him, thus killing a believer for an unbeliever, and so I should go to hell."[354]

Abdullah ibn Ubayy was a great man among his people, and the Medinans respected their old chief. This was now a tough situation. Permitting a son to murder his own father, a father like ibn Ubbay, could have unpleasant consequences. What if his son was testing the veracity of the rumor to turn against him and rise in defense of his father? Muhammad wisely decided to let go of his macabre design. Ibn Ubayy's son's gesture, however, is praised by Muslim historians and commentators and is regarded as an example of true faith. This was the level of control he exerted on his followers. He made them spy on each other and created an atmosphere of fear in which every dissent was nipped in the bud.

When Abdullah ibn Ubayy died, his son begged Muhammad to say his father's funeral prayer. Because of ibn Ubay's stature, Muhammad felt it is expedient to oblige. As he got up to pray for the deceased, Umar, who remembered Muhammad's reluctance to pray at the grave of his own mother, caught hold of his garment and said, "Allah's Messenger, are you going to conduct prayer for this man,

[354] Ibn Ishaq. Sira

whereas Allah has forbidden you to offer prayer for unbelievers?" He replied, "Allah has given me an option as He has said: *Ask pardon for them, or ask not pardon for them; if you ask pardon for them seventy times, God will not pardon them* (Q.9:80) and I am going to make an addition to the seventy."[355] It is ironic that Muhammad should call ibn Ubay "hypocrite" when that title best suited him. He hated Ibn Ubay, but now that he had died, it was time to ingratiate himself with his son and his tribe and say one more prayer to change God's mind. Why he would not say that extra prayer for his mother and uncle and save them from hellfire?

The following hadith is one example of the anger that Muhammad expressed for those who dared to question him. This happened when he was distributing all the booty confiscated in the war of Hunain among the chiefs of Mecca to, as he put it, "sweeten Islam in their mouths," and "soften their hearts." He gave nothing to those who had helped him conquer Mecca and win the war against the Hunain. A man said: "O Allah's Apostle! Do Justice." The Prophet said, "Woe to you! Who could do justice if I did not? I would be a desperate loser if I did not do justice." Umar said, "O Allah's Apostle! Allow me to chop his head off."[356]

This man was from Banu Tamim. His tribe was not Muslim. They had joined the expedition for a share in the loot. Now that Muhammad had become victorious, and had the support of the Quraish, he had no use for the Tamim anymore and did not feel the need to honor his promise. This man was not familiar with the Prophet's character. His life suddenly threatened for his criticism of Muhammad. The experience must have been sobering for him and all those who were present. The lesson learned was that one is not allowed to question the Prophet even when he is unjust. Anyone who questioned him met his wrath. Only sycophancy was approved.

Is there a lesson in this for the leftists? The Left has allied itself with Islam in the hope that they would help them to grab the power. That is a pipe dream. The leftists who supported the Islamists in Iran during the 1979 revolution were the first to be hanged. Forming an alliance with one group to conquer another and then turning against them, was Muhammad's modus operandi.

Osherow continues, "Conditions in the People's Temple became so oppressive, the discrepancy between Jim Jones's stated aims and his practices so pronounced, that it is almost inconceivable that members failed to entertain questions about the church. But these doubts were not reinforced. There were no allies to support one's disobedience of the leader's commands and no fellow dissenters to encourage the expression of disagreement with the majority. Public disobedience or dissent was quickly punished. Questioning Jones's word, even in the company of family or

---

[355] Bukhari, 6: 60:192

[356] Bukhari, 4: 56: 807

friends was dangerous. Informers and 'counselors' were quick to report indiscretions, even the relatives."

Like Jones, Muhammad relied heavily on his spies and informers, which as Osherow says, "This not only stifled dissent; it also diminished the solidarity and loyalty that individuals felt toward their families and friends."

Muslims are asked to keep a watch on each other lest one of them deviates from the "right path." This is called *Amr bil ma'roof* (injunction to do right) and *Nahi min al munkar* (forbiddance of wrong). The right and wrong, however, are not what commonsense and the Golden Rule dictate. They are what Muhammad enjoined and forbade. In Islam, everyone is required to correct the conduct of the fellow believers and report them to authorities in grave cases. In Iran, after the Islamic revolution, children were encouraged to report any un-Islamic activity by their parents. Also several youths were reported by their fathers and were executed. The informers were lauded and praised to encourage others to do the same.

Osherow says: "While Jones preached that a spirit of brotherhood should pervade his church, he made it clear that each member's personal dedication should be directed to "Father."

In Islam the believers are supposed to be brothers to each other, but their first loyalty is to Muhammad, or as he put it, to the company of "Allah and his messenger." The moment you leave Islam, those very "brothers" in faith will not hesitate to slit your throat. In fact even your brother in blood may kill you.

The similarities between Jim Jones' cult and Islam are astounding. This is the natural expression of the psychopathic mind of all narcissists. All totalitarian polities, from Nazism to fascism, from communism to Islam, share the same characteristics that George Orwell described in his novel.

Destruction of Family Ties

Jim Jones believed: "Families are part of the enemy system," because they hurt one's total dedication to the "Cause."[357] The "Cause" was of course none but himself. Thus, a person called before the membership to be punished could expect his or her family to be among the first and most forceful critics.[358]

Muhammad split families by stating that the believers must pay their allegiance first to Allah and his Messenger and disobey their parents if they come in between. He said, "*Now We have enjoined on man goodness towards his parents; yet (even so) should they endeavor to make you commit Shirk (disbelief) with Me of something which you have no knowledge of, obey them not.*" (Q. 29:8)

[357] Mills, J. *Six years with God.* New York: A & W Publishers, 1979.

[358] Cahill, T. In the valley of the shadow of death. *Rolling Stone.* January 25, 1979.

You also recall the love story of Muhammad's daughter Zeinab and her husband Abul Aas mentioned in chapter two and how he ordered her to leave her husband because he had not converted to Islam.

If a woman converts to Islam her marriage to her unbelieving husband becomes void. The intent is to coerce the husband to convert.

A heart wrenching story is that of Mus'ab ibn Umair, a youth of Mecca. His parents loved him dearly. His mother was Khunaas, a wealthy and influential lady. She donned him with the best and finest cloths, indulged him with the most expensive perfumes and bought him the most elegant and fashionable shoes. Mus'ab was one of the early converts in Mecca. He must have been about 14 years old when he became a Muslim. He kept his faith a secret. When his mother learned about it she was distraught. She impeded him from going out. When Muhammad ordered his followers to go to Abyssinia Mus'ab was among them. Upon his return, Khunaas tried again to persuade him to leave Muhammad. Her cries fell on deaf ears. She stopped giving him money. Mus'ab was undeterred. He wore tattered cloths and remained steadfast in his faith. Muhammad sent him to Medina to preach. He was successful and managed to convert more than seventy people. These are the same seventy who visited Muhammad at Aqaba and pledged to support him.

When Mus'ab returned to Mecca he did not go to see his mother. When she heard that her son was in town and had not come to see her, she felt saddened and sent him a message saying, how ungrateful can you be to your mother? You came to the city where I reside and did not come to see me? He responded, I would not go to anyone's house before visiting the house of the Prophet. When he visited her, she pleaded with him to stay. He said, "Don't insist mother, for if you attempt to block me leaving I will have no choice but to kill you." The heart broken mother said you may go, while fighting back her tears. Mus'ab told her, "I want your own good mother. Attest that there is no god but Allah and Muhammad is his messenger." Khunaas responded, "by the brilliance of the stars I will not abandon my faith, but you are free to do as you please." Mus'ab left and soon after, he migrated to Medina. He took part in Muhammad's raids and robberies and was killed in the Battle of Uhud.[359] Khunaas was present in that battle and saw her son's death and cried bitterly.

Muslims narrate this story and praise the mindless devotion of Mus'ab as an example to be followed. One Muslim wrote, Musa'b's story "is a pride of all mankind." But it is only a sad tale of a brainwashed youth and the anguish and grief of a heartbroken mother. When one converts to Islam, they sever their ties with their loved ones and their cries fall on deaf ears. The love is gone. The beautiful innocent child is transformed into a heartless zombie. It is as if his soul is snatched.

---

[359] Ibn Sa'd, Tabaqat V. III p. 100-102

I know of hundreds of such cases, each one, a painful story of a parent, a spouse or a sibling who has lost a loved one to Islam and writes to me in desperation, as if I can help. If this has happened to you, try to persuade your Muslim to read this book. If you succeed, you will have them back. This is a promise. It has worked every time. The problem is that it is nearly impossible to convince one who falls prey to Islam to read this book.

Muhammad was not coy about his wishes to be loved above everyone. A hadith reports him saying, "By Him in Whose Hands my life is, none of you will have faith till he loves me more than his father and his children."[360] It's this "love" that makes Muslims murder anyone who criticizes Muhammad and Islam.

I quoted the story Mus'ab for all those mothers who write to me with broken hearts and tell me their tales of sorrow. Cults are dangerous. Protect you child before they fall prey to them. Ask them to read this book before they go out and take a Muslim as friend. Start early because cults prey on the very young. Education is the best protection you can provide for your children. In a society, diseased by multiculturalism and crippled by political correctness, don't expect the media or the school to educate your child. This is your responsibility.

Muslims are actively preying on young people. Search "love jihad" on Google and you'll find shocking stories of young Muslim men luring inexperienced non-Muslim girls on the Internet, with promise them love, only to use them either as prostitutes of convert them to Islam.

Let your children know there are predators out there. The cute little Muslim girlfriend of your teenager daughter can be a wolf in sheep clothing. The predatory mentality is so natural to Muslims that it would be foolish to trust any of them. They have to spread Islam. This is how they are programmed. They are themselves victims, but as long as they carry the virus of Islam you should be wary of them. Let others call you prejudiced, Islamophobe or even racist. It is much better that you are thus defiled than to lose your son or daughter to this dangerous cult.

Dissention Prohibition

"Why didn't more people leave?" Osherow asks. "Once inside the People's Temple, leaving was discouraged; defectors were hated. Nothing upset Jim Jones so much; people who left became the targets of his most vitriolic attacks and were blamed for any problems that occurred. One member recalled that after several teen-age members left the Temple, 'We hated those eight with such a passion because we knew any day they were going to try bombing us. I mean Jim Jones had us totally convinced of this.'"[361]

---

[360] Bukhari, 1: 2: 13

[361] Winfrey, C. Why 900 died in Guyana. *New York Times Magazine,* February 25, 1979.

A Muslim can't hate anyone more than the apostates. Apostates, freethinkers, and critics are threatened and killed. Muslim dissenters are accused of blasphemy. They and lynched or executed. This comment was left in my blog by a Muslim. Notice the intensity of his rage. "Mr Ali sena ..... I wish that if i can get you some time in my life, and i promise to god i will killl you , kill you an kill you." It is not that this person does not know how to write in English. When their cherished faith is slighted, blood rushes to their head and somehow they forget how to write. Muslims can hate no one more gutturally than the apostates. I know this makes you Jews out there envious. But sorry, not even the Jews can beat that.

Osherow writes, "Defecting became quite a risky enterprise, and, for most members, the potential benefits were very uncertain. Escape was not a viable option. Resistance was too costly. With no other alternatives apparent, compliance became the most reasonable course of action. The power that Jim Jones wielded kept the membership of the People's Temple in line, and the difficulty of defecting helped to keep them in."

The Quran makes it clear that apostasy is not an option. "*If you renounced the faith, you would surely do evil in the land, and violate the ties of blood. Such are those on whom God has laid His curse, leaving them deaf and sightless.... Those who return to unbelief after God's guidance has been revealed to them are seduced by Satan and inspired by him...*" (Q. 47:23-28) Here Muhammad is promising Divine chastisement for the apostates, along with punishment in this world. Bukhari reported, "Allah's Apostle said, 'The blood of a Muslim who confesses that none has the right to be worshipped but Allah and that I am His Apostle, cannot be shed except in three cases: In Qisas for murder, a married person who commits illegal sexual intercourse, and the one who reverts from Islam (apostate) and leaves the Muslims.'" [362]

Another hadith says a few apostates were brought to Ali and he burned them. When the news of this brutality reached Ibn 'Abbas, he said, "If I had been in his place, I would not have burnt them, as Allah's Apostle forbade it, saying, 'Do not punish anybody with Allah's punishment (fire).' I would have killed them according to the statement of Allah's Apostle, 'Whoever changed his Islamic religion, then kill him.'"[363]

The Power of Persuasion

What attracted people to join Jones's church in the first place? Let us analyze this question and compare it to what attracts converts to Islam.

---

[362] Sahih Bukhari Volume 9, Book 83, Number 17
[363] Bukhari, 9: 84: 57

7- When Sane People Follow Insane People

Osherow credits Jones's charismatic personality to his oratory power, aided by his genius in manipulating people who were most vulnerable. With promises and carefully honing his presentation to appeal to each specific audience he would easily win their hearts and imagination. In the words of Cicero "Nothing is so unbelievable that oratory cannot make it acceptable."

Muhammad was fully aware of the power of oratory. He believed that "in eloquence there is magic"[364] and used to say, "Some eloquent speech has the influence of magic (e.g., some people refuse to do something and then a good eloquent speaker addresses them and then they agree to do that very thing after his speech)."[365]

Elsewhere he bragged, "I have been given the keys of eloquent speech and given victory with terror."[366] He used the power of oratory for persuasion, and terror for intimidation.

Osherow writes, "The bulk of the People's Temple membership was comprised of society's needy and neglected: the urban poor, the black, the elderly and a sprinkling of addicts and ex-convicts."[367]

Compare that to the early followers of Muhammad in Mecca. They were mostly poor, disfranchised slaves, rebellious youths, and a few disaffected women. He told the slaves to insult the religion of their masters. To the youths he said, rebel against their parents, and to women said if their husband does not convert their marriage is void. He spoke of social equality and the brotherhood of all the believers, but the exclusion of disbelievers. He promised rewards in the afterlife for those who were harsh to his enemies and encouraged sedition and discord.

The three historians, Tabari, Ibn Sa'd, and Ibn Ishaq agree that only a few of the early believers converted to Islam out of faith. The majority converted for greed and for a share in the booty. Nonetheless, irrespective of their intent, they made Islam victorious. The companions of Muhammad, the *Salafs*, were a bunch of ruffians, thugs, raiders, highway robbers, and murderers. Today's devout Muslims are no different. The more they believe, the more dangerous they become.

Claims of Grandiosity

Cult leaders have megalomaniac personalities. Both Jim Jones and Muhammad had hyper-inflated egos. To attract new members, Jones held public services in various cities. Leaflets distributed read, "*Pastor Jim Jones... Incredible!*

---

364 Sunnan Abu Dawud; *41: 4994*

365 Bukhari, 7: 62: 76

366 Bukhari, 9: 87: 127

367 Winfrey, C. Why 900 died in Guyana. *New York Times Magazine,* February 25, 1979.

Miraculous! Amazing! The Most Unique Prophetic Healing Service You've Ever Witnessed! Behold the Word Made Incarnate In Your Midst!"[368]

Muhammad made many similar lofty claims about himself. His sock puppet deity oft praised him glowingly.

> *We sent you not, but as a Mercy for all creatures.* (Q.21:107)
> *And surely you [Muhammad] have sublime morals.* (Q.68:4)
> *Indeed in the Messenger of Allah you have a good example to follow.* (Q.33:21)
> *Verily this is the word of a most honorable Messenger.* (Q.81:19)
> *But no, by the Lord, they can have no (real) faith, until they make you judge in all disputes between them, and find in their souls no resistance against your decisions, but accept them with the fullest conviction.* (Q. 4:65)

The last verse makes it clear that Muhammad was seeking absolute obedience and frowned at any criticism or disagreement.

Osherow writes:

> Members learned to attribute the apparent discrepancies between Jones's lofty pronouncements and the rigors of life in the People's Temple to their personal inadequacies rather than blaming them on any fault of Jones. As ex-member Neva Sly was quoted: 'We always blamed ourselves for things that didn't seem right.'[369] A unique and distorted language developed within the church, in which 'The Cause' became anything that Jim Jones said.[370] Ultimately, through the clever use of oratory, deception, and language, Jones could speak of death as 'stepping over,' thereby camouflaging a hopeless act of self-destruction as a noble and brave act of 'revolutionary suicide,' and the members accepted his words.

This is so typical in Islam. Muslims volunteer to take the blame for anything that goes wrong and credit Allah for everything that goes right. Also, notice the incredible similarity between the followers of Muhammad and those of Jim Jones in their approach to death.

The origin of the statement "we love death more than you love life," with which Osama Bin Laden began his infamous letter to America is to be found in the Battle of Qadesiyya in the year 636, when the commander of the Muslim forces, Khalid ibn Walid, sent an emissary with a message from Caliph Abu Bakr to the Persian commander, Khosrau. The message stated, "You [Khosrau and his people] should convert to Islam, and then you will be safe, for if you don't, you should know

---

[368] Suicide Cult: The Inside Story of the Peoples Temple Sect and the Massacre in Guyana (201P) by Marshall Kilduff and Ron Javers (1978)
[369] Winfrey, C. Why 900 died in Guyana. *New York Times Magazine,* February 25, 1979.
[370] Mills, J. *Six years with God.* New York: A & W Publishers, 1979

that I have come to you with an army of men that love death, as you love life." This account is recited in today's Muslim sermons, newspapers, and textbooks.

Claim to Secret Knowledge

Cult leaders try to impress their followers by performing miracles and claiming to have the knowledge of the unknown. Jim Jones performed many miracles. Among them was his ability to reveal something about the new members or the guests that no one except them knew. To perform this "miracle" he would send one of his confidants beforehand to search the belongings of the guest, go through his private letters or eavesdrop on their conversations and inform him of their findings. Then he would surprise them with his "secret knowledge" about them.

For his secret knowledge, Muhammad sent spies everywhere and when tipped off, he would claim "Gabriel informed me..."

In Chapter Two, I discussed the scandal of Muhammad's sexual affair with Mariyah, Hafsa's reaction to it, and Muhammad's oath to prohibit that slave girl to himself, which he later broke, because Allah rebuked him for prohibiting something that he liked just to appease his wives. Relevant to our discussion is the verse that followed that incident. This verse talks about Muhammad ordering Hafsa not to reveal the secret of his sexual affair with Mariyah to anyone. Unable to keep her mouth shut, Hafsa, divulged the secret to Aisha. Muhammad became outraged. It does not take a lot of intelligence to know that if the secret was out, Hafsa must have spoken. However, Muhammad claimed that it was Allah who informed him that Hafsa had disobeyed him. "*And when the prophet secretly communicated a piece of information to one of his wives-- but when she informed (others) of it, and Allah made him to know it, he made known part of it and avoided part; so when he informed her of it, she said: Who informed you of this? He said: The Knowing, the one Aware, informed me.*" (Q.66:3)

The maker of the Universe first takes the role of a pimp to procure sex for his prophet with the woman he lusts for. Then he gossips and informs him about what his wives said behind his back. There is no point in discussing the silliness of this story. The point is that Muhammad claimed to have received information from Allah when the fact that Hafsa had divulged his secret was quite obvious.

Performing Miracles

What is surprising is that cultists often become willing collaborators of the leader's scams.

Jeanne Mills, wrote about Jim Jones's miracle of multiplying the food:

> There were more people than usual at the Sunday service, and for some reason the church members hadn't brought enough food to feed everyone. It became apparent that the last fifty people in line weren't going to get any meat. Jim announced, 'Even though there isn't enough food to feed this multitude, I am blessing the food that we have and multiplying it just as Jesus did in Biblical times.'
>
> Sure enough, a few minutes after he made this startling announcement, Eva Pugh came out of the kitchen beaming, carrying two platters filled with fried chicken. A big cheer came from the people assembled in the room, especially from the people who were at the end of the line.
>
> The "blessed chicken" was extraordinarily delicious, and several of the people mentioned that Jim had produced the best-tasting chicken they had ever eaten.
>
> One of the men, Chuck Beikman, jokingly mentioned to a few people standing near him that he had seen Eva drive up a few moments earlier with buckets from the Kentucky Fried Chicken stand. He smiled as he said, "The person that blessed this chicken was Colonel Sanders."
> During the evening meeting Jim mentioned the fact that Chuck had made fun of his gift. "He lied to some of the members here, telling them that the chicken had come from a local shop," Jim stormed. "But the Spirit of Justice has prevailed. Because of his lie Chuck is in the men's room right now, wishing that he was dead. He is vomiting and has diarrhea so bad he can't talk!"
>
> An hour later a pale and shaken Chuck Beikman walked out of the men's room and up to the front, being supported by one of the guards. Jim asked him, "Do you have anything you'd like to say?"
>
> Chuck looked up weakly and answered, "Jim, I apologize for what I said. Please forgive me."
>
> As we looked at Chuck, we vowed in our hearts that we would never question any of Jims "miracles," at least not out loud. Years later, we learned that Jim had put a mild poison in a piece of cake and given it to Chuck. [371]

Now, to perform this "miracle" Jones had to rely on the collaboration of Eva. Why would this woman, knowingly participate in that scam? Cultists are willing participants in self-deception.

There are similar miracles attributed to Muhammad. In one hadith, a Muslim claims to have witnessed a miracle. "I saw Allah's Apostle when the 'Asr (evening) prayer was due and the people searched for water to perform ablution but they could not find it. Later on (a pot full of) water for ablution was brought to Allah's Apostle.

[371] Mills, J. *Six years with God.* New York: A & W Publishers, 1979

He put his hand in that pot and ordered the people to perform ablution from it. I saw the water springing out from underneath his fingers till all of them performed the ablution (it was one of the miracles of the Prophet).[372] Another hadith says Muhammad multiplied the bread.[373] Elsewhere we read he struck a huge solid rock with his spade and the rock became like sand.[374] Or, he blessed a meal that was barely enough for four or five and with it he fed an army.[375]

There are hundreds of miracles attributed to Muhammad. Some of them were claimed by himself. There are miracles that no one but he saw. One such miracle is his claim to have spent a night in the town of the jinns. In another place he said that a group of jinns in Medina had embraced Islam.[376] In an story that I quoted in Chapter Two, he claim that he struggled with Satan and subdued him. His famous story of Mi'raj is recorded in the Quran.

These stories were either hallucinations or concocted to impress the gullible. Ibn Sa'd quotes a story narrated by Abu Rafi, one of the believers, who said that one day Muhammad visited him and he killed a lamb for dinner. Muhammad liked shoulder so he served him a shoulder. Then he asked for another and when he finished, he asked for another. [How much appetite he had?] Abu Rafi said, "I gave you both shoulders; how many shoulders does a lamb have?" to which Muhammad responded, "Had you not said this, you could give me as many shoulders as I had asked."[377]

Despite these claims, when challenged by the sceptics, the self-anointed prophet repeatedly denied being able to perform miracles. He admitted that although other prophets before him were given the power to perform miracles, his only miracle was the Quran. "The Prophet said, There was no prophet among the prophets but was given miracles because of which people had security or had belief, but what I was given was the Divine Inspiration which Allah revealed to me."[378]

So, why would the believers insist to attribute miracles to their prophet? Once people become convinced of the truth of a faith, they justify everything including lies. People with strong faith willingly lie, participate in fraud, abuse and even kill others, to support their belief. The "cause" to them is so important that it overshadows every other consideration. When people become so convinced of the truth of a cause that they are willing to die for it, then to lie for it is a synch. The end justifies the means. Pascal, the French philosopher and mathematician wrote, "Men never do evil so completely and cheerfully, as when they do it from religious

---

[372] Bukhari, 1: 4: 170
[373] Bukhari, 5: 59: 428
[374] Bukhari, 5: 59: 427
[375] Bukhari, 7: 65: 293
[376] Muslim, 26: 5559
[377] Tabaqat, V.1, P. 375
[378] Bukhari, 9: 92: 379

conviction." History is witness to the truth of Pascal's words. A lot of crimes have been perpetrated in the name of religion. Faith blinds and absolute faith blinds absolutely.

Imam Ghazzali's[379] authority in Islam is indisputable. He said: "When it is possible to achieve such an aim by lying but not by telling the truth, it is permissible to lie if attaining the goal is permissible".[380]

Kasindorf wrote, "Jim Jones skillfully manipulated the impression his church would convey to newcomers. He carefully managed its public image. He used the letter-writing and political clout of hundreds of members to praise and impress the politicians and press that supported the People's Temple, as well as to criticize and intimidate its opponents."[381]

If any newspaper writes something that Muslims find objectionable, thousands of them flood the offices of the editor to voice their complaint. They will continue with their harassment until an apology is issued publicly and the edition is withdrawn. How can we forget the riots and killing of innocent people when the Danish newspaper, Jyllands-Posten, published a few cartoons of Muhammad, or when Pope Benedict XVI quoted a Byzantine emperor who said, "Show me just what Mohammed brought that was new?"[382]

Distrust of Outsiders and Self -Blame

Osherow writes: "Jones inculcated a distrust of any contradictory messages, labeling them the product of enemies. By destroying the credibility of their sources, he inoculated the membership against being persuaded by outside criticism."

This is also typical of Muslims, who accuse their critics of being Zionists and/or paid agents of "the enemies of Islam." Now, there is nothing wrong in being a Zionist, considering the fact that the most despicable people are anti-Zionist, to Muslims this is an insult. The critics of Islam are sued, vilified, harassed and attacked *ad hominem,* but never contested logically. A group of Muslim "intellectuals" wrote a rebuttal to the Pope's speech, knowing well that after the mayhem that their brethren caused there will be no response from the Pontiff. Will

---

[379] Abu Hamid Muhammad al-Ghazzâlî (1058-1111) known as Algazel is one of the most celebrated scholars in the history of Islamic thought. Born in Iran, he was an Islamic theologian, philosopher, and mystic. He contributed significantly to the development of a systematic view of Sufism and its integration and acceptance in mainstream Islam.

[380] Ahmad Ibn Naqib al-Misri, *The Reliance of the Traveler*, translated by Nuh Ha Mim Keller , Amana publications, 1997, section r8.2, page 745

[381] Kasindorf, J. Jim Jones: The seduction of San Francisco. New West, December 18, 1978.

[382] Speech of Pope Benedict XVI in münchen, altötting and regensburg (september 9-14, 2006)

a Muslim ever write a rebuttal to this book? Don't hold your breath. In fact, if they read this book chances are that they will leave Islam.

"In Jonestown," writes Osherow, "any contradictory thoughts that might arise within members were to be discredited. Instead of seeing them as having any basis in reality, members interpreted them as indications of their own shortcomings or lack of faith." This is so typical of Muslims who although they realize that their lives are a living hell and their countries are in shambles, blame themselves and their lack of adherence to "true Islam" for their miseries, when Islam is the source of most of their pains.

Unbounded Devotion

Jim Jones created an atmosphere of total domination and control. Osherow says, "Analyzing Jonestown in terms of obedience and the power of the situation can help to explain why the people acted as they did. Once the People's Temple had moved to Jonestown, there was little the members could do other than follow Jim Jones's dictates. They were comforted by an authority of absolute power. They were left with few options, being surrounded by armed guards and by the jungle, having given their passports and various documents and confessions to Jones, and believing that conditions in the outside world were even more threatening. The members' poor diet, heavy workload, lack of sleep, and constant exposure to Jones's diatribes exacerbated the coerciveness of their predicament; tremendous pressures encouraged them to obey."

We know that Muhammad was not pleased with those who deserted him. As we can see, there is little difference between Muhammad's way of thinking and that of Jones. However, it would be a mistake to assume that cultists stay only because they are coerced physically. Psychological coercion is much more effective. The victims become willing, even grateful participants in their own abuse and enslavement.

Osherow writes, "By the time of the final ritual, opposition or escape had become almost impossible for most of the members. Yet even then, it is doubtful that many wanted to resist or leave. Most had come to believe in Jones. One woman's body was found with a message scribbled on her arm during the final hours: 'Jim Jones is the only one.'[383] They seemed to have accepted the necessity, and even the 'beauty' of dying. Just before the ritual began, a guard approached Charles Garry, one of the Temples hired attorneys, and exclaimed, 'It's a great moment... we all die.'"[384]

---

[383] Cahill T. In the valley of the shadow of death. *Rolling Stone*. January 25, 1979.
[384] Lifton, R. J. Appeal of the death trip. *New York Times Magazine*, January 7, 1979.

A survivor of Jonestown, who happened to be away at the dentist, was interviewed a year following the deaths: "If I had been there, I would have been the first one to stand in that line and take that poison and I would have been proud to take it. The thing I'm sad about is this: that I missed the ending."[385]

What is it that drives normal people to these extremes? Once people accept someone as a divine being, they become the extension of his psychopathic mind, and willful participants in their own abuse. The victim and victimizer merge. A symbiosis of sadomasochistic co-dependency is created where the victim wants to be victimized. The cultist wants to prove his devotion by showing how much he is willing to be abused and accepts all hardships joyously. Several early followers of Muhammad were youths from well to do families. They left all that comfort, emigrated from their homes and endured hardship both in Abyssinia and in Median. In the early days, before Muhammad's raids became successful, his followers often slept with no food in their stomach. At the same time they vied with each other to show their love for their leader. In one hadith we read, "Allah's Apostle came to us at noon and water for ablution was brought to him. After he had performed ablution, the remaining water was taken by the people and they started smearing their bodies with it (as a blessed thing)."[386]

Muhammad encouraged this cultic devotion. One hadith says, "Ali was suffering from eye-trouble, so the Prophet applied saliva to his eyes and invoked Allah to cure him. He at once got cured as if he had no ailment."[387]

Muhammad could not cure his own ailments and was in constant physical pain. But he wanted his follower to believe that his saliva was panacea of their ailments. It is also likely that in some instances it worked. It is called placebo effect. Faith heals. The object of faith is not important. Many Iranians used to claim that they were healed by praying at the tomb of Khomeini. That man was a mass murderer.

Isolationism

Osherow describes isolationism as "the aspect of Jonestown that is perhaps the most troubling." He says, "To the end, the vast majority of the People's Temple members believed in Jim Jones. External forces, in the form of power or persuasion, can exact compliance. But one must examine a different set of processes to account for the members internalizing those beliefs. Although Jones's statements were often inconsistent and his methods cruel, most members maintained their faith in his leadership."

---

[385] Gallagher, N. Jonestown: The survivors' story. *New York Times Magazine,* November 18, 1979.

[386] Bukhari, 1: 4: 187

[387] Bukhari, 4: 52: 253

7- When Sane People Follow Insane People

Muhammad was unable to perform miracles. His awareness was rudimentary. His teachings were prosaic. He did not have any secret knowledge. And as we can see from the Quran, his revelations were asinine. What his followers saw in him that they were ready to sacrifice everything for him?

One explanation is provided by Osherow. He wrote, "Once they were isolated at Jonestown, there was little opportunity or motivation to think otherwise; resistance or escape was out of the question. In such a situation, the individual is motivated to rationalize his or her predicament; a person confronted with the inevitable tends to regard it more positively. For example, social psychological research has shown that when children believe that they will be served more of a vegetable they dislike, they will convince themselves that it is not so noxious,[388] and when a person thinks that she will be interacting with someone, she tends to judge a description of that individual more favorably."[389]

Cult leaders often barricade their followers in order to reduce their contact with the outside world. Jim Jones built his own "Jonestown." in the jungles of Guyana, Muhammad chose Yathrib as his compound, killed and expelled those who did not accept him and renamed it, *Medinat ul-Nabi* (Prophet's town). He corporally punished, publicly humiliated and assassinated anyone who defied his authority. Medinat ul Nabi was very much like Jonestown. Muhammad was the absolute authority. Any dissent was severely punished. Once a person entered that town as a believer, there was no going back.

Abdullah ibn Sa;d ibn Abi Sarh, was a scribe of Muhammad. He was more educated than his prophet. He often would correct his "revealed" verses and suggest better wordings. Muhammad accepted his suggestions. Abdullah realized that the Quran is not revealed and that Muhammad was making the verses up. He escaped to Mecca and told everyone about it. When Muhammad conquered Mecca, despite having given assurances of amnesty to everyone if the Meccans surrender, he ordered the beheading of Ibn Abi Sarh. He was spared thanks to Othman's intercession and Muhammad's inability to communicate properly his wishes through signals. When Othman pleaded with Muhammad to not kill his foster brother, Muhammad remained silent. His companions assumed that he has agreed and Othman took Ibn Abi Sarh away. After they left, Muhammad complained that he did not wish to turn down the request of Othman, but he had hoped his companions would kill his foe. Talk about hypocrisy!

Ibn Ishaq explains, "The reason he ordered him to be killed was that he had been a Muslim and used to write down revelation. Then he apostatized and returned

---

388 Brehm, J. Increasing cognitive dissonance by a *fait-accompli. Journal of Abnormal and Social Psychology,* 1959, 58, 379-382.

389 Darley, J. and Bersceild, E. Increased liking as a result of the anticipation of personal contact. *Human Relations,* 1967, 20, 29-40.

to Quraish [Mecca]... He was to be killed for apostasy but was saved through Othman's intercession."[390]

The atmosphere in Medina was tense. Islam and Jihad had become the focus of the lives of everyone. People had lost every vestige of privacy and private life. They had to go to the mosque and pray in congregation, not once or twice, but five times a day. Their lives were changed. There was no work. They had become marauders -- constantly raiding, plundering, and waging war.

There is a hadith which shows the level of coercion that Muhammad exerted on his followers. He is reported saying, *"I thought that I should order the prayer to be commenced and command a person to lead people in prayer, and I should then go along with some persons having a fagot of fuel with them to the people who have not attended the prayer (in congregation) and would burn their houses with fire."*[391]

In this hadith Muhammad is expressing his wish to burn the houses of those who were not attending the mosque regularly, with their occupants inside. One does not have to be a psychologist to see the Prophet was not sane. Despite that his followers did not object and did not desert him, not because all of them were incapable of seeing the monstrosity of his thoughts, but because expressing their thoughts freely, was suicide.

Muhammad actually did burn a mosque with all the people inside it. Muslims of Zarrar (a place close to Medina) had built a mosque (a temple). They invited him to come and bless it. He told them that he would come after the raid of Tabuk. When he returned from Tabuk some malicious people told him that the Muslims of Zarrar had invented their own version of Islam and were not following the Islam of the Prophet. Muhammad did not try to investigate. He ordered his men to burn the mosque with the worshippers inside. Then he revealed a verse to justify his hideous crime. "*And there are those who put up a mosque by way of mischief and infidelity – to disunite the Believers – and in preparation for one who warred against Allah and His Messenger aforetime. They will indeed swear that their intention is nothing but good; But Allah doth declare that they are certainly liars.*" (Q.9:107)

Life in Medina had completely changed. Prior to the arrival of Muhammad, the people of Yathrib were farmers, artisans and tradesmen. The bulk of the industry was in the hands of the Jews.. The Arabs were illiterate, lazy, and indolent. They had few skills and worked for the Jews. When the Jews were exterminated, there were no more businesses where people could work and earn a livelihood. The economy of the town had collapsed. The citizens relied entirely on plunder for their sustenance. There was no going back. They had become dependent on Muhammad and the spoils of his raids. Even those who did not believe in him, like Abdullah ibn Ubbay and his followers joined his raids, not because they wanted to

---

[390] Sirat, p. 550
[391] Muslim, 4: 1370; and Bukhari, 1: 11: 626

support Islam, but because marauding had become their only source of income. Like the members of People's Temple, Muslims in Medina were confronted with an inevitable situation, which in turn led them to accept their condition more favorably.

The Arab population of Medina was ignorant, impoverished, and a superstitious lot. For them, even owning one camel and one robe was considered wealth. They worked as journeymen for the Jews. Several hadiths report that their first wealth was acquired through spoils of war. There was also plenty of sexual booty. Women captured in the raids provided an added incentive for the believers, particularly the Immigrants who were mostly young and single.

Once the Jews were killed and banished, the impoverished Arabs of Medina had no alternative but to enlist in Muhammad's army. The main incentive for these early believers to sally forth in jihad was wealth and sex. Isolationism and group pressure made them accept things that they would have otherwise considered objectionable, and even abhorrent. An isolated group, controlled by a charismatic cult leader, sets its own laws. The norms of the outside world don't apply there. What the leader says and does becomes the law. He defines what is moral, ethical, right, and wrong and the cultists agree. As Muslims often say, one should not measure Muhammad by the standard of the Golden rule, but rather rules must be measured by his standard.

Gradual Absorption

The life of a believer is an arduous life of constant inner battle and mindless religious rituals. They submit to this life gradually. Osherow says, "A member's involvement in the Temple did not begin at Jonestown, it started much earlier, closer to home, and less dramatically. At first, the potential member would attend meetings voluntarily and might put in a few hours each week working for the church. Though the established members would urge the recruit to join, he or she felt free to choose whether to stay or leave. Upon deciding to join, a member expended more effort and became more committed to the Peoples Temple. In small increments, Jones increased the demands made on the member, and only after a long time did he escalate the oppressiveness of his rule and the desperation of his message. Little by little, the individual's alternatives became more limited. Step by step, the person was motivated to rationalize his or her commitment and to justify his or her behavior."

Ex-converts to Islam report similar experiences. As they become more involved, the bar of expectations is raised gradually. Women new converts are told that it is not mandatory to cover their hair, but it would be meritorious to do so. New believers are asked to refrain from certain foods, eat halal, perform the obligatory prayers, fast and give zakat – minor requirements that can be easily observed. Gradually, they are introduced to the virtues and rewards of jihad.

Because the newcomers are eager to belong and be accepted in the group, they strive to outperform the born Muslims and as the proverb goes, become "more catholic than the Pope."

According to a poll by the Pew Research Center, the most dangerous Muslims in America are the black converts. "Fully 28% of U.S.-born black Muslim respondents said "suicide bombings and other violence against civilians can be justified sometimes or at least in rare cases. That compares with 9% of foreign-born Muslims who hold the same view. Pew also found that 11% of black Muslims living in the U.S. have a favorable opinion of al-Qaida – more than double the share of U.S. Muslims overall who hold that view."[392]

The indoctrination is so gradual that the converts feel they are undergoing these changes voluntarily. They finally end up doing things that they thought they would never do. An American born ex-Muslim woman told me that when she first saw a group of Muslim women, all covered in black veils, she laughed and felt sorry for them. When she converted to Islam she started wearing the strictest form of veil that covers even the eyes (*neqab*). I came to know this lady online because she had created an Internet site "Khadijah in niqab,"to promote Islam. Her favorite pastime was to malign me and tell other Muslims not to read my articles. However, she read them. Finally, she came to her senses and left Islam. She explained how she had been sucked into Islam to the extent that at one point she asked her non-Muslim husband to convert and take another wife.

I have met Muslim women (virtually) who had become so brainwashed that they defended Muhammad's saying that women are deficient in intelligence and inferior. Paradoxically, at the same time, they were convinced that Islam liberates women. Faith is a mind-numbing narcotic.

Those who convert to Islam, soon start disliking the Jews and then their own country. They are fed with conspiracy theories and in no time will find themselves hating their non-Muslim parents and cut their ties from their unbelieving friends and relatives.

A Canadian who converted to Islam, after apostatizing wrote of his experience:

> An unadulterated Islam was difficult for the kuffaar (unbelievers) to digest so deviants evidently had a higher success rate in their propagation of Islam (da'wah) as they modified principles "to suit the nafs" (carnal self) of recipients. The moderate and sanitized version of Islam that initially brought me to conversion had to be reassessed. Through the local masjid (mosque), always available was a handshake and anticipated hug. This was a comfort unavailable at home, especially from a mother always unsatisfied with my performance and father unconcerned with my progress. Encouraged by my Muslim brothers, I desired to excel in my religion; possibly get

[392] Poll stunner: These American blacks OK with violent attacks www.wnd.com/?pageId=339793#ixzz1XoUgd8GE

married, master the Arabic language and be a mujaahid (partaker in jihaad) and shaheed (martyr).

Reverts to Islam, ever so gullible and naive, were easily susceptible to the prevalent dysfunctional behaviour and propaganda infecting most Muslim societies. By striving not to conform to the kuffaar, we duly had to be ignorant by circumnavigating anything unislamic. One revert declared that Osama bin Laden was better than "a million George Bushes,' and 'a thousand 'Tony Blairs' simply because he's a Muslim. Arrogantly speaking, we Muslims were 'the best of peoples ever raised up for mankind.' (3:110) So, when an atrocity occurred that was obviously committed by Muslims in the name of Allah, my fellow brothers and sisters were complacent. We obsequiously forsook the human rights violations in Muslim countries, even when the victims were Muslims. The conspiracy theories widespread in my Muslim society were outright delusion. Not even the moderate Muslims, who neglected salaat and committed zinaa (illegal sex; fornication, adultery, etc.), could accept the Muslim identities of the 9/11 pilots. As my Afghani classmate remarked, 'It was the Jews!' When the opportunity arose for self-criticism, inevitably, we instead blamed the Jews, our favorite scapegoat. Homogenizing oneself into the Islamic ummah was ostensibly clinched if one supported the latest Arab-Muslim agenda, grew an outstanding beard, expressed hatred for the Jews, uttered the word 'bid'ah' (denouncing the modernists) occasionally, and repudiated the modern state of Israel. We proudly acknowledged the jihaad, yet acted stupid if questioned by a kaafir and responded to their accusations with, for example, 'How do you know it was done by Muslims? Where is the evidence?' Although they were not blind to the videotaped confessions by boasting Muslim terrorists, they chose to be. Not all Muslims were terrorists, although it was unequivocally but agonizingly true that most terrorists were Muslims. If some Americans or Jews died, there was sympathetic joy and I observed this particular behavior genially absorbed by one Muslimah just five years old. Reverts hopelessly adopted a rigid interpretation of Islam taught by immigrants from oppressive theocracies that incarcerated ijtihaad (free discussion) to keep freethinking and dissent criminal and their rule immutable.[393]

John Walker Lindh, was a young man who went to Afghanistan to serve in al Qaeda and kill American soldiers. He did not become a terrorist overnight. John's interest in Islam began when he was just 12 years old. His mother took him to see Spike Lee's film, *Malcolm X.* She said, "He was moved by a scene showing people of all nations bowing down to God."[394]

No one cared or knew enough to warn this young man of the dangers of Islam. Time Magazine wrote, "John's parents were pleased to see that their son had found something that moved him. And at a time when other parents they knew were

---

[393] www.faithfreedom.org/Testimonials/Abdulquddus.htm

[394] By Timothy Roche, Brian Bennett, Anne Berryman, Hilary Hylton, Siobhan Morrissey And Amany Radwan The Making of John Walker Lindh. http://www.time.com/time/magazine/article/0,9171,1003414-5,00.html

coping with their kids' experimentation with drugs, booze, and fast driving, it all seemed fairly innocent. Marilyn (John's mother) would drop young John off at the mosque for Friday prayers. At the end of the evening, a fellow believer would drive John home."[395]

The tolerant American society also did not see anything wrong or alarming about a young American converting to Islam. He would stroll with his awkward Islamic outfit up and down the streets, and the good American folks did not get especially worked up. "It was just another kid experimenting with his life, with his spiritual side, certainly nothing to fear or loathe," wrote Time Magazine.

Cults are a lot more dangerous than drugs, booze, and fast driving. Instead of investigating the truth about Islam, John's father allowed himself to be fooled by what he defined as the "Islamic custom of hospitality for fellow believers," which in itself is a giveaway of its cultic nature. "Islamic hospitality" is a mask. Cultists are exceptionally friendly towards those whom they want to woo to their faith or from whom they want to gain concessions. Once they no longer need you they step over you and oppress you as they do to minorities among them. Muslims are all smiles for the media. Then they laugh at how they fooled the journalists.

Unbeknownst to his parents, this impressionable teenager was gradually becoming brainwashed and indoctrinated into hating his country. Time magazine quoted, a language teacher in Yemen who said, "Lindh came from the U.S. already hating America." The magazine writes: "Lindh's correspondence from Yemen evinces an ambivalence toward the U.S. In a letter to his mother dated Sept. 23, 1998, he refers to the bombing of the U.S. embassies in Africa the previous month, saying the attacks 'seem far more likely to have been carried out by the American government than by any Muslims.'"

Non-Muslims are becoming familiar with the Islamic tactic of committing the crime and blaming the victim. The fantastic story of "4000 Jews not showing up for work on the fateful morning of 9/11/2001," is rehashed to this day. This conspiracy theory blames the CIA and the Mossad for what Bin Laden boastfully claimed as his victory. John was gradually led to believe that Islam is the only real religion. He tried to learn it and practice it with sincerity and eagerness. He studied and memorized the Quran. In his notebook he wrote, "We shall make jihad as long as we live."[396] The origin of this sentence is attributed to the companions of Muhammad, who while digging the trench around Medina, sang, "We are those who have given a pledge of allegiance to Muhammad that we will I carry on Jihad as long as we live."[397]

[395] Time magazine September 29, 2002 edition
[396] Ibid.
[397] Bukhari, 4: 52: 88

7- When Sane People Follow Insane People

Once a Muslim, John Walker Lindh entered in Muhammad's narcissistic bubble universe. On the one hand he denied that 9/11 was the work of Muslims and on the other hand he was vowing to make jihad as long as he lives.

John cut himself from the rest of his countrymen. According to the Quran, Muslims are not supposed to make friends with unbelievers. (Q.9:23) They are asked to fight those who do not believe (Q.9:29) and murder them. (Q.9:123)

When John wrote to his mother, after the U.S. presidential election in 2000, he referred to George W. Bush as "your new President" and added, "I'm glad he's not mine." A Muslim cannot accept the rule of an unbeliever. He must disobey them, fight against them, and endeavor to kill them. (Q.25:52)

John Walker Lindh and many other young people who have fallen prey to Islam are victims of political correctness. There are also those who, perhaps for personal gain, deliberately deceive the public.

As required summer reading for his first-year students, Prof. Michael Sells of the University of North Carolina compiled a book titled Approaching the Quran where according to his own statement the "nice" teachings of the Quran, pertaining to the early Meccan period were handpicked and published. He left out the violent and gory verses that churn the stomach. Why? Why teach half-truths? It is not hard to see that the goal was to deceive the alumni and make Islam look benign to them. Similar deception can be seen in the works of Karen Armstrong, John Esposito, and a host of other "experts" of Islam.

Why these people deliberately hide the truth? Do they do this out of ignorance or is something more sinister at work? The public is hoodwinked. Innocent people fall into the trap of Islam and are victimized. Aren't these deceivers responsible? Are we supposed to believe that Armstrong who has left Christianity can't see that Islam is not only a bad copy of Judaism, but also evil? She wrote, "There is far more violence in the Bible than in the Qur'an; the idea that Islam imposed itself by the sword is a Western fiction, fabricated during the time of the crusades when, in fact, it was Western Christians who were fighting brutal holy wars against Islam." [398] This is a blatant lie. What does this former nun and convert to Sufi Islam find attractive in Islam that she talks about it so glowingly?

Once people convert to a cult, they enter an underworld of illusions, ignorance, and fear, where fantasy takes the form of reality and evil is perceived as divine. Their values disintegrate and they enter into a twilight zone where the distinction between wrong and right becomes blurred. Islam unfolds like a creeping paralysis, slowly corrupting minds and spirits, until it produces the best of all Muslims, the jihadi.

Osherow gives a thorough psychological explanation of this phenomenon.

---

[398] Andrea Bistrich, "Discovering the common grounds of world religions," interview with Karen Armstrong, Share International, Sept. 2007, pp. 19-22.

> According to dissonance theory, when a person commits an act or holds a cognition that is psychologically inconsistent with his or her self-concept, the inconsistency arouses an unpleasant state of tension. The individual tries to reduce this 'dissonance,' usually by altering his or her attitudes to bring them more into line with the previously discrepant action or belief. A number of occurrences in the People's Temple can be illuminated by viewing them in light of this process. The horrifying events of Jonestown were not due merely to the threat of force, nor did they erupt instantaneously. That is, it was not the case that something 'snapped' in people's minds, suddenly causing them to behave in bizarre ways. Rather, as the theory of cognitive dissonance spells out, people seek to justify their choices and commitments. Just as a towering waterfall can begin as a trickle, so too can the impetus for doing extreme or calamitous actions be provided by the consequences of agreeing to do seemingly trivial ones. In the People's Temple, the process started with the effects of undergoing a severe initiation to join the church, was reinforced by the tendency to justify ones commitments, and was strengthened by the need to rationalize ones behavior.
>
> Once involved, a member found ever-increasing portions of his or her time and energy devoted to the People's Temple. The services and meetings occupied weekends and several evenings each week. Working on Temple projects and writing the required letters to politicians and the press took much of one's 'spare' time. Expected monetary contributions changed from 'voluntary' donations (though they were recorded) to the required contribution of a quarter of one's income. Eventually, a member was supposed to sign over all personal property, savings, social security checks, and the like to the Peoples Temple. Before entering the meeting room for each service, a member stopped at a table and wrote self-incriminating letters or signed blank documents that were turned over to the church. If anyone objected, the refusal was interpreted as denoting a 'lack of faith' in Jones. Each new demand had two repercussions: In practical terms, it enmeshed the person further into the People's Temple web and made leaving more difficult; on an attitudinal level, it set the aforementioned processes of self-justification into motion. As Mills (1979) describes: 'We had to face painful reality. Our life savings were gone. Jim had demanded that we sell the life insurance policy and turn the equity over to the church, so that was gone. Our property had all been taken from us. Our dream of going to an overseas mission was gone. We thought that we had alienated our parents when we told them we were leaving the country. Even the children whom we had left in the care of Carol and Bill were openly hostile toward us. Jim had accomplished all this in such a short time! All we had left now was Jim and the Cause, so we decided to buckle under and give our energies to these two.'"

The same could be said of the early Muslims. Those who followed Muhammad to Medina had nothing to fall back on. They had no jobs and no homes. Muhammad had asked the Ansar [Helpers, the believers native to Medina] to accommodate the Immigrants and share whatever they had with them. This, of course, was not an easy life for either party. There is a curious story of an Ansar offering his wife to an Immigrant.

> Abdur Rahman bin Auf said, when we came to Medina as emigrants, Allah's Apostle established a bond of brotherhood between me and Sa'd bin Ar-Rabi'. Sa'd bin Ar-Rabi' said (to me), 'I am the richest among the Ansar, so I will give you half of my wealth and you may look at my two wives and whichever of the two you may choose I will divorce her, and when she has completed the prescribed period (before marriage) you may marry her.' A few days later, 'Abdur Rahman came having traces of yellow (scent) on his body. Allah's Apostle asked him whether he had got married. He replied in the affirmative. The Prophet said, 'Whom have you married?' He replied, 'A woman from the Ansar.[399]

Muslims quote this story to brag how Muhammad had fostered brotherhood among believers, but it also shows how they had been overcome with zealotry. They disregarded their own privacy and even the sanctity of their marriage. Their freedom and their independence were all but gone. In most cases, they willingly relinquished their independence. Those who could see the problem did not dare to talk about it. The Immigrants could not go back. No one could complain. Anyone could be an informer. They could be assassinated as there was no dearth of zealot believers who would report and happily kill an unruly fellow believer. Those who could see the problem had no other option but to buckle under and play along.

In one hadith we read:

> A blind man had a slave-woman who used to abuse the Prophet and disparage him. …So he took a dagger, placed it on her belly, pressed it, and killed her. A child who came between her legs was smeared with the blood that was there. When the morning came, the Prophet was informed about it. He assembled the people called on the man to explain why he committed such horrendous murder. The man stood up while trembling and said: 'I am her master; she used to abuse you and disparage you. I have two sons like pearls from her, and she was my companion. Last night she began to abuse and disparage you. So I took a dagger, put it on her belly and pressed it till I killed her.' Thereupon the Prophet said: 'Oh be witness, no retaliation is payable for her blood.'[400]

This man committed double murder and all he had to say to go free was that his victim had insulted the Prophet. In such an atmosphere of terror, how could anyone disagree with Muhammad? What if that blind man was lying to avoid punishment? The message that Muhammad wanted to send was clear: Don't dare to insult me or you will be killed. One can only imagine how many murderers have walked away

[399] Bukhari *3:34: 264*
[400] Sunan Abu-Dawud, 38: 4348

with this alibi. Today, in Islamic countries, minorities are killed over personal disputes and all that the killer has to say is that the victim insulted the Prophet and walk free or get a lenient sentence.

Pakistan has become a madhouse. Salman Taseer, a prominent politician who fought for human rights and against the blasphemy law was gunned down by his own bodyguard. His murderer said he wanted to teach an apostate a lesson. He became a national hero to the many Pakistanis, who kissed and garlanded him and showered him with rose petals. Prominent lawyers offered to represent him for free.

Section 295-C of Pakistan's Penal Code says: "Whoever by words, either spoken or written, or by visible representation, or by any imputation, innuendo, or insinuation, directly or indirectly defiles the sacred name of the Holy Prophet Muhammad shall be punished with death and shall also be liable to a fine."

Muhammad was so desperate and keen to enforce respect for himself that when a group of Arabs came to visit him and did not pay him the reverence that he thought he was entitled to, he made his deity say, "*O ye who believe! Raise not your voices above the voice of the Prophet, nor speak aloud to him in talk, as ye may speak aloud to one another, lest your deeds become vain and ye perceive not. Those that lower their voices in the presence of Allah's Messenger, their hearts has Allah tested for piety: for them is Forgiveness and a great Reward. Those who shout out to thee from without the inner apartments - most of them lack understanding.*" (Q.49:2-4)

The evolution from being a moderate Muslim to a terrorist Muslim is gradual and often imperceptible. New converts are taught the "beauties of Islam." They are told that Islam is an easy religion, of peace and equality and the worship of a single God. They are led to believe that Islam is accepting of other religions, especially Judaism and Christianity, and only disagrees with the believers of these religions in that they have corrupted their faith. They are then led to believe that Islam is the only religion that has remained pristine. Consequently, it is the only true religion accepted by God. Those who don't believe in Islam are rejecting the truth. They are sinners. Eventually they are told that the *Isa* and *Musa* of the Quran are not the same as Jesus and Moses of the Bible. They are told that the people of other faiths are envious of Muslims. They see the truth of Islam and yet deny it because their hearts are diseased. They reject Islam out of spite. They are the enemies of Allah. Because of that Allah hates them. It follows that the believers should not love those whom God hates. Only Muslims are brothers. Others are kafir, filthy, and enemies of God.

As the new convert is gradually brainwashed, they develop a sense of victimhood. They lose their own identity and become an anonymous part of the amorphous *ummah*, slaves of Allah. They even adopt new Islamic names. They start seeing the world differently. The feeling of "us" versus "them" becomes stronger every day. "They" are the evil ones, the oppressors, the enemies of God. "Us" are the Muslims the oppressed ones, the victims.

It may take very little time for a new convert to be transformed into a fully-fledged terrorist seeking revenge for all that perceived injustices that non-Muslims do to

Muslims. Gradual indoctrination is the modus operandi in all cults, where the core truth and the real agenda of the cult is concealed and is slowly spoon-fed to the believer.

Demanding Ultimate Sacrifice

What the narcissist ultimately wants is control over life and death. This makes him feels like God. The cult leader becomes so obsessed with obedience that he demands his followers to prove their loyalty by sacrificing everything, including their lives. The cause is a pretext. The Quran offers great rewards for martyrs and encourages Muslims to give up their lives.

> Think not of those who are slain in Allah's way as dead. Nay, they live, finding their sustenance from their Lord. They rejoice in the Bounty provided by Allah...the (Martyrs) glory in the fact that on them is no fear, nor have they grieve. They rejoice in the Grace and the Bounty from Allah, and in the fact that Allah suffers not the reward of the Faithful to be lost (in the least). (Q.3:169)

> The Prophet said, "Paradise has one hundred grades which Allah has reserved for the Mujahidin (Muslim fighters) who fight in His Cause."[401]

> The Prophet said, "Nobody who enters Paradise likes to go back to the world even if he got everything on the earth, except a Mujahid who wishes to return to the world so that he may be martyred ten times because of the dignity he receives (from Allah). Our Prophet told us about the message of our Lord that 'Whoever amongst us is killed as a martyr will go to Paradise' Umar asked the Prophet, 'Is it not true that our men who are killed will go to Paradise and theirs (i.e. those of the Pagan's) will go to the (Hell) fire?' The Prophet said, 'Yes.' [402]

Osherow says, "Ultimately, Jim Jones and the Cause would require the members to give their lives. What could cause people to kill their children and themselves? From a detached perspective, the image seems unbelievable. In fact, at first glance, so does the idea of so many individuals committing so much of their time, giving all of their money, and even sacrificing the control of their children to the People's Temple. Jones took advantage of rationalization processes that allow people to justify their commitments by raising their estimations of the goal and minimizing its costs."

Muhammad convinced his followers that everyone is created for the sole purpose of believing in him and worshiping the god that spoke to him. *"I have only created Jinns and men that they may worship me"* (Q.51:56). According to a hadith

[401] Bukhari, 4: 5: 48
[402] Bukhari, 4: 52:72

qudsi, (believed absolutely to be true) the purpose of life is to know Allah and to worship him, made possible only through his messenger Muhammad. Since believing in Muhammad is the sole purpose of the creation, promoting his cause is regarded as the most important endeavor. In this quest, everything, including crime is permissible.

Former Scientologist Amy Scobee, in her interview with Mike Hess Posted on Popeater.com said:

> Something dangerous about Scientology is that they truly believe that they are the "only salvation" for mankind. They therefore consider they can do all sorts of things -- even if it breaks the law -- because it's "the greatest good" and forwards their overall mission to ensure everyone's future eternity. Crush a critic into silence, lie on national television, beat a staff member who is not behaving as you'd like, blackmail people using family disconnection and other threats to keep them in line, use personal information obtained on people to smear their name, hide evidence that could be damning if it were discovered -- on and on. They are fanatics about being the ONLY salvation and the end justifies the means.

Osherow writes, "Much as he gradually increased his demands, Jones carefully orchestrated the members' exposure to the concept of a 'final ritual.' He utilized the leverage provided by their previous commitments to push them closer to its enactment. Gaining a 'foot in the door' by getting a person to agree to a moderate request makes it more probable that he or she will agree to do a much larger deed later, as social psychologists and sales people have found.[403] Doing the initial task makes something that might have seemed unreasonable at first appear less extreme in comparison, and it also motivates a person to make his or her behavior appear more consistent by consenting to the larger requests as well."

Osherow then explains how Jones prepared his followers to commit mass suicide:

> He started by undermining the member's belief that death was to be fought and feared and Jones directed several 'fake' suicide drills. These became tests of faith, of the member's willingness to follow Jones even to death. Jones would ask people if they were ready to die and on occasion would have the membership 'decide' its own fate by voting whether to carry out his wishes. An ex-member recounted that one time, after a while Jones smiled and said, 'Well, it was a good lesson. I see you're not dead.' He made it sound like we needed the 30 minutes to do very strong, introspective type of thinking. We all felt strongly dedicated, proud of ourselves. Jones taught that it was a privilege to die for what you believe in, which is exactly what I would have been doing.[404]

---

[403] Freeman, J., AND Fraser, S. Compliance without pressure: The foot-in-the-door technique. *Journal of Personality and Social Psychology,* 1966, 4, 195-202.
[404] Winfrey, C. Why 900 died in Guyana. *New York Times Magazine,* February 25, 1979.

7- When Sane People Follow Insane People

Muhammad did not advocate suicide. Instead, he greatly praised martyrdom. He was more pragmatic than Jones. Suicide was of no use to him. He needed his followers alive so they could raid and plunder and conquer for him. He glorified martyrdom and death on battlefields. The pragmatism of Muhammad can also be appreciated in the fact that while Jones and many other cult leaders committed suicide and died along their followers, Muhammad rarely took an active role in any battle. His personal safety was of paramount importance to him. In this sense he was less insane than many cult leaders.

While any sane person can easily see killing in the name of God is insane, no Muslim can see that. Jihad is a pillar of Islam and any Muslim who disagrees with it is not a Muslim anymore. The term "moderate Muslim" is an oxymoron. No one can be moderate and subscribe to an ideology that prescribes killing.

Osherow writes, "After the Temple moved to Jonestown, the 'White Nights,' as the suicide drills were called, occurred repeatedly. An exercise that appears crazy was a regular, justifiable occurrence for the People's Temple participant."

The members of People's Temple were normal people. They were not insane or crazy. However, since they had placed their intelligence in the hands of a crazy man, they followed him blindly into his madness. The same holds true about Muslims.

Osherow says, "The reader might ask whether this [the fake drills] caused the members to think that the actual suicides were merely another practice, but there were many indications that they knew the poison was truly deadly on that final occasion. The Ryan visit had been climatic, there were several new defectors, the cooks who had been excused from the prior drills in order to prepare the upcoming meal were included, Jones had been growing increasingly angry, desperate, and unpredictable, and, finally, everyone could see the first babies die. The membership was manipulated, but they were not unaware that this time the ritual was for real."

Self- Justification

Osherow explains that under such conditions, people are apt to justify their actions, to comply with what their leader dictates. "A dramatic example of the impact of self-justification," he wrote, "concerns the physical punishment that was meted out in the People's Temple. As discussed earlier, the threat of being beaten or humiliated, forced the member to comply with Jones's orders. A person will obey as long as he or she is being threatened and supervised. To affect a person's attitudes, however, a mild threat has been demonstrated to be more effective than a severe threat [405] and its influence has been shown to be far longer lasting.[406] Under a mild

[405] Aronson, E. , and Carlsmith, J. M. Effect of the severity of threat on the devaluation of forbidden behavior. *Journal of Abnormal and Social Psychology,* 1963, 66. 584-588.

threat, the individual has more difficulty attributing his or her behavior to such a minor external restraint, forcing the person to alter his or her attitudes in order to justify the action. Severe threats elicit compliance, but, imposed from the outside, they usually fail to cause the behavior to be internalized. Quite a different dynamic ensues when it is not so clear that the action is being imposed upon the person. When an individual feels that he or she played an active role in carrying out an action that hurts someone, there comes a motivation to justify ones part in the cruelty by rationalizing it as necessary or by derogating the victim by thinking that the punishment was deserved."[407]

This point is crucial. In Jonestown believers themselves would condemn the non-conforming members, especially their own family, and punish them. Acts of cruelty for normal people are traumatic. To alleviate the pangs of their conscience, they try to rationalize their cruelty by derogating the victim and considering them, deserving of the punishment. Muslims are required to wage war even against their kin. These cruelties are justified and rationalized. Believers are taught that their harshness against the unbelievers is God's will, and not only acceptable, but will be rewarded.

Jeanne Mills, who managed to defect two years before the Temple relocated in Guyana, begins her account, *Six Years with God* (1979), as follows: "Every time I tell someone about the six years we spent as members of the People's Temple, I am faced with an unanswerable question: If the church was so bad, why did you and your family stay in for so long?" Osherow says, "Several classic studies from social psychological research investigating processes of self-justification and the theory of cognitive dissonance[408] can point to explanations for such seemingly irrational behavior."

Self-justification is what Islam is all about. Muslims commit all sorts of crimes and abuses, and they justify them all.

A story is told of Abu Hudhaifa, a young Meccan believer who participated in the battle of Badr while his father, uncle and brother were on the opposite side, in the ranks of the Quraish. It is reported that when Muhammad instructed his followers to spare Abbas, his own uncle, who was his spy among the Quraish, Hudhaifa raised his voice, "What? Are we to slay our fathers, brothers, uncles, etc., and to spare Abbas? No, verily, but I will slay him if I find him." Upon hearing this impertinent remark, Muhammad became red with anger. He turned to Umar and said, "Oh Lion of God! Ought the face of the Apostle's uncle to be marked with the

---

[406] Freedman, J. and Long-term behavioural effects of cognitive dissonance. *Journal of Experimental Social Psychology, 1965,* 1, 145-155.

[407] Davos, K., AND Jones, E. Changes in interpersonal perception as a means of reducing cognitive dissonance. *Journal of abnormal and Social Psychology,* 1960, 61, 402-410.

[408] *See Aronson*, E. *The social animal* (3rd ed.) San Francisco: W. H. Freeman and Company, 1980. AND Aronson, E. The theory of cognitive dissonance: A current perspective. In L. Berkowitz (ed.), *Advances in experimental social psychology.* Vol. 4, New York: Academic Press, 1969.

sword?" Umar, in his usual sycophantic gesture of loyalty, unshielded his sword and replied, "Let me off with his head. By God the man is a false Muslim."[409]

This threat had an immediate effect. A dramatic change happened in Abu Hudhaifa and we see him after the battle, a completely subdued and different person. When he saw his father slain and his corpse unceremoniously being dragged to be dumped into a well, he was overwhelmed and started crying. "What?" asked Muhammad, "Are you saddened for the death of your father?" "Not so, O Allah's Prophet!" responded Abu Hudhaifa, "I do not doubt the justice of my father's fate; but I knew well his wise and generous heart, and I had trusted that God would lead him to the faith. But now that I see him slain, and my hope destroyed! -- it is for that I grieve." Muhammad was pleased with his response, comforted and blessed him; and said, "It is well."[410] Abu Hudhaifa used to say, "I never felt safe after my words that day."

The displeasure of Muhammad at Abu Hudhaifa's irreverence in defying his authority and the swift reaction of Umar threatening to kill him on the spot, despite him being an early convert, were so powerful that Abu Hudhaifa immediately changed his attitude and a day later he even saw the "justice" in the slaying of his father. Once Hudhaifa lost his father, in whose killing he had conspired by ganging up with his murderers, there was no going back for him. He had to justify what he had done and rationalize the murder of his loved ones. Coming to his senses and facing his guilty conscience would have been painfully mortifying. He had to continue in his chosen path and convince himself that Islam is true or face a lifetime of remorse.

Tolstoy said, "Both salvation and punishment for man lie in the fact that if he lives wrongly he can befog himself so as not to see the misery of his position."[411]

Dissociation from Responsibility

Thousands of ordinary Germans perpetrated horrendous atrocities under the Nazis and became accomplices in the Holocaust. In their trial they defended themselves by saying they were following orders. Yale University psychologist Stanley Milgram decided to put that claim to test. In 1961 he devised a psychological experiment to prove that Eichmann and his accomplices had intent, in at least with regard to the goals of the Holocaust and shared a mutual sense of morality.

---

[409] Muir; The Life of Mohammet Vol. III Ch. XII, Page 109. (Sirat Ibn Ishaq p. 301)
[410] Muir; The Life of Mohammet Vol. III Ch. XII, Page 109; (Waqidi, p. 106; Sirat p. 230; Tabari, p. 294)
[411] The Kreutzer Sonata

He created an electric 'shock generator' with 30 switches. The switches were marked in 15 volt increments, ranging from 15 to the lethal 450 volts. The subjects were made to experience 45 volts shock, which was painful. The 'shock generator' was in fact phony and would only produce sound when the switches were pressed. Subjects were recruited via a newspaper ad. They were told they were going to participate in an experiment about 'memory and learning'.

The subject met an 'experimenter', the person leading the experiment, and an actor confederate of the experimenter, who posed as another subject.

The two subjects (the real subject and the actor) drew slips of paper to indicate who was going to be a 'teacher' and who was going to be a 'learner'. The lottery was fixed and the real subject would always get the role of 'the teacher'.

The teacher was shown the learner being strapped to a chair and electrodes were attached to his wrists. The subject was then seated in another room in front of the shock generator, unable to see the learner.

Milgram wanted to know for how long someone will continue to give shocks to another person if they are told to do so, even though they knew they were hurting them.

Remember that the subjects had met and conversed with the other person, a likable stranger, and that they thought that it could very well be them who were in the learner-position receiving shocks.

The subject was instructed to teach word-pairs to the learner. When the learner made a mistake, the subject was instructed to punish the learner by giving him a shock, 15 volts higher for each mistake.

The learner never received the shocks, but pre-taped audio was triggered when a shock-switch was pressed. The teacher could hear the learner screaming in pain and saying he does not want to participate anymore.

When the subject (teacher) contacted the experimenter, seated in the same room, he would answer with predefined 'prods' ("Please continue", "Please go on", "The experiment requires that you go on", "It is absolutely essential that you continue", "You have no other choice, you must go on"), starting with the mild prods, and making it more authoritarian for each time the subject contacted the experimenter.

If the subject asked who was responsible if anything would happen to the learner, the experimenter answered "I am responsible". This gave the subject a relief and many continued.

During the experiment, many subjects showed signs of distress. Yet although they were uncomfortable doing it, most of them continued with the experiment giving what they believed to be painful and even lethal shocks to the learner.

The conclusion shocked the world. Before the experiment, experts thought that 1 - 2% of the subjects would continue giving the shocks. They thought only psychopaths would obey inhumane orders. The experiment proved that 65% of people will commit the most evil crimes when obeying someone they believe to be an authority – which in the case of Milgram's Experiment, was just a man in white coat. None stopped, even when the "learner" complained about having heart-trouble. This experiment can be seen on Youtube.

Stanley Milgram's Experiment sheds light on a dark side of our human mind. It shows that most of us are capable of committing horrendous atrocities when obeying orders. If people are capable of killing when obeying orders from another human in authority, what they are capable of doing when believing that the authority is God? There lies the danger of Islam. This explains why ordinary Muslims abuse the non-Muslims, and why they feel no remorse killing non-believers.

Once a person believes that someone has divine authority, they surrender their intelligence and stop thinking. A mani told me that if there is a discrepancy between what he perceives as right and what the messenger of God says, he would not hesitate to forgo his judgment and follow what the messenger says. He emphasized that should the messenger of God say, day is night and night is day, he would believe him more than he would believe his own eyes. He reasoned that human perception is flawed, whereas God's wisdom is perfect. This is the nature of faith. Believers of all faiths shave similar views. This belief may not be immediately dangerous if the teachings of the religion are not. But the teachings of Islam are dangerous.

The Thugs in India believed that their deity, Kali, had ordered them to kill all those who did not belong to their faith. When a group of them was arrested, during the interrogation, they expressed their pride for the murders that they had committed.

One Thug who boasted to have murdered over nine hundred and thirty travellers was asked whether he ever felt remorse for murdering in cold blood for those whom he had beguiled into a false sense of security and who had laid their trust him him. "Certainly not!" replied Buhram (the Thug), "Are not you yourself a hunter, and don't you enjoy the thrill of the stack, the pitting of your cunning against that of an animal, and are not you pleased at seeing it dead at your feet? So with the Thug who indeed, regards the stalking of men as a higher form of sport. Remorse? Never! Joy and elation? Often![412]

Thugs were not common criminals. They were devoutly religious people who considered murder a divinely punishable offence. They picked their victims only when they received "favorable omens" from their deity. William Sleeman, the British administrator in India who hunted the Thugs and ended their 500 year reign of terror, interrogated a group of them:

> Sleeman: And do you never feel sympathy for the persons' murdered – never pity or compassion?"
> Sahib Khan: (with great emphasis) "Never."

[412] Thug or a Million Murders by Brigadier – General Sir William T. F. Horwood, p 7

> When Sleeman asked Faringea who had strangled a beautiful young woman, if he had not felt pity for her, he replied, "we all feel pity sometimes, but the sweetness of gur (a raw sugar the Thugs ate after killing their victims) of the sacrifice changes our nature.[413]
> Sleeman: When you have a poor traveller with you, or a party of travellers who appear to have little property and you hear or see a very good omen, do you not let them go in the hope that the virtue of the omen will guide you to better prey?
> Dorgha: Let them go? Never, never! (with great emphasis)
> Nasir: How could we let them go? Is not the omen the order from heaven to kill them, and would it not be disobedient to let them go? If we did not kill them how should we ever get any more travellers?
> Morlee: Certainly not! The travellers who are in our hands when we hear a good omen must never let go, whether they promise little or much; the omen is unquestionably the order (from God) as Nasir says.[414]
> Sleeman: But you think that no man is killed by man's killing? That all who are strangled are strangled in effect by God?
> Nasir: Certainly.[415]

The similarity between the Thugee mindset and the jihadi conviction is inescapable. Believers abandon reason. The good news is that all religions are not evil. When the teachings of a religion are evil and the followers blindly believe in it, we have a recipe for holocausts. Islam is evil and Muslims are zealot believers. Hence the world is in great peril.

Muhammad reassured his followers that when they raid and kill their victims, it is God who does the killing and they are mere instruments in the hand of God. "*You killed them not, but Allah killed them. And you (Muhammad) threw not when you did throw, but Allah threw, that He might test the believers by a fair trial from Him. Verily, Allah is All Hearer, All Knower.*" (Q. 8:17)

With that assurance, the believer can dissociate himself from his crimes. He can shift the responsibility and is not bothered by his conscience.

Total Mind Control

There is a story narrated by Abdullah ibn Ka'b bin Malik that demonstrates the kind of control Muhammad exerted on his followers. Ibn Ka'b says he was a devout believer and had accompanied Muhammad on all his expeditions and that thanks to the proceeds of those raids he had become a wealthy person. But when Muhammad called his followers to prepare for the raid of Tabuk, it was a hot summer, the fruits were ripe, and so he procrastinated and stayed behind. Upon returning, Muhammad called on those who had not gone and enquired the reason.

---

[413] ibid. p. 41
[414] ibid. p. 38-40
[415] ibid. p.33

7- When Sane People Follow Insane People

Many gave legitimate excuses. Muhammad was not sure about that. He reluctantly forgave them but called them liars and condemned them to hell fire. Ibn Ka'b and two other staunch believers did not dare to lie in order to excuse themselves. Ibn Ka'b wrote:

> 'Really, by Allah, there was no excuse for me. By Allah, I had never been stronger or wealthier than I was when I remained behind you.' Then Allah's Apostle said, 'As regards this man, he has surely told the truth. So get up till Allah decides your case.' Allah's Apostle forbade all the Muslims to talk to us, the three persons out of all those who had remained behind in that Ghazwa. So we kept away from the people and they changed their attitude towards us till the very land (where I lived) appeared strange to me as if I did not know it. We remained in that condition for fifty nights. As regards my two fellows, they remained in their houses and kept on weeping, but I was the youngest of them and the firmest of them, so I used to go out and witness the prayers along with the Muslims and roam about in the markets, but none would talk to me, and I would come to Allah's Apostle and greet him while he was sitting in his gathering after the prayer, and I would wonder whether the Prophet did move his lips in return to my greetings or not. Then I would offer my prayer near to him and look at him stealthily. When I was busy with my prayer, he would turn his face towards me, but when I turned my face to him, he would turn his face away from me. When this harsh attitude of the people lasted long, I walked till I scaled the wall of the garden of Abu Qatada who was my cousin and dearest person to me, and I offered my greetings to him. By Allah, he did not return my greetings. I said, 'O Abu Qatada! I beseech you by Allah! Do you know that I love Allah and His Apostle?' He kept quiet. I asked him again, beseeching him by Allah, but he remained silent. Then I asked him again in the Name of Allah. He said, 'Allah and His Apostle know it better.' Thereupon my eyes flowed with tears and I returned and jumped over the wall.
>
> When forty out of the fifty nights elapsed, behold! There came to me the messenger of Allah's Apostle and said, 'Allah's Apostle orders you to keep away from your wife,' I said, 'Should I divorce her; or else! What should I do?' He said, 'No, only keep aloof from her and do not cohabit with her.' The Prophet sent the same message to my two fellows. Then I said to my wife. 'Go to your parents and remain with them till Allah gives His Verdict in this matter.' Ka'b added, 'The wife of Hilal bin Umaiya came to Apostle and said, 'O Allah's Apostle! Hilal bin Umaiya is a helpless old man who has no servant to attend on him. Do you dislike that I should serve him?' He said, 'No you can serve him, but he should not come near you.' She said, 'By Allah, he has no desire for anything. By, Allah, he has never ceased weeping till his case began till this day of his.'
>
> On that, some of my family members said to me, 'Will you also ask Allah's Apostle to permit your wife to serve you as he has permitted the wife of Hilal bin Umaiya to serve him?' I said, 'By Allah, I will not ask the permission of Allah's Apostle regarding her, for I do not know what Allah's Apostle would say if I asked him to permit her to serve me while I am a young man.' Then I remained in that state for ten more nights after that till the period of fifty nights was completed starting from the time when Allah's Apostle prohibited the people from talking to us. When I had

> offered the Fajr prayer on the 50th morning on the roof of one of our houses and while I was sitting in the condition which Allah described (in the Quran) my very soul seemed straitened to me and even the earth seemed narrow to me for all its spaciousness, there I heard the voice of one who had ascended the mountain of Sala' calling with his loudest voice, 'O Ka'b bin Malik! Be happy by receiving good tidings.' I fell down in prostration before Allah, realizing that relief had come. Allah's Apostle had announced the acceptance of our repentance by Allah when he had offered the Fajr prayer. The people then went out to congratulate us. The people started receiving me in batches, congratulating me on Allah's Acceptance of my repentance, saying, 'We congratulate you on Allah's Acceptance of your repentance.[416]

Muhammad refers to this story in the Quran: "(*He turned in mercy also) to the three who were left behind; (they felt guilty) to such a degree that the earth seemed constrained to them, for all its spaciousness, and their (very) souls seemed straitened to them,- and they perceived that there is no fleeing from Allah (and no refuge) but to Himself. Then He turned to them, that they might repent: for Allah is Oft-Returning, Most Merciful.* (Q. 9:118)

This is the kind of control Muhammad exerted over his followers. The atmosphere of Medina was charged. The psychological control was so intense that some dreaded lying or making excuses. Muhammad had made Muslims believe that his god was aware of their innermost thoughts and therefore rendered them helpless. They were completely under his sway. This is the ultimate control. The invisible "Big Brother" is not only watching you, he is also monitoring your thoughts. There is nothing more crippling than this. Freedom to think is the most vital human faculty. It is what makes us human. Believers give up that faculty.

About those who had legitimate excuses, Muhammad made his Allah say, "*They will swear to you by Allah, when ye return to them, that ye may leave them alone. So leave them alone: For they are an abomination and Hell is their dwelling-place, a fitting recompense for the (evil) that they did. They will swear unto you, that ye may be pleased with them but if ye are pleased with them, Allah is not pleased with those who disobey.*" (Q. 9:95-96)

He had no way to verify the legitimacy of these men's alibis. He was reluctant to accept their excuses for if they were lying, it would have been a giveaway that he can be fooled and therefore, his claim to prophecy would be exposed as a lie. So he said, I let you go unpunished, but if you think you fooled me you are mistaken.

Mind control works as long as one believes. Once the person stops believing, they are set free. The fear of hell has paralyzed the thinking ability of Muslims. The very thought of doubting makes them tremble in fear and they dismiss it instantly.

Osherow says:

---

[416] Bukhari, 5: 59: 702

7- When Sane People Follow Insane People

> The processes going on at Jonestown obviously were not as simple as those in a well-controlled laboratory experiment; several themes were going on simultaneously. For example, Jim Jones had the power to impose any punishments that he wished in the People's Temple, and, especially towards the end, brutality and terror at Jonestown were rampant. But Jones carefully controlled how the punishments were carried out. He often called upon the members themselves to agree to the imposition of beatings. They were instructed to testify against fellow members, bigger members told to beat up smaller ones, wives or lovers forced to sexually humiliate their partners, and parents asked to consent to and assist in the beatings of their children."[417] The punishments grew more and more sadistic, the beatings so severe as to knock the victim unconscious and cause bruises that lasted for weeks. As Donald Lunde, a psychiatrist who has investigated acts of extreme violence explains: 'Once you've done something that major, it's very hard to admit even to yourself that you've made a mistake, and subconsciously you will go to great lengths to rationalize what you did. It's very tricky defense mechanism exploited to the hilt by the charismatic leader.'"[418]

A more personal account of the impact of this process is provided by Jeanne Mills. At one meeting, she and her husband were forced to consent to the beating of their daughter as punishment for a very minor transgression. She relates the effect this had on her daughter, the victim, as well as on herself, one of the perpetrators:

> As we drove home, everyone in the car was silent. We were all afraid that our words would be considered treasonous. The only sounds came from Linda, sobbing quietly in the back seat. When we got into our house, Al and I sat down to talk with Linda. She was in too much pain to sit. She stood quietly while we talked with her. 'How do you feel about what happened tonight?' Al asked her. 'Father was right to have me whipped.' Linda answered. 'I've been so rebellious lately, and I've done a lot of things that were wrong. I'm sure Father knew about those things, and that's why he had me hit so many times.' As we kissed our daughter goodnight, our heads were spinning. It was hard to think clearly when things were so confusing. Linda had been the victim, and yet we were the only people angry about it. She should have been hostile and angry. Instead, she said that Jim had actually helped her. We knew Jim had done a cruel thing, and yet everyone acted as if he were doing a loving thing in whipping our disobedient child. Unlike a cruel person hurting a child, Jim had seemed calm, almost loving, as he observed the beating and counted off the whacks. Our minds were not able to comprehend the atrocity of the situation because none of the feedback we were receiving was accurate.
>
> The feedback one received from the outside was limited, and the feedback from inside the Temple member was distorted. By justifying the previous actions and commitments, the groundwork for accepting the ultimate commitment was established.

---

[417] Mills, 1979; Kilduff and Javers, 1978

[418] Newsweek, 1978a

> Only months after we defected from Temple did we realize the full extent of the cocoon in which we lived. And only then did we understand the fraud, sadism, and emotional blackmail of the master manipulator.[419]

The testimony of Jeanne Mills is in many ways identical to those of former Muslims. Ex-Muslims admit that they were not aware of the abuse that they were subjected to when they were believers. It is only after they left Islam that they realized the enormity of the abuse and mind control. A Muslim woman married a Muslim man is subject to the same domestic violence that a non-Muslim woman who marries a Muslim man. However, the former is often unaware of the abuse. She is used to abuse because she grew up with it. She saw her mother, aunts, and other women she knows were all abused. This is normal to her and she has accepted it as part of her womanhood. Non-Muslim women, who marry Muslim men, often come from families where women are not denigrated, beaten and abused. For them, the marriage to a Muslim man is much more oppressive.

Christians, Jews and Hindus, also leave their faiths. However, there is not much anger and resentment in them towards the faith they leave behind. When Muslims leave Islam, they leave it with bitterness in their hearts. It is only then that they see the extent of their victimization. For a Muslim the awakening is painful.

Osherow says, "A few hours before his murder, Congressman Ryan addressed the membership: "I can tell you right now that by the few conversations I've had with some of the folks, there are some people who believe this is the best thing that ever happened in their whole lives." [Cheers and applause can be heard in the background] (Krause, 1978). The acquiescence of so many and the letters they left behind indicate that this feeling was widely shared or at least expressed by the members."

Islam, like the People's Temple, attracts the vulnerable, those who are downtrodden and in need of a sense of purpose. In the Western society, where individuality is taken to the extreme, there is a sense of loneliness. Islam gives the new convert a sense of belonging. It gives them an alternative way of viewing their lives, a direction and a sense of transcendence. But it does so at a terrible cost. It alienates them from their own selves to the extent that they disown their families and friendships and plot the downfall of their country.

Islam, like People's Temple, teaches its members to fear anything and anyone outside of their faith and regards nonbelievers as "the enemy." True Muslims hate the possibility of any other lifestyle. Islam to them is the only correct way and everything else must perish. Muslims are increasingly suspicious of non-Muslims and are fervent believers of the conspiracy theories about the "wicked West".

---

[419] Mills, J. *Six years with God.* New York: A & W Publishers, 1979.

7- When Sane People Follow Insane People

Control of Information

Osherow writes:

> Within the People's Temple, and especially at Jonestown, Jim Jones controlled the information to which members would be exposed. He effectively stifled any dissent that might arise within the church and instilled distrust in each member for contradictory messages from outside. After all, what credibility could be carried by information supplied by 'the enemy' that was out to destroy the People's Temple with 'lies?' Seeing no alternatives and having no information, a member's capacity for dissent or resistance was minimized. Moreover, for most members, part of the Temples attraction resulted from their willingness to relinquish much of the responsibility and control over their lives. These were primarily the poor, the minorities, the elderly, and the unsuccessful. They were happy to exchange personal autonomy (with its implicit assumption of personal responsibility for their plight) for security, brotherhood, the illusion of miracles, and the promise of salvation. Stanley Cath, a psychiatrist who has studied the conversion techniques used by cults, generalizes: 'Converts have to believe only what they are told. They don't have to think, and this relieves tremendous tensions.' (Newsweek, 1978a)"

The above, perfectly describes the condition of Muslims as well, especially in Islamic countries where any information slightly contradicting the official creed is censored and the believers are allowed only one view, the one provided by the authorities. In fact Muslims try hard to censor any anti-Islamic message even in non-Muslim countries. If a book or an article is published that they don't like, they protest and try to force the "offender" to withdraw his publication and apologize. One can only imagine the kind of control and censorship that Muhammad exerted over his followers in his compound.

Jeanne Mills commented:

> I was amazed at how little disagreement there was between the members of this church. Before we joined the church, Al and I couldn't even agree on whom to vote for in a presidential election. Now that we all belonged to a group, family arguments were becoming a thing of the past. There was never a question of who was right, because Jim was always right. When our large household met to discuss family problems, we didn't ask for opinions. Instead, we put the question to the children, 'What would Jim do?' It took the difficulty out of life. There was a type of 'manifest destiny' which said the Cause was right and would succeed. Jim was right and those who agreed with him were right. If you disagreed with Jim, you were wrong. It was as simple as that.[420]

Osherow says:

> Though it is unlikely that he had any formal exposure to the social psychological literature, Jim Jones utilized several very powerful and effective techniques for

---

[420] Mills, J. *Six years with God.* New York: A & W Publishers, 1979

> controlling people's behavior and altering their attitudes. Some analyses have compared his tactics to those involved in 'brainwashing,' for both include the control of communication, the manipulation of guilt, and power over people's existence,[421] as well as isolation, an exacting regimen, physical pressure, and the use of confessions.[422] But using the term brainwashing makes the process sound too esoteric and unusual. There were some unique and scary elements in Jones's personality paranoia, delusions of grandeur, sadism, and a preoccupation with suicide. Whatever his personal motivation, however, having formulated his plans and fantasies, he took advantage of well-established social psychological tactics to carry them out. The decision to have a community destroy itself was crazy, but those who performed the deed were 'normal' people who were subjected to a tremendously provocative situation, the victims of powerful internal forces as well as external pressures."

This definition explains how it is possible for a multitude of sane people to follow an insane man. It happened in Germany. Hitler was insane. Yet the millions of Germans that followed him were not.

The grip, the psychopath cult leader has over his followers is mind-boggling. Ibn Ishaq tells a story about Orwa's observation of the treatment that the followers of Muhammad conferred on him. He was a negotiator of the Meccans who visited Muhammad in his encampment at Hudaibiyah, on the outskirts of Mecca.

Muhammad was aloof and Abu Bakr was speaking on his behalf. Orwa, became more earnest, and in accordance to the Bedouin custom, stretched forth his hand to take hold of Muhammad's beard. This was a token of friendship and familiarity and not an act of disrespect. "Back off!" cried a bystander, striking his arm. "Hold off your hand from the Prophet of Allah!" Orwa was startled at the youth's interruption and asked, "And who is this?" "It is your nephew, Moghira," responded the youth. "Ungrateful!" exclaimed Orwa (alluding to his having paid compensation for certain murders committed by his nephew), "it is but as yesterday that I redeemed your life."

Orwa was impressed by the degree of reverence and devotion that Muhammad's followers showed their prophet. Upon returning to Mecca he reported that he had seen many kings, the Khosrow, Caysar, and Najashi, but never had witnessed such attention and homage as Muhammad received from his followers. "They rushed to save the water in which he had performed his ablutions, to catch up his spittle, or seize a hair of his if it chanced to fall."[423]

Muhammad had built a personality cult around himself. He was the personification of his god. Obedience to him was obedience to Allah and disobeying him was disobeying Allah. This is everything a narcissistic psychopath

---

[421] Lifton, R. J. Appeal of the death trip. *New York Times Magazine,* January 7, 1979.
[422] Cahill, T. In the valley of the shadow of death. *Rolling Stone.* January 25, 1979.
[423] Ibn Ishaq, Sira, p.823

craves for – to be God incarnate. Muhammad manipulated everyone until he ascended to the throne of Allah and became the de facto God.

Three months after the horrendous event in Jonestown, Michael Prokes who was spared because he was assigned to carry away a box of People's Temple funds, called a press conference in a California motel room. After claiming that Jones had been misunderstood and demanding the release of a tape-recording of the final minutes [quoted earlier], he stepped into the bathroom and shot himself in the head. He left behind a note, saying that if his death inspired another book about Jonestown, it was worthwhile. (Newsweek, 1979) Doesn't this shed light on the psychopathology of the suicide bomber?

Jeanne and Al Mills were among the most vocal critics of the People's Temple following their defection, and they topped an alleged "death list" of its enemies. Even after Jonestown, the Mills had repeatedly expressed fear for their lives. Well over a year after the People's Temple massacre, they and their daughter were murdered in their Berkeley home. Their teen-age son, himself an ex-People's Temple member, testified that he was in another part of the large house at the time. There are indications that the Mills knew their killer. There were no signs of forced entry, and they were shot at close range. Jeanne Mills had been quoted as saying, "It's going to happen; if not today, then tomorrow." On the final tape of Jonestown, Jim Jones blamed Jeanne Mills by name, and promised that his followers in San Francisco "will not take our death in vain." (Newsweek, 1980)

Muslims consider it their duty to kill anyone who leaves Islam. Their hatred for apostates is unbelievably intense. If you leave Islam and keep it to yourself, you may get away with it, but if you commit the impudence of speaking against it, every Muslim considers it to be their duty to hunt you and will kill you in the cruelest way. There is nothing that a Muslim hates more feverishly than those who renounce Islam and then speak against it. Those who dare to defy Islam do so at their own peril. Muhammad's orders are unequivocal: "*But if they turn renegades, seize them and slay them wherever ye find them.*" (Q. 4:89).

Chapter Eight

The Psychology of Fear

In order to understand a narcissist, it helps to learn a thing or two about psychopaths. Narcissistic traits are subtle and the narcissist is quite apt in dissimulation. The psychopath shows the same traits of a narcissist in a magnified form. Once we understand these traits, it becomes a lot easier to detect them in their subtle manifestations and hence identify a narcissist.

Psychopath and sociopath are colloquial terms. The term used in psychiatry is antisocial personality disorder (ASPD). In this chapter I will stick to the colloquial terms.

NPD manifests as a pathological craving for attention. Socio/psychopathy manifests as a pathological craving for self-gratification. The latter is perhaps the less inhibited and less sophisticated manifestation of the former. Some researchers suggest that there is a hybrid between the two - the "psychopathic narcissism". What is important to know is that despite their nuances, narcissism, psychopathic narcissism and antisocial personality are different gradations of the same disorder.

Vaknin says, "Psychopaths, like narcissists, lack empathy but many of them are also sadistic: they take pleasure in inflicting pain on their victims or in deceiving them. They even find it funny!" In his book "Malignant Self Love - Narcissism Revisited" Vaknin writes:

> As opposed to what Scott Peck says, narcissists are not evil – they lack the intention to cause harm (mens rea). … Narcissists are simply indifferent, callous and careless in their conduct and in their treatment of others. Their abusive conduct is off-handed and absent-minded, not calculated and premeditated like the psychopath's…. When the egocentricity, lack of empathy, and sense of superiority of the narcissist cross-fertilizes with the impulsivity, deceitfulness, and criminal tendencies of the antisocial, the result is a psychopath, an individual who seeks the gratification of selfish impulses through any means without empathy or remorse.

> Like narcissists, psychopaths lack empathy and regard other people as mere instruments of gratification and utility or as objects to be manipulated. Psychopaths and narcissists have no problem to grasp ideas and to formulate choices, needs, preferences, courses of action, and priorities. But they are shocked when other people do the very same.
>
> Most people accept that others have rights and obligations. The psychopath rejects this quid pro quo. As far as he is concerned, only might is right. People have no rights and he, the psychopath, has no obligations that derive from the "social contract". The psychopath holds himself to be above conventional morality and the law. The psychopath cannot delay gratification. He wants everything and wants it now. His whims, urges, catering to his needs, and the satisfaction of his drives take precedence over the needs, preferences, and emotions of even his nearest and dearest.[424]

These traits were all present in Muhammad. He recognized no rights for others. Everyone had to submit to his will or perish. His decisions were God's decisions and disobeying him was regarded as disobeying God. He did not present logical arguments to support his claim, but issued ultimatums and threats. He demanded that his followers abandon their own will and submit to him completely and unhesitantly. He expected others to fight for him, sacrifice their comfort, wealth, and life. As far as he was concerned he had the last word and no one was allowed to express an opinion contrary to his.

> *But no, by the Lord, they can have no (real) faith, until they make you judge in all disputes between them, and find in their souls no resistance against your decisions, but accept them with the fullest conviction.* (Q. 4:65).
>
> *No believing man and no believing woman has a choice in their own affairs when Allah and His Messenger have decided on an issue.*(Q.33:36).

Vaknin says, "Psychopaths feel no remorse when they hurt or defraud others. They don't possess even the most rudimentary conscience. They rationalize their (often criminal) behavior and intellectualize it. Psychopaths fall prey to their own primitive defense mechanisms (such as narcissism, splitting, and projection). The psychopath firmly believes that the world is a hostile, merciless place, prone to the survival of the fittest and that people are either "all good" or "all evil". The psychopath projects his own vulnerabilities, weaknesses, and shortcomings unto others and forces them to behave the way he expects them to (this defense mechanism is known as "projective identification"). Like narcissists, psychopaths are abusively exploitative, and incapable of true love or intimacy." [425]

---

[424] http://samvak.tripod.com/personalitydisorders15.html
[425] Ibid.

8- The Psychology of Fear

Muhammad felt no qualm in deceiving his victims, in taking them off-guard and raiding them, in murdering innocent people for no other reason than the fact that they were not his followers, and in regarding them as enemies, deserving to be subdued, enslaved, raped, humiliated, and killed. He justified all these crimes with divine justification.

The best way to understand the mind of a psychopath is through example. The following is the story of Cameroon Hooker as narrated by Katherine Ramsland.[426] You may wonder what this story has to do with Muhammad. But read on to the end and the shocking similarities will begin to emerge.

In 1977, 20 year old Coleen Stan left her home in Oregon to visit a friend in California, 400 miles away.

She hitchhiked and when a car stopped to pick her up, she saw a clean-cut friendly couple with a baby, she felt comfortable and got into the back seat.

The family, whose last name was Hooker, and Coleen, had an amiable conversation and when the husband, Cameron Hooker, mentioned they were close to some spectacular ice caves and suggested they should stop and have a look, Coleen did not felt threatened.

They drove down a dirt road and then they stopped in the middle of nowhere. Hooker got out of the car, pulled Coleen out of the car and put a knife on her throat. He told her that if she does not cooperate he would kill her. Coleen froze in fear and agreed. He then handcuffed and blindfolded and gagged her. He then encaged her head in a box made of plywood. She was in total darkness and could hardly breathe. She was then placed in the trunk of the car and taken to the Hookers' house. Janice, the wife of Cameron cooperated with her husband fully. During the trip Coleen wondered whether she would ever see her family again.

Inside the house, Cameron removed the heavy box from Coleen's head and took her to cellar, where he disrobed her and made her stand on an ice chest. He told her to lift her hands over her head and with a leather strap, tied her wrists to an overhead pipe while still blindfolded. This was just the beginning of what awaited her.

Cameron then removed the chest supporting Coleen, so now she was hanging in the air suspended by her writs. When she screamed he told her to go ahead and scream and that in other such situations, he'd just cut the vocal chords of his captive and if she kept it up, he'd do the same to her.

He then started whipping her, both front and back. The more he shrieked for help them more sadistic he became and the harder he beat her. He then placed something beneath her feet, barely high enough for her toes to touch and left. Looking beneath her blindfold, Coleen could see a pornographic magazine lay on the floor, with a naked woman hung up just as she was.

---

[426] Katherine Ramsland
http://www.trutv.com/library/crime/criminal_mind/psychology/sex_slave/4.html

Shortly after that Cameron and his wife Janice came back and had sex right there in the cellar. Then he took her down from her hanging position. Her arms were sore and her body hurt from beating. Then he made her sit inside another tight box and placed the head box back on her head. She was now completely immobilized and barely able to breathe. When she screamed he placed a strap over her chest that constricted her breathing even more, and she could no longer scream. Then he left her like that for a very long and frightening night. She thought she was going to die. Coleen's nightmare had just begun.

Cameron and Janice were an ordinary couple who did not stand out. They were quiet and kept to themselves. Cameron was working in a local lumber mill and was considered dependable. They lived in a rented house from an elderly couple who lived next door and did not notice anything strange in them.

Cameron met Janice in 1973 when she was 15. An epileptic and with very little self-esteem she was malleable and yielding to whatever he said. She wanted to have a man at any cost. Cameron introduced Janice to violent pornography and tortured her with her with her consent, enacting a sadomasochist relationship. Janice agreed to all sorts of abuses as long as she got his attention.

Roy Hazelwood and Ann Burgess conducted a study on 20 women accomplices of sexual sadists and concluded that the male's sexual fantasies often become shared by their female partners. As he progressively isolates her she becomes more dependent on him, sharing his deviances and sadistic fantasies.

The same synergy exists between a cult leader and his followers. The fantasies of the cult leader are bequeathed to his votaries. They become paranoid and suspicious of outsiders and share their leader's ambition of grandiosity. They negate their own individuality, in fact sacrifice their own needs and desires, but feel grandiose as extensions of the cult leader.

"It is important to understand," Hazelwood writes, "that the ritualistic and heterosexual sadist inherently believes that all women are evil. Consequently, if and when these men set out to prove this hypothesis they select nice, middle-class women who are apparently normal." They use a process that exploits the woman's vulnerability to turn her into a compliant accomplice.

This is not dissimilar to how cult leaders view human beings in general. They see people as inherently sinners and naturally prone to do evil. Their message is often in the form of warnings and calls to repent.

Muhammad had a very similar conception of women. He thought women are deficient in intelligence and in faith, that they are prone to go astray and sin, and need to be contained. The veil is a symbol of that containment.

Everyone views the world from their own perspective. Honest people think others are also honest and vice versa. This is known as Projection. According to Sigmund Freud, projection is a psychological defense mechanism whereby one "projects" one's own undesirable thoughts, motivations, desires, and feelings onto someone else. "Emotions or excitations which the ego tries to ward off are 'split out' and then felt as being outside the ego... perceived in another person." Muhammad believed that everyone has a natural tendency to sin and the only way to deter them is through fear of punishment. He projected his own narcissistic traits on others. A narcissist will break all laws if he can get away with them. The only thing that stops a narcissist is fear of being caught and punishment. Therefore to control others, the narcissist uses fear.

Cameron controlled everything and Janice submitted. If she didn't he would threaten to leave her or to harm her and she complied. The cult leader has the same kind of control over his followers. Their threats are mostly given in the form of admonitions, divine retributions, and call to repentance. But it can also be corporal, involving beating, torturing, maiming, and beheading; it depends how much control a cult leader has over his followers and to what extent he can get away with his whims. In a lawless society, like the Seventh Century Arabia, and especially in Medina where Muhammad ruled supreme, he could get away with anything. He represented God. His authority was supreme.

The sadist is never satisfied. The sadist is always after new conquests and new trills. Cameron decided he needed to have a sex slave and asked Janice to help him acquiring one. She feared if she did not agree, he would leave her. She was ready to tread over her own conscience as long as she could have a family and pretend living a normal life. She also thought that if he had a sex slave, he would satisfy his sadistic fantasies with her and would leave her in peace.

This symbiotic relationship between the psychopath and his co-dependent is quite similar to that of a cult leader and his cultist followers. The cult leader strips the identity of his followers who don't see any worth in themselves except as submissive slaves of the leader who often presents himself as the representative of God. The cultists are charged only when basking in the leader's glory and feel negated when deprived of it. They will do anything to gain his pleasure. The relationship between the cult leader and his followers is neither fear nor love. It is a combination of both at their extreme. The biggest fear of a cultist is not corporal punishment, but abandonment and rejection. To gain the pleasure of the cult leader, the cultist will do anything. They will commit murder and suicide, and willingly offer themselves, their wives and their children for their guru's sexual gratification.

The next morning Cameron removed the head box and then pulled Coleen out of the body box. Finally she could breathe easily, but her ordeals were not over. He made her starve for the rest of the day and finally gave her some water and potatoes. Then he hung her to the pipes for a while and then removed. After that Cameron placed the head box back on her head and stretched her out on a rack where she lay immobile for hours. All this was designed to make her fear him.

The narcissist cult leader is more subtle in gaining the submission of his followers. He instills in them the fear of the afterlife and the torments that await them in the pending doomsday. He warns them that if they don't submit, terrible things will happen to them. Both narcissists and psychopaths use fear as a tool for domination. The following hadith will make the point clear:

> Narrated Abu Said Al-Khudri:
> Once Allah's Apostle went out to the Musalla (to offer the prayer) o 'Id-al-Adha or Al-Fitr prayer. Then he passed by the women and said, "O women! Give alms, as I have seen that the majority of the dwellers of Hell-fire were you (women)." They asked, "Why is it so, O Allah's Apostle?" He replied, "You curse frequently and are ungrateful to your husbands. I have not seen anyone more deficient in intelligence and religion than you. A cautious sensible man could be led astray by some of you." The women asked, "O Allah's Apostle! What is deficient in our intelligence and religion?" He said, "Is not the evidence of two women equal to the witness of one man?" They replied in the affirmative. He said, "This is the deficiency in her intelligence. Isn't it true that a woman can neither pray nor fast during her menses?" The women replied in the affirmative. He said, "This is the deficiency in her religion."[427]

This hadith is reported by many chains of narrators and is recorded by several collectors. To make women fill his coffer Muhammad instilled in them fear and called them to repent. Fear is the most primitive and the most effective way to makes others do your bidding.

Note that the above hadith is also anachronistic. According to Muhammad's eschatology, people who die, including prophets, will stay in their graves until they are resurrected in the Day of Judgment, whereupon they will receive their verdict and will be sent either to hell or to heaven. Ergo, Muhammad could not possibly have seen anyone in hell which is not going to be in operation until after the Day of Resurrection. By the same token, his claim of his assentation to Heaven and meeting the past prophets is also false.

Could possibly Muhammad have travelled in time and the story of Mi'raj is futuristic? This hypothesis is also untenable because he claimed that upon his arrival the prophets were already in heaven who greeted him. Yet, this cannot be possible because according to his own claim, after Israfil (Rafael) will sound his sûr (horn), sending out a "blast of truth," Muhammad will be the first to be brought back to life and the first to enter paradise.

Back in Hookers' house! Another day passed before Coleen was allowed to eat again. She was given egg salad. She ate, but could not finish it. She was in pain and the air was hot and humid. He angrily reminded her that she ought to be grateful. She said she was full. This prompted him to teach her a lesson that a slave must not argue with her master. He then hung her up again with her wrists and whipped her so much until she passed out. When she regained her consciousness he

[427] Sahih Bukhari 1:6:301

forced her to finish her food, then he tied her up, replaced the head box on her and left.

Time passed and Coleen was left chained, blindfolded and stretched out naked on the rack. She saw very little of Janice and the baby. Cameron visited her frequently and whipped her sadistically. He took a pervert pleasure in her pain. Every once in a while he'd hold Coleen's head under water until she would lose consciousness. Coleen would frequently ask him whether he would let her go and he would say "yes, Soon."

Realizing that keeping Coleen chained to a rack all day could harm her health, he made a box that looked like a coffin. It had double walls with insulation between them to muffle her screams. The coffin had a hole and a fan for ventilation. He placed a sleeping bag in the coffin and forced Coleen inside it. He then plugged her ears with ear plugs and chained her before closing her inside. Then he shoved the coffin under the bed where he and Janice slept and that became Coleen's home for the next seven years. She would eat there and had a bedpan for her necessities. She was not allowed to shower. She lost twenty pounds and stopped menstruating. Her world became the box. Living in total darkness she learned to approximate the time of day by the temperature inside the box.

To increase the torture, Cameron used a heat lamp to burn Coleen's skin and sometimes would electrocute her. Sometimes he would strangulate her and the whipping was administered daily. All these tortures sexually excited him and he would end the sessions by molesting her, but he did not have intercourse with her.

Eventually he decided to put her to work and constructed a tiny cell under the staircase where Coleen was allowed to stay unshackled. Her new duty was to shell nuts or do macramé. This tiny cell became her small realm of liberty.

Physical Control vs. Mind Control

Narcissists and sociopaths are predators. They want to control others. Having control over life and death gives them the sensation of godhood. This is the ultimate power. Their means of gaining control are different. The sociopath's ways are cruder. He traps his prey physically. He stalks them like an animal. He plays with his victims and tortures them like a cat playing with a mouse before killing it. The narcissist lures his prey by promising them the nirvana and controls them psychologically with fear of hell and divine retribution. Despite this difference, they are eerily similar.

A year passed. Coleen spent her birthday in the coffin, just as she did the Christmas and the New Year. Eight months after her kidnapping, Cameron subscribed to an underground sadomasochistic newspaper. It contained an article titled, "They Sell Themselves Body and Soul When They Sign THE SLAVERY CONTRACT."

A lamp went on Cameron's head and he set about to create a contract, one for Coleen. He made Coleen sign with her new slave name, "K" and he signed the contract himself as "Michael Powers." When he read the bogus contract that gave him total control over Coleen, she thought it was utterly evil. But he told her if she did not sign he would make her wish that she had. So she complied.

The contract set the rule of her conduct and that from there on Cameron had to be called "master". She had to have her body "open" to him at all time for anything he wished to do with her. If she did not comply, the company had the option to take her away and give her to someone who might not be as nice as Cameron.

The irony is that the narcissist and the sociopath have a very high opinion of themselves. Every detail of the life of Muhammad is filled with ruthlessness, crime and sheer evil, and yet he thought he was the perfect human, the best example to follow.

Cameron told Coleen that he had paid $1,500 to register her with something called the Slave Company. He made her believe that spies from the company were watching them all the time, and they had even bugged the house. They knew who Coleen's relatives were and would kill them if she ever violated the terms of the contract. He said that Janice was also his slave, and should either of them attempt to escape, the company would punish them by nailing their hands to a beam and hanging them up for days. Janice corroborated Cameron's lies and Coleen believed that. "He always had things to back up his stories," Coleen later reported, "and I believed what he said."

Physical control has its limitation. The prey will escape her captor in the first opportunity. But when the chains are psychological, the slavery is permanent. Physical chains are easier to break than the psychological ones.

Cameron realized that in order to have total control over his prey he needed a fictitious ally. Someone who sees everything but cannot be seen, who hears everything but cannot be heard, is omnipresent, omnipotent and fearsome. The narcissist/psychopath can control his prey to the extent that he can convince them of the existence of this powerful imaginary ally.

Cult leaders use God as their imaginary ally. Most people believe in God. They believe He is all powerful, all seeing, all hearing, omnipotent and omnipresent. Once a cult leader convinces his followers that he is a representative, a messenger, a prophet of God, he can have unlimited power over them.

By signing the slavery contract, Coleen was no longer the slave of Cameron; she now belonged to the invisible Company that was far more powerful and fearsome than him. Invisible entities are more awe striking than the ones you can see.

Once Coleen believed in the Company, she lost her freedom to escape. She feared to talk to others. She feared that anyone can be a spy of the Company. Nevertheless, she was still free to think and to escape from her reality through her thoughts. She knew that the Company was evil and she was free to despise it. This is a luxury cultists don't have. Muslims won't question Allah. Even though they can see he is evil, they will not let that thought cross their minds.

Resigned to slavery and given up hope, Coleen learned to shut down her emotions. "The more I played his game," she told a journalist, "the better it was for me. If I fought, it went on forever." She learned that begging for mercy only further incited him, so she stopped asking. She used her imagination to escape her situation. No one could stop her dreaming.

Replace The Company with Allah. Allah can see and hear everything. But he has powers that Cameron's fictitious company did not have. Allah can read one's mind. Coleen knew that the "Slave Company" could not read her thoughts. Muslims believe that their thoughts are open book to Allah. When Coleen could dream about freedom, a Muslim will not allow himself to have such dreams. The slavery in Islam is absolute.

This is an awesome power in the hand of the cult leader. What makes us human is our ability to think, to question and to doubt. *Cogito ergo sum,* (I think, therefore I am) said Descartes. If someone can control your thoughts, he can control your life. A person who fears to think, to question and to doubt is no longer a person. He is a zombie. Allah can read people's thoughts and he has a tormenting fire for those who doubt him. Is there a more paralyzing technique of mind control than this?

Cameron's "Slave Company" could only punish the slaves for a short time. No matter how painful torture may be, death is always a relief. Allah can read the minds of his slaves and he will burn them for eternity, pour in their mouths boiling water, chop their fingers and make them eat puss and poisonous fruits for thinking the wrong thoughts. All one has to do to deserve these never ending torments is to doubt what Muhammad said.

Once a person believes in this yarn, he surrenders his thinking. There is no escape for him. Muslims have signed their contract of slavery to Muhammad and to his imaginary deity for as long as they believe in his whoppers. It is not a coincidence that Muhammad called his followers *ibad*, (slaves).

All Muslims have to do to set themselves free is to question whether a compassionate and merciful God would torture humans in such a sadistic way and the whole charade of Islam will fall apart. How can God burn people for not believing in absurdities and in illogical claims of a man who lived a despicable life of thuggery? Only a moment of rational thought will set Muslims free. But once you have signed your contract of slavery, and allow fear to cloud your judgment that moment is hard to come.

A Muslim woman wrote hurling at me a lot of insults and said I don't understand the truth. I told her Muhammad said women are deficient in intelligence; please tell me whether you agree or disagree. I often ask this question from Muslim women. They don't respond. This Muslima wrote back defiantly, "I agree with everything the prophet Muhammad said, and you won't change my mind even in a hundred years." She wrote back again and after calling me stupid she added, "All the women in my family agree with everything the prophet Muhammad has said about women, and it's true, women are deficient in their thinking."

This is the perfect case of brainwashing. Believers stop thinking and surrender to the cult leader. They cannot be considered free people, or human for that matter.

Assuming God exists, we can never know him nor can we know his attributes. The gods that we envision are figments of our imagination. No one would say their god is evil. Making vacuous claims about Allah being merciful and compassionate are meaningless when all his teachings are about fighting, murdering, deceiving, and subduing. To envision God as a sadist, someone who runs a hell to burn humans and who ruthlessly tortures them for eternity because they did not worship him, is the abyss of stupidity. Attributing such insanity to the maker of the universe is nothing short of blasphemy.

Good people envision good gods and evil people envision monstrous gods. The Muslim world is hellish, because Muslims believe in a sadistic god, the figment of the mind of a psychopath.

Those who believe in evil gods will do evil things. The Aztecs sacrificed up to 20,000 humans every year at the altar of their god Huitzilopochtli. The Indian Thugs were also accredited with about 40,000 murders every year, for Kali, a deity that they believed had ordered them to murder all those who were not of their kind. With the massacre of 280 million non-Muslims since Muhammad, the number of people Muslims have sacrificed at the altar of Allah exceeds 200,000 per year. The 20th Century was an exception. In that century Muhslims had empoverished and therefore and since the possibility of winning was limited, they had put a truce to jihad. Thanks to immigration to western countries and oil, now they feel empowered again and are back in business. Muslims are promised incommensurable rewards when they kill non-believers (those who are not of their kind).

> *Let those (believers) who sell the life of this world for the Hereafter, fight in the Cause of Allah; and whoso fights in the Cause of Allah and is killed or gets victory, We shall bestow on him a great reward.* (Q.4:74)

Outright Slavery

Ramsland writes, "Eventually Coleen, now referred to in the house as K, was allowed to do household chores such as cooking, washing dishes, and cleaning up. Yet whenever Cameron yelled "Attention!" she was to strip off her clothes, stand on her tiptoes, and reach her hands to the top of the doorway between the living room and dining room."

The similarities between the mind of a sociopath and that of Muhammad are inescapable. In one hadith Muhammad is reported saying, "if a man calls his wife to his bed, let her respond, even if she is riding her camel."[428] Elsewhere he said, she should rush to please her husband even if she is busy at the oven.[429] Let the bread burn, but don't let your horny husband waiting for you. And what will happen if she delays? "By Him in Whose Hand is my life," he swore, "when a man calls his wife to his bed, and she does not respond, the One Who is in the heaven is displeased with her until he (her husband) is pleased with her.[430] And if "he goes to sleep angry with her, the angels will curse her until the morning.[431]

I don't want to interfere in Allah's business, but in my humble opinion this is a waste of resources. Why would Allah instruct angels to lobby him so he can damn woman who don't please their husband in bed? It just seems there is too much similarity between the slavery of Muslims and that of Coleen.

"Coleen wore a slave collar," writes Ramsland, "and was supplied with a registration card, supposedly from the slave company. Cameron would tell her horror stories of things that had happened to slaves who'd disobeyed. One had her tongue taken out with a soldering gun, he claimed, another pulled limb from limb, and another, her fingers torn off."

Compare this to how Muhammad described the punishment in hell and in the grave. In the grave the detractors' corpse will be crushed while they are conscious and feel the pain, and in hell, they will burn. Once their skin is consumed they will grow a new one to burn again. They will be dismembered, devoured, and made to drink puss and boiling water. A billion otherwise normal people believe in this asininity and they demand respect.

Finally, Cameron decided to bring Coleen into the marriage bed. Janice was fully cooperative. By assimilating his insanity she had lost ever trace of humanity and had become an extension of her sociopathic husband. After a while, however, she went to another room. That night Cameron raped Coleen and since then had regular sex with her.

Note that for nearly a year or perhaps more, Cameron did not have sex with Coleen. Sex for the psychopath is only a way to exert domination. Psychopath narcissists want to control their victim. They are not driven by sex or by money. They are driven by lust for power. They want slaves. They want people to submit to them, to obey them, and not to question their authority.

Some cult leaders live an austere life. Many of them endured persecution, imprisonment and death. None of these are proof of the validity of their claim. In the quest for power, the narcissist is willing to endure any hardship.

Eventually, Cameron gave his slave some freedom. Coleen could stay longer in her cell under the stairs and even sleep there. But that freedom was short-lived. The

---

[428] Majma' al-Zawa'id, 4/312.
[429] Tirmidhi, 2/314, abwab al-rida', 10, and by Ibn Hibban, Sahih, 9,473, kitab al-nikah.
[430] Muslim, 8: 3367
[431] Muslim, 8: 3368

Hookers moved to a trailer where space was at premium and the coffin under the waterbed became Coleen's home again and a bedpan, her toilet.

She was allowed out of her box for an hour each day to brush her teeth, eat, clean her bedpan, and sometimes wash her hair. And on days that Cameron had off from work and could keep an eye on her, she could work in the yard.

He had convinced that the company was watching her every move. So she did not try to escape, or ask for help from the neighbors when occasionally she talked to them. She even went jogging and always came back.

Coleen had become an obedient slave, but sometimes she would make a mistake. For that she would be punished with electrical wires that left many scars on her skin, which helped the prosecutors to convict Cameron.

One year Coleen asked for a Bible for Christmas and Cameron complied. This became her only solace. She would read it whenever she had the freedom to do so.

When Janice lost her job, Cameron decided to put his slave to work. By then he was confident that she would not attempt to escape and took her to a neighboring town to work as beggar. It was humiliating, but Coleen did it and still did not try to escape nor did she exploit the ample opportunities she had to ask for help.

Psychological enslavement is far more constrictive than physical enchainment. The main shackle that keeps Muslims in Islam is fear, fear of Allah, fear of the punishment in the grave and a hell that Muhammad relished describing in sanguinary detail.

> As for those who disbelieve, garments of fire will be cut out for them; boiling fluid will be poured down on their heads. Whereby that which is in their bellies and their skins too, will be melted, and for them are hooked rods of iron. Whenever, in their anguish, they would go forth from thence they are driven back therein and (it is said unto them): Taste the doom of burning (Q. 22: 19-22) in scorching wind and scalding water, and shadow of black smoke, neither cool nor refreshing. (Q. 56:42 -44) The tree of Zaqqum, the food of the sinner, like molten brass, it seethes in their bellies as the seething of boiling water. (And it will be said): Take him and drag him to the midst of hell, then pour upon his head the torment of boiling water, Now taste! You forsooth the mighty, the noble! Lo! This is that whereof you used to doubt. (Q. 44: 43 -50) What is the tree of Zaqqum? Lo! We have appointed it a torment for wrong-doers. It is a tree that springs in the heart of hell. Its crop is as it were the heads of devils. And lo! They verily must eat thereof, and fill (their) bellies therewith. And afterward, they have a drink of boiling water And afterward, lo! their return is surely unto hell (Q. 37: 62 -68). Indeed, it is the flame (of Hell), plucking out (his being) tight to the skull! (Q. 70:11-16) And he shall be given to drink of festering water: He shall sip it in and shall not be able to swallow it easily. And death shall come to him from every quarter, yet he shall not die. And besides that there shall be for him a severe chastisement. (Q. 14: 16-17) Those who reject the Book and that with which We sent our messengers: but soon shall they know, When the yokes (shall be) round their necks, and the chains; they shall be dragged along in the boiling fetid fluid: then in the Fire shall they be burned. (Q. 40: 70-72) Every time their skins are roasted through We will replace them with other skins so they may taste the

> punishment. Indeed, God is ever Exalted in Might and Wise. (Quran 4:56) Their refuge is Hell; every time it subsides We increase them in blazing fire." (Quran 17:97) The Fire will burn their faces and they will grin therein, their lips displaced. (Quran 23:104) The Day they are dragged into the Fire on their faces (it will be said), 'Taste the touch of Hell.' (Q. 54:47-48)) The Day their faces will be turned over in the Fire, they will say, 'How we wish we had obeyed God and obeyed the Messenger. (Q 33:66)

All these await those who doubt Muhammad. When one believes in these tales, even slightly, he is enslaved for life, crippled by fear and can no longer doubt.

Shakila is a lady I helped to leave Islam. She told me about her Pakistani grandmother who lamented that despite reading the Quran all her life she had never read its translation and at 82 her eyes were not good for the task. Hoping for *ajr* (rewards), her daughter in-law volunteered to read it to her. When this old lady understood what the Quran says, she was overtaken by fear. She remembered that she had missed prayers and sometimes neglected fasting and even disobeyed her husband. She became convinced that she will have to spend sometimes in hell before she can go to paradise. She lived the remaining four years of her life terrified of the prospect of what she thought was awaiting her. Although bed ridden, she never miss a prayer again, which she performed with difficulty.

That is why "moderate Islam" is a charade. You can't believe in the Quran and remain moderate. Once you believe in Muhammad's hell you'll do anything to avoid it. The only sure way, according to the Prophet, is to hate, to fight and to kill the unbelievers. If you are a Muslim you must join the jihad and become a terrorist. The reason most Muslims are not terrorists is because they don't know their religion.

Carlos Bledsoe was an all American kid raised in a loving family with a promising future. He converted to Islam, changed his name to Abdul Hakim Mohamed, went to Yemen to receive his terrorist training and returned having been transformed into a jihadi murderer. He targeted the Jewish community and unsuccessfully attempted to bomb a rabbi's house. Then, in June 2009 he shot and killed William Andrew Young, a 19 years old soldier and injured another. Abdul Hakim has no remorse for his crime. He said, "I don't think it was murder. Murder is when a person kills another person without justified reason. What I did was Islamic justified. And it was justified by commonsense." This is what Islam does to people. Those who deny this fact are deceiving the public. The fathers of Carlos and Andrew have created a website, *losingoursons.com* to warn the world of the threat of Islam and tell the truth that the Obama administration and the leftist media are hiding. Make sure to visit that site.

Let us continue with our story. To keep the fear alive, Cameron told Coleen that he had paid the company $30,000 to jack up the surveillance of her 24/7. He said this was for him a huge financial sacrifice, so she had better behave. He told her the company had bugged the cars, homes, and phone lines of all the members of her family, to make sure she did not contact them to get help.

One day, Cameron told Coleen to say goodbye to the neighbors telling them she was going to South Carolina. In fact she was going to be confined to the trailer. Even then she complied, and lied to the neighbors instead of asking for help.

Coleen missed her family. Cameron told her he would allow her to write to them as reward for her obedience. He checked the letters' content before sending them. He even allowed her to phone her family from a payphone and eventually agreed that she visit them. He said it was rare that the company allowed such a thing, and they would be monitoring it carefully.

She was kept inside the box for a full week before being taken out to go on her trip. Cameron gave her a description of the company's museum of skeletons from runaway slaves and told her that if she said anything to anyone about her situation, they would rush in and grab her.

On March 20, 1981, three and a half years into her captivity, Cameron provided Coleen with a cover story about him being her fiancé and took her to meet with her parents and sisters.

Cameron dropped Coleen and left without waiting to introduce himself. Her family noted her thin and haggard appearance, but afraid that they had offended her in some way to have made her run away they walked on eggshells, leaving their many questions unspoken. Coleen remained vague about where she had been, but she was overjoyed to see them all and wanted to make every minute count.

"She gave us no information on where she'd been," Her sister recalled, "or on where she'd be going. We were all afraid to sit her down and get it out of her. We were afraid we would lose her again."

The next morning, she went accompanied her mother to the church and then it was over. "Mike" called and said he would be there soon to pick her up. After only 24 hours, he had decided to cut her visit short.

Once in the trailer, Cameron put her back in the box where she stayed most of the time for the next three years of her confinement. Her health declined, her hair fell out and she became thinner. Cameron talked about wanting more slaves and decided to build a dungeon and Coleen helped him to dig a deep hole in the yard. He put a floor and brick walls and moved her into it, but was forced to abandon the project when the hole was flooded. Coleen was forced again to the box under the bed.

Cameron had more frequent sex with Coleen and Janice grew jealous of her. For solace she started reading the Bible and gradually felt ashamed over her life. She began attending a local church and Coleen sometimes went with her. Interestingly Cameron too was biblically inspired, but the parts that attracted his interest were female submission. Quoting the story of Abraham, Sara and their slave, Hagar, he would say that this arrangement was what God wanted.

8- The Psychology of Fear

It is important to note that almost all sociopaths have a religious streak. They often believe in God, form a cult and recruit followers. They justify their crimes and convince their followers that their perversity is not perversity at all and that they should not be judged with the same yardstick that others are judged.

When I published an article exposing the Canadian cult leader, John de Ruiter, one of his followers wrote. "Dear Ali, Is it possible that sexual expression takes on a different meaning to one who has let go of attachments and needs? When you find Truth in yourself, all kinds of desires and needs no longer hold sway over you, but they simply become a natural expression of a body or vehicle... like eating or sleeping with no deeper meaning, no narcissistic supply for your ego."

This explains why Muslims are not perturbed when they hear about Muhammad's crimes and his depraved nature. It is not that they are unable to distinguish between good and bad and don't know murder, theft, rape and pedophilia are wrong. But like this benighted follower of De Ruiter, they believe that Muhammad's expressions of lust and rage were of different kind. When Muhammad raped women, it was not rape. When he massacred unarmed men and plundered them it was not terror and theft. The psychopath and the cult leader don't want to be judged by the same standards that they judge others. Whatever they do should be evaluated under a different parameter. Their followers agree.

Janice talked about her situation as a hypothetical case to other church members. They all told her such relationship is sinful. The Pastor confirmed what others had told her and she finally decided to pluck out the sin from her life.

On August 9, 1984, Janice picked up Coleen from work and told her that there was no company and the slavery contract was just a lie. Coleen listened to this and realized that nothing now bound her to Cameron. He had suddenly lost all control over her.

She called Cameron from the bus station and told him she knew about the lies and she was leaving. Cameron cried, but Coleen, now retrieving her real name, and with it her identity as a fee person, was not to be deterred. She walked away from seven years of forced captivity to try find her life again. "I got on the bus and I left," she told the reporters. Truth set her free.

This mind numbing story gives us a glimpse into the mind of the malignant narcissist and the psychology of their victims. Understanding it allows us to understand how cults operate, what drives the cult leader and why cultists submit to their irrational and evil demands.

The sociopath traps his victim through violence. The malignant narcissist cult leader lures them with promises of heavenly rewards. The former restrains them physically. The latter ensnares them psychologically. Both cripple the will power of their victims through fear.

The story of the Slave Company made no sense. Coleen was already an adult. In normal situations she would not have believed it. But she believed Cameron because she was deprived of her liberty, cut off from the world, had endured horrendous torments, and Janice had backed up the story.

These are factors that allow cultists to believe in doctrines that are irrational and evil. Take the doctrine of Jihad. Muslims are told that the highest form of worship is waging war for the sake of God and murdering those who don't believe. Any rational person can see this is evil. But Muslims' ability to reason is crippled. What distinguishes humans from beasts is their ability to reason. Muslims have abdicated that ability.

I receive countless angry and threatening emails from Muslims. The recurring theme in all of them is the fear of hell. Even educated Muslims cannot escape from this irrational fear that has been instilled in them since childhood. If phobia is an irrational fear, Islam is nothing but *infernophobia.*

Then there is the conformity factor. The absurd, violent, and evil teachings of the Quran are confirmed by all Muslims, and if one wants to belong to that community, one must conform. Cultists will deny their own judgment in order to conform.

In 1950s, psychologist Solomon Ash conducted an experiment that showed how people will side against their own perception in order to conform to the group.

His subjects were shown an image of a few straight lines of different lengths. Then another image was shown to them of one line that matched one of the lines in the first image and they were asked to find that line. Subjects had no difficulty giving the right answer, until they were placed in a group of actors posing as subjects who conspired to give a wrong answer. Subjects were disconcerted by the discrepancy between their perception and the answers given by others. After a few times, most caved to conform and started giving the wrong answers. Only 29% of Ash's subjects refused to join the bogus majority. Daring to stand out in a crowd and be different requires courage.

Stockholm syndrome

The control that cult leaders and psychopaths exert on their followers is so powerful that sometimes it lasts even when their victims escape. The victims seem to develop a sense of loyalty to their captors.

Coleen returned to her parents, but did not report Cameron. She didn't even tell her family. She stayed in touch with Janice Hooker by phone, even though she had been just as ruthless and cruel to her as her sociopath husband. Janice asked her to keep the whole thing quiet and she complied.

Cameron and Janice began to get rid of any evidence that Coleen had ever been there at their home. Coleen kept calling them. Cameron begged her to come back, but she refused. Yet she assured them that she would not go to the police.

8- The Psychology of Fear

As she dropped hints about her ordeal to her parents, they urged her to turn these people in. Her cousins made threatening calls to the Hookers but Coleen reassured them that she had forgiven them and that she would pray for them to stay away from their life of sin.

Considering her ordeals, Coleen's forgiveness of Cameron sounds incomprehensible. The Hookers were dangerous. Cameron told Coleen that he had murdered a girl before her. Janice had confirmed his story. This couple was a threat to the society. So why wouldn't Coleen turn them in?

Then Janice left Cameron. Her fear and guilt had eaten away at her. She needed to talk with someone and she chose the receptionist at a doctor's office who thought she was asking for help. She encouraged Janice to tell her what was really bothering her, and Janice let the truth out. Having told one person, and having become frightened about what might happen to her two daughters, Janice went straight to her Pastor to confess everything. He was stunned, and with her permission, he phoned the police.

Janice told Police about the other young woman that they had abducted, in much the same way, but because she did not obey and was screaming, Cameron cut her vocal cords, then strangulated her and dumped her body somewhere far. A young woman, matching the description given by Janice was missing, but Police could not find her body and Cameron was not charged for that crime.

Janice told them about Coleen and how her husband had brainwashed her to keep her under his control. She provided more details, including how she had helped to destroy evidence. The detectives went out to investigate. One team questioned neighbors, who insisted that Cameron was "nice," "normal," and "good-tempered," while the police officer who talked with Coleen found her disturbingly detached. She corroborated Janice's story, but deputy district attorney found real problems: Coleen had had many opportunities to escape and upon getting back home, she'd never even contacted the police.

During the trial, Coleen had a quiet demeanor showing no sign of any sense that she wanted revenge to the extent that the prosecutors feared the case may be thrown out of the court. Troublesome for the prosecution was a tape on which Coleen told Cameron that she loved him. Fortunately, the judge decided there was sufficient evidence for a trial, and Cameron Hooker was convicted and sentenced to consecutive terms for a total of 104 years imprisonment.

I know of former Muslims, who despite having rejected Islam still feel a sense of loyalty towards Muhammad. Hassan is someone I met online in 1999. He was an educated man and used to debate with me defending Islam. Some years later he left Islam and became friendly. On many occasions he advised me that I should tone down my rhetoric against Muhammad. When I sent him an article I wrote about Muhammad's abusive childhood, he felt sympathy for that mass-murderer. Virtually all criminals have had abusive childhood. This may explain, but never justify their crimes, and feeling sympathy for these monsters is out of place. Hassan was offended when someone spoke opprobriously of Muhammad. In his words, "On a personal note, leaving Islam was enormously difficult." He withdrew from Faithfreedom.org forum in anger and started a new ex-Muslim organization where he criticized Islamic extremism and me, as if we are the two sides of the same coin. He wrote, "We are only against the Islamists and harsh, literalist and violent interpretations of Islam and those who seek to impose it on others." He wanted to ignore the fact that the literalists are the true Muslims, not those who interpret Islam as they wish.

When he left Islam, he wrote his testimony under a pseudonym and sent it to me for publication. Some times later, he had a change of heart and asked me to remove it. I didn't. Instead I published his recantment. I wanted people to see Islam's psychological trapment of Muslims. I never revealed his identity.

Hassan's loyalty to Muhammad, the one who had enslaved his mind all his life was greater than his gratitude to me, who liberated him. Not only he never thanked me, he remained scornful of me and vilified me at every turn. He wrote, "Anyone who understands the power religion can have over people who are born to a faith will know that from a very early age it forms their whole identity, place in the world, meaning to their life and comfort zone. Rejecting it is not simply an intellectual process, but one that tears your whole world apart. It means losing your identity and meaning for life, it means losing family and friends and it means depression and emotional trauma - not to mention abuse intimidation and even death threats in some cases." I wholeheartedly agree with Hassan. In an article titled Seven Valleys from Faith to Enlightenment[432], I described my own ordeal of leaving my faith, and yet I feel no loyalty to Muhammad. I detest him. Most ex-Muslims do.

However, Hassan's case is not uncommon. This inexplicable loyalty towards one's captor is known as Stockholm syndrome. In 1974 Patricia Hearst, a 19-year old girl from an affluent family was kidnapped. During her captivity she developed such a sense of loyalty towards her captors that she helped them to rob a bank and identified herself with them completely.

Cultists develop a misplaced sense of loyalty towards their leader. You are not free until you realize that the person towards whom you feel loyalty has been your captor, an evil soul who deserves not your sympathy, but you scorn.

Hassan's story has a happy ending. In 2012 he sent me an email where he wrote, "I just wanted to say that I must credit you for giving me the slap in the face many years ago that I needed to wake up from the religious delusion I was in as a Muslim. Although it took me several years to finally leave Islam, it was my exchanges with you, years earlier that set the ball in motion. At the time of course it was a very painful and shocking experience - but I needed that slap in the face and so I wish to thank you for that now - something I couldn't do at the time."

---

[432] http://alisina.org/seven-valleys-from-faith-to-enlightenment/

8- The Psychology of Fear

I am very glad for this email. This means a lot to me as Hassan meant a lot to me and I am very proud of him. He is indeed a shining light.

Psychologist Chris Hatcher who was called to testify for the prosecutor in the case of Hooker explained to the jury how mind-control works. He addressed the dynamics of sadomasochism, and the dominant and submissive personalities involved—particularly the excitement factor for the "master" in getting someone to submit to his whims. Hatcher then talked about how the effects of sudden kidnapping, death threats, being housed in a dark tomb that disturbed daylight patterns, the physical abuse, the loss of control over necessary bodily functions, and the lack of communication were collectively effective in breaking down Coleen's will. In other words, her values, her identity, and her whole way of looking at the world had been changed.

In Islam there are many absurd, but strict rules that are aimed to do just that. The following extract from the testimony of a woman who converted to Islam and finally left it is an example of how Muslims live under constant psychological stress, striving to comply with the rituals. She wrote, "I must wake up in the middle of the night to get up, wash myself, pray, and then somehow get back to sleep and manage my life with lack of sleep (because apparently praying is so much better than sleeping). I have a baby also. When my baby decides she wants to nap or sleep and it is prayer time, I can't just leave the baby to scream and howl for me, just so I can go and make *wudu* (ablution) before the sunset, lest I be committing a sin of not praying on time. It is exhausting enough being a mother, so I must also sleep when the baby sleeps, otherwise I would get next to no sleep. How can this be right, when I personally get extremely sick and rundown if I don't sleep well? How can this be beneficial to my life?"[433]

The above is only a token of the psychological entrapment devised by Muhammad to cripple the believers' will and to destroy their individuality. Muslims are never concerned about helping another soul and acts of kindness are alien to Islamic mentality. Showing kindness is not a requirement of their faith. They give more to their "charities" than anyone else, but all that money is earmarked for jihad and the spread of Islam, not to help someone in need. Muslims main preoccupation is how to perform the rituals, how not to miss a prayer, how to do *wudu*, how to enter the toilet, what to say upon entering the toilet and how to clean their keister. It is all about rituals, halal and haram and to endure suffering in exchange for reward. The bigger the suffering, the greater will be the reward. This is the extent of the religiosity of Muslims. This is their definition of piety. This sums up the morality of Islam. Suffering equals Reward.

Muslims are encouraged to lose their identity and accept their nothingness. Rumi says, "For how long will you be concerned about clothing? Abandon your

---

[433] http://www.faithfreedom.org/features/letters/soon-to-be-ex-muslimah/

body so you won't need clothing." This is the highest expression of spirituality for a Muslim.

Cults devalue life. They call the body a "container," a "vehicle" the real self being the spirit. Although Muhammad made no mention of spiritual world and his afterlife is all corporal, he taught that this life has no value – it is only a testing ground. One should live in function of the next world.

A Palestinian mother, whose infant's life was saved thanks to a donation of $55,000 by an Israeli Jew, verbalized the Islamic concept of worthlessness of life most eloquently.

The baby was being treated and needed bone marrow transplant. Shlomi Eldar, the Gaza correspondent for Israeli Channel 10 News, was assigned to make a documentary about the operation called "Precious Life." But when he met Raida Abu Mustafa, the mother of the child, she launched into a painful monologue about the culture of the *shaheeds* (martyrs) and admitted, during the complex transplant process, that she would like to see her son perpetrate a suicide bombing attack in Jerusalem.

"Jerusalem is ours," she declared. "We are all for Jerusalem, the whole nation, not just a million, all of us. Do you understand what that means – all of us?"

She also explained exactly what she had in mind. "For us, death is a natural thing. We are not frightened of death. From the smallest infant, to the oldest person, we will all sacrifice ourselves for the sake of Jerusalem. We feel we have the right to it. You're free to be angry, so be angry."

Eldar asked, "Then why are you fighting to save your son's life, if you say that death is a usual thing for your people?" she smiled at him and said, "It is a regular thing. Life is not precious. Life is precious, but not for us. For us, life is nothing, not worth a thing. That is why we have so many suicide bombers. They are not afraid of death. None of us, not even the children, are afraid of death. It is natural for us. After Mohammed gets well, I will certainly want him to be a shaheed. If it's for Jerusalem, then there's no problem. For you it is hard, I know; with us there are cries of rejoicing and happiness when someone falls as a shaheed. For us a shaheed is a tremendous thing."

Like most cults, Islam is a cult of death. Muslim's entire thought revolves around their death. They are told that the fastest way to Paradise is to die while killing someone else.

Stockholm syndrome occurs under stress in captivity, where there may be torture and a high degree of uncertainty. A Muslim's life is filled with uncertainty. He can never be certain whether he has earned the acceptance of God or whether he will be thrown into hell.

8- The Psychology of Fear

This uncertainty is enshrined in the Quran. Although, at times Muhammad claimed that on the Day of Judgment he would be sitting next to God advising the Almighty whom to reward and whom to punish,[434] at other times he claimed that he did not know what would happen to him. "*I am no bringer of new-fangled doctrine among the messengers, nor do i know what will be done with me or with you. I follow but that which is revealed to me by inspiration; I am but a Warner open and clear.*" (Q. 46:9)

This is confirmed in a hadith where he said "By Allah, though I am the Apostle of Allah, yet I do not know what Allah will do to me."[435] Note that the above contradicts verses 48:1-2 were Muhammad claims all his past and future sins will be forgiven. He said what he needed to say, as situation dictated. The only certainty that Muslims have for salvation is when they take part in jihad and become a martyr.

Kidnapped victims, abused spouses, and tortured prisoners are most prone to Stockholm syndrome, and so are the cultists. The captive appears to become involved with his or her captor, and even consent to abuse and captivity. They may express feelings of affection towards their captor in a way that surprises outsiders and makes them wonder at just how captive and abused they really are.

Muslims are the primary victims of Islam, and yet few of them recognize it. They are defensive of it and viciously attack those who try to help them.

Katherine Ramsland wrote, "What appears to occur, according to experts who have studied the phenomenon, is that the person 'freezes' as a way to avoid further torture, and then yields to try to appease the captor. If the captor then takes care of basic needs, the captive may feel gratitude bordering on affection. Such victims become susceptible to suggestion, and having their own world shrink to that shared with the captor, they may become sympathetic. Identifying with the captor and seeing no way to escape, it becomes easier to acquiesce, even to the point of acting as if they love their captors. They are trying to arrange their otherwise unsafe and difficult world for maximum comfort and safety."

No one is more trapped than Muslims. They are convinced that Allah can read their minds and record their every thought; that he has a torture house for all those who doubt Muhammad and that his punishment is severe and lasting. With so much fear how can one dare to doubt? Without doubt how can one come to the truth? The greatness of man is in his ability to doubt, not in his blind faith.

Allah, like Huitzilopochtli, is ruthless and bloodthirsty. You don't want to be on the wrong side of this fearsome deity. The Aztecs loved their god. They sacrificed countless lives at his altar. Hundreds of millions have been sacrificed at the altar of Allah and the counting continues.

---

434 Sahih Muslim, 1:367 and 4:266

435 Bukhari Volume 5, Book 58, Number 266

It makes no sense to love a god as evil as Huitzilopochtli, Kali and Allah. These terrifying deities are loved, not because they are worthy of love, but because they are feared. After all, it is wise to be friendly with the crocodile if you must drink from the same pond. Complex is indeed human mind.

Unlike the crocodile, fearsome gods are figments of human imagination. They are no more real than the monster beneath a child's bed. However, as long as they are believed to be real their followers will continue wreaking havoc and doing evil in their names. The believers are captives of their own imagination. Only truth will set them free.

Who Is Attracted to Cults?

The behavior of Janice, Cameron's wife, is also worthy of study. She was a woman with low self-esteem. She would do anything to appease her man so she could stay with him. Although a victim herself, Janice participated in the kidnapping of Coleen and of the girl before her. She was an accomplice in the first girl's murder and was abusive to Coleen. Janice did not help Coleen to escape out of compassion, but because she had become jealous of her.

The psychology of people converting to Islam is not dissimilar to that of Janice. Most converts to Islam are prison inmates and youths wanting to belong, or are women with low self-esteem, desperate for love. Smart people hardly become attracted to a religion like Islam. Islam is repulsive to intelligent people. Converts to Islam have low IQ, low self-esteem, or are deceived. They are impressionable and easily misled. Most of them leave Islam after they come to their senses.

Muslims are victims and victimizers at once. Muhammad is dead. All the crimes perpetrated in his name and in the name of his deity are committed by his followers. They cling to Islam for the same psychological need that made Janice cling to Cameron. They abuse others for the same reason that Janice abused Coleen. Muslims are psychological hostages of a seventh century psychopath. Although dead and his corpse his turned into dust, Muhammad's lies still entrap people and still produce victims. Muslims collectively suffer from low self-esteem. They are not the only evil doers in the world, but most human rights abuses, violence, and terrors are perpetrated by them.

The dignity of us humans is in our freedom of thought. Stripped from that freedom, we lose our humanity. When one submits to a demonic god one becomes a devil.

Look at Pakistan, Saudi Arabia, and Egypt! Look at all Muslim countries. They all abuse the minorities living among them and no one protests. Abuse of minorities is seen as normal. Where is the outcry of the so called moderate Muslims? A few may murmur some complaints and blame the "radicals" but no one will raise a finger to defend the abused .They see all this evil in Islam and they still believe in it – they still defend it. You show them the hateful verses of the Quran and they close their eyes and refuse to denounce them.

Numerous innocent souls are jailed and tortured in Pakistan accused of blasphemy. Once a person is accused of this charge it is up to him to prove his innocence. Meanwhile, they are regularly beaten and often put to death with the full vigor of the law. And the "moderates" hide their heads in the sand and keep defending Islam.

The blasphemy law is savagery. The silent majority are just as guilty for their silence as those who commit those crimes. Where is their outcry? Where is the protest of the so called moderate Muslims? They are either the perpetrators of crimes against mankind or defenders of Islam that is the inspiration behind those crimes.

Nations, who were once the lights of the world and cradles of mighty civilizations, are now followers a madman, worshippers of the Devil, and chasers of a mirage. These once cribs of glorious cultures, have become cesspools of the world.

Muslims are aware of their misery, but in denial of its cause. The facts are clear, but they refuse to see. Like an addict who seeks refuge in his deadly substance to escape his misery, the more wretched they become, the faster they cling to Islam - as if the lunacy of a madman can bring them salvation.

Salvation comes through knowledge, not through ignorance. It can be attained when Muslim countries unblock websites such as faithfreedom.org and books such as this and allow dialogue and scrutiny into Islam. Islam will be destroyed where truth is not suppressed. With the end of Islam will come, the freedom of Muslims and their prosperity.

Chapter Nine

Ripples and Effects

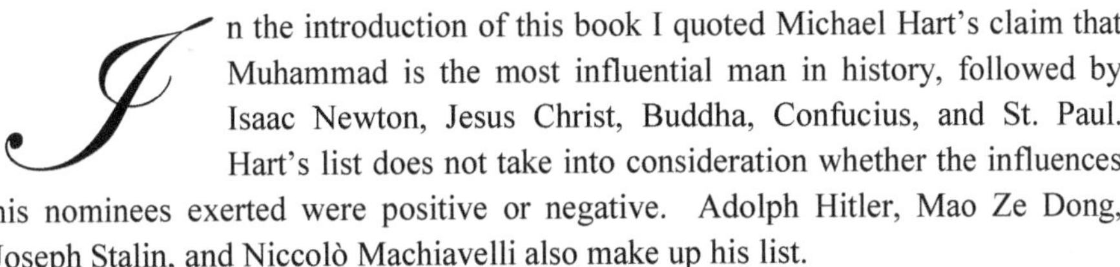

In the introduction of this book I quoted Michael Hart's claim that Muhammad is the most influential man in history, followed by Isaac Newton, Jesus Christ, Buddha, Confucius, and St. Paul. Hart's list does not take into consideration whether the influences his nominees exerted were positive or negative. Adolph Hitler, Mao Ze Dong, Joseph Stalin, and Niccolò Machiavelli also make up his list.

I don't dispute Hart's claim about Muhammad. However, it is important to recognize that Muhammad's influence on the world has not been positive.

Muhammad's Influence on Nazism

Muhammad's notion of a super religion with undisputed authority was the inspiration for Hitler's super race. Albert Speer, Hitler's wartime Minister of Armaments and Munitions, records in his memoirs that Hitler regretted the fact that Muslims failed to penetrate beyond France into Central Europe, during the eighth century:

> Had the Arabs won the battle the world would have been Mohammedan today, for theirs was a religion that believed in spreading the faith by the sword and subjugating all nations to that faith. The Germanic peoples would have become heirs to that religion. Such a creed was perfectly suited to the Germanic temperament. Hitler said that the conquering Arabs, because of their racial inferiority, would in the long run have been unable to contend with the harsher climate and conditions of the country. They could not have kept down the more vigorous natives, so that ultimately not Arabs but Islamized Germans could have stood at the head of this Mohammedan Empire.
>
> Hitler usually concluded this historical speculation by remarking, 'You see, it's been our misfortune to have the wrong religion. Why didn't we have the religion of the Japanese, who regard sacrifice for the Fatherland as the highest good? The Mohammedan religion too would have been much more compatible to us than Christianity. Why did it have to be Christianity with its meekness and flabbiness?[436]

---

[436] A. Speer, Inside the Third Reich, pp. 142-143

There is no doubt that Hitler admired Muhammad and found Islam appealing. He was attracted by the penchant for violence through which Islam expanded. There was also a common connection of Jew-hatred.

In 1940 the Nazi Germany produced a movie in the form of documentary called "The Eternal Jew" that served to dehumanize the Jews and prepare for Hitler's "Final Solution." The film compared the Jewish people to rats. Why rats? "Abu Huraira reported that Allah's Messenger said: A group of Bani Isra'il was lost. I do not know what happened to it, but I think (that it 'underwent a process of metamorphosis) and assumed the shape of rats."[437]

The movie characterized the Jews as wandering cultural parasites and depicted them as finding pleasure in money and a hedonist lifestyle. This too was based on the Quran 2:96 that says Jews are the greediest of all humankind, who like to live 1000 years.

Carl Jung, in an interview conducted in 1930s, referring to the rise of Nazism in Germany said, "We do not know whether Hitler is going to found a new Islam. He is already on the way; he is like Muhammad. The emotion in Germany is Islamic; warlike and Islamic. They are all drunk with a wild god. That can be the historic future."[438]

Elements of Islamic militarism found their way into Hitler's ideology. Like the prophet of Islam, Hitler believed that might is right. He regarded the Arian race to be the master race who would "create mastery and avoid comforting lies." This is eerily similar to Muhammad's concept of Islam being the master religion, and that it would dominate the world, replacing and subduing all religions.

Muhammad's Influence on Communism

Communism also owes its world view to Muhammad. Bertrand Russell in *The Practice and Theory of Bolshevism*, published in 1920 wrote, "Bolshevism combines the characteristics of the French Revolution with those of the rise of Islam....Marx has taught that Communism is fatally predestined to come about; this produces a state of mind not unlike that of the early successors of Mahommet....Among religions, Bolshevism is to be reckoned with Mohammedanism, rather than with Christianity and Buddhism. Christianity and Buddhism are primarily personal religions, with mystical doctrines and a love of contemplation. Mohammedanism and Bolshevism are practical, social, unspiritual, concerned to win the empire of this world."[439]

---

[437]Sahih Muslim Book 042, Number 7135

[438] Carl Jung. *The Collected Works Volume 18, The Symbolic Life*, 1939, Princeton, Princeton University Press p. 281.

[439] Bertrand Russell. The Practice and Theory of Bolshevism. London: George Allen and Unwin, 1920 pp.5,29,114.

9- Ripples and Effects

Jules Monnerot called Communism the Twentieth-Century Islam. Monnerot wrote that the ultimate aim of Soviet Communism was "the most absolute tyranny ever conceived by man; a tyranny that recognizes no spatial limits (except for the time being those of the planet itself), no temporal limits (communist believers generally refuse to contemplate any post-communist ages), and no limits to its power over the individual: its will to power claims total possession over every man it wins, and allows no greater freedom in mental than in economic life. It is this claim that brings it into conflict with faiths, religions, and values, which are older than itself or developing independently; and then the battle is joined. We are the battle".[440] "Communism," says Monnerot, "takes the field both as a *secular religion* and as a *universal State*; it is therefore more comparable to Islam than to the Universal Religion that began by opposing the universal State in the Hellenistic and Roman worlds, and which can be said to have drawn men's hearts away from the State to itself....Soviet Russia...is not the first empire in which temporal and public power goes hand in hand with a shadowy power that works outside the imperial frontiers to undermine the social structure of neighboring States."[441]

Bernard Lewis wrote in his essay, "Communism and Islam"

> I turn now from the accidental to the essential factors, to those deriving from the very nature of Islamic society, tradition, and thought. The first of these is the authoritarianism, perhaps we may even say the totalitarianism, of the Islamic political tradition.... Many attempts have been made to show that Islam and democracy are identical-attempts usually based on a misunderstanding of Islam or democracy or both. This sort of argument expresses a need of the up- rooted Muslim intellectual who is no longer satisfied with or capable of understanding traditional Islamic values, and who tries to justify, or rather, re-state, his inherited faith in terms of the fashionable ideology of the day. It is an example of the romantic and apologetic presentation of Islam that is a recognized phase in the reaction of Muslim thought to the impact of the West.... In point of fact, except for the early caliphate, when the anarchic individualism of tribal Arabia was still effective, the political history of Islam is one of almost unrelieved autocracy...It was authoritarian, often arbitrary, sometimes tyrannical. There are no parliaments or representative assemblies of any kind, no councils or communes, no chambers of nobility or estates, no municipalities in the history of Islam; nothing but the sovereign power, to which the subject owed complete and unwavering obedience as a religious duty imposed by the Holy Law. In the great days of classical Islam this duty was only owed to the lawfully appointed caliph, as God's vicegerent on earth and head of the theocratic community, and then

---

[440] Jules Monnerot. Sociologie du Communisme, Paris: Gallimard, 1949. [English translation by Jane Degras and Richard Rees. Sociology and Psychology of Communism, Boston: Beacon Press, 1953]

[441] Jules Monnerot's footnote and emphases: In intention but not in fact. The universal State is a sort of collective fantasy; the totalitarian State's image of itself projected into the future.

> only for as long as he upheld the law; but with the decline of the caliphate and the growth of military dictatorship, Muslim jurists and theologians accommodated their teachings to the changed situation and extended the religious duty of obedience to any effective authority, however impious, however barbarous. For the last thousand years, the political thinking of Islam has been dominated by such maxims as "tyranny is better than anarchy" and "whose power is established, obedience to him is incumbent."
>
> ...Quite obviously, the Ulama of Islam are very different from the Communist Party. Nevertheless, on closer examination, we find certain uncomfortable resemblances. Both groups profess a totalitarian doctrine, with complete and final answers to all questions on heaven and earth; the answers are different in every respect, alike only in their finality and completeness, and in the contrast they offer with the eternal questioning of Western man. Both groups offer to their members and followers the agreeable sensation of belonging to a community of believers, who are always right, as against an outer world of unbelievers, who are always wrong. Both offer an exhilarating feeling of mission, of purpose, of being engaged in a collective adventure to accelerate the historically inevitable victory of the true faith over the infidel evil-doers. The traditional Islamic division of the world into the House of Islam and the House of War, two necessarily opposed groups, of which- the first has the collective obligation of perpetual struggle against the second, also has obvious parallels in the Communist view of world affairs. There again, the content of belief is utterly different, but the aggressive fanaticism of the believer is the same. The humorist who summed up the Communist creed as "There is no God and Karl Marx is his Prophet!" was laying his finger on a real affinity. The call to a Communist Jihad, a Holy War for the faith-a new faith, but against the self-same Western Christian enemy-might well strike a responsive note.[442]

Muhammad's Influence on Fascism

The influence of Islam on fascism is also undeniable. Fascism is a reactionary, authoritarian political ideology. The same can be said about Islam. Benito Mussolini said, "Fascism, which was not afraid to call itself reactionary... does not hesitate to call itself illiberal and anti-liberal." But reaction to what? "Fascism was based on a rejection of the social theories that formed the basis of the 1789 French Revolution," writes American investigative journalist, Chip Berlet. "Fascists particularly loathed the social theories of the French Revolution and its slogan: Liberty, Equality, Fraternity."[443]

Islam was born as a reactionary movement against the authority of the Meccans and their religious system, which was based on polytheism. Polytheistic religions are by their very nature, pluralistic, and tolerant of other people's beliefs.

---

[442] *International Affairs*,Vol. 30, No. 1(Jan., 1954), pp. 1-12]

[443] http://www.remember.org/hist.root.what.html

9- Ripples and Effects

Muhammad could not tolerate that. He wanted his authority to reign supreme and unchallenged. In their demonstrations in Europe, Muslims carry placards that read, "Freedom Go to Hell", and "Democracy is Hypocrisy".

American Iranian journalist Amir Taheri points out, "There was no word in any of the Muslim languages for democracy until the 1890s... If it wasn't on their tongues, it's likely that it was not on their minds either. Democracy is based on equality. The idea is unacceptable to Islam. For the non-believer cannot be equal of the believer. Even among the believers only those who subscribe to the three so-called Abrahamic religions: Judaism, Christianity and Islam are regarded as fully human."[444]

Here is the hierarchy of human worth in Islam:

At the summit are free male Muslims.

Next come Muslim male slaves.

Then come free Muslim women.

Next come Muslim slave women.

Then come free Jewish and /or Christian men.

Then come slave Jewish and/or Christian men.

Then come slave Jewish and/or Christian women.

The fraternity in Islam does not extend to non-Muslims. In the treaty that Muhammad enforced on all the citizens of Medina, including non-Muslim Arabs and Jews, he wrote that his followers are one *umma* (community), to the exclusion of all men. The Quran say, "The believers are harsh against unbelievers but compassionate amongst each other" (Q. 48:29). This is the core belief of fascism.

Inspired by the Quran, Muslim groups employ sectarian violence to achieve political ends. The first group was Kharijiyya. The Kharijiyya insisted on two things. First, that the Islamic community must be based on the Quran. The second point emphasized the ascendancy of the Islamic state over the individual rights. Motivated by many verses of the Quran (32.13, 76:29-31, 3:39, 3:159, 16:93, 2:6-7, 4:88, etc.), they maintained that God's will, must supersede men's will and claimed the community must be the bearer of the values that constitute meaningfulness. In other words, man's life has meaning only if he belongs to the Muslim community. These ideas were based on the Quran and were eventually adopted by the rest of the Muslims. This is how fascism came to define the position of the individual vis-à-vis the state.

There are many similarities between Islam and fascism. Both divide people in two camps, "us" and "them," while identifying goodness and superiority with "us," and evil with "them." This process involves scapegoating, dehumanizing, and blaming all societal problems on "them," and presupposes a conspiracy of these

---

444 http://www.timesonline.co.uk/tol/news/article430160.ece

enemy evildoers and holds them responsible for emasculating and humiliating the community.

In fascism as in Islam, unity is achieved by instilling victimhood in the community and hatred of the outsider. Sigmund Freud writes, "It is always possible to unite considerable numbers of men in love towards one another, so long as there is still some remaining as objects of aggressive manifestations."[445]

Islam shares the following hallmarks with fascism, as highlighted by Berlet.

- Jingoism and excessive devotion to the nation (*umma*).
- Mindless heroism and martyrdom.
- Militarism and glorification of war.
- Use of violence or threats of violence to impose views on others.
- Silencing the critics.
- Complete reliance on an authoritarian leader not accountable to the people.
- Cult of personality around a charismatic leader.
- Reaction against change and Modernism.
- Dehumanization and scapegoating of the enemy, – seeing the enemy as inferior and subhuman, perhaps involved in a conspiracy that justifies eradicating them.
- The self-image of superiority.
- Abandonment of any consistent ideology in a drive for absolute power and world domination.[446]

Fascism and Islam discourage individualism and promote the state/caliphate. In the words of Mussolini, "If classical liberalism spells individualism, Fascism spells government." That holds true also for Islam.

Like Islam, fascism promoted principles of masculine heroism, militarism, and discipline while rejecting cultural pluralism and multiculturalism.

Like Muhammad, Mussolini perceived women's primary role as child-bearers, while men are to be warriors. He said, "war is to man is what maternity is to the woman."[447]

The influence of Muhammad on fascism and Nazism comes through Friedrich Nietzsche whose philosophy was the inspiration for these political ideologies. Nietzsche was himself influenced by Islam and particularly by the Ismailia sect "The Order of Assassins." In section 24 of *On the Genealogy of Morality*, Nietzsche points to the worthlessness of Judeo-Christian values and proposes a transvaluation of values, i.e., to transcend the inherited Jewish and Christian politics, psychology and ethics of ressentiment or guilt. He aimed at going beyond the categories of good and evil

---

[445] http://www.writing.upenn.edu/~afilreis/50s/freud-civ.html

[446] http://www.remember.org/hist.root.what.html

[447] Bollas Christopher. 1993. Being a Character: Psychoanalysis & Self-Experience. P.205.

since they suppress the full potential of the strong and talented. Nietzsche heralded the arrival of the so-called 'free spirits' who no longer believe in truth. Thus, they alone are capable of redeeming the world of the modern ills of comfort, mediocrity, and nihilism. This is distinctively an Islamic concept where truth, good and evil are appraised, not based on their intrinsic values but in relation to how they serve Islam.

Nietzsche wrote, "When the Christian crusaders in the Orient came across that invincible Order of Assassins – that order of free spirits *par excellence* whose lowest order received, through some channel or other, a hint about that symbol and spell reserved for the uppermost echelons alone, as their secret: 'nothing is true, everything is permitted'. Now *that* was *freedom* of the spirit, *with that*, belief in truth itself was *renounced*."[448] He was talking of the sect of Hassan Sabbah, of whose followers' blind obedience, to the point of committing suicide at his command, I spoke earlier.

Sir Bertrand Russell describes Nietzsche with contempt and says "he condemns Christian love because he thinks it is an outcome of fear. It does not occur to Nietzsche, as possible, that a man should genuinely feel universal love, obviously because he himself felt almost universal hatred and fear which he would feign disguise as lordly indifference. His "noble man," who is him-self in his daydreams, is a being wholly devoid of sympathy, ruthless, cunning, cruel, concerned only with his own power". This is also a perfect description of Muhammad. It is easy to see that Nietzsche was greatly influenced by Muhammad and admired him? Like his seventh century Arab hero, he too was a malignant narcissist.

Charles Watson, G.-H. Bousquet, Bertrand Russell, Jules Monnerot, Czeslaw Milosz, Carl Jung, Karl Barth, Saeed Amir Arjomand, Maxime Rodinson, and Manfred Halpern are among those who noted Islam's similarities to fascism, Nazism, and communism.

Islam and the Demise of the Classical Civilization

In his ground breaking book, *Holy Warriors: Islam and the Demise of Classical Civilization* John O'Neill demonstrates that the destruction of the Roman civilization was due to Arab invasion and not the spread of Christianity or the invasion of Barbarians as it is commonly believed. He writes:

> After the Germanic and Asiatic Invasions of the fifth century, the peoples of Western Europe, we are told, reverted to living in thatched, wattle-and-daub huts. Cities were destroyed and abandoned, the art of writing virtually lost, and the mass of the population kept in a state of ignorance by an obscurantist and fanatical Church, which effectively completed the destructive work of the Barbarians. Into this darkened stage,

[448] On the Genealogy of Morals, Friedrich W.Nietzsche, Walter Arnold Kaufmann. p. 150

the Arabs arrived in the seventh and eighth centuries like a ray of light. Tolerant and learned, they brought knowledge of the science of antiquity back into Europe and under their influence the Westerners began the long journey back to civilization... It is a version of the past that is completely and utterly false. Indeed, it would be difficult to imagine a narrative further removed from what actually happened. And, shocking as it may seem, historians have known this for several generations.

The truth is that when the Arabs reached southern Italy and Spain they found not a bunch of primitive savages, but a highly sophisticated Latin civilization, a civilization rich in cities, agriculture, art and literature, and presided over by completely Romanized Gothic kings. How do we know this? Well, the Arabs themselves said so; and their testimony has been proven categorically by both documentary and archaeological evidence.

Yet, having said all that, it is true that by the end of the seventh century, or at the very latest by the start of the eighth, this flowering Classical civilization came, rather suddenly, to an end; and the medieval world we are all familiar with took shape: cities and towns declined and were sometimes abandoned, trade diminished, life became more rural, the arts declined, illiteracy prevailed, and the feudal system, which fragmented the kingdoms of Western Europe, took shape. In the years which followed, the Church became the sole vehicle of learning and administration, and a barter economy largely replaced the monetary system in place shortly before. What coins were issued, were minted in silver, rather than the gold used till the start of the seventh century. The Middle Ages had begun."

Who or what had produced this situation? As early as the 1920s Belgian medievalist Henri Pirenne located the proverbial smoking gun. But it was not in the hands of the Goths or Vandals, or the Christian Church: it was in the hands of those people whom it had, even then, become fashionable to credit with *saving* Western Civilization: the Arabs. The evidence, as Pirenne was at pains to show in his posthumously published *Mohammed and Charlemagne*, was incontrovertible. From the mid-seventh century the Mediterranean had been blockaded by the Arabs. Trade with the great centers of population and culture in the Levant, a trade which had been the mainstay of Western Europe's prosperity, was terminated. The flow of all the luxury items which Pirenne found in the records of the Spanish Visigoths and the Merovingians of Gaul, came to an abrupt end, as Arab pirates scoured the seas. The flow of gold to the West dried up. Gold coinage disappeared, and the great cities of Italy, Gaul, and Spain, especially the ports, which owed their wealth to the Mediterranean trade, became mere ghost towns. Worst of all, perhaps, from the perspective of culture and learning, the importation of papyrus from Egypt ceased. This material, which had been shipped into Western Europe in vast quantities since the time of the Roman Republic, was absolutely essential for a thousand purposes in a literate and mercantile civilization; and the ending of the supply had an immediate and catastrophic effect on levels of literacy.

These dropped, almost overnight, to levels perhaps equivalent to those in pre-Roman times."[449]

Is history repeating itself? Muslims have invaded the west again, this time under the guise of immigration and westerners are drunk or sleep. This invasion is lot more dangerous, because the victim is not even aware. In the first invasion, the west was awake and able to defend itself. The Europeans had their religion; they clung to it and expelled the enemy. This time, the leftist diseases of political correctness and cultural relativism have left them no moral bones. They don't know who they are and what they stand for anymore. On the other hand Muslims perfectly know who they are and what they want. Aristotle said nature abhors vacuum. This allows Muslims to fill the void and destroy the western civilization from within.

Viruses though small, are more dangerous than a wild beast. The Islamic immigration should be likened to the invasion of viruses. The problem is that the host has lost its immunity. Things are so bad that when Douglas Carswell, a Tory British MP defected to UKIP, in his speech he bragged, "What was once dismissed as political correctness gone mad, we now recognize it as just straight forward good manners." Political correctness is not good manners. The term was associated with the dogmatic application of Stalinist doctrine, debated between formal Communists and Socialists. It means one must lie when truth is contrary to the communist party line. It means lies are preferable to truth when they are more expedient from the leftist Marxist perspective.

Political correctness is the acquired immune deficiency syndrome of the white man. The west can defeat Islam, but not with the leftists culture of godlessness, immorality, moral and cultural relativism. Unless the westerners defeat the Left in all its manifestations, they should prepare themselves for an Islamic take over. Muslims can see this weakness and are already celebrating their victory.

Lest I am misunderstood, I should make it clear that the disease of political correctness has corrupted the conservative parties too. If there is any hope, it will be in new parties that won't be afraid to name the enemy and won't bow to the tyranny of political correctness. Geert Wilders' Freedom Party in Netherlands is a ray of hope.

Islam's Influence on the Modern West

Thoughts are viral. Ideas pass from one person to another and from one society to the next. They mutate and adapt to the environment. Today, in many Western countries, it is dangerous to criticize Islam. The Dutch parliamentarian Geert Wilders was charged with hate speech for speaking against Islam. He was acquitted of the charges. Yet the fact that such charge was made against him shows that

[449] Holy Warriors: Islam and the Demise of Classical Civilization p. 1-2

Europe is gradually giving in to the Sharia law. In the UK, Andrew Ryan, 32, was jailed for 70 days for burning a Quran. Going to jail for criticizing a religion or burning a book was unthinkable thirty years ago. It is clear that Islam's intolerance of freedom of speech is spreading amongst the Westerners. The following episode is a glaring example.

When in April 2011, Terry Jones, a pastor of a very small congregation burned a copy of the Quran, Muslims in Afghanistan rioted and killed 20 U.N. workers of different nationalities who had nothing to do with the Quran burning. The leading elite of the U.S. and the media did not find the savagery of the Afghans reprehensible; instead they vilified Pastor Jones for burning a book made of paper and ink. The West is changing. It is clear that freedom of speech is rapidly giving way to respect for Islam. Churchill must be turning in his grave. In his book, *The River War*, written in 1899, when he was 24 years old, he wrote these prophetic notes:

> How dreadful are the curses which Mohammedanism lays on its votaries! Besides the fanatical frenzy, which is as dangerous in a man as hydrophobia in a dog, there is this fearful fatalistic apathy. The effects are apparent in many countries. Improvident habits, slovenly systems of agriculture, sluggish methods of commerce, and insecurity of property exist wherever the followers of the Prophet rule or live....A degraded sensualism deprives this life of its grace and refinement; the next of its dignity and sanctity. The fact that in Mohammedan law every woman must belong to some man as his absolute property, either as a child, a wife, or a concubine, must delay the final extinction of slavery until the faith of Islam has ceased to be a great power among men.
>
> Individual Moslems may show splendid qualities ... but the influence of the religion paralyses the social development of those who follow it. No stronger retrograde force exists in the world. Far from being moribund, Mohammedanism is a militant and proselytizing faith. It has already spread throughout Central Africa, raising fearless warriors at every step; and were it not that Christianity is sheltered in the strong arms of science, the science against which it had vainly struggled, the civilisation of modern Europe might fall, as fell the civilisation of ancient Rome.[450]

Influence on the Catholic Church

Just as Islam is changing Europe and the western civilization today, it changed the Church of the middle Ages.

O Neil writes,

> Having examined Islam and the nature of Muslim culture, we return to Europe and an examination of the West's response. This was, in fact, multi-faceted, both in material and ideological terms. Perhaps the most obvious, and certainly the most controversial, European response was military: the Crusades. The average non-academic, influenced by a politically-correct popular media, now imagines the Crusades to be an almost

[450] *The River War*, first edition, Vol. II, pp. 248-50

> incomprehensible adventure launched by the aggressive warrior-aristocracy of Europe against a quiescent and cultured Islamic Middle East. But this is far from being the case. The Crusades were in fact a European response to Islamic conquest, and they began not in Palestine at all, but in Spain and Sicily. In fact, the Spanish and southern Italian crusades were ongoing from the first arrival of Islamic armies on European soil, and there never was a time when this war ended or even paused. Fighting was not always intense, but it was incessant. By the end of the tenth century the war for Spain had reached a crucial stage, and early in the eleventh century the monks of Cluny in southern France called upon the kings of Europe to intervene. From this point onwards a continual stream of French, German and Burgundian knights made their way across the Pyrenees to engage the Moors, and the tide of battle turned. Yet just as Islam began to lose ground in the west, it gained spectacular new victories in the east; and it was these that eventually led to the launching of what is known as the First Crusade.
>
> It is perfectly clear from this that the Crusades were not launched by an aggressive and expansionist Christendom against a peaceful and inoffensive Muslim world. They were, as commonsense in any case suggests, defensive actions against an aggressive and relentless foe. Having said that, it does seem strange that Christendom should wait almost four centuries after the initial Muslim expansion, which saw the loss of all the Christian lands of the Middle East and North Africa, before producing anything like an organized and full-scale response. So, here again, we must mention an apparent chronological inconsistency; and the same anomaly is encountered when we consider the most important political consequence of Islam's appearance: the re-establishment of the Western Empire.

There is no justification in the Bible, for the crusades or for the Inquisition. They were inspired by Jihad and *Mihna.* Mihna means Inquisition. It was devised by Abbasid Caliph al-Ma'mun in 833 CE to impose his theological views on his subjects.

Thanks to Islamic ideas imported to Europe, the Universal Church assumed temporal powers and put a halt on science and reason. Enlightenment was stalled for a millennium.

Jesus did not advocate seizing worldly powers. He said his Kingdom is not of this world. The Church was inspired by Islam, and to a great extent forced by it, to take up arms and defend itself.

The influence of Islam in Persia, Egypt, India, and countries that succumbed to it has been more devastating. The cultures of these countries were wiped out and in many cases people lost their language and their identity. The Western civilization will go the same route if the present trend continues and Islam is allowed to gain more grounds unchecked.

Islam's Influence on Secret Societies

Secret societies, like the Shriners, the Rosicrucian, the Freemason, the Illuminati, and the Mafia, were inspired by Islam and owe their organizational structure to the Order of Assassins, founded by Hassan Sabbah in the 11th century.

The illuminati secret society was modeled after Roshaniya. Roshaniya (literally illuminati), was a 16th century Afghan secret society, founded by Pir Roshan (Illumined Saint). Pir Roshan preached the transmigration of souls and the representation of God through individuals. This was the core of the doctrine of Hassan Sabbah. Sabbah understood that the essence of Islam was the glorification of one man, and that God was Muhammad's tool to dominate the unenlightened. This knowledge was his secret. The masses were to be encouraged to sacrifice and have complete devotion to the illumined leader. They were to believe that the leader is the manifestation of God. But the leader knew that all devotions are to him and God is a pretext, an instrument to mobilize the masses and through them gain power. The leader would present himself as a holy man, the representative of God on Earth and preach goodly teachings while at the same time he would encourage thuggery, murder and assassination. The disciple was taught that truth cannot be attained through his own endeavor nor perceived by his conscience. He needed the guru to discern right from wrong. What he says is good and truth even when they appear otherwise. It is not up to the disciple to question the wisdom of the manifestation of God. He is the only person who possesses the secret knowledge and hence the only one who can discern between good and evil.

This "secret" did not start with Sabbah. Ja'far, the seventh Shiite holy Imam is reported to have said. "Our cause is a secret (*serr*) within other secret, the secret of something that remains hidden - a secret that only another secret can reveal. It is a secret about a secret that is based on a secret."[451]

This "secret" became the cornerstone of all secret societies. The Freemasons recruit new members by portraying Freemasonry "as a voluntary, fraternal organization, composed of men of good will, good character and good reputation, whom in most jurisdictions around the world, believe in an Almighty Creator and practice the spirit of universal brotherhood to man. They are loyal to their country and devote their time to the principles of friendship and fellowship. Their focus is to be of service to all mankind."[452]

It sounds noble. What the 6,000,000 ordinary members of the fraternity don't know is that those at the highest echelon hold the same secret held by Muhammad, Imam Ja'far, and Sabbah that God is an instrument to gain power, that truth does not exist.

---

[451] Henri Corbin, *Historia de la Filosofia Siglo XXI* editores. V.3 p.253

[452] http://www.masonic-lodge-of-education.com/become-a-free-mason.html

9- Ripples and Effects

According to the Guinness Book of Records the Thuggee cult in India was responsible for approximately 2,000,000 deaths. They claimed to have originated from seven Muslim tribes. The earliest authenticated mention of the thugs is found in Ziya'-ud-Din Barani, History of Firuz Shah, dated about 1356.

The practice of Thuggee consisted in deceiving travellers and then strangulating them and robbing them. Their patron god was the goddess Kali. Kali represents time. Time gives birth, nurtures and then destroys. Given a personality, it becomes a ruthless mother. Kali took the characteristics of Allah. From there on she started feeding on death and would have to be offered blood sacrifices.

In 1816, Dr. Robert C. Sherwood published an article in the Madras Literary Gazette where he wrote, "In the more northern parts of India, these murderers are called Thugs, signifying deceivers. In the Tamul language, they are called Ari Tulucar or Mussulman noosers."

The word 'thug' is believed to come from the Sanskrit root *Sthag*, to conceal. Curiously, the Arabic word taqiya sounds the same as Thuggee and it also means the same – to conceal. In practice, the cult of Thuggee is very similar to the cult of the Assassins and taqiya was what Muhammad practiced. He deceived his victims, concealed his intention, then ambushed them, massacred them, and robbed them.

The Thugs were fanatical killers. Like Muslims, they eliminated any who spoke out against them. They believed that murder is their most sacred mission. This was a Muhammad's idea who taught nothing is more praiseworthy than jihad - to fight and to kill for Allah.

The evidence of the influence of the Ismailia Assassins on the Thuggee cult can be found in their hierarchy and organizational structure.

Mamluk ,(Owned): 1st level; Includes only Thuggee apprentices or mundane worshippers.

Askar, (army): 2nd-3rd level; anyone who has slain at least one victim.

Faris, (cavalier): 4th-9th level; the holy warriors.

Kahin, (priest): 10th-12th level; a head of the local cult.

Ghool, (giant) 13th-14th level; each of these Ghuls controlled the cult branches in their country.

Caliph: 15th level; head of the entire cult.

These titles are Arabic, which implies that the root of Thuggee is in Islam.

The Mafia also owes its existence to Islam. Muslims conquered Sicily and Malta in 902 and ruled the Islands until 1061, when they were evicted, following the Norman Conquest, the local gangsters moved in to fill their gap. Extorting money, in exchange for "protection," is what Muslims practiced in south Italy. It is by understanding this connection that we can understand how the Mafia can reconcile their religiosity with their crimes.

All totalitarian regimes, all fascistic forms of government, all systems that disregard the Golden Rule and use ideology as a tool for domination are either directly or indirectly, influenced by Islam.

Islam and the Loss of a Millennium

The idea of the Golden Age of Islam is nothing but a deception. Although the Umayyad and the Abbasid caliphs used Islam as a pretext to raid other countries annex them to their empire, they were not believers. Mu'awiya and his family had fought against Muhammad for two decades and many of them, including his grandfather and uncle were killed by him. They were forced to submit to Islam when Muhammad raided Mecca. The options were, to convert or to die. It is not rational to believe that they became devout Muslims by force. They came to power, because they were close relatives of Othman, the third caliph. After Othman's death, they ceased the power and started killing Muhammad companions and relatives, including his grandsons. Islam was not their goal but a means to conquer and to build their empire. This is also true in the case of the believers. Their incentive was to loot, to take women as slaves and to enrich themselves.

The Omayyad and the Abbasid rulers were secular kings. The caliphate gave them divine authority. Their interest was not to spread Islam. Their profession of faith was merely for political convenience. Unlike Umar who was wont of destroying the libraries and the culture of the vanquished, the Omayyad rulers preserved them. They gave total autonomy to their Christian and Zoroastrian subjects and trusted the administration of their empire to them.

During these first two centuries, when Islam was only a name and an excuse to raid and conquer. Scientists and philosophers of the conquered countries were not bothers and they could continue with their scientific works. They had to change their name to Arabic and nominally call themselves Muslim, so they could escape the status of dhimitude. Beyond that they were free to even call Muhammad a charlatan and the prophets, Billy goats, as Zakaria Razi was wont of doing.

O'Neill dispels many long held beliefs and false assumption regarding the claim that Islam contributed to science. He wrote:

> We find too that, far from being a force for enlightenment, Islam was, from almost the beginning, hostile to the very concept of science and learning. And to describe the science that existed throughout the Middle and Near East in the seventh and eighth centuries as "Arabic" or "Islamic" is quite ridiculous. The Arabs themselves who, by the middle of the seventh century had come to control all the great and ancient centers of culture in the region – including Egypt, Syria, Mesopotamia, and Persia – were illiterate or semi-literate nomads, who had little or no understanding of the learning of the peoples of those regions. But they did not, to begin with at least, destroy it. They merely installed their religion and with it their language in the corridors of power. The result was that by the eighth century, many or most of the alchemists, mathematicians, astronomers and physicians based in those regions were known by Arab names. But they were not Arabs, nor were they, in most cases, even Muslims. The vast majority were Christians, Jews and Zoroastrians, who continued to practice their own faiths, though they now labored under an Islamic regime and Arab masters, and were compelled to publish their findings in the Arabic language. Nor should it be forgotten

> that virtually all of the scientific and technical innovations which Europeans have traditionally described as "Arab", actually originated in China and India, and made their way westwards to the Near East via Persia. Such, for example, was the case with the compass, paper, and the use of the zero in mathematics. It is possible, even probable, that several of these had already reached Sassanid Persia by the reign of Chosroes II, ie. just before the Islamic takeover, and the Arabs simply used ideas and technologies already in place. This was admitted even by such writers as Briffault.
>
> With or without the Arabs, these things would have made their way to Europe. The only Arab contribution was to impede this process. Having closed the Mediterranean to their trade, thus impoverishing Europeans materially, the Arabs also prevented the rapid adoption of the new Chinese and Indian inventions by the besieged westerners. And they would not long suffer the spirit of rationalism and scientific enquiry to survive even in their own lands. Within a short time – a very short time indeed – Muslim theologians were declaring that all scientific and philosophical enquiry was contrary to Allah's will, and the flourishing sciences which the Arabs found in Egypt, Syria, Mesopotamia and Persia, were crushed under the weight of a totalitarian theocracy. Thus by the twelfth century at the latest, Europe – without the aid of paper and with limited and very late access to the ideas and technologies which reached the Near East from China and India much earlier – had taken the lead, a lead that was never to be relinquished. Thus we find that when the Turks besieged Constantinople in the fourteenth and fifteenth centuries they were compelled to find European armorers who could cast for them the cannons to breach the walls of the city – this in spite of the fact that both gunpowder and firearms were Asiatic inventions which reached the West much later than they had reached the Arab world.

A group of thinkers under the domination of Islam flirted with rationalism for a short time. They called themselves Mu'tazelis. They claimed reason is above revelation. Their school was vehemently opposed and became extinct. The Mu'tazelis were attacked by Ash'ariyya school to which al-Ghazzali and the celebrated poet Jalaleddin-e Rumi belonged. Rumi mocked the rationalists and said they stand on "wooden legs."

The Ash'ariyya glorified irrationality and remained faithful to the Quran. They blamed the rationalists for forsaking religion and for detracting from God and his revelation. Rational objectivism was quashed with mockery and violence. The rationalists' books were destroyed and rationalists themselves had to hide for their safety. The Ash'ariyya won because they had the Quran on their side. With the Ash'ariyya's unconditional embrace of the authority of revelation and exaltation of irrationality, rationalism was nipped in the bud.

In an article titled, "Is Rumi What We Think He Is?" Massoume Price quotes Dr. Shaffiee Kadkani who wrote, "Unfortunately, the emergence of geniuses such as Rumi and other *urafa* (religious mystics) who unconditionally supported

Ash'ariyya, did not give freedom of thought a chance. If it wasn't because of Ash'ariyya our history might have evolved differently".[453]

Price contends:

> It is not a coincidence that in Mathnavi, Rumi attacks all thinkers including atheists, naturalists and philosophers etc.... When Ibn Khadon [Khaldun] said Africans are black because of geographical and environmental conditions, it was the Ash'ariyya who ended such scientific observations by declaring people are black because God created them as such. When Physicians tried to find the connection between the brain and hand's movements, it was Imam Muhammad Ghazzali who mocked scientific inquiry and stated "hands move because God wants them to move" (Alchemy of Happiness, Kimiyaya Saadat). It was Ash'ariyya who imposed inquisition culture that still exists today and haunts us even in North America.[454]

The great, so called "Muslim thinkers" were not Muslim at all. About prophets, Mohammad ibn Zachariah al-Razi (Rhazes) (865 – 925) wrote:

> The prophets—these billy goats with long beard cannot claim any intellectual or spiritual superiority. These billy goats pretend to come with a message from God, all the while exhausting themselves in spouting their lies, and imposing on the masses blind obedience to the "words of the master." The miracles of the prophets are impostures, based on trickery, or the stories regarding them are lies. The falseness of what all the prophets say is evident in the fact that they contradict one another: one affirms what the other denies, and yet each claims to be the sole depository of the truth. As for the Quran, it is but an assorted mixture of 'absurd and inconsistent fables,' which has ridiculously been judged inimitable, when, in fact, its language, style, and its much-vaunted 'eloquence' are far from being faultless.[455]

Abu Ali Sina (Avicenna) (980-1037) rejected the central Islamic doctrine of resurrection of the dead and was denounced by the theologians of Islam like al-Ghazzali as "apostate".

The blind Arab philosopher/poet Al-Ma'arri (973-1057) wrote, "Religions are noxious weeds and fables, invented by the ancients, worthless except for those who exploit the credulous masses. Do not suppose the statements of the prophets to be true. Men lived comfortably till they came and spoiled life. Their 'sacred books' are only such a set of idle tales as any age could have and indeed did actually produce.

---

[453] Creation and History, (Afarinesh va Tarikh, p.50)

[454] http://www.ghandchi.com/iranscope/Anthology/Culture/RumiMassoume.htm

[455] Al-Razi wrote three books dealing with religion: (1) *The Prophet's Fraudulent Tricks*, (2) *The Stratagems of Those Who Claim to Be Prophets* (Arabic حيل المتنبيين), and (3) *On the Refutation of Revealed Religions* (Arabic مخارق الانبياء). None of his books have survived. Bits and pieces of what he wrote were quoted by an Ismaili Muslim while refuting him. That is what has survived.

9- Ripples and Effects

Hanifs (Muslims) are stumbling, Christians all astray.
Jews wildered, Magians far on error's way.
We mortals are composed of two great schools.
Enlightened knaves, or else religious fools."

Umar Khayyam objected to the notion that every particular event and phenomenon was the result of the intervention of God. He mocked the idea of resurrection, Judgment Day or rewards and punishments in an alleged afterlife.

Some for the Glories of this World; and some,
Sigh for the Prophet's Paradise to come;
Ah, take the Cash, and let the Credit go,
Nor heed the rumble of a distant Drum!"

Muhammad ibn Musa al-Khwarizmi (780 -850), mathematician, astronomer, astrologer, and geographer, and the Father of Algebra, was, as Tabari noted, a Zoroastrian.

Ibn Rushd (Averroes), Al-Biruni, Yaqub ibn Ishaq al-Kindi, considered to be "one of the twelve greatest minds of the Middle Ages", Abul Qasim Khalaf ibn al-Abbas al-Zahrawi (Abulcasis) and many other so called "Muslim" thinkers did not believe in Islam and expressed their disdain of its prophet in various ways.

With men of science such as Muhammad Zachariah Razi, Al Khwarizmi, Khayyam, Abu Ali Sina, al Farabi and many others, Persia was about to become the cradle of the Age of Reason, seven hundred years before it happened in Europe. Enlightenment was stalled, both in Europe, and in Iran, thanks to Islam.

Imagine where we would be today if humanity had come to the Age of Reason, one thousand years earlier.

Nazism, communism, fascism, the destruction of the Classical Civilization, the corruption of the Catholic Church, the Crusades, the Inquisition, the secret societies, the Mafia, the holdup of the Enlightenment for one thousand years, countless wars, and hundreds of millions of deaths, are all influences of Islam. There is no doubt that Muhammad has been the most influential person in history. However, it can be argued that without him the world would have been a much better place.

Muhammad taught his followers to hate, to wage war, to raid, to rape and to murder in exchange for a free pass to a heavenly brothel. What is good in that?

Islam and Muslims' Backwardness

Although Islam has been a curse to everyone, Muslims are its primary victims. In a 2005 article titled "What Went Wrong," Dr. Farrukh Saleem, a Pakistani writer, wrote:

> The combined annual GDP of 57 Muslim countries remain under $2 trillion. America, just by herself, produces goods and services worth $10.4 trillion; China $5.7 trillion, Japan $3.5 trillion and Germany $2.1 trillion. Even India's GDP is estimated at over $3 trillion (purchasing power parity basis).

Oil rich Saudi Arabia, U.A.E., Kuwait and Qatar collectively produce goods and services (mostly oil) worth $430 billion; Netherlands alone has a higher annual GDP while Buddhist Thailand produces goods and services worth $429 billion.

Muslims are 22 percent of the world population and produce less than five percent of global GDP. Even more worrying is that the Muslim countries' GDP as a percent of the global GDP is going down over time. The Arabs, it seems, are particularly worse off. According to the United Nations' Arab Development Report: "Half of Arab women cannot read; One in five Arabs live on less than $2 per day; Only 1 percent of the Arab population has a personal computer, and only half of 1 percent use the Internet; Fifteen percent of the Arab workforce is unemployed, and this number could double by 2010; The average growth rate of the per capita income during the preceding 20 years in the Arab world was only one-half of 1 percent per annum, worse than anywhere but sub-Saharan Africa."

The planet's poorest countries include Ethiopia, Sierra Leone, Afghanistan, Cambodia, Somalia, Nigeria, Pakistan and Mozambique. At least six of the poorest of the poor are countries with a Muslim majority.

Conclusion: Muslims of the world are among the poorest of the poor.

Fifty-seven Muslim majority countries have an average of ten universities each for a total of less than 600 universities for 1.4 billion people; India has 8,407 universities, the U.S. has 5,758. From within 1.4 billion Muslims Abdus Salam and Ahmed Zewail are the only two Muslim men who won a Nobel Prize in physics and chemistry (Salam pursued his scientific work in Italy and the UK, Zewail at California Institute of Technology). Dr Salam in his home country is not even considered a Muslim.

Over the past 105 years, 1.4 billion Muslims have produced eight Nobel Laureates while a mere 14 million Jews have produced 167 Nobel Laureates. Of the 1.4 billion Muslims less than 300,000 qualify as 'scientists', and that converts to a ratio of 230 scientists per one million Muslims. The United States of America has 1.1 million scientists (4,099 per million); Japan has 700,000 (5,095 per million).

Fact: Of the 1.4 billion Muslims 800 million are illiterate (6 out of 10 Muslims cannot read). In Christendom, adult literacy rate stands at 78 percent.

Consider, for instance, that Muslims constitute 22 percent of world population with a 1 percent share of Nobel Prizes. Jews constitute 0.23 percent of world population with a 22 percent share of Nobel Prizes.

What really went wrong? Muslims are poor, illiterate and weak. What went wrong? Arriving at the right diagnosis is extremely critical because the prescription depends on it.

The diagnosis is simple. The problem with Islamic countries is Islam. The more a country becomes Islamic the more backward it becomes.

9- Ripples and Effects

Professor Pervez Hoodbhoy, a Pakistani nuclear physicist, wrote that Israel has almost twice as many scientists as all the 57 Muslim countries put together. Islam, with a fifth of the world's population, accounts for less than 1% of the world's scientists.[456]

In an article published in The New York Times, Tariq Ahmad, a Muslim doctor at Brigham and Women's Hospital in Boston had an ingenious idea.[457] After admitting "I am by no means an expert on the topic of Islam or Muslims," he suggested, "To defeat the threat of radical Islam, I suggest that the answer lies among the people who are the least Muslim. It is only the secular forces within Islam that can subdue the screams of radicalism."

In other words, the solution to the problem is in the hands of those who know Islam less and practice it least. Does Dr. Ahmad also believe the best persons to practice medicine are those who dropped out of med school?

Ahmad is not alone. His, is the prevalent idea. The fact is that for 1400 years the "least practicing Muslims" have been unable to end the virulent Islam. They can't because once they accept the authority of the Quran they give all the power to the true Muslims - the radicals and the terrorists.

Those who know Islam better know that violence is part of it. Khomeini knew Islam well. He wrote. "Those who know nothing of Islam pretend that Islam counsels against war. Those are witless. Islam says: Kill all the unbelievers just as they would kill you all! … Islam says: Kill them, put them to the sword. People cannot be made obedient except with the sword![458]

Khomeini's views are based on Islamic scriptures and are shared by all Muslim scholars. When those who are "less Muslim" decide to become good Muslims, they become jihadi terrorists.

Numbers don't count. Whoever has the "Divine Authority" on his side has the last word. In Islam, the fundamentalists will always prevail.

Lukewarm Muslims are not the solution. They are a massive part of the problem. By identifying themselves as Muslim they give legitimacy to the Quran and to the terrorists who put that book to practice.

The majority of Germans did not agree with the holocaust. Nonetheless, millions perished because silent majority don't count. They gave legitimacy to the criminals in power.

If Islam is good why practice it minimally. If it is bad why practice it at all? Poison, taken in small doses, may not kill you, but why take it?

---

[456] *Islam* and *Science, Religious Orthodoxy and the Battle for Rationality. 1991*
[457] http://www.nytimes.com/2009/12/05/opinion/05iht-edahmad.html?_r=2
[458] Khomeini: *Islam Is Not a Religion of Pacifists (1942)*

Muhammad's Influence on Misogyny

Islam has been a negative influence in the world, yet none has been as baleful as its misogyny. Women prior to Islam, enjoyed more rights and privileges.

When Muhammad heard the news that Persians had made the daughter of Khosrau their Queen, he said, "Never will succeed such a nation as makes a woman their ruler."[459] No woman has ever ruled Iran after it succumbed to Islam.

Muslims claim that in Arabia women were considered so low that Arabs buried their new born daughters alive. This goes against commonsense and human nature. Women in pre-Islamic Arabia enjoyed far more respect and status than they ever had after Islam. A good example is Khadijah, who was a successful merchant and employed men. Khadijah was not an exception. Khunaas, mother of Mus'ab ibn Umayr, was also a successful merchant no less powerful than Khadijah.

At the time of Muhammad, a woman by the name of Sijah claimed to be a prophetess and led an army of 30,000 men in a war against Muslims. For an Arab today, it is inconceivable to follow a woman.

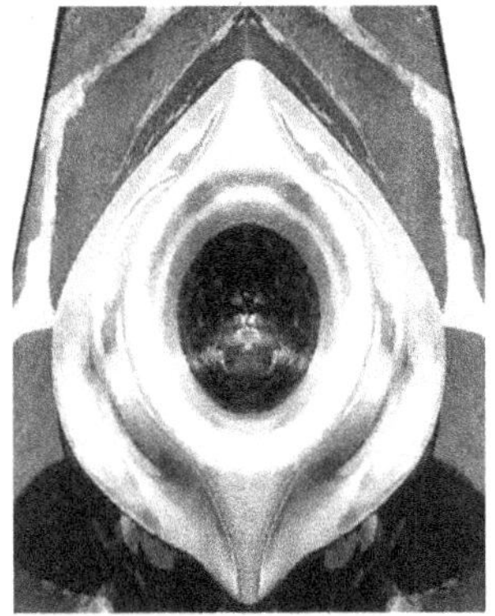

The Sacred Yoni of Sheba, the goddess of Ka'ba

Pre-islamic Arabs worshiped Al Lat (literally 'the goddess') with triple aspects, each representing a phase of the moon - Qure, the crescent moon or the maiden; the full moon and the mother aspect, Al'Uzza, (literally 'the strong one'); and Al'Manat, the waning, but wise goddess of fate, prophecy and divination. Later, these three personalities of the triune god came to be known as 'daughters of Allah'. Another deity, Hubaal, became known as Allah (literally 'the god'). Muhammad thought it is denigrating for God to have daughters. He said, "*What? for you the males and for Him the females? This indeed is an unjust division!*" (Q. 53:21-22)

Bob Trubshaw says, "At Mecca the Goddess was Shaybah or Sheba, the Old Woman, The sacred Black Stone now enshrined in the corner of Ka'ba was her feminine symbol, marked by the sign of the yoni and covered by a veil. The Black Stone rests in the Haram, 'Sanctuary', cognate of 'harem,' which used to mean a Temple of Women: in Babylon, a shrine of the Goddess Har, mother of harlots. Hereditary guardians of the Haram were the Quraishites, 'children of Qure'. The holy office was originally held by women, before it was taken over by male priests

[459] Bukahri, 9. 88. 219

calling themselves, Bani Shayban, 'Sons of Sheba' - the famous Queen Sheba of Solomon's times."[460]

Worshipping goddesses and veneration of female genitalia, the symbol of fertility, suggests Arabs had high respect for women. Muslims still kiss the symbol representing her yoni, without knowing its origin.

Muslim historians report the story of two extraordinary women, Umm Qirfa and her daughter Salma. Umm Qirfa was the leader of Bani Fadara. Zayd, the foster son of Muhammad, raided her tribe. Under her leadership, her men defeated the raiders. Many Muslims were killed and Zayd himself was wounded. Zayd swore that he would take his revenge. When he recovered Muhammad sent him back with more force. He fought the Bani Fazara, killed some of them and took Umm Qirfa, and her beautiful daughter as hostage. The Sira of Ibn Ishaq says Zayd killed Umm Qirfa, "cruelly." The details of this cruel killing is omitted by Ibn Hisham who edited Ibn Ishaq's Sira. Tabari explains that her legs were tied to two ropes and each rope was pulled by a camel until she was ripped in two. Ibn Ishaq says, "She held a position of honor among her people, and the Arabs used to say, 'Had you been more powerful than Umm Qirfa you could have done no more'". Such was the courage of this woman that she had become a legend among Arabs.

Umm Qirfa's daughter Salma was enslaved. Salma, proved to be no less a superwoman than her mother. After her captivity she was employed to do the domestic work for Aisha. But this princess had blue blood in her veins. After the death of Muhammad, many Arabs left Islam. Abu Bakr waged a savage war against the apostates (War of Apostasy) and killed hundreds of thousands of them. He burned them, stoned them to death, threw them into well or cast them off from cliffs, until he brought them back into submission. Tabari says a Muslim named Ilyas left Islam and fought against Muslims (for his freedom). When he was captured Abu Bakr ordered to ignite a fire in the middle of the mosque in Medina and threw the wretched man in the fire alive.[461]

Salma persuaded Aisha to allow her to go to the remainder of her people and convert them to Islam. Once freed, she travelled to villages and towns and assembled a huge army. She posed such a threat to Muslims that Abu Bakr sent his most savage general, Khalid ibn Walid, with a large army who brought her down in the most un-chivalrous cowardly way.

Tabari reports "the defeated apostates regrouped around Salma, daughter of Malik ibn Hudhaifa, who like her mother was valiant and honored. She rode the camel of Umm Qirfa and roused people to fight. As men became heartened they gathered around her. When Khalid ibn Walid learned that Salma is raising fund and preparing an army he went to fight her. A fierce battle broke. During the battle

---

[460] http://mysteryofthelnquity.wordpress.com/2011/04/04/the-black-stone-at-mecca/

[461] Tabari, v. 4, p. 1390

Salma was standing on the top of her mother's camel, and like her, she was courageous, respected and honored."[462] Her story is reported below in more detail.

> When after the defeat of Taleaha, many of his followers sought refuge with Umm Zummal (Salma), she decided to avail of the opportunity, and lead a coalition against the Muslims. She moved from tribe to tribe and exerted them to hostility against the Muslims. She mustered a considerable force, which assembled at her headquarter Zafar at the western edge of the Salma range, a rugged mountain named after her. When Khalid came to know of the hostile intentions of Umm Zummal, he led a Muslim force from Buzakha to Zafar. Immediately on arrival at Zafar, Khalid took the initiative and launched the attack. Umm Zummal and her forces offered stiff resistance. It was by all accounts a hard battle. Mounted on a camel, Umm Zummal personally led the charge, and her undaunted courage was a source of great inspiration for her followers. Failure of his first effort to dislodge the apostates made Khalid reassess the situation. He saw that the center of the apostates was led by Umm Zummal who rode on a magnificent camel which belonged to her mother. She exhorted her followers to fight bravely. She was surrounded by a ring of warriors who fought desperately, fired with a determination to win or die. For long the result of the confrontation remained uncertain. Khalid realized that the moral strength of the apostate force lay in the leadership of Umm Zummal, and unless she was eliminated somehow the chances of the Muslim victory were not very bright. Khalid directed his archers to aim at the camel on which Umm Zummal was riding. Every bow was bent and every spear of the Muslim was directed towards the camel. The camel was pierced with countless wounds, and it fell. Then Khalid with a picked group of warriors made a determined thrust towards the center, and as the litter carrying Salma alias Umm Zummal fell to the ground she was killed immediately. The Muslims made free use of their swords and spears. Umm Zummal lay dead on the battlefield, and around her lay the dead bodies of her bodyguards who had fought to the last in her defense. With the death of Umm Zummal all resistance of the apostates collapsed and the battle of Zafar was won by the Muslims. That was in October 632 C. E. The apostate bibles offered submission and were re-admitted to the fold of Islam. Considerable booty fell into the hands of the Muslims which was sent to Madina.[463]

Compare the bravery of this young woman to the cowardice of Muhammad who wore two coats of mail and stood away from any danger, protected by his bodyguards.

Even Aisha led an army against Ali. In the early years of Islam Muslims had not yet shed their ancestral chivalry and women had not lost all their status. It took a couple of generations for women to be reduced into chattels, animals and objects.

How can women thrive in an Islamic society? How can they succeed when they are shrouded in a veil? Muslims claim that veil is cultural. Not so. Tabari says, "When the hostages of Badr were brought to Mecca Sauda, the wife of the Prophet

---

[462] Tabari, v. 4, p. 1393

[463] http://forum.ziyouz.com/index.php?topic=1358.115;wap2

was at the home of the Afra with their sons, as at this time the law of veiling had not yet been ordained.[464] This ordinance is in the Quran 33.59.

Muhammad said women are deficient in intelligence and their testimony should not be trusted because their brain does not work properly (they forget). The Quran 4:34 makes women eternally subservient to men and says Allah has made men excel over women, and women should be obedient to men. The Quran 2:228 says that women have some rights but men have a degree of advantage over them.

After Islam we don't see any Khadijah, Umm Qirfa and Salma in any Islamic country. Muslim women were degraded. The effect of Muhammad's misogyny is eloquently expressed by Fakhruddin al-Razi (1149-1209 not to be confused with the rationalist Zakaria Razi) who in At-Tafsir al-Kabir, commenting on Q. 30:21wrote:

> His saying 'created for you' is a proof that women were created like animals and plants and other useful things, just as the Most High has said 'He created for you what is on earth' and that necessitates the woman not to be created for worship and carrying the Divine commands. We say creating the women is one of the graces bestowed upon us and charging them with Divine commands to complete the graces bestowed upon us, not that they are charged as we men are charged. For women are not charged with many commands as we are charged, because the woman is weak, silly, in one sense she is like a child, and no commands are laid upon a child, but for the grace of Allah upon us to be complete, women had to be charged so that they may fear the torment of punishment and so follow her husband, and keep away from what is forbidden, otherwise corruption would be rampant.

In other words women hare the rights of animals but they can be punished most severely. They have no rights but all the responsibilities.

Rehashing the biblical fable about the creation of Eve, Muhammad said "Woman is like a rib. When you attempt to straighten it, you would break it. And if you leave her alone you would benefit by her, and crookedness will remain in her."[465]

The consequence of Muhammad's misogyny is more ruinous than all his other influences. Women in Islamic countries are equated to animals. Their bodily fluids are deemed to be filthy and they are thought to be of the devil because they tempt men. How can one respect and love a person he regards so lowly? How can you love a woman when you can buy them in quantities and dispose of them when you please? Prior to Islam the Persian and the Arab poets composed beautiful love poems for women. After Islam you rarely find a love story or a love poem for a woman. Instead, Islamic literature is full of love lyrics for young boys.

Women are denigrated, discriminated against, beaten, raped and honor killed. The Muslim world languishes, because half of its population is barred from contributing.

---

[464] Tabari v. 3, p. 977
[465] Sahih Muslim 8. 3466

Women are denied education. Uneducated women are ignorant and lack self-esteem. But women are also mothers. They project their sense of inferiority on their children. Their sons inherit their mother's low self-esteem and grow up to build the Islamic world with inadequacy and incompetence – fighting constantly with their inner demons, the demons of fear, hurt pride and humiliation. As the result, the Muslim world is plunged into darkness of ignorance, of self-pity and of dictatorship.

Dr. Mahathir, the ex- Prime Minister of Malaysia summed up this sentiment eloquently when in the 10th summit of the Organization of Islamic Conference he said, *"We are all Muslims. We are all oppressed. We are all being humiliated."*

This sense of inferiority, however, is not the fault of the "Zionists," as Dr. Mahathir misdiagnosed, but the outcome of how women are treated in Islam.

The feeling of inferiority torments the Muslim. He can function either in the role of a bully/dictator or a sycophant, but never as equal. That is why there can't be a long lasting democracy in any Islamic country. He seeks power. He is in constant need to show off and to compensate for his sense of inferiority. He feels neglected, humiliated and victimized and seeks revenge. This too was echoed by Dr. Mahathir who called upon the Muslims to acquire "*guns and rockets, bombs and warplanes, tanks and warships"* to humiliate their "*detractors and enemies*".

The moderate Muslim Dr. Mahathir was right! Muslims are oppressed and humiliated. However, their humiliation has nothing to do with their perceived "detractors," but with their religion. It has to do with how they are raised and how their mothers were raised. It has to do with how Islam treats women. Women who have no self-esteem can't raise sons with high self-esteem. They raise men with bruised egos who sublimate their shame in anger and express it in violence. Is it any wonder that Osama bin Laden's mother was the least favorite of her husband's numerous wives? Osama grew up with a mother with low self-esteem and inherited her sense of inferiority. This petty man was striving to compensate his own feeling of worthlessness by becoming a hero to his fellow Muslims.

Men with low self-esteem are dangerous. They cover up their shame with violence. They seek "martyrdom" for its perceived glory. The thought of becoming heroes, their pictures published in the newspapers and shown to the world, for a young man who sees no worth in his life can be exhilarating. He is nobody in life, but he can become famous and even a hero in death.

The self-anointed prophet of Arabia could never imagine that his obsession to control his young wives would one day bring the world to the brink of destruction, as if a narcissist like him would have given a damn!

Thanks to his misogyny, Muhammad sired a sick society of emotionally scarred men, with humongous egos, unable to function harmoniously in a world of equals and incapable of being happy and at peace. They fail in relationships with their spouses and their children, unless it is patriarchal. They fail in the society unless it is dictatorial. They perpetuate the cycle of abuse, humiliation and dictatorship ad infinitum. Little men, who are hurt inside wear masks of grandiosity; hide inside their inflated and inflammable egos; are explosively dangerous to themselves, and in such a large numbers, to the world.

Among all Muhammad's influences none is more malefic than his misogyny. Muhammad's misogyny has victimized every Muslim - women and men alike. A sick society has "evolved" with timid men, self-pitying men, arrogant, ego-centered, violent and angry men, hate mongers, and war mongers.

The Increase of Intolerance on Non-Muslims

For every action there is a reaction. When you hit someone, again and again, eventually he will hit you back. Muslims abuse, rape, terrorize and kill their non-Muslim hosts in many countries. It would be foolhardy to think their continuous assaults will remain uncontested forever.

The victims of Islam are becoming restless and are reacting. Remember that the crusades were a reaction to over 400 years of jihad. When in 2002 Gujarat Hindus rioted, killed the Muslims and burned their mosques, it was because Muslims had burned a train full of Hindu pilgrims, killing nearly 80 women and children.

Nigeria, Africa's most populous country, has seen tens of thousands die in the violence between Christians and Muslims since it gained independence from Britain in 1960. While members of the two faiths have perpetrated atrocities against each other, we must not forget the fact that Muslims started this violence and Christians responded in kind. The same was true in Serbia and Somalia. The instigators of all savageries are always Muslims.

People in countries under attack by Muslims, which is virtually all the countries where a substantial number of Muslims reside, are becoming radicalized. Andres Behring Breivik the 32 year old extremist who bombed a government building in Oslo that resulted in eight deaths, and shot 69 mostly teenagers in a camp of the Workers' Youth League (AUF) of the Labor Party may have been a lone wolf, a sick individual suffering from narcissism and delusions of grandiosity. However, the anger against Islam and the liberals who blindly support it is going main stream.

On one hand Muslims are transforming the non-Muslim countries into, as Orianna Fallaci put it, kasbahs. They piss and defile the picturesque cities of Europe. They refuse to integrate. They build ghettos and no-go zones for the locals, including the police. They assault non-Muslims, rape their women and try to shove their Sharia and their barbaric way of life on their hosts and at the same time demand respect. On the other hand their leftist allies are aiding them. Together they have formed an alliance to destroy the Judeo-Christian foundation of the western civilization.

There is a limit to forbearance. Muslims interpret tolerance as a sign of weakness and if not stopped, will increase their violence. It is only natural for their victims to react. So far violence has been one sided – perpetrated by Muslims. It's only a matter of time for it to become reciprocal.

Europe is becoming intolerant. Ironically, that is a good thing, because tolerating intolerance will only encourages it. If Islam is not stopped, Europe will be lost and the western civilization will be lost. Let us be honest; the modern world is owed to the western civilization. A newly Islamized Europe will be more radical than the present Islamic countries.

It would be a mistake to see this anger as anything other than a reaction to Islamic invasion, and it would be foolish to try to suppress it. The anti-Islam sentiment cannot be suppressed, because it is legitimate. But it can be directed so it does not turn violent. Suppressing it will make it explode. Muslims have been very clear in stating their intent, which is to subdue and to dominate their hosts and even to rape their women. People hear their message and see what they do. They can't pretend the elephant is not in the room.

Instead of blaming the reaction we must remove its cause. The cause of this intolerance is Islam and the stubborn denial of the leftist-controlled media and multiculturalist governments. Denial will only aggravate the problem. I am not against multiculturalism. I love humus, falafel and babaghanush, and did I say belly dancing? That is culture. Female genital mutilation, honor killing, wife beating, hand chopping and eye gouging that are based on the Sharia are barbarity. Islam is not a culture any more than fascism and communism, or for that matter Christianity and Buddhism are. Islam is an ideology.

To quote Wafa Sultan, civilizations don't clash; they compete. It's barbarity that clashes with civilization. Are Indian culture, Chinese culture, African culture or any culture in war with any other culture? Islam is in war with all cultures, because it is not a culture. It is the antithesis of culture.

I support Geert Wilders and his effort to stop Islam in Europe. Wilders is our best hope. If people like him are silenced, the anti-Islam sentiment will turn violent. There will be bloodshed and Muslims will be the losers. To avoid such a dreadful scenario, Wilders must be supported. I urge ex-Muslims to join him and demonstrate that we are part of the West. We cherish its values and defend its freedom. This is not a war between races, even though Muslims and their leftist lackeys want to make it look that way. This is a war between two ideologies – an ideology of freedom, of pluralism, of tolerance and of equality and an ideology of slavery, of supremacy, of intolerance and of domination.

Chapter Ten

Where Are We Headed?

Muslims try to be like Muhammad in every way. The mullahs, study for years to learn their Prophet's sunnah, and then teach that to believers, who in turn, do their best to emulate him. Through the sunnah, Muslims learn how Muhammad prayed, washed his face, cleaned his teeth, nose, and ears. How he ate, which fingers he licked after eating, which foods he liked, on which side he slept, what was the shape and material of his clothing, and how long was his beard. Did he wash before sex or after? With which foot he entered the toilet? Did he urinate standing or squatting? Which direction he faced when defecating? On which foot did he place his weight when squatting? With which hand did he clean his private parts? To a Muslim, doing these is piety. The Quran says "Verily, you have in the Prophet of Allah an excellent example." (Q. 33:21)

Ibn Sa'd reports a hadith from a companion of Muhammad who tried to show off his piety by saying that he saw Muhammad liked squash and since then he too loves this vegetable.[466]

Muslims' thoughts reflect those of Muhammad and their actions mirror his. They strive to lose their selfhood and become clones of their prophet. It is false to say Muslims are a diverse group of people. To the degree that they emulate Muhammad they are all his mini replicas. This determines their level of "piety" as well as violence.

There are also good people who call themselves Muslims. They are often denounced by the real Muslims as hypocrites, or like Salman Taseer, the governor of Punjab who opposed the blasphemy law, they are assassinated.

The "soft" Muslims make up the bulk of the Umma, but their voices are silenced because they find no support for their views in the Quran. They sheepishly trail behind the zealot minority. If Umma were a dog and the "extremists" its tail, the tail wags the dog.

466 Tabaqat Volume 1, Page 374

Actually there are no extremists in Islam. Extremists and radicals exist in other faiths, but not in Islam. Muslims can be divided in three categories – the good, the bad, and the hypocrites.

The *good Muslims* are those who follow Muhammad to the letter. They disdain the world and seek martyrdom. We call them terrorists. They call themselves Salafi – followers of the Sunnah of Muhammad and his companions.

The *bad Muslims* are those who don't follow Islam properly. They are wishy-washy Muslims. Their faith is weak and their knowledge of Islam is deficient. Instead of seeking martyrdom they strive to better their lives. They are ignorant of Islam and confess to their ignorance and lack of devotion. Most of them are overtaken by guilt and hope that one day they will renounce the world and become good Muslims.

Then there are the *hypocrites*. These are the ones who know the truth, but hide it. They claim that Islam has been hijacked by a few "radicals" (the good Muslims). Their argument is that Islam is a great religion, as long as it is not practiced. They call themselves devout Muslims, but disagree with the Sharia. Zuhdi Jasser, Tarek Fatah, Tawfik Hamid Maajid Nawaaz and Irshad Manji are among the most vociferous proponents of this Islamic ruse in the West. They repudiate everything that Islam teaches and say this is not the real Islam. Their goal is to convince the victim that Islam is not the enemy. They are guilty of false labeling Islam. While they call themselves "reformers, they don't write for Muslims who know Islam well and will never buy their charade. They write for the westerners.

Secret Pakistan: Double Cross, is a documentary made by BBC (available on Youtube) that shows how Pakistan, while openly acting as an ally of the West secretly supported the Taliban. Once in a while they would capture low ranking al Qaida commanders to keep the Americans happy and secure their billions of dollars share of aid, but secretly they protected the Taliban and aided them to continue to fight. Thousands of American soldiers were killed as the result of Pakistan's duplicity.

The so called "moderate" Muslims are playing the same game of deception. They criticize everything Islam teaches, and say this is not Islam. In my view they are more dangerous than the terrorists. Islamic reformation is a smoke screen.

Truth was spoken by Turkey's Prime Minister Erdogan who condemned the term "moderate Islam", often used in the West to describe his party AKP, and said, "These descriptions are very ugly, it is offensive and an insult to our religion. There is no moderate or immoderate Islam. Islam is Islam and that's it."[467]

Although the efforts of those who speak of moderation in Islamic countries are laudable, to do the same in the western countries is deception. Firstly, in the west there is freedom to speak the truth and secondly, it's the Muslims who have to believe Islam is moderate and stop supporting terrorism; the non-Muslims can made their mind through the actions of Muslims.

---

[467] http://www.thememriblog.org/turkey/blog_personal/en/2595.htm

10- Where Are We Headed?

The so called "moderate" Muslims are the silent accomplices of their jihadi co-religionists. It is their adherence to Islam that makes this faith the second largest religion and legitimizes it. The result is a hellish society that has little hope of recovery, where everyone suffocates, and no one knows how to extricate themselves. Ironically, the more they suffer, the more they cling to their faith.

If we adopt a submissive peaceful posture vis-à-vis Muslims, they will be emboldened and we lose. We lose our freedom, our democracy, our civilization and everything humanity has achieved since Enlightenment. Science will be enslaved by an obscurantist religion and the world will sink in the quagmire of Talibanization.

This will not be the end of the story. Since Muslims know no other way to resolve their disagreements except through fighting, in an eventual Islamic world everyone will be fighting with everyone else and there will be mass slaughters worldwide. With the world's reserves of nuclear weapons in the hands of Muslims, you can imagine what will be the future of mankind.

Muslims will start killing each other because each considers others to be heretic. A Good example is what is happening in Gaza. Muslims in this tiny piece of land are in perpetual war with Israel. Meanwhile, they persecute the Christians and have splinted in numerous groups, fighting among each other.

Muslims are divided into thousands of groups. They are all hostile to each other, killing one another and calling each other kafir and heretic. The only thing that unites Muslims is their hatred of non-Muslims and particularly the Jews. If Islam conquers the world, this is where we are heading: Constant war and the assured destruction of mankind.

This division between Muslims appears to be by design. It is as if Muhammad wanted his followers to be disunited, fight and kill one another. Muslims will jump to differ and will quote the surah 3:103 where Muhammad exhorts his followers: "*And hold fast, all of you together, to the rope of Allah and be not divided.*" That was probably what he hoped. However, thanks to his lack of wisdom he laid the foundation of disunity among his followers.

Imam Abu Dawood quoted a Hadith concerning the division of the Muslims into seventy-three sects. He siad, "The Apostle of Allah stood among us and said': 'Beware! The People of the Book before (you) were split up into 72 sects, and this community will be split up into 73, seventy-two of them will go to Hell and one of them will go to Paradise.'"'[468]

This hadith is reported also by others. It is an authentic hadith. The implication is clear. It follows that Muslims will split into many sects and since all but one are false, all but one are heretics. How the righteous Muslims should deal with heretics? That too is prescribed. Heretics must be killed.

---

[468] Sunnan Abu Dawud, 3:4580

But which one of these 73 sects is the right one? That depends on whom you ask. When every Muslim believes to be rightly guided and those who disagree with him are heretics, doesn't it follow that Muslims are required to fight with each other?

The truth is that Islam is divided into thousands of sects. Let us assume, for the sake of argument, that Satan is real and determined to destroy mankind. What better way could he find than inventing a religion like Islam and making people kill one another?

More lives have been lost because of Islam than for any other cause. If Hitler's insanity caused the death of fifty million people, Muhammad's cost hundreds of millions of lives. The pain caused by Hitler is history. The wounds caused by Islam have been bleeding for 1,400 years.

The primary victims of Islam are its believers. Their minds are filled with superstitions, their hearts are hardened with hatred, their lives are tormented with suffering, and their brains are paralyzed with fear. They are the most pitiable people of the world and yet believe others envy them.

One educated Muslim lady who left Islam and encouraged her husband to do the same after reading the above passage in an earlier edition of this book wrote the following:

> Once we visited my brother's family. They are typical devout Muslims. Their children respect the parents. They rarely have heated arguments about anything. They are socially and financially stable and healthy – a typical perfect family. Thinking about them, how could I have an idea that they could be the ones you described here? It seemed impossible for my brother and his family to have a heart filled with hatred, until when we heard of three Ahmadis murdered by a mob of 200 jihadists. When we asked his opinion about the murder of the innocent people, his response increased my repulsion of Islam and confirmed what you said. He said that it was not the mistake of the Jihadist; it was the victims who are to be blamed, for they ignored the noble principles of Islam. Even though violence was unacceptable, he said, in this circumstance the anger of Muslims is understandable. The same tone came from his wife, his children, my colleagues, and even from many prominent figures on TV, including one of the members of National Human Rights Committee. Our President condemned the attack, but he too blamed the Ahmadis for insisting to call themselves Muslim. (The Ahmadis are regarded as heretics by the mainstream Muslims.)

An article titled, "*Jihad: The Forgotten Obligation*" that can be found with a Google search on several Islamic sites writes:

> *Provision, Under the Shade of the Spear*: Narrated Ibn Umar (ra) that the Prophet (saw) said, "*My livelihood is under the shade of my spear, and he who disobeys my orders will be humiliated.*" (Bukhari, p.408, vol.1) The virtue of the spear has been mentioned in this hadith and we have been informed that the livelihood and provision of the Prophet (saw) lies in the spear (jihaad). This is why the muhaditheen have stated that the best earning is that of war booty and it is clearly proven by this hadith

> that booty has been made permissible for this Ummah. Note: the term "humiliation for the kuffar" in the hadith, means paying jizya.[469]

The above is a clear demonstration of the utter lack of morality in Muslims. A hadith says Muhammad earned his livelihood through robbery; as the result Muslim scholars and *muhaditheen* (collectors of hadith) have concluded that booty is permissible and the best earning is the one that comes from robbery. Today, Muslims lament that the obligation of jihad has been forgotten and think they should earn their livelihood by plundering and forcing the non-Muslims to pay jizyah. This is the true Islam. It can't be changed because it is the sunnah of Muhammad.

Talking about her own conversion, this lady wrote, "After reading your articles, I was terribly confused and depressed. I felt so much languish and I was so angry. I felt sad. I was in a nightmare for days and nights. I kept searching and reading other related sources frantically. I kept telling my husband how abhorrent Islam is. He asked me to stop reading, but how could I? It is hard to believe how people can become so monstrous."

Islam blinds people. It destroys their humanity. Nonetheless, when Muslims leave Islam they are transformed. I have received countless emails from people who told me that after they left Islam, for the first time they saw mankind as one family. The distrust and the hatred had evaporated overnight. Now they could love everyone without guilt. There is goodness in everyone. The light is there; it is only covered. Once the cover is removed, it will shine again.

This lady said she is in charge of 1000 students. Although impossible for her to speak openly, she vowed to sow the seed of inquisitiveness in their young minds. That is great, but while she has to do this surreptitiously and with a great risk to her life, the mullahs can spread their hate and ignorance freely to millions.

Muslim societies are dysfunctional, their countries are dictatorial and their lives are in shambles. It's up to them to end their denial and face the painful truth that Islam is the main cause of their miseries.

Non-Muslims are guilty of naiveté. By tiptoeing around the truth, lest they offend Muslims' petal delicate sensitivity, they are accomplices in keeping them ignorant. When they accept Islam as a legitimate religion, they validate it.

Non-Muslims have allowed unrestricted propagation of this cult in their countries. Islam does not recognize any other religion or system as legitimate. It aims to abolish all other systems, and take control over the lives of every living being. How can such a thing be tolerated?

---

[469] Fath ul Bari, p.116, vol.2

Muslim immigrants are flooding the Western countries with the intent to colonize them. Shortsighted and unscrupulous politicians bend over backwards to welcome them. Some have gone as far as to support the "blasphemy law" and have passed laws to prosecute the critics of Islam.

Thanks to immigration and Muslims' high birth rate, their numbers in the West is on the rise. The entire water of the ocean can't sink a ship unless it gets inside it. Similarly, large populations of Muslims in Islamic countries pose little threat to the world. But their growth in the West is a serious threat to mankind. If Muslims multiply in their own countries they will only become poorer. They will fight among each other and will be weakened. They can only hurt themselves. Eventually, they will give up Islam, as most Iranians have. However, their increased number in the West will undermine democracy and this means the death of human civilization.

If the western civilization falls, humanity will revert to a dark age from which there will be no recovery. This is the most serious threat mankind has ever faced. Had Hitler won the war, his reign of terror could not have lasted long. It would have fallen like communism fell in Russia. But the reign of terror of Islam can last indefinitely.

Muslims in the West are more "evangelical" and more militant than their co-religionists back home. Democracy provides them a fertile ground to be virulent. Radical Muslims are jailed in most Islamic countries, while they roam freely in the West.

Those who think kindness can win the hearts and minds of Muslims are in grave error. No amount of kindness will ever soften the hearts of Muslims and make them accepting of non-Muslims. Their hatred is deeply rooted in their faith.

Wool Wafa Samir, a 21 year old Palestinian woman, tried to enter Israel. Security cameras were fixed on her as she was questioned by the Israeli guards from a distance. She had a medical certificate and a pass to enter Israel. A year and a half earlier Wafa was injured in her house when a gas canister went off. The medical treatment in Gaza only worsened her condition. So she was given permission by Israel to be treated at Soroka Hospital in Beersheba for her burns treatments. This time Wafa was not coming for treatment. She was carrying 10 kg of explosives fastened to her thighs, with the intent to kill her doctor, nurses, and other patients in the hospital that treated her.

Those who read the history of Islam know that early Muslims prided themselves for murdering their friends. Islam had changed their hearts. Showing kindness to Muslims in the hope that they may reciprocate, belies the ignorance of the reality of Islam.

Is Islam compatible with democracy and Western values? Are we going to be safe if Muslims grow in our midst? Does multiculturalism mean that ideologies that are openly against other cultures, pluralism, and democracy should also be welcomed?

Multiculturalism assumes that every culture has something valuable to offer. It presupposes that all cultures can co-exist in harmony, and that they are all the same.

10- Where Are We Headed?

Islam has a proven record of creating isolated communities which often, if not always, are antagonistic and in conflict with those around them. Islam is not a culture, nor is it capable of meaningful integration with other cultures. It is a belief system that promotes hate. It is no different than Nazism. Is there a benefit in recognizing Nazism as a legitimate ideology, and allowing its practice and its spread? Should we be tolerant of doctrines that are intolerant, promote inequality, foment hate and encourage terrorism? How rational is it to let a belief system thrive in our countries when the very tenets of that belief call for our subjugation?

Islam is not a culture. It is a doctrine that aims to subsume all cultures. It is not another color in the rainbow of religions. It is the dark void of night that wants to devour all colors.

If any culture needs to be protected, it is the Western Helleno-Judeo-Christian culture. It is this culture that is facing extinction. It is to this culture alone that we owe the Enlightenment, individual freedom and democracy. These are the foundations of our modern world. It would be a terrible mistake not to protect this culture. If we do nothing, we face a future where democracy and tolerance will fade and Islam's primitive instincts will subjugate humanity.

All cultures are not made equal. A "culture" that advocates subjugation of women and minorities is not on parity with one that promotes equality of all people. Islam is the antithesis of culture. It is savagery and incivility. We owe our freedom and modern civilization to the Western culture. It is this culture that is now under attack and needs protection.

In his book *Slavery, Terrorism and Islam: The Historical Roots and Contemporary Threat*, Dr. Peter Hammond explains how Islamization occurs when there are sufficient Muslims in a country to agitate for their so-called "religious rights."

> When politically correct and culturally diverse societies agree to 'the reasonable' Muslim demands for their 'religious rights,' they also get the other components under the table. Here's how it works (percentages source CIA: The World Fact Book (2007)).
>
> As long as the Muslim population remains around 1% of any given country they will be regarded as a peace-loving minority and not as a threat to anyone. In fact, they may be featured in articles and films, stereotyped for their colorful uniqueness. (United States --1.0%; Australia --1.5%; Canada --1.9%; China --1%-2%; Italy --1.5%; Norway --1.8%)
>
> At 2% and 3% they begin to proselytize from other ethnic minorities and disaffected groups with major recruiting from the jails and among street gangs. (Denmark --2%; Germany --3.7%; United Kingdom --2.7%; Spain --4%; Thailand --4.6%)
> From 5% on they exercise an inordinate influence in proportion to their percentage of the population. They will push for the introduction of halal (clean by Islamic standards) food, thereby securing food preparation jobs for Muslims. They will

increase pressure on supermarket chains to feature it on their shelves --along with threats for failure to comply. (France --8%; Philippines --5%; Sweden --5%; Switzerland --4.3%; The Netherlands --5.5%; Trinidad &Tobago --5.8%)

At this point, they will work to get the ruling government to allow them to rule themselves under Sharia, the Islamic Law. The ultimate goal of Islam is not to convert the world but to establish Sharia law over the entire world.

When Muslims reach 10% of the population, they will increase lawlessness as a means of complaint about their conditions (Paris --car-burnings). Any non-Muslim action that offends Islam will result in uprisings and threats (Amsterdam-Mohammed cartoons). (Guyana --10%; India --13.4%; Israel --16%; Kenya --10%; Russia --10-15%)

After reaching 20% expect hair-trigger rioting, jihad militia formations, sporadic killings and church and synagogue burning. (Ethiopia --Muslim 32.8%)

At 40% you will find widespread massacres, chronic terror attacks and ongoing militia warfare. (Bosnia --40%; Chad --53.1%; Lebanon --59.7%)

From 60% you may expect unfettered persecution of non-believers and other religions, sporadic ethnic cleansing (genocide), use of Sharia Law as a weapon and Jizya, the tax placed on infidels. (Albania --70%; Malaysia --60.4%; Qatar --77.5%; Sudan --70%)

After 80% expect State run ethnic cleansing and genocide. (Bangladesh --83%; Egypt --90%; Gaza --98.7%; Indonesia --86.1%; Iran --98%; Iraq --97%; Jordan --92%; Morocco --98.7%; Pakistan -97%; Palestine --99%; Syria --90%; Tajikistan --90%; Turkey --99.8% United Arab Emirates --96%)

100% will usher in the peace of 'Dar-es-Salaam' --the Islamic House of Peace --there's supposed to be peace because everybody is a Muslim. (Afghanistan --100%; Saudi Arabia --100%; Somalia --100%; Yemen --99.9%)
Of course, that's not the case. To satisfy their blood lust, Muslims then start killing each other for a variety of reasons.

It is worth repeating: Muslim demographic explosion is not a threat to the world. The danger is when they immigrate to non-Muslim countries, refuse to integrate and try to make Islam dominant. To protect the West and the human civilization, it is imperative to halt Muslim immigration, ban the Sharia, and send those who have no desire to integrate, back to where they, their parents or grandparents came from.

Muslims don't consider the Western countries as theirs, even when they are born there. The Pakistani kids in UK, even the second and third generations, still see themselves as Pakistanis. This is true for all Muslims. Indian Muslims take always the side of Pakistan. Muslims can't have allegiance to a country ruled by non-Muslims. They must be sent back to where they feel belonged.

Minority Rules

Muslims in the West are still a small minority. But that can change rapidly. In fact it is possible that Islam become the dominant religion in only a few short decades.

Scientists at Rensselaer Polytechnic Institute, America's oldest technological university have found that when just 10 percent of the population holds an unshakable belief, their belief will always be adopted by the majority of the society. The scientists, who are members of the Social Cognitive Networks Academic Research Center (SCNARC) at Rensselaer, used computational and analytical methods to discover the tipping point where a minority belief becomes the majority opinion. The finding has implications for the study and influence of societal interactions ranging from the spread of innovations to the movement of political ideals.[470]

"When the number of committed opinion holders is below 10 percent, there is no visible progress in the spread of ideas. It would literally take the amount of time comparable to the age of the universe for this size group to reach the majority," said SCNARC Director Boleslaw Szymanski, the Claire and Roland Schmitt Distinguished Professor at Rensselaer. "Once that number grows above 10 percent, the idea spreads like flame."[471]

The findings were published in the July 22, 2011, early online edition of the journal Physical Review in an article titled "Social consensus through the influence of committed minorities." The study shows how the prevailing majority opinion in a population can be rapidly reversed by a small fraction of randomly distributed committed agents who consistently proselytize the opposing opinion and are immune to influence.

Islam encourages zealotry. Virtually every Muslim is a proselytizer. Say something against Muhammad to the most liberal Muslim and he will suddenly want to behead you. A much larger percentage of Muslims are committed to their faith than the followers of any other religion. That is the reason Islam is spreading. It's not spreading because it has any merit. It is spreading because Muslims are fanatically convinced of it. Their conviction convinces others. Zealotry is contagious.

To stop Islam we need an army of dedicated warriors, committed to oppose it, with the same religious fervor that Muslims have in spreading it. Indifference and

---

[470] Gabrielle DeMarco; http://news.rpi.edu/update.do?artcenterkey=2902
[471] http://www.rpi.edu/about/index.html

inaction will only lead to our defeat. We have to speak against Islam with courage and make it clear to Muslims among us that they are welcome, but their cult of domination is not. Muslims can't have it both ways. They can't be, as a Persian proverb says, the friend of the caravan and the partner of the bandits.

I believe Islam can be eradicated in a very short time. But we need a medium to tell the truth about Muhammad to a large audience. We have to find a way to reach to hundreds of millions, or even billions of people. This can be done through an epic biopic on his life. Not a documentary. Documentaries attract only a small audience. We need to make a feature film, something that can be seen, for its entertainment value, by everyone. I have written the script of such movie and I am looking for people who might be interested to help me produce it. Today we can do things that were not possible a few years ago. We can, for example, disguise the features of the actors so they can't be recognized and we can distribute the movie via Internet, so we don't have to worry about theaters being bombed. Such movie can be downloaded and viewed even in Mecca.

Defeating Islam Politically

I wrote this book with two goals in mind, to help Muslims see the truth, leave Islam, leave their hatred, and join the rest of mankind as fellow humans, and to warn the world of the threat of Islam. Islam must be banned, but how can we ban a religion? Isn't freedom of belief guaranteed in a democratic society? Isn't it a cornerstone of human rights? Wouldn't that make us just as intolerant as Muslims?

Islam portrays itself as religion and uses religious terminology, but its goal is world domination. This is the same goal pursued by Nazism and communism. Islam's ambition is worldly and political. Its alleged "spiritual message" is icing on the cake. Since the ultimate agenda of Islam is political, it must be classified as a political ideology. We can ban Islam's political side, and that would be the end of Islam. Without its political agenda of world domination Islam has no reason to exist.

Islam is about domination. Its method is to rouse the believers to action and make them eager to fight for its imperialistic objectives. Most people are oblivious of this threat. All one has to do to be aware of it is to listen to what Muslims say. Read their placards during their protests. They are the writings on the wall. Freedom has never been so vulnerable to attack as it is today.

Freedom does not come free. Westerners enjoy freedom because their forefathers fought Islamic aggression. Had the crusaders failed to defend their countries, as the Persians and the Egyptians did, the Europe of today would have been just as dystopian a land as are the Middle East and the rest of the Islam infested world.

10- Where Are We Headed?

The raiders are back, this time under the guise of immigrants and economical refugees. They are the Trojan horse of Islam. If we don't eliminate this threat in time, we stand to lose everything. The danger is real and time is running out.

There are three options before us. Option one is to do nothing. This will allow Muslims become the majority in Europe in a few short decades. Muslim immigrants on average produce four times more children than Europeans. These children are often raised with the tax money of their hosts in the hope that their "investment" in them will eventually pay dividends when these little Muslims grow up and support the pensions of those who paid for their upbringing. This is an illusion. Muslims will never pay to support non-Muslims. As soon as they become the majority, they will take over, scrap the pension plan. Non-Muslims will be reduced to dhimmis and will have to pay tribute to their Muslim rulers. The madrassas fill the minds of Muslim kids with hate. Westerners are nurturing their own nemeses.

The Common Cuckoo it is a brood parasite. This bird lays its eggs in the nest of another smaller species of bird. When the chicks are born the cuckoo chick ejects its foster siblings out of the nest to their death, leaving the foster parents, moved by their parental instinct, to nurse this murderous brat. Muslim immigrants in the West are brood parasites. The western civilization will become extinct unless these parasites are removed. The second and third generation Muslims in the Western countries, are more radicalized than their parents.

The second option is to wait until Muslims become a formidable force and fight back when they start taking control of their host countries. That would be a losing fight. When it comes to violence no one can beat Muslims. We can't kill people because they have a different faith. We can't kill children because their parents are Muslims. But Muslims have no such qualms. Good Muslims can kill any number of non-Muslims, including children, with total freedom of conscience. Remember Beslan? No one but Muslims could have murdered so many children in cold blood.

On Feb. 13, 2007, the CBC published the results of an Environics poll. According to this poll, fully 12% of Canadian Muslims said the aborted terrorist plot – that included kidnapping and beheading the Canadian prime minister and blowing up the Parliament and the CBC – was justified. 12% of 700,000 Muslims living in Canada means 84,000 Canadian Muslims support terrorism. On February 25, 2007, the UK Telegraph reported that the director general of M.I.5 warned there were more than 1,600 "identified individuals" actively engaged in plotting terrorist attacks, and 200 known networks involved in at least 30 terrorist plots. It is thought that the number of British citizens of Islamic persuasion involved in plots could be well in excess of 2,000. The situation is no different in other countries where there is a large Muslim conclave. The *sunnah* of Muhammad and Muslims' normative lack of conscience give them an edge over their opponents. It was thanks to this lack of conscience that Muhammad and a handful of his warriors subdued much larger empires, more sophisticated and advanced. When civilization and barbarity collide, brute force always wins. History is full of cases where large empires were conquered by a bunch of swordsmen and robbers.

The third option is to ban the Sharia, end the Muslim immigration, deport those who refuse to integrate, and fight Islam ideologically before freedom of speech is lost forever.

It is easy to see that the third alternative is better. Our fight is against darkness. We don't draw a sword against darkness; we lit a light. Lies can be defeated with truth. Fighting Islam with violence is fighting Muslims in their turf. When it comes to violence Muslims have the upper hand. No one can be as ruthless as one who is motivated by his faith. Violence is the strength of Islam, but logic is its weakness.

If Islam is defeated ideologically, ex-Muslims will turn against it. Former Muslims are the best allies the world has in this war. They know the truth about Islam, they know the value of freedom and they are determined to defend it.

This would be a win/win war. We win because we convert the enemy into a friend, and Muslims win over their demon and are set free. There is no need for bloodshed. No bullets need be fired. By destroying Islam we will eliminate the source of hate.

Lest I am misunderstood, let me clarify that I am not proposing pacifism. Turning the other cheek emboldens the bully. Muslims understand the language of strength. If not at your feet, they will be at your throat. Islamic violence must be stopped with force of such a magnitude that will make Muslims to reconsider the timing of Jihad.

Muslims are required to wage jihad when they are strong and make *hudnah* (truces), when weak. Imam Suyuti, in Itqan Fi 'Ulum al- Qur'an (Certainty in the science of the Quran) wrote: "The command to fight the infidels was delayed until the Muslims become strong, but when they were weak they were commanded to endure and be patient."[472]

Muslims interpret tolerance as weakness. Islamic violence can only be stopped with strength. When we are attacked we must strike back. We can never win the hearts and minds of Muslims with appeasement. Our objective should never be to win their hearts. This will never happen. Our objective must be to stop their advancement and to eradicate Islam. However, Islam cannot be eradicated by force. The only way to eradicate Islam is by upholding the truth.

Islam cannot stand probing. It is held together, like a house of cards, glued with lies. Appeasement of Muslims and walking on eggshells lest we hurt their religious sensitivity, which is always sour like an open wound, is showing them weakness.

Vaknin says: "The narcissistic bully very often gets his way,... his misdeeds are overlooked, his misbehavior tolerated. This is partly because, narcissists are

---

[472] Sobhy as_Saleh, Mabaheth Fi 'Ulum al- Qur'an, Dar al-'Ilm Lel-Malayeen, Beirut , 1983, p. 269

excellent liars with considerable thespian skills - and partly because no one wants to mess around with a thug, even if his thuggery is limited to words and gestures."[473] How accurately the above defines Muslims! They riot, threaten with lawsuit and assassination, to intimidate those who dare criticizing Islam.

Tolerance does not mean approval and it is not a one way street. If Muslims want tolerance from us, they must first show it where they are the majority. Let them allow a church in Saudi Arabia before we allow them to build one more mosque in the West. Muslims will not allow a non-Muslim close to Mecca and Medina because they are considered filthy, and this is an injunction of the Quran.

The Fifth Column among Us

Truth about Islam is difficult to find. Islamic apologists like Karen Armstrong and John Esposito have taken it upon themselves to portray a one-sided and deceptively rosy image of Islam. The mainstream liberal media finds their narrative more convenient to promote.

On the other hand, Muslims are convinced that they will take over the Europe and the west. In 1999, Archbishop Giuseppe Bernardini recalled a talk he had with a Muslim leader: "Thanks to your democratic laws, we will invade you," the Muslim leader told Bernardini. "Thanks to our religious laws, we will dominate you."[474]

I am always suspicious of non-Muslims who defend Islam. I find it hard to believe that any honest person would side with this faith of hate and terror, unless they are ignorant. There are many politicians in the West that are defensive of Islam. These people are most likely bought. An example is former US congressman Mark D. Siljander who began his career as a zealous evangelical Christian and then went on to write a book, *A Deadly Misunderstanding*, to "bridge the Muslim-Christian divide." He argued that Christian and Muslim religious texts are "surprisingly compatible," when studied in their original languages – a preposterous claim since he does not know either of the languages? Truth came out on July 7, 2010 when Siljander pleaded guilty to two counts of receiving money from Muslims and supporting Muslim terrorists. He was indicted in January 2008 on charges of money laundering, conspiracy, and obstruction of justice. It is not always the useful idiots that defend Islam, sometimes they are hardcore traitors.

Another bizarre case was the enthusiastic support of the mayor of New York, Michael Bloomberg, for the construction of a 13 story mega mosque, only two blocks away from where 19 Muslims killed 3000 Americans. How could he be

---

[473] Narcissism in the Workplace: online conference transcript healthyplace.com/Communities/Personality_Disorders/Site/Transcripts/narcissism_workplace.htm

[474] http://www.meforum.org/448/we-will-dominate-you

so insensitive to the families of the victims of that tragedy and to all Americans? Mr. Bloomberg's ardent support of the project was so intense that he went on to insult the intelligence of the nation and said that allowing the mosque project to go forward would be a victory over the forces that attacked America on 9/11. Really?

This was the argument originally presented by Faisal Abdul Rauf, the imam behind this "Cordoba Initiative." However, Rauf in his interview with Soledad O'Brien on CNN contradicted himself and said he can't move the Islamic center because of "national security concerns." He said the Muslim world would be violently inflamed at the news of its relocation. "If we do move," Rauf said, "it will strengthen the argument of the radicals to recruit, and their increasing aggression and violence against our country. If this is not handled correctly, this crisis could become much bigger than the Danish cartoon crisis, which resulted in attacks on Danish embassies in various parts of the Muslim world." He warned, "It could become something which could really become very, very, very dangerous indeed."

How can both these contradictory statements be true? Do the "extremists" want the Ground Zero Mosque or not? How can they hate it and at the same time become radicalized if its construction is stopped? It is amazing to see the extent of deception that Muslims and their supporters use to advance their agenda.

According to polls 71% of Americans opposed the construction of the Islamic Centre. Disregarding that Bloomberg retorted, "To cave to popular sentiment would be to hand a victory to the terrorists, and we should not stand for that." Bloomberg's position defies logic until one learns the story behind the story. The United Arab Emirate online newspaper, The National, in October 2008 revealed that Mr. Bloomberg owns a financial news service with significant share in the Middle East. His company has had a presence in Dubai for over a decade, and was about to quadruple in size in 2009. It has also developed an "Islamic finance portal."

How much is at stake? At that time Bloomberg's company serviced about 300,000 terminals worldwide, bringing in about US$5 billion in annual revenues. That is billion with "B". It had news bureaus throughout the GCC, including in Bahrain and Kuwait, and was in the process of opening offices in Saudi Arabia and Qatar. A news bureau was also planned for Abu Dhabi.[475]

Only when we learn the facts, can we understand why Bloomberg was so supportive of such an outrageous project.

Those who defend Islam are the fifth column among us. They are selling us out. They are opening the gates of our countries to the enemy. They have no scruple, no patriotism, and no shame. It is up to us to protect our countries. The liberal media and the leftist parties are in bed with the enemy. The irony is that Bloomberg is the Jew. But I assume his real religion is money.

---

[475] www.thenational.ae/article/20081029/BUSINESS/302158245/1005

10- Where Are We Headed?

The public is awakening. It is almost funny to read the major Internet based media, repeatedly publishing articles apologetic of Islam, while the overwhelming number of comments posted below those articles show that ordinary people are no longer buying their charade. People have woken up, while the media and the corrupt politicians keep beating the same old drum.

Throughout history, Islamic forces have deceived their victims, making them think Islam and Muslims are peace-loving, only later to find the opposite. One example of this deception happened in 635 CE when Damascus fell to Muslims because the invaders tricked and bribed its Bishop who opened the city gates at night.

When a politician or a "scholar" stands up for Islam, preaches "tolerance" and "community cohesion," and ignores the fact that there is no tolerance in Islam, follow the money trail. Chances are that you'll find a skeleton in their closet.

Whilst the misleading politically correct voices attempt to defend the indefensible, angry Muslims show the true face of Islam with their constant readiness to harass, intimidate, and assassinate anyone who stands in their way or slights their religion.

To defeat Islam we need public awareness. Politicians can be changed and consequently, government policies. If the outcry from the public is loud enough, someone will step up to make those voices heard. We owe it to our children. It is our responsibility to make sure that their world will be safe and free. George Orwell wrote, "In a time of universal deceit, telling the truth becomes a revolutionary act." We need revolutionaries.

How to illegalize Islam, Legally

I am being frequently ask, how to combat the emerging threat of Islam. In 2001, I predicted that Islam will be defeated in our own time. Since then Islam has advanced. Mosques are mushrooming everywhere in the West and the population of Muslims has grown. Muslims have infiltrated into western governments and even into the White House. Anyone who still does not know the fraudulent president of America, Barak Hussein Obama is a Muslim sympathizer must have his head examined.

This advancement of Islam was expected. Muslims have been planning for decades for their takeover of the West. The non-Muslims were completely oblivious of that fact and were taken by surprise. Many of them, particularly those on the Left, are still in denial. It took nearly a decade since 9/11 for most of the world to wake up. Those who haven't, have cotton in their ears. Now that the masses of people are realizing Islam is not just another religion, but a threat to mankind, we can stop it.

However, there is a problem. Islam is a religion. Banning a religion goes against freedom of belief, which is an integral part of democracy. But there is a way. Islam is multi-dimensional. All other religions have one dimension. Let us call it the vertical line that unites man with God. Islam has a width and a depth that are purely this worldly. They are its social and political dimensions.

This sociopolitical base of Islam is defined by the Sharia law. It regulates every aspect of human relations, e.g. the relationship between husband and wife. Under the Sharia law, a husband has the right to beat his wife. He can divorce her at will and in absentia. To him belong the children. He can marry as many as four wives, etc.

The Shaira law does not apply only to Muslims. It also regulates the rights of non-Muslims. Non-Muslims in Muslim majority countries must be reduced to dhimmis, subdued and humiliated and they must pay a penalty tax that can be as high as half of their earning. This was the amount Muhammad exacted from the surviving Jews of Khaibar, after raiding them and killing their able bodied men.

Under the Sharia, women's rights are half of those of men. They are deemed to be deficient in intelligence and their testimony in court is also worth half. Homosexuals must be killed and adulterers must be stoned to death, even if they are victims of rape. If a raped woman can't produce four male witnesses, her testimony against her assailant is not admissible in the court and therefore, according to the Quran 24-13 she is a liar, and according to verse 4 of the same sura, she should be flogged with eighty stripes. If she gets pregnant as the result of the rape, it would be proof that she has had extra-marital sex and consequently she should be stoned for adultery.

The political dimension of Islam is its most important dimension. Without it Islam ceases to exist. The foremost objective of Islam is to "reclaim" the earth and establish Allah's law on it. The means to do that is through jihad. The goal is not to convert everyone, but to make the Sharia dominant. Even Islamic countries that are not 100% Sharia compliant are legitimate targets of jihad.

All Muslims are automatically members of the Umma and subjects of the universal Islamic state. Today, this state exists in a virtual form. It is the duty of every Muslim to bring it into the realm of reality. Leaving Islam is considered an act of treason against the Islamic state.

Under these three dimensions nothing is left to the individual. Every aspect of the life of a believer is regulated. As Muslims keep telling us, Islam is a complete way of life. It is a totalitarian Orwellian system that dominates every aspect of everyone's life. These three dimensions are indivisible. They form the trinity of Islam.

The Chinese sage Sun Zi said, know your enemy and you will not be defeated. Muslims know us and they use our system to penetrate into our countries and to defeat us from within. They have their allies among us – the useful idiots and the fifth columns.

Muslims know how to use our democracy and our civil liberties against us. The Westerns on the other hand don't know Islam and as the result they are losing the battle.

10- Where Are We Headed?

Once we understand this Islamic trinity it will be easy to defeat it. We cannot ban Islam as a religion, but we can ban it as a political system. As a political system Islam is incongruent with democracy and our laws. For example, Islam does not recognize the equality of all men before the law. It does not grant equal rights to both genders. It also does not recognize the freedom of Muslims to leave their faith. On these grounds Islam is in violation of our laws and as such it can be banned.

Let us take a closer look at the Sharia law. Former Muslim Nonie Darwish, author of *Cruel and Usual Punishment: The Terrifying Global Implications of Islamic Law*, in an article titled, *Sharia for Dummies* highlights a few of those laws.

1. Jihad defined as "to war against non-Muslims to establish the religion" is the duty of every Muslim and Muslim head of state (Caliph). Muslim Caliphs who refuse jihad are in violation of Sharia and unfit to rule.
2. A Caliph can hold office through seizure of power meaning through force.
3. A Caliph is exempt from being charged with serious crimes such as murder, adultery, robbery, theft, drinking and in some cases of rape.
4. A percentage of Zakat (alms) must go towards jihad.
5. It is obligatory to obey the commands of the Caliph, even if he is unjust.
6. A caliph must be a Muslim, a non-slave, and a male.
7. The Muslim public must remove the Caliph in one case, if he rejects Islam.
8. A Muslim who leaves Islam must be killed immediately.
9. A Muslim will be forgiven for murder of: 1) an apostasy 2) an adulterer 3) a highway robber. Making vigilante street justice and honor killing acceptable.
10. A Muslim will not get the death penalty if he kills a non-Muslim
11. Sharia never abolished slavery and sexual slavery and highly regulates it. A master will not be punished for killing his slave.
12. Sharia dictates death by stoning, beheading, amputation of limbs, flogging and other forms of cruel and unusual punishments even for crimes of sin such as adultery.
13. Non-Muslims are not equal to Muslims and must comply to Sharia if they are to remain safe. They are forbidden to marry Muslim women, publicly display wine or pork, recite their scriptures or openly celebrate their religious holidays or funerals. They are forbidden from building new churches or building them higher than mosques. They may not enter a mosque without permission. A non-Muslim is no longer protected if he commits adultery with a Muslim woman or if he leads a Muslim away from Islam.
14. It is a crime for a non-Muslim to sell weapons to someone who will use them against Muslims. Non-Muslims cannot curse a Muslim, say anything derogatory about Allâh, the Prophet, or Islam, or expose the weak points of Muslims. However, the opposite is not true for Muslims.
15. A non-Muslim cannot inherit from a Muslim.
16. Banks must be Sharia compliant and interest is not allowed.
17. No testimony in court is acceptable from people of low-level jobs, such as street sweepers or a bathhouse attendant. Women in such low level jobs such as professional funeral mourners cannot keep custody of their children in case of divorce.
18. A non-Muslim cannot rule even over a non-Muslims minority.
19. Homosexuality is punishable by death.

20. There is no age limit for marriage of girls under Sharia. The marriage contract can take place anytime after birth and consummated at age 8 or 9.
21. Rebelliousness on the part of the wife nullifies the husband's obligation to support her, gives him permission to beat her and keep her from leaving the home.
22. Divorce is only in the hands of the husband and is as easy as saying: "I divorce you" and becomes effective even if the husband did not intend it.
23. There is no common property between husband and wife and the husband's property does not automatically go to the wife after his death.
24. A woman inherits half what a man inherits.
25. A man has the right to have up to 4 wives and she has no right to divorce him even if he is polygamous.
26. The dowry is given in exchange for the woman's sexual organs.
27. A man is allowed to have sex with slave women and women captured in battle, and if the enslaved woman is married her marriage is annulled.
28. The testimony of a woman in court is half the value of a man.
29. A woman loses custody if she remarries.
30. To prove rape, a woman must have 4 male witnesses.
31. A rapist may only be required to pay the bride-money (dowry) without marrying the rape victim.
32. A Muslim woman must cover every inch of her body which is considered "Awrah," a sexual organ. Some schools of Sharia allow the face and some don't.
33. A Muslim man is forgiven if he kills his wife caught in the act of adultery. However, the opposite is not since he "could be married to the woman he was caught with."

These laws are universally accepted by both Sunnis and Shiites and are the basis of the laws in Islamic countries. The Sharia derives from the Quran and the hadith. These are the laws that Muslims want to bring into the West.

Cyanide looks like granulated sugar. But it would be a deadly error to mistake it with sugar. Comparing Islam to other faiths, because of some similarities between them is also a lethal mistake. Cyanide contains carbon atom triple-bonded to a nitrogen atom. These elements, in isolation, are harmless. Bonded together they become deadly. Politics and religion are harmless in isolated form. Mixed together they are lethal. If the bond between carbon and nitrogen is broken, cyanide ceases to exist. If we ban the political Islam, Islam will cease to exist.

Muslims organizations, mosques and imams should be required to sign a pledge not to preach the Sharia. If they refuse to do so they would be in violation of our laws and as such their organization should be dismantled and they should be deported.

All Madrassas should be closed and Muslim children should be enrolled in ordinary schools. How can we expect these kids to integrate in the society when we segregate them from childhood and teach them to hate the country that they live in?

Surveillance cameras should be installed in all mosques. If any hate speech or antigovernment statement is made the preacher should be expelled and the mosque should be shut down. If Islam cannot be banned as a faith, it can be banned as a subversive political ideology.

Christians can easily draw a line between their faith and politics. Jesus was clear that he wanted no part in politics when he said my kingdom is not of this world. Politics and Islam are indivisible. Muhammad said *Al Islamo deenun wa dawlah* (Islam is religion and government). Here lies the vulnerability of Islam. One cannot serve two masters. Muslims must choose between Islam and the country that they live.

Most Muslims are not aware of what the Sharia entails. Iranians paid a hefty price for this ignorance when they supported Khomeini in the revolution of 1979. We would be doing a great favor to Muslims by educating them about their religion.

Muslims have a romantic idea of Islam that has no basis in reality. Highlighting the laws of the Sharia will help many of them to see the truth and abandon their faith. Thanks to the Internet, millions of Muslims have left their faith in recent years. It is important that we keep in mind that Muslims are not the enemy. The enemy is Islam. Yet Islam is an ideology. Ideologies can't hurt us. It is the people who believe in them that hurt. A person infected by a deadly virus must be quarantined.

If you read this book you already know that Islam poses a huge threat to mankind. Many Muslims and non-Muslims are rubbing their sleepy eyes and are aghast at the sight of this monstrosity disguised as religion. Truth will set us free. The problem is that truth has become a hostage to political correctness and is condemned as hate speech. Islam thrives thanks to ignorance. Unless we speak out, this ignorance will be perpetuated. Silence is deadly.

Index

Index